If Truth
Be Told

If Truth
Be Told

The Politics of
Public Ethnography

Didier Fassin, editor

DUKE UNIVERSITY PRESS   *Durham and London*   2017

Designed by Matt Tauch
Typeset in Garamond Premier Pro by Westchester
Publishing Services

Library of Congress Cataloging-in-Publication Data
Names: Fassin, Didier, editor.
Title: If truth be told : the politics of public
    ethnography / Didier Fassin, editor.
Description: Durham : Duke University Press, 2017. |
    Includes bibliographical references and index.
Identifiers:
LCCN 2017006739 (print)
LCCN 2017008864 (ebook)
ISBN 9780822369653 (hardcover : alk. paper)
ISBN 9780822369776 (pbk. : alk. paper)
ISBN 9780822372875 (ebook)
Subjects: LCSH: Ethnology—Philosophy. |
    Ethnology—Methodology. | Publicity.
Classification: LCC GN345 I34 2017 (print) |
    LCC GN345 (ebook) | DDC 305.8001—dc23
LC record available at https://lccn.loc.gov
    /2017006739

Chapter 11 © 2016 by the American
Anthropological Association. Originally published
as "The Postneoliberal Fabulation of Power"
in *American Ethnologist* 43, no. 3 (2015).

Cover art: Prapat Jiwarangsan, *Dust under Feet*,
2012, installation view. Photographs and magnifier,
120 × 150 cm. *Dust under Feet* is composed of some
3,000 tiny, thumbnail-size photographs of figures
from Thailand's political history—including prime
ministers, generals, protestors, democracy activists,
and martyrs of massacres—and a magnifying
glass, to prompt the viewer to scrutinize the tiny
portraits up close.

Contents

Part III. Tensions

Introduction

When Ethnography Goes Public

DIDIER FASSIN

Ethnography has long been regarded essentially as a method, which was characterized by the emblematic approach to fieldwork subsumed under the phrase "participant observation." *Argonauts of the Western Pacific* established its mythical foundation. Emphasis was later placed on ethnography as writing, which led to a reflexive stance on what was at stake in the translation of empirical material into a text that was supposed to represent it. *Writing Culture* disenchanted the positivist illusion of a transparent process. In parallel with this dual dimension, the existential aspect of ethnography, namely the experience of the ethnographer through interaction with his or her subjects and the related exercise of introspection, was given more salience, via diaries, memoirs, or even scientific works, when it became an object of inquiry in its own right. *Tristes tropiques* epitomizes the meditative contemplation on this journey. But whether considered from the perspective of method, writing, or experience, it seemed relatively self-evident that ethnography ended with ethnographers going home or, at best, correcting the final proofs of their manuscript. Most of the time what happened afterward was largely ignored, as if the only relevant production of knowledge concerned what went on in the field and how the collected data were organized and interpreted.

Yet once a book, an article, or a film is out, a new phase begins for the ethnographer: the encounter with a public or, better said, multiple encounters with various publics. Indeed, rare are the ethnographic works that escape the fate of becoming, at some point, public, whether it is a scholarly piece known to only a few colleagues or an acclaimed essay arousing wide interest. The very word "publication" clearly indicates the passage from a private to a public space, and one certainly publishes texts in order to be read and discussed by others. However, authors grant little attention—or at least rarely admit they do—to the challenges and stakes related to the dissemination, promotion, reception, and utilization of their intellectual production. Their teaching, lecturing, debating with colleagues, intervening in the media, being solicited by policymakers or activist groups or professionals, and sometimes being questioned by those about whom they write or speak remain a blind spot, a sort of mundane after-sales service posing practical problems to be solved personally but of no relevance for the discipline.

Of course such a general statement should be tempered, and exceptions deserve to be mentioned. Among classical examples, one could cite the chapter "Ethical and Bureaucratic Implications of Community Research" that Arthur Vidich and Joseph Bensman added to the new edition, ten years later, of their 1958 *Small Town in Mass Society*, and the article "Ire in Ireland," written by Nancy Scheper-Hughes more than two decades after her 1977 *Saints, Scholars and Schizophrenics*; the collection *When They Read What We Write*, edited by Caroline Brettell and published in 1993, proposed a series of case studies about the mishaps experienced by anthropologists after the publication of their work; the lecture "When Natives Talk Back," delivered by Renato Rosaldo in 1985, offered a stimulating reflection on the problems posed by the way anthropologists reacted to the reactions to their writings of those they study. Most of these contributions shed light on the often controversial reception of ethnographies among the people who are the subjects of the research, but this is only one aspect of the interactions with publics. A broader analysis remains to be done of what we could call, paraphrasing Talal Asad, *ethnography and the public encounter*. The present volume is a collective endeavor to fill this gap by exploring in its diversity the public afterlife of ethnography.

As Thomas Hylland Eriksen has convincingly argued, the "public presence" of anthropology is anything but new, even if it has been subject to a long partial eclipse. Indeed from the early days of the discipline, with James Frazer, W. H. R. Rivers, and Bronislaw Malinowski in Britain, Franz Boas, Ruth Benedict, and Margaret Mead in the United States, Marcel Mauss, Michel Leiris, and Alfred Métraux in France, anthropologists have intervened in the public sphere, generally as scholars, sometimes as engaged intellectuals, occasionally as novelists or poets. Such positioning was not limited to the Western world, and the boundaries between scientific work and public life were even more blurred in the case of pioneers such as Jean Price-Mars in

Haiti, Jomo Kenyatta in Kenya, Gilberto Freyre in Brazil, and Nirmal Kumar Bose in India, who were all deeply involved in the politics of their country. With the professionalization and institutionalization of their discipline, however, anthropologists tended to refocus their activity within the academic realm. There were exceptions to this trend, with works destined for large audiences and sometimes provoking public controversies, most notably Oscar Lewis's *La Vida*, Napoleon Chagnon's *Yanomamö: The Fierce People*, and Colin Turnbull's *The Mountain People*. In recent years public anthropologies have taken a critical turn, addressing contemporary issues such as epidemics with Paul Farmer's *AIDS and Accusation*, drugs with Philippe Bourgois's *In Search of Respect*, and immigration with Seth Holmes's *Fresh Fruit, Broken Bodies*. But today, for the most part, at a global level, anthropology seems increasingly confined within the perimeter of the scholarly world, and anthropological works have almost disappeared from the shelves of bookstores, where what is presented under the corresponding section is popular essays by evolutionary biologists like Jared Diamond and Richard Dawkins. Interestingly there exist national variations in this transformation of the public presence of the discipline, the most remarkable case being that of Norway, where anthropologists have maintained a form of intellectual activism for the past half-century; as Signe Howell argues, the reasons for this rarity are multiple, including the general interest in social issues, the high level of education within the population, the links between the academic and political worlds, the relatively easy access scholars have to the media, and the presence of respected figures such as Fredrik Barth, who in the 1970s had a very popular television series, *Their Lives and Our Own*, which certainly familiarized people with different cultures and worlds. The decline of the public life of ethnography thus may not be ineluctable—unless one deems this outlier as the remnant of the discipline's past glory.

At this point a clarification may be necessary. In the past decade much has been written and debated regarding public social science. On the one hand, Michael Burawoy's famous presidential address at the 2004 American Sociological Association meeting calling for a "public sociology" has given rise to discussions, objections, and rejoinders. According to its promoter, public sociology is distinct from "professional," "critical," and "policy" approaches to sociology, which are involved, respectively, in comforting established knowledge, questioning foundational issues, and responding to political demands for expertise. It encompasses a "traditional" dimension, through popular publications, media interventions, and teaching, and an "organic" dimension, through a personal engagement with local associations, social movements, labor unions, or human rights organizations. On the other hand, Rob Borofsky's launching of a book series on "public anthropology" at the University of California Press signaled a renewed interest to "engage issues and audiences beyond today's self-imposed disciplinary boundaries" and "address broad critical concerns in ways that others beyond the discipline are able to understand." This public anthropology dissociates itself from "specialized anthropology," which corresponds to the dominant "narrow" approach in the field but "dances an ambiguous minuet with applied anthropology," the less legitimate branch of the discipline. Although public sociology has benefited from a more developed conceptualization than public anthropology, they have many features in common, in terms of both their external distancing (notably from academic norms and habits) and their internal differentiation (whether addressing general audiences or working with specific groups). But above all those who use these formulations share the same normative commitment: to speak of public sociology or public anthropology implies simultaneously contesting a certain intellectual order criticized for its scholarly enclosure and advocating for an engaged practice open to the world and its problems.

Although most, if not all, of the authors in the present volume would adhere to the project of a public sociology or a public anthropology—certainly with variations—our collective enterprise is of a distinct nature. It does not consist in affirming that the social sciences should have a public presence but rather in analyzing what difficulties, complications, and contradictions, as well as dares, expectations, and imaginations this public presence involves. Ours is definitely a move from the prescriptive to the descriptive. When using the phrase "public ethnography" we do not intend to coin a new creed or a novel realm; we propose it for two main reasons. First, we are specifically interested in the fact that what is made public is ethnography, in other words not any form of practice of social sciences but one defined by its method, its writing, and its experience. What difference does ethnography make when the findings, the style, and the world of the ethnographer are transported into the public domain? This is the first question that underlies our analysis. Second, we are particularly keen on producing a form of ethnography of the very scenes where the social sciences are rendered public by recounting the events that take place and dissecting the issues that are at play with some detail. What happens in the encounter between the ethnographers and their publics? This is the second point we address. Public ethnography thus refers to what is publicized and how such a process can be apprehended: *it is simultaneously an ethnography made public and the ethnography of this publicization.*

The intellectual engagement that derives from this characterization of public ethnography is consequently more on the side of the "specific intellectuals" in Foucault's terms than of the "universal intellectuals" embodied by Sartre. The relevance and legitimacy claimed by public ethnography stem from the sort of work conducted and knowledge produced. Adopting this perspective one does not comment on any topic or speak about any issue but limits oneself to one's domain of competence acquired through exacting work—which does not prevent one from drawing general conclusions. The scientific authority invoked is circumscribed—which does not mean, of course, that it should not be questioned. Public ethnographers are thus modest intellectuals, confident in their findings but cautious not to exceed their limits. Moreover, as specific intellectuals, they recognize that, although they take full responsibility for their analyses and statements, they owe much of their understanding to the people they study and work with. They are both *independent* and *indebted*. In this sense the practice of public ethnography can be regarded as a democratic exercise on two counts: because the intellectual production of social scientists is open to public discussion and because the social intelligence of the public is acknowledged.

If we therefore call publicization the process in which ethnographic works encounter various publics, we can distinguish two dimensions to this process: popularization and politicization. *Popularization*, which has been analyzed by Jeremy MacClancy, consists of two complementary aspects: making ethnography accessible to and likeable by the public. This dual endeavor precedes publicization. It is involved in the choice of the topic of research and, even more, in the way to present it. It includes the refusal of scientific jargon and more generally of scholarly customs and rules whose function is to affirm one's belonging to the group of learned peers and bar laypersons from this exclusive circle. Willingly resorting to literary forms, it is attentive to the style, privileges, narratives, and descriptions, integrates theory within the stories and scenes rather than treating them as separate textual blocks. All these decisions are taken before rendering the work public precisely in anticipation of its potentially wider reception. Because of the cost of such strategies in terms of academic career, popularization has often taken the form, notably among French anthropologists, of what Vincent Debaene has called a "second book," written for large audiences in parallel with a more technical publication destined for one's scientific community. *Politicization*, as can be derived from C. Wright Mills, also consists of two possible operations, which can be connected or not: contributing to debate and action. Indeed the idea of politicizing should be understood here in the sense of the Greek polis, a public space where individuals exercise their rights as citizens for the realization of the common good. In the case of public ethnography, the first operation—debate—entails, on the side of the ethnographer, the translation and dissemination of knowledge and, on the side of the public, its appropriation and contestation, while the second operation—action—involves the transformation of the knowledge thus discussed into practical orientations and decisions, which can be taken by institutions or individuals. Politicization therefore has affinities with the public sphere and communicative action analyzed by Habermas, although it does not preclude conflicts.

The two dimensions of publicization are often associated, but they do not need to be. Ethnographers may want to popularize their work without a particular intention of politicizing it: when Jean Malaurie launched his new series "Terre humaine" in 1955 with the publication of his ethnography of the Inuit society poetically titled *Les Derniers rois de Thulé*, his project, which became one of the most successful in the editorial history of the social sciences, was primarily to render anthropology accessible and likeable. Conversely ethnographers may try to politicize their work but not be preoccupied by the idea of popularizing it; whereas Pierre Clastres has been influential among leftist intellectuals for his description and analysis of stateless societies based on his work with the Guayaki, one would not argue that *La Société contre l'État*, published in 1974, is characterized by a specific effort of legibility. Finally, some may consider popularization instrumental to the success of politicization, as is the case, for instance, with David Graeber's *Debt: The First 5,000 Years*. An interesting model is the strategy developed by certain economists who publish their serious and impenetrable scientific work in the top journals of their discipline and write easy-to-read books for wide audiences. This strategy does not account, however, for the international success of Thomas Piketty's *Capital in the Twenty-First Century*, which is not exactly a page-turner.

Until now the *public* of public ethnography has been assumed to be implicitly self-evident, even in its plural form. But who composes this public, and what do we know about it? As Michael Warner writes, "it is an obscure question," and although "publics have become an essential fact of the social landscape, it would tax our understanding to say exactly what they are." They can be the audience of a talk or a film, the readership of a book or an article, the students attending a class, or the scholars at a conference; the policymakers in search of practical solutions to their problems or the journalists expecting short answers to their questions; the people with whom the ethnographer has worked and the broader social or professional group to which they belong—and many others. Attention can therefore vary considerably as well as expectation and comprehension. Yet what is perhaps the most constant fact about this public is that we know very little about who it is and how it has received or will use the ethnography. Only a few voices, which surely do not form a representative sample, will express themselves in reviews or blogs, in private conversations or public debates, but the great majority of those who have been exposed to the work will remain silent and anonymous, unknown to the author. Even this exposition cannot be ascertained, as it can rely on direct as well as indirect access to the work, through commentaries or comments read in the newspapers, heard on the radio, or simply caught in a conversation. The information most people have regarding the work of a social scientist is filtered through these mediations, and their opinion is based on the latter more than the former. Needless to say this unpredictable journey of public ethnography may give rise to surprising reactions that have only a very distant relation with its content, when criticisms or praises are based on what people say rather than on what the author wrote. In the end ethnographers have not only little knowledge of but also little hold on what becomes of their work in their direct or indirect encounters with publics. One can think of the publicization of one's work as a form of dispossession or, better expressed, alienation. This does not imply, however, that one should renounce the project of inquiring about these publics, not least to critique the common view of their self-evidence.

But *ethnography* in the phrase "public ethnography" does not deserve less consideration. The point is to discuss not what it is but what public impact it has as such. What does ethnography do that other modes of apprehending social worlds may not do or may do in a different way? It is possible to distinguish four specific and linked effects produced by ethnography. The first one is an effect of veridiction: the presence of the ethnographer in the field is assumed to attest to the veracity of his or her account of facts and events. The second is a symmetrical effect of reflexivity: the personal involvement of the researcher and author with his or her work and the people who inhabit it calls for a critical take on the deceptive transparency of what is related. The third is an effect of realism: description and narration generate more concrete, suggestive, and lively knowledge than other rhetorical forms do. The fourth is a connected effect of proximity: readers or auditors find themselves immersed in the scenes and circumstances depicted. Each of these effects can definitely be discussed or contested—the recent controversy regarding Alice Goffman's ethnography of poor neighborhoods in Philadelphia has revived debates about the reliability of this approach—but their combination gives ethnography a form of intellectual authority that has resisted rather well its questioning by the natives and by the textualist turn.

What is therefore at stake in the project of a public ethnography is the sort of truth that is produced, established, and, in the end, told.

———————

Beyond the general features that have been analyzed thus far, ethnography's encounters with its publics may take multiple forms and raise diverse issues. The present volume reflects this multiplicity and this diversity.

Ethnographers are engaged with a wide range of publics, including journalists for Gabriella Coleman and Unni Wikan, policymakers for Manuela Ivone Cunha and Vincent Dubois, political actors for Ghassan Hage and João Biehl, legal experts for Kelly Gillespie and Jonathan Benthall, local populations for Federico Neiburg and Lucas Bessire, and even scholars for Nadia Abu El-Haj and Sherine Hamdy—although most of them deal at some point with other social agents. Their role varies from intervening as experts for Benthall and Dubois, to serving as mediators and translators in the case of Coleman and Neiburg, proposing intellectual companionship for Hage and Bessire, reframing interpretations of social phenomena in the case of Gillespie and Cunha, shedding light on controversial topics for Wikan and Hamdy, and even responding to tense confrontations in the case of Biehl and violent attacks in the case of Abu El-Haj—although for each of them the form of engagement changes with time as problems are redefined and places are renegotiated. Finally, the relationships and interactions that the authors have with the national communities to which the publics belong differ: they can be a member of this community, like Coleman, Gillespie, and Dubois; present themselves as a sympathetic foreigner, in the case of Hage, Neiburg, and Bessire; occupy intermediate positions, like Benthall, Abu El-Haj, and Sherine Hamdy; or even move from one context to another, like Cunha, Wikan, and Biehl. Each of these positions is uncertain and changeable, with important consequences in terms of the legitimacy and efficacy of the public presence.

Yet whatever the configuration of this presence, the contributors to this volume all strive with the same objective of communicating a certain truth, or perhaps better said, *a conception of the truth* grounded in their empirical and theoretical work against prejudices, interests, powers, and sometimes simply common sense. They acknowledge that there is no absolute and definitive truth and that their approach is not the only one possible—their version of the truth could be and needed to be discussed and even disputed—but they are convinced that something essential is at stake in both the production of an ethnographic understanding of the world and its public dissemination. For Coleman this means correcting the simplified representation of hackers such as Anonymous; for Hage, resisting the trivialization and instrumentalization of the idea of resistance among Palestinian leaders; for Gillespie, acknowledging the moral sense of popular justice among poor South Africans; for Cunha, revealing the targeting of the poor and the downgrading of judicial practices underlying incarceration in Portugal; for Neiburg, identifying the legitimate expectations rather than mere violence of residents in the marginal neighborhoods of Port-au-Prince; for Bessire, denouncing the complicity of anthropologists and nongovernmental organizations in their construction of a culturalist and primitivist image of Ayoreo people. Similarly Benthall argues that Islamic charities and intellectuals are unjustly discredited by experts and lobbies; Dubois shows that the alleged aggressiveness of people confronting the welfare bureaucracy is to be understood as a response to the social violence they are subjected to; Abu El-Haj unveils the ideological and political stakes at the heart of the constitution of archaeology as an academic discipline in Israel; Wikan challenges the dominant discourse of successful Norwegian multiculturalism in light of growing inequality and discrimination affecting immigrants; Biehl demonstrates that the judicialization of health cases in Brazil is not a manipulation of the system by the wealthy but a demand for treatment access and state accountability on the part of the underprivileged; and Hamdy analyzes the environmental and economic conditions of the dramatic increase in kidney failures in Egypt. In each case the ethnographer goes against the grain, contesting accepted evidence, disturbing established assertions, defending both a different truth and a different way of accessing it—via critical inquiry, empirical research, and fieldwork presence.

In doing so the contributors are obviously *taking a risk*. Speaking truth to power, as the motto goes—whether this power is academic or political—is a perilous exercise. It implies being ready "to raise embarrassing questions" and "to confront orthodoxy and dogma," as Edward Said says of intellectuals. It may lead to unpleasant moments when those who feel threatened try to delegitimize the social scientist, discredit his or her work, block his or her career, prosecute him or her, or prevent the continuation of his or her program, especially when it is conducted in a foreign country. But the risks of going public often take more subtle and ambivalent forms. They reside in the compromises accepted, sometimes not very honorable ones, when the researcher becomes the official expert for public authorities or private corporations. They lie in the difficulties of translating complex issues into simple, and potentially simplistic, ideas as the ethnographer interacts with the media or even general audiences. They ultimately originate in the suspicion existing within the scholarly domain toward both popularization and politicization of scientific work. This wide range of risks—some of them stemming from external forces, others coming from the social scientists themselves and their professional community—frequently results in a form of intellectual prudence that amounts to renunciation. Self-censorship is probably more common than censorship, at least in democratic contexts. The courage of truth, as Foucault phrases it, is primarily a struggle against one's own reluctance to go public for fear of being attacked or, perhaps more often, of losing some of one's legitimacy or authority. There is a cost to publicization, and one has to decide whether one is ready to pay it. But there is also a value to it—of which the present essays bear witness.

The first part of this book illustrates some of the more or less successful *strategies* deployed by the authors in their interactions with various publics. Coleman describes herself alternatively as a translator, gopher, and trickster as she responds to solicitations by journalists. Studying a secretive network of hackers rendered both her knowledge and her mediation particularly coveted. Her public contribution mainly consisted in explaining as well as rehabilitating Anonymous and its members since they aroused a combination of curiosity and suspicion. This investment had double returns: she gained recognition among the hackers, and she used the journalists to transform the image of the activist network. Interestingly, in time her relation with the media seemed to gain serenity and mutual trust. Hage recounts how he was asked to deliver a lecture at a Palestinian university and discusses the tensions he experienced as he was preparing his intervention. Whereas he perceived that the role of the intellectual in such circumstances is less to affirm new ideas than to confirm what his or her audience already knows, thus manifesting support for their cause, he nevertheless took the opportunity of this public presence to challenge the conventional topic of resistance and assert that empowerment is not an end but a means. To the heroic discourse, which masks games of power and reproduces the attitude of the oppressor, he opposed the everyday practices of resilience. Gillespie analyzes the conditions under which her testimony was requested at a commission investigating police brutality in the South African township of Khayelitsha. While she was expected to confirm the commonsense idea according to which the development of vigilantism in poor neighborhoods was a response to the inefficacy of law enforcement agencies, she used her ethnographic work to complicate the picture, showing that violence had broader grounds in postapartheid society, that popular anxieties regarding insecurity had multiple causes, and that demands for social justice were not limited to the single issue of policing. Yet in the end she realized that her discourse was instrumentalized to validate the commission's ready-made arguments. Cunha compares two experiences in which her ethnography, although not policy-driven, became relevant for policies. After her research on a Portuguese correctional facility, she had a hearing before the national commission in charge of prison reform, to which she was able to explain the flaws in the justice system, especially those related to the application of the drug laws that had led to a dramatic increase of the incarcerated population; this analysis later served to inform changes in legislation and judicial illicit drug control. By contrast the study conducted on vaccine acceptability, which underlined the complexity of dissenting processes, did not benefit from such privileged circumstances, but it was also able to contribute to modifying the scientific framing predefined by the epidemiologists and public health experts who had initiated the program. Elements intrinsic to ethnography may therefore have weighed more heavily than extrinsic elements to account for the receptiveness of policy-oriented publics in both cases.

The second part of the volume discusses the various forms of *engagements* more or less sought from ethnographers by their publics. For Neiburg the involvement was direct with the people he was working with in Haiti, as his assistance was requested to help solve conflicts in the urban area where he was carrying out his research. Responding positively was both an ethical necessity and a pragmatic attitude to be able to pursue the research safely. It generated new openings for the ethnography as well as criticisms from outsiders and frustrations among insiders. But on the whole, albeit unexpected and unprepared, this observant participation in a process of local pacification enriched and deepened the understanding of the logics of war and peace on an island that is chronically subjected to political as well as everyday violence. Bessire's long-term presence among the Ayoreo Indians, who are regarded as one of the most recently contacted ethnic groups and who live in dire conditions on the border between Bolivia and Paraguay, put him in the delicate position of intermediary between this population and the local nongovernmental organizations representing it before international agencies. Conflictive relationships developed between native leaders and their self-proclaimed advocates, and the question soon became one of legitimacy and relevance when multiple discourses, including those of missionaries, ranchers, government officials, and indigenous peoples themselves, expressed the supposed needs and will of the latter. More specifically a tension arose between two public ethnographies: one, tactical, which consisted in using ethnographic authority to impose the paradigm of a traditional society to be defended; the other, reflexive, which critically analyzed such authority and proposed instead an indigenized version attentive to the voices of those directly concerned. In his role of expert witness Benthall was confronted with a radical impasse of public ethnography. Having studied Islamic charities in the West Bank for years, he was called to testify in a court case in which the defendant was accused of using humanitarian assistance for terrorist activities. Not only was his testimony obsessively scrutinized in the hope of discrediting it, but the whole case fell under an absolute prescription of confidentiality. In other words, his ethnography was treated with suspicion and prevented from any publicization. Instead of this impossible account, two related cases, which take place in the United States, are presented: one in which the anthropologist produced an expert affidavit in a lawsuit in favor of Tariq Ramadan, whose visa had been denied allegedly because of his small donations to a Swiss charity funding Palestinian aid committees; the other a trial in which a distinguished judge and part-time political blogger seems to have prejudged an important issue. Linking the two instances the author discusses the assumptions of a popular book on Hamas written by a counterterrorist expert who has been instrumental in trials leading to heavy prison sentences for charity organizers in the United States. It is a less tense situation that Dubois faces with his essay on the bureaucracy of welfare in France. The national context of the social sciences is important to take into consideration insofar as it is characterized by the public funding of most scientific programs, with institutions defining issues but guaranteeing the autonomy of the researcher, and by a certain porosity between the academic domain and the public sphere, with scholars commonly writing opinion articles for newspapers. The interactions developed with the agents of the organizations were therefore based on a certain mutual acknowledgment of the expectations and limits of the collaboration. Yet it would be a mistake to subsume policy ethnography under the category of applied social science and oppose it to critical approaches, as is often assumed. In reference to Pierre Bourdieu's analogy of sociology with a contact sport, the author argues that, like the practitioner of martial arts, the ethnographer studying policies can use his or her knowledge and skill to manipulate the force of those in power rather than directly confronting them.

The third part of this collection analyzes cases in which *tensions* more or less provoked occurred in the course of the publicization of ethnography, often threatening the researcher himself or herself. The attacks to which Abu El-Haj was subjected show how far the menace can go. After the publication of her book on the political significance of Israeli archaeological practices in Palestine, Zionist scholars and networks campaigned to deny her tenure and attempted to discredit her empirical work as methodologically flawed and her theoretical approach as ideologically biased. Beyond her research, it was ethnography itself that was at stake as epistemological questions were raised about the protection of her sources and the generalization of her findings. While these questions must certainly be, and actually are, addressed by ethnographers, it is remarkable that they would be brought up only when ethnographers uncover uncomfortable truths about sensitive issues. Abu El-Haj had touched on the most shielded topic in Western societies, the one that has been euphemized under the official call for civility and on which censorship and self-censorship have become extreme in recent years. Although the subject Wikan deals with is not quite as dangerous, it too exposes those who study it to difficult ordeals: the relationships between Muslim migrants and their host national communities in Europe. She experienced this peril with two of her books, which generated fierce criticisms; one contested the widely celebrated success of multiculturalism in Norway, and the other accounted for an honor killing in a migrant family from Kurdistan. In such cases of polarized moral passions, the efforts to render the complexity of the situation and maintain a critical stance are met with suspicious or even hostile reactions from all sides. Yet it should be noted that Norwegian anthropologists have been particularly successful in their endeavor to produce public debates on contemporary social and cultural issues, as mentioned earlier. But the objects arousing emotional responses also vary across countries, as Biehl realized when he carried out his collective project on the judicialization of health in

Brazil. While the country was praised worldwide for its management of the HIV epidemic, the multiplication of lawsuits by patients suffering from a wide range of health conditions and unable to access treatment amid precarious infrastructure raised concerns among public authorities. By contesting, on the basis of their empirical data, the official discourse that discredited those who used this alternate path to access medicine, the anthropologist uncovered simultaneously the failure of the state to fulfill its obligations and the falsehood of its arguments against those who tried to unveil it. In response he was confronted with the criticisms of his Brazilian collaborators regarding the validity of his findings and the reliability of his method. It is a comparable form of nationalism that Hamdy faced when she presented the results of her research on medicine, religion, and health in Egypt at a conference on Islamic bioethics in Qatar. Because her analysis was critical of health inequalities, especially in the domain of organ transplantation, it was virulently dismissed by Egyptian scholars, their reaction generating in turn protests from North American participants who interpreted it as religious instead of political. As is almost always the case, the positions of both critics and critics of critics were largely determined by historical background, cultural prejudice, and power structure. But this scene becomes the starting point of a meditation on the quandary of doing anthropology in the Middle East with the singular tensions between hope and cynicism, cheerfulness and negativity that undermine political debates.

The epilogue proposes a broad discussion regarding the public afterlife of ethnography, which is based on my experience of research conducted in South Africa and France on topics as different as the AIDS epidemic, urban policing, and the prison system; in contexts as diverse as classrooms, conference amphitheaters, radio broadcasts, television programs, newspaper interviews, online interactions, court cases, and art exhibitions; and with audiences as distinct as students, scholars, journalists, policymakers, members of nongovernmental organizations, agents from the areas and institutions I studied, and lay persons politically motivated by or simply interested in the subject I treated. This final account can be viewed as an illustration of the variety of ethnography's public encounters and of the multiplicity of issues raised on each occasion. It can also be read as a reflection on the responsibility that ethnographers have toward their publics. Etymologically the word *responsibility* stems from Latin *respondere*, which means both "to make a reply" and "to promise in return." By going public ethnographers thus repay society for the knowledge and understanding they have acquired while answering questions that may have been explicitly formulated or are merely superficial. The settlement of this intellectual debt is, if truth be told, their ultimate political and ethical commitment.

Note

The conception and preparation of this volume started in a workshop I convened at the Institute for Advanced Study in Princeton. The event benefited from the financial support of the Fritz Thyssen Foundation. I am grateful to Beth Brainard and Donne Petito for their assistance in the organization of the meeting, and to Laura McCune for the revision of the manuscript. I thank the two anonymous reviewers of the manuscript for their comments and suggestions.

References

Asad, Talal, ed. 1973. *Anthropology and the Colonial Encounter*. London: Ithaca Press.
Borofsky, Rob. 2011. *Why a Public Anthropology?* Hawaii Pacific University, Center for a Public Anthropology, http://www.publicanthropology.org/books-book-series /why-a-public-anthropology/.
Bourgois, Philippe. 1996. *In Search of Respect: Selling Crack in El Barrio*. Cambridge: Cambridge University Press.
Brettell, Caroline, ed. 1993. *When They Read What We Write: The Politics of Ethnography*. Westport, CT: Bergin and Garvey.
Burawoy, Michael. 2005. "For Public Sociology." *American Sociological Review* 70.1: 4–28.
Chagnon, Napoleon. 1968. *Yanomamö: The Fierce People*. New York: Holt McDougal.
Clastres, Pierre. (1974) 1987. *Society against the State: Essays in Political Anthropology*. New York: Zone Books.
Clifford, James, and George Marcus. (1986) 2010. *Writing Culture: The Poetics and Politics of Ethnography*. Berkeley: University of California Press.
Debaene, Vincent. (2010) 2014. *Far Afield: French Anthropology between Science and Literature*. Chicago: University of Chicago Press.
Eriksen, Thomas Hylland. 2006. *Engaging Anthropology: The Case for a Public Presence*. Oxford: Berg.
Farmer, Paul. 1992. *AIDS and Accusation: Haiti and the Geography of Blame*. Berkeley: University of California Press.
Foucault, Michel. 1984. "Truth and Power." In *The Foucault Reader*, edited by Paul Rabinow, 51–75. New York: Pantheon Books.
———. (2008) 2011. *The Courage of Truth: Lectures at the College de France, 1983–1984*. Houndmills, UK: Palgrave Macmillan.
Goffman, Alice. 2014. *On the Run: Fugitive Life in an American City*. Chicago: University of Chicago Press.

Graeber, David. 2011. *Debt: The First 5,000 Years*. New York: Melville House.

Habermas, Jürgen. 1989. *The Structural Transformation of the Public Sphere: An Inquiry into a Category of Bourgeois Society*. Cambridge, MA: MIT Press.

Holmes, Seth. 2013. *Fresh Fruit, Broken Bodies: Migrant Farmworkers in the United States*. Berkeley: University of California Press.

Howell, Signe. 2010. "Norwegian Academic Anthropologists in Public Spaces." *Current Anthropology* 51.S2: 269–77.

Lévi-Strauss, Claude. (1955) 1992. *Tristes tropiques*. New York: Penguin Books.

Lewis, Oscar. 1966. *La Vida: A Puerto Rican Family in the Culture of Poverty—San Juan and New York*. New York: Random House.

MacClancy, Jeremy. 1996. "Popularizing Anthropology." In *Popularizing Anthropology,* edited by Jeremy MacClancy and Chris McDonaugh, 1–57. London: Routledge.

Malaurie, Jean. (1955) 1985. *The Last Kings of Thule: With the Polar Eskimos, as They Face Their Destiny*. Chicago: University of Chicago Press.

Malinowski, Bronislaw. (1922) 2014. *Argonauts of the Western Pacific: An Account of Native Enterprise and Adventure in the Archipelagoes of Melanesian New Guinea*. Abingdon, UK: Routledge.

Mills, C. Wright. 1959. *The Sociological Imagination*. New York: Oxford University Press.

Piketty, Thomas. 2014. *Capital in the Twenty-First Century*. Cambridge, MA: Harvard University Press.

Rosaldo, Renato. 1986. "When Natives Talk Back: Chicano Anthropology since the Late Sixties." In *Renato Rosaldo Lecture Monograph Series 2*, 3–20. Tucson: University of Arizona Press.

Said, Edward. 1994. *Representations of the Intellectual*. New York: Vintage Books.

Scheper-Hughes, Nancy. 2000. "Ire in Ireland." *Ethnography* 1.1: 117–40.

Turnbull, Colin. 1972. *The Mountain People*. New York: Simon and Schuster.

Vidich, Arthur, and Joseph Bensman. (1958) 1968. *Small Town in Mass Society: Class, Power, and Religion in a Rural Community*. Princeton: Princeton University Press.

Warner, Michael. 2002. "Publics and Counterpublics." *Public Culture* 14.1: 49–90.

Part I

—Strategies

1

Gopher, Translator, and Trickster

The Ethnographer and the Media

GABRIELLA COLEMAN

Three days after a pair of brothers stormed the editorial offices of *Charlie Hebdo* and brutally gunned down scores of journalists during the magazine's morning meeting in Paris, the countercultural digital activists known as Anonymous launched #OpCharlieHebdo. In a video announcing this political maneuver, a Flemish branch of Anonymous declared, "It's obvious that some people don't want, in a free world, this sacrosanct right to express in any way one's opinions. Anonymous has always fought for the freedom of speech, and will never let this right be smirched by obscurantism and mysticism. *Charlie Hebdo*, historical figure of satirical journalism has been targeted."[1] The effect was pretty much immediate. A bevy of journalistic outfits—stretching from the most mainstream of establishments to the most boutique of niche technological blogs—churned out stories about the intervention, deeming it unusual for at least one reason: Anonymous, so often taking a confrontational stance toward Western governments, this time appeared to be bolstering those very governments' interests.

As became customary following any large or distinctive Anonymous intervention, about half a dozen media requests came my way, in this case, regarding the retaliatory operation. By this time I had found the vast majority of these queries to be predictable: equipped with basic information about Anonymous, journalists would ask probing questions about the specific intervention in question, presumably with the aim of filling in the gaps of their knowledge (and also acquiring a tasty sound bite). This time, however, one journalist deviated from this norm—and not in a laudable fashion. On January 11, 2015, a reporter for one of the major three-lettered U.S. national networks contacted me by email, and it wasn't long before we connected on the phone. Like so many other journalists laboring under a looming deadline, he cut right to the chase, asking me to connect him to a participant in the collective willing to speak that evening on the national news telecast.

The request, while difficult to fulfill, was not unusual; by that time I had introduced Anonymous participants to journalists at least a couple of dozen times. What was exceptional was his stubborn insistence on the particular Anonymous participant he wanted to interview: "the Julian Assange figure of Anonymous." Stunned by this ill-informed solicitation (the vast majority of journalists had studied enough to learn that Anonymous was premised on an ideal of leaderlessness or were at least more aware of the gaps in their knowledge), I first had to muzzle my laughter before transitioning into a role I had once occupied fairly often, that of a cultural translator and ambassador. I offered a version of the following explanation: because Anonymous eschews leadership there is no "Julian Assange figure." I hammered deeper into this point, drawing from years of anthropological research. Participants are so quick to ostracize leaders and fame seekers, I continued, that it has prevented the development of an official leader, and even the emergence of a spokesperson is rare. While many Anons respect Assange and have supported him and his causes, there is no equivalent Assange figure in Anonymous. I finished by telling him that while Anons have appeared on TV before, it took some measure of work to earn their trust, so it was not likely that I or he could convince someone to agree to an interview in a single day.

Seemingly undeterred and unconvinced by my explanations, he became more aggressive in his pursuit by attempting to bribe me, suggesting that if I helped him a producer might later seek me out to publicly comment on matters related to hacking. Now annoyed, I opted to offer help but only in a roundabout manner, as a sort of test. Would he, I wondered, put in the effort to seek out Anonymous for himself, based only on counsel? I offered to facilitate his contact with the operatives by teaching him how to get on their chat channel. I sent an email with basic instructions for how to join their communication infrastructure, Internet Relay Chat (IRC), attached to a promise of further help once he was there. Unsurprisingly he failed the test. I never saw him on the channels nor heard back from him.

The wake of this exchange provided an ideal moment to reflect on my many years of interactions with journalists, an incidental byproduct of my multiyear anthropological study of Anonymous, which culminated in a popular ethnography on the topic published by a trade press. This case was striking for being anomalous; after my brief exchange with the reporter, I recall thinking that he was not only the single most clueless, uninformed journalist I had ever spoken to but, thankfully, had become the exception. That day it dawned on me that just as my view of Anonymous changed after being in the trenches with them, so too did my views on journalists shift after clocking so many hours with them. Fieldwork, which at first centered almost exclusively on interactions with activists, very quickly came to involve a near constant engagement with the journalistic field: over a roughly five-year period I was interviewed by around three hundred journalists, wrote numerous op-ed pieces, and eventually contributed extensive background information for a series of investigative articles, documentaries, and a web-based television documentary series. My book, while rooted foremost in an ethnographic sensibility, also adopted several journalistic conventions. Initially skeptical of the general enterprise of journalism, especially its most commercial or mainstream incarnations, I had grown not only to respect many journalists but had also become deeply entangled with the fourth estate.

In what follows I recount the distinct roles I adopted during my interactions with journalists, most often the roles of a translator and gopher, eventually a prolific broker, and on occasion a trickster. I occupied these positions for multiple reasons that shifted over time. Initially I traded my access to media outlets for the promise of publicity to the attention-hungry Anonymous activists I was studying. Eventually the task of shaping popular understandings of Anonymous via established media channels became more interesting as a political end in itself. And ultimately, as I wrote my book, I saw journalism as indispensable for publicizing the plight of Anonymous activists, especially hackers, rounded up by the state.[2] I conclude by reflecting on why the contemporary moment is especially ideal for experts to engage with journalistic publics.

My Ethnographer's Magic

My involvement with journalism was an entirely coincidental byproduct of my primary field of academic study. Droves of journalists sought me out not because I was a technology pundit or public figure but because I was one of the few experts researching Anonymous, a confusing and tricky political phenomenon to describe, at least in any straightforward or compact fashion. At this point, after years of activity, there are a few definitive things that can be said about Anonymous. While increasingly recognizable as advocates for social justice and stewards of disruption and direct action, employing a recognizable roster of tools and tactics (including freezing websites, doxing, hacking, leaking, publishing coordinated Twitter alerts) across various "ops," Anonymous is nevertheless whimsical, making it impossible to predict its next steps. Because participants refuse to establish an ideological or political common denominator, Anonymous is not best thought of as a traditional social movement, for no matter how internally diverse such movements always are, for instance exhibiting radical and moderate wings and a diversity of tactics, they still tend to be oriented toward a single issue or cause, such as fighting for the environment or civil rights.[3] Anonymous is far more plastic. It functions as an improper name—Marco Deseriis's term—which is an alias anyone can deploy for whatever purpose. Anonymous, in specific, combines a general idea—that anyone can be anonymous—along with a set of tactics and iconography around which different groups around the globe have coalesced to take action.[4] In the past five years the majority of Anonymous interventions have been geared toward concrete political and progressive causes, for example, their role in supporting the Occupy Wall Street and Arab Spring movements; their commitment to domestic social justice issues, seen in engagements against rape culture and police brutality; and their exposure of the shadowy world of intelligence and security firms. But when journalists first reached out to me in 2010 Anonymous was far more baffling and I happened to be one of the few people who had spent time with participants and publicly ventured any conclusions on the subject. This only intensified as my perceptions and interpretations of Anonymous evolved in step with its ability to generate increasingly prominent and newsworthy activities.

My research on Anonymous commenced in January 2008. It was the month when participants first targeted the Church of Scientology, an intervention that began as a fierce pranking endeavor but then morphed, quite surprisingly, into a long-standing protest campaign named Project Chanology. Prior to this campaign the name Anonymous had been used almost exclusively for sometimes devilish and gruesome attacks, sometimes playful and jocular hijinks. Between then and 2010 my research on Anonymous could be described as a part-time curiosity rather than a full-blown ethnographic study. After a dramatic surge of politically motivated direct action activity among Anons, in December 2010 I switched to full-time fieldwork research.

The blizzard of Anonymous activity began soon after WikiLeaks published a cache of classified U.S. diplomatic cables, a move that prompted the U.S. government to target the WikiLeaks founder Assange and pressure companies like Amazon and PayPal to halt the processing of all services to his organization. The AnonOps node of Anonymous, angered by this act of censorship, rallied in support of WikiLeaks. In keeping with an Anonymous tradition, in early December 2010 they launched a multiday distributed denial of service (DDoS) campaign against every company they identified as having caved to U.S. government pressure. (A DDoS attack momentarily disables access to a website by clogging the targeted website with more data requests than it can handle.)

After this op Anonymous never let up, demonstrating an incredible run of activism between 2011 and 2013. For instance, it dramatically and assiduously intervened in each of the 2011 revolts that so intrigued the public: in solidarity with the Tunisian people, Anonymous hacked their government's websites; the Spanish *indignados* beamed Anonymous's signature icon, the Guy Fawkes mask, on the façade of a building in the Plaza del Sol; and after playing a crucial role by disseminating the earliest calls to occupy Wall Street, Anonymous further developed its propaganda techniques in service to Occupy as the movement attracted more and more people to join its encampments.

Back in December 2010, in the midst of its initial surge of direct action activity, I installed myself in nearly a dozen of the Anonymous chat channels that then proliferated on IRC and rarely logged off any of them in the next two years. In contrast to their knowledge of WikiLeaks—a constituted entity with clear objectives—journalists were understandably perplexed by Anonymous's origins, motives, and organizational style. Even as I began to tease out its cultural and ethical logics, throughout most of the winter of 2011 I found Anonymous deeply bewildering; while it was clear that many participants were galvanized to act in order to expose corruption and remedy injustices, many of their activities seemed to stem rather directly from a rowdy and often offensive culture of humor. Furthermore, even as I gained access to many Anons and witnessed some operations, I also became increasingly aware of an inaccessible underworld where sometimes illegal activity was hatched. While I began to recognize that Anonymous had settled into a few predictable patterns, it also was clear that mutability and dynamism are core features of its social metabolism and development; it was difficult to forecast when or why Anonymous would strike, when a new node would appear, whether a campaign would be successful, and how Anonymous might change direction or tactics during the course of an operation.

With the exception of technology journalists capable of finding Anonymous for themselves, the great majority of reporters in 2010 and much of 2011 knew so little about the collective—and so little about the basic functioning of the Internet technologies it relied on—that they imagined the participants were entirely beyond reach, as if they were deliberately hiding in the digital equivalent of a black hole. Almost immediately I dispelled the myth of Anonymous's incognito status and did so by acting as a gopher. It was really only a question of logging on to their chat services, I explained time and again. I taught the willing, a couple dozen journalists, how to use Internet Relay Chat—a text-based communication platform invented in 1988 and popular among hackers of all stripes for communication—so they too could spend hours of their day chatting to participants directly. (Generally those who took my advice were far too busy with daily grind of deadlines to spend as much time as I did on the IRC channels.)

Although far less common today, the idea that Anonymous is out of reach still occasionally crops up among non-technologically oriented journalists covering it for the first time. Take, for example, a July 2015 request from a Washington-based reporter specializing in Canada-U.S. relations. After Anonymous leaked classified Canadian government documents that revealed the existence of twenty-five spying stations located around the world, he sent me an upbeat electronic missive: "You might imagine how I might find some of this Anonymous stuff about CSE [Canadian Security Establishment] spying in the U.S. incredibly intriguing. If only Anonymous had a 1–800 media hotline!" I replied that they do have something similar to a hotline, but it is in the form of a series of chat channels devoted to internal organization as well as media inquiries and communications. I passed along the information he would need to seek out participants.

This "hotline"—the variegated network of Anonymous IRC servers and channels—acted as my home base throughout these years of intense fieldwork. One of the most bustling IRC servers at the time, hosted by AnonOps, even maintained a channel named #reporter, dedicated to communications with the press. As I did my research I witnessed journalists conduct dozens of interviews with participants, especially those reporters willing to do so in public. (Most were unwilling to conduct public group interviews for fear of being scooped.) Some of these early journalists had found their own way onto IRC. But it was and remains gratifying to teach the ones who reach out for technical assistance so they can interact with Anonymous themselves. (I also enjoyed watching them discover that portions of the so-called dark web are far more accessible and less creepy and sinister than many had initially imagined.).

While the gophering was often enjoyable, nearly everything else about my early media interactions felt more like a chore and, ultimately, a losing battle. It was particularly discouraging to see that, from the beginning, many journalists, even those working for reputable outfits, were publishing pieces that flattened out the complexities of Anonymous and its tactics by confining it in a straitjacket of well-worn stereotypes. Even as Anonymous insisted there was no formalized single point of leadership—a point my research bears out—a handful of these early journalists, especially in the United Kingdom and the United States, became obsessed with identifying the mastermind or leader pulling the Anonymous strings. Another common distortion concerned Anonymous's composition. Some journalists declared with certainty that it was composed primarily of juvenile, white, male hackers. At the time this struck me as particularly reckless and anti-empirical, as no participants had yet been arrested and unveiled. Given the painfully obvious—Anonymous intentionally obfuscated itself via technical anonymity—these declarations could be based only on conjecture and ingrained assumptions about the type of person the journalist assumed would be attracted to this style of activism. (Granted, at times the style of talk employed by some Anonymous participants could appear quite juvenile, but this was more an artifact of the entity's subcultural trolling origins than a reflection of the individuals behind the keyboards; upon arrests it was clear that, though some of the participants were young white hackers, many were neither young nor white.) Another predilection common to this early period of journalistic writing was a refusal to entertain the notion that Anons were driven by any activist sensibility, instead slanting reporting to emphasize sinister, criminal, or chaotic elements. Finally, journalists repeatedly misrepresented the DDoS campaign as a species of hacking; the truth is its deployment requires only the most rudimentary computer knowledge, and its use is the equivalent of accessing a public web page rapidly and in succession—a far cry from computer intrusion, much less data destruction that sometimes follows bona fide hacking.

I became so exasperated by these early representations that I wrote two critical blog entries and one op-ed with the sole purpose of picking apart and debunking the most problematic media representations of Anonymous then floating about.[5] Yet even as I sought to demolish these representations, I expected no less of the media. The continual deployment of these misconceptions simply reinforced some of the most negative views and ingrained assumptions I held about the journalistic endeavor writ large.

Walking a Fence, Walking on Eggshells

In spite of being annoyed by these media representations and believing there was not a thing I could do to prevent them, much less change them, I resolved to continue interacting with journalists; my initial labor of gophering and cultural translation was simply too beneficial, aiding me in two interrelated ways. The first was to enable the participant component of the participant-observation method, the sine qua non of anthropological research. While anthropologists can be more or less involved with and more or less sympathetic toward their subjects—some identify with their subjects unconditionally, even militantly, while others are more distant and critical in their analysis[6]—it is routine to embed ourselves deeply and participate in some capacity within the domain of study. This type of entanglement is driven partly by mundane practicalities. It is, after all, very hard to be present for years in a group of people without either feeling the desire to do something useful or simply being put to work.

But, more than that, it is also a sacred anthropological mantra that knowledge should be shored up directly from the wellspring of experience. "More than any other discipline in the human sciences," Tim Ingold notes in a tract on the distinctiveness of anthropological fieldwork, "[anthropology] has the means and the determination to show how knowledge grows from the crucible of lives lived with others."[7] Given Anonymous's serious penchant for breaking the law, I wanted to steer clear of anything straight-up illegal or that could be construed as such; since a hefty portion of the entity's energy was dedicated to making propaganda—as they themselves call it—and interacting with journalists on their chat channels, contributing to their own media efforts seemed like an ideal and safe way to participate in Anonymous.

The second reason to forge ahead with my media work was more selfish—and also exceeded my role as a participant within Anonymous. As my facilitation led to more and more appearances in the media, many participants came to see me as useful. Undoubtedly this was a crucial component in my ongoing access, justifying my presence to those skeptical of my position and giving me increased proximity to deliberative processes. As I transitioned from gopher to academic source and media commentator, it became evident that the respect only grew—especially following those occasions when I succeeded in publicly demolishing a particularly noxious or persistent myth. The following compliment, bestowed on me in July 2011 after I was interviewed on PBS, was typical of the Anonymous reactions I received in this period: "I'm far more impressed that you actually understood the essence of anon and were able to articulate it far better than anyone else I've seen on TV media thus far."

But even as my media presence facilitated my research, it also felt insanely precarious, as if I were walking on eggshells. During those early months of research, when so much remained hidden from me, whether intentionally or because of my own bewilderment, it was rather hard to authenticate information. (Once I was entrusted with leaked logs or accessed court documents, which included chat conversations, I was able to verify many of the statements offered during Internet and face-to-face interviews.) I remained acutely aware that if I tendered a statement that was revealed to be false, my public reputation could be irrevocably tarnished. So I tended to stick to a narrower band of information whose veracity I felt certain of. But this did not eliminate my anxiety about being misquoted by a journalist or lessen my fears regarding my own inability to boil down complex ideas into the pithy statements so often required by news organizations. When journalists asked hard-hitting, difficult-to-answer questions, as Bob Garfield did on the NPR show *On the Media*, there was a brief window of response time in which to be precise and on point:

B.G.   We were talking about individuals under the banner of Anonymous creating mischief. What happens if, for example, a country engaging in cyber warfare decides to do so masquerading as Anonymous?

G.C.   While anyone can take the name, people who are familiar with Anonymous, which includes journalists, people like me, other interested parties, could come about and say, look, this may be Anonymous but it did not spring forth from the networks whereby Anonymous is currently organizing themselves. And so you can sort of respond in the media and say, well, it is, but in name alone.[8]

My primary worry, especially during the first six months of active research, was losing Anonymous's respect by saying something that drew its ire. Many Anons actively seek media attention to further their cause. They also care about their portrayal. Aware that they were critically assessing—even dissecting—every statement I made (and they still are), I was ruthlessly deliberate during every interview I conducted in those first six months. It was not that I felt muzzled or cowed into silence. (In fact I could be very blunt about a class of issues; for instance, I contested early on the pervasive idea that Anons operated as an unthinking swarm, instead emphasizing the importance of transitional styles of leadership and, especially, the role of close-knit teams.) Nor was I afraid of being hacked or attacked by Anons if I said something off-putting to them; by that time the collective had explicitly professed its commitment to a free press by refusing to target journalists and media commentators, even those they vehemently disagreed with, a rule they generally followed. But still I did not feel reassured by the existence of this norm. Most concerned about losing access, I was always excruciatingly mindful of how and when to make public statements.

Indeed I exercised such restraint, delicacy, and caution during those early interviews that one could almost describe my behavior at the time as trickery or cunning. Most often this stance came from attempts to be diplomatic when commenting on a sensitive issue. In other instances it manifested as a careful effort not to comment at all—largely because of my own knowledge on a given subject was too patchy and incomplete to benefit anyone. In yet other instances I withheld information when I could not control the narrative or was not afforded the space to tell a fuller story. This is the situation I found myself in in March 2012, when *Fox News* published the news, previously unbeknown to me, that one of the most charismatic and prominent hackers in Anonymous, Sabu, had been working as a government informant for nine months, forcibly assigned by the FBI to shadow the collective around the clock. As the news ricocheted across social media and especially on the Anonymous IRC channels, no one from Anonymous knew I had met Sabu on a handful of occasions in person in New York City. Meanwhile I had confided this sensitive information to a few friends and a couple of journalists. One of them, a *New York Times* journalist, writing a story about Sabu after the *Fox News* stories had been broadcast, made a valiant attempt to coax a comment out of me about Sabu's life and personality. (Days later, when I wrote her without this personal nugget, instead offering an apology and asking if I was too late, she responded, "Yes, the beast was hungry Thursday.") I also had a window of opportunity to write an op-ed for a prominent news outlet, discussing the implications of his deceit from a personal vantage point. As tempting as these opportunities were, I remained silent on the matter for a very long time. A minuscule quote in a brief article could hardly provide the full context of my meetings with Sabu. Even an op-ed could not afford the space I needed. The semisecret remained mine for a year and a half, until I could recount the whole story in my book.

My craftiness in those days took one final and pleasurable form. Although I was the only professor hanging out with Anonymous on chat channels—at least knowingly the only one doing research, as there were ostensibly a couple present in their free time as participants—I was far from the only outsider. A handful of journalists had taken to covering Anonymous so frequently, and with such perceptiveness, that they had come to occupy a position similar to mine: that of trusted outsider. Mutually beneficial, the relationship between outsiders and insiders was built on unstated understanding. Anonymous would provide a bit of extra access, and we would transmit messages participants could not always send on their own or by themselves. For the most part hoaxing was rare; Anonymous activists wanting their pet causes and issues covered in the news were largely forthcoming in their dealings with us, but as a confederacy of outsiders we also maintained an acute awareness that we could be manipulated if we were not careful. Some of us outsiders became close confidantes, even friends. Not only was it a relief to discover empathetic human outlets for complaining about Anonymous—which was only to be expected in an arena difficult to study and maneuver—but we also relied on each other to verify information and share warnings about shady characters. For instance, one core Anonymous participant loved to boast about his manipulation skills. He regularly told me how easy it was for him to social-engineer (hacker jargon for "manipulate") some of the reporters. It became clear that this confession itself was part of a higher-order social engineering he was working on me, designed to make me feel I was part of the club. As exhausting as it was, I played along, working his confidence right back, even as his shenanigans became a frequent subject of discussion, alongside many other topics, among us outsiders.

Ultimately these small, routine, required deceptions added up, until I realized that I myself had become a trickster—one of the master tropes I use to frame Anonymous in my book.[9] This conniving spirit became apparent in the way I handled myself on all matters related to Anonymous during my first year of research in interactions with participants, public lectures, and interviews with journalists. Yet I thought it curious that this craftiness emerged not merely as an extension of its integral role in the community under study, a collective in many ways defined by its occasionally spinning webs of guile and subterfuge. Rather tricksterism can be considered a fundamental attribute of anthropological research itself precisely because we are "invariably caught between the dimensions of involvement and detachment," as Toon van Meijl has put it.[10] With multiple masters—our subjects, the scholarly community, and also, for some of us, the public at large—anthropologists hold multiple allegiances, far more, it seems, than journalists do. We must be adept in the art of code shifting as we traverse boundaries and craft our writing to speak to multiple audiences.

Thus public anthropology—especially when it involves being public at the very start of research—introduced some particularly thorny situations that I had not expected. The most difficult aspect of my media work was having to speak authoritatively during the early stages of research, before patterns, much less conclusions, became evident. Commenting about Anonymous, already a perplexing entity, felt premature but also, due to the general gulf of public understanding, somehow necessary, just one more example of the myriad complexities that defined this period. Either Anonymous could be described by those without any firsthand experience interacting with the collective (and there are plenty of technology pundits happy to do so), or it could be described by me, someone who had at least been around long enough to have an inkling of what made this phenomenon special and how it might function without a single leader, or any of the other tropes so fervently sought by journalists in the quest to provide their readers with easy understanding. What my engagement with Anonymous and journalists demanded of me above all else was a willingness to be at ease with some degree of uncertainty regarding my area of study.

From Trickster to Broker and Media Maker

Even if in retrospect it remains impossible for me to identify the exact date, my relationships with both Anonymous and the journalists covering it were drastically transformed for the better sometime late in 2012. My interactions with reporters ceased to feel hostile and instead began to take on a more collaborative character. I had become more media-savvy, able to forecast and take control of most situations, especially interviews. In many cases this was facilitated by a shift in the journalists themselves, many of whom had been paying attention and asked sophisticated, sound, and probing questions. Increasingly my exchanges with them became rewarding experiences in their own right, and I came to admire many aspects of their craft, especially their ability to transmit complex ideas in accessible and lively language. My brokering activity became quite common: I routinely and quite openly advised reporters who they should trust and who should be avoided within Anonymous, cleared up any persistent falsehoods, helped facilitate dozens of exchanges and interviews, and even began to contact journalists proactively about stories they might be interested in pursuing, which I continue to do today.

Even my trickery and caution when proffering public statements about Anonymous waned. By establishing firmer relationships with participants and by harvesting more and more knowledge about the collective, I could make definitive statements without fear of making a major mistake or angering participants. Coming to know many Anonymous activists on a personal level certainly helped; for instance, during interviews and public talks I came with the ammunition needed to firmly and confidently contest the pesky and still rather tenacious myth, held by the media and the public alike, that Anonymous is primarily composed of white male juvenile hackers.[11] As my relationship with Anonymous also became more secure, it enabled me to be more frank in both on-the-record and off-the-record interviews. Take, for instance, an interview in November 2011, where I openly suggested that Anonymous may be manipulating me:

> There are things about Anonymous that I currently can't write about because I don't understand it well enough. You have to have some discretion because there are some back-room politics, and they need time to develop before you make a claim about it. I'm aware that I am operating within webs of duplicity. While I've come to trust certain Anons and have more empathy than less, I'm also well aware that duplicity is the name of the game—misinformation and social engineering—and I'm being caught up in it myself. But, if it was clear cut and transparent, it wouldn't be as effective politically.[12]

To be sure, on occasion I still read articles that struck me as problematic, but I generally found myself tearing apart pieces less frequently. The nature of the reporting had shifted, and generally for the better. For instance after 2012 it was rare for journalists to identify a leader of Anonymous, well aware that a multiplicity of individuals and groups—some at war with each other—made use of the collective alias. However, journalists still sometimes resorted to grossly sensationalist accounts. For instance, in January 2012 Anonymous mounted a colossal DDoS campaign against the copyright industry following the takedown of the popular file storage site MegaUpload and the arrest of its owner, an Internet hacker and entrepreneur named Kim Dotcom. Afterward Molly Wood, a journalist working for the respected online technology news website CNET, wrote a piece about the campaign that could have been published on the parody website *The Onion* for how it equates DDoS with nuclear war. Wood begins, "With #OpMegaUpload, Anonymous launches the equivalent of thermonuclear cyber war," and continues, "In the aftermath of Wednesday's SOPA/PIPA blackout protests, the Internet community amassed quite a bit of goodwill, flexed its muscles in a friendly, humorous, civil-disobedience kind of way, and, remarkably, even managed to change quite a few minds. Just twenty-four short hours later, Anonymous legions nuked that goodwill and took cyber security into thermonuclear territory."[13] Readers unaware of how a DDoS attack works might come away from such an article with the deeply dubious notion that a large-scale DDoS attack is one of the most destructive forces online or off.

Journalists of this period also continued to routinely assess Anonymous on distinctly ethical terms—some pieces were neutral, many still tilted toward more negative assessments, and a minority were positive without qualification—but the sort of ridiculous distortions like the one reflected in the CNET piece had become rare, or at least increasingly isolated to the tabloid press, especially in Britain. In late 2011 outlets like the *Huffington Post, Rolling Stone,* and the *New York Times Magazine* increasingly began to publish longer pieces about Anonymous that exhibited nuance and precision.[14] Journalists tasked with covering Anonymous were afforded the time—in some cases up to six months—and the generous word count they needed to address socio-logical factors, accommodate varying perspectives, and tell fuller and more dynamic stories. (The exceptions were a couple of longer stories, all written by the same author, that puffed up and overstated the role of single individuals, which quite understandably drew Anonymous's fury; after all, Anonymous campaigns are collective efforts, and any individual self-promotion is univer-sally loathed.)[15] Many shorter articles described Anonymous more accurately as well. I was quite pleased, for instance, when a journalist working for one of the most reputable journalistic outfits contacted me in 2012 to ask whether the following definition of Anonymous, which he wanted to include in their style guide, was accurate: "Anonymous: An amorphous movement of on-line activists and other Web rebels who periodically coalesce around a cause or campaign. Although some within Anonymous are skilled computer users, many are not. Avoid the terms 'hackers' or 'hacking movement' when describing the movement as a whole."

The stakes of journalistic reporting became clearer to me when law en-forcement officers began arresting increasing numbers of Anonymous activ-ists. From late 2011 to 2012 arrests intensified—a period I dubbed "the nerd scare" in my book. Yet even though I was one of the world's experts on Anon-ymous, there was next to nothing I could do to meaningfully publicize the difficult plight of these Anonymous activists; the impact of a couple of op-eds about state crackdowns could only be fleeting, reaching a limited one-time audience. Journalists, however, could inform the wider public about this cre-scendo of arrests and also interpret their significance.

They had the ability to reach millions of citizens—but only if they chose to cover these crackdowns at all. A small cadre of journalists would write about the arrests and trials in specialized, niche publications covering technology news, such as *Wired* and *Ars Technica*. But their appearance—and, perhaps more significant, their characterization of the events—remained more uncertain in the national North American papers with large circulations. I even deliberated whether it was better for them to ignore the story and avoid the potential for negative characterizations. After all, pejorative associations have long been used to tar and feather hackers.

As it turned out journalists covered in great detail the arrests and eventual convictions of a trio of Anons: Barrett Brown, Jeremy Hammond, and Matt DeHart. (The coverage did not extend infinitely, however, as others who spent time in prison, such as John Anthony Borell and Higinio O. Ochoa III, received barely any press.) A portion of this coverage came in longer pieces, appeared in prominent mainstream sources, such as *Newsweek* in the United States, the *Guardian* in the United Kingdom, and the *National Post* in Canada, and was sympathetic or neutral in tone. Most significant, these articles paint these Anons as activists working on behalf of a political and social movement and never resort to crass demonizations of either their actions or the movement at large.[16] I deemed it vital to contribute to this effort that drew attention to the injustices inherent in the U.S. prosecutorial system and the dubious legislation, the Computer Fraud and Abuse Act, designed to target hackers. So in 2012 I assumed the roles of broker and collaborator with more frequency and intensity. It was in this period that I learned how to pitch stories and even succeeded in landing one on the front cover of a major national U.S. newspaper. I encouraged participants and their relatives who were initially and understandably reluctant to share stories with journalists (concerned as they were with losing control of their narrative) and offered advice on who to trust and how to proceed. I wrote a handful of op-eds and spent more time in behind-the-scenes work with investigative journalists, providing background information, and brokering contacts between Anonymous and journalists. For a couple of pieces I put in over a dozen hours explaining to journalists Anonymous's history and confusing organizational dynamics. I connected them to Anonymous participants and former participants whose knowledge about specific operations was essential to their reporting. It became clear that some journalists were receptive to advice from specialists and that collaboration with outside experts was an essential component of the investigative process.

By the end of 2012 my engagement with so many journalists from so many publishing outfits—*Mother Jones*, BBC, *Wired*, CBC, PBS, *Maclean's*, *Time*, *Al Jazeera*, *New York Times*, *Rolling Stone*, *New Yorker*, *Vice*, *Motherboard*,

Huffington Post, Ars Technica, and a dozen others—meant I could no longer cling to my earlier facile perceptions of a singularly oriented, unitary sphere called "the media." I had spent so many hours with these professionals that I couldn't help but observe journalism from an ethnographic perch. Direct experience forced me to approach the field with more nuance, and I began to differentiate among styles of journalism and specialized arenas while also making assessments on a yet more granular level based on the integrity and corpus of specific individuals.

In fact I began to perceive this domain much in the same way I saw Anonymous: not as a monolith that was good or bad but as a multilayered, complex, heterogeneous, and at times contradictory venture. Anonymous participants are fond of declaring "Anonymous is not unanimous," and of course the same could and should be said about the field of journalism. If my past dissatisfaction with journalists was premised on the way so many of them in 2011 fell back on generalizations and stereotypes, it became apparent that it was hypocritical of me to do the same to them.

Even if my views of journalists shifted, what could be said more generally about the impact of my media input and output? Did my counsel, commentary, and public writings contribute to sculpting a positive public image of Anonymous as a politically minded collective that should be taken seriously, that possesses a legitimate agenda? These questions are harder to answer, given how notoriously difficult it can be to ascertain something as diffuse as public opinion in relation to Anonymous, especially in the absence of a large-scale sociological survey on the topic. Even harder to gauge is my own role in shaping public perceptions of Anonymous. Still what can be said with some degree of confidence is that with a handful of exceptions, the great majority of articles that relied on my feedback were generally accurate—even if, again, ethical assessments veered in distinct, at times opposing directions.

Obviously many pieces were written without my (or any expert's) input. Initial findings based on a comprehensive analysis of two hundred media articles on Anonymous establish that the majority of pieces published between 2012 and 2013 in one way or another minimized or at least questioned the legitimacy of Anonymous activism, typically by framing its operations as pranksterism, vigilantism, or cyber threats.[17] The very general strokes of the study appear sound, although follow-up research could be more nuanced and concise. After all, some media outlets are more influential than others. Nor does the study adequately distinguish between short pieces and long investigative articles, the latter of which tend to carry more weight.[18] Perhaps most significant, the survey ignores the immense power of entertainment and pop culture representations to shape the political life of ideas.[19] When assessing the influence of Anonymous it is especially vital to include an analysis of popular films, graphic novels, and television series, such as *Mr. Robot* and *Who Am I*, which have integrated explicit and implicit references, many of them quite positive, to hacktivism in general, and Anonymous in particular.[20]

Downplaying the legitimacy of Anonymous can also be understood as part and parcel of a much longer trend in American journalism to altogether ignore or marginalize radical political interventions.[21] Given this context, what may be most remarkable is that journalists chose to write on Anonymous so extensively at all. (The reasons compelling so many reporters to write about Anonymous could be the subject of another article.) If we compare the coverage Anonymous receives to, say, radical animal rights activism, which is featured in specialty news outlets catering to these issues but otherwise is generally ignored by mainstream journalists, Anonymous stands out for the ample coverage it has received in the past five years.

It is also critically relevant (and a relief) that journalists rarely framed Anonymous as cyberterrorists. Indeed one of the most vigorous attempts to suture Anonymous to extremism failed.[22] Had this connection been successfully forged, the entire movement could have been discredited. Still the possibility that under the right conditions government officials could paint Anonymous as cyber extremists has always struck me as a real threat. Elsewhere I have theorized why Anonymous managed to escape the clutches of cyberterror and warfare imaginary, a story that is too complex to recount here.[23] Given the political misuse of terrorism rhetoric, especially in the context of the environmental movement, the sheer pervasiveness of cyber warfare rhetoric, and under ambiguous conditions, suffice it to say that it is conceivable state actors or law enforcement could have successfully placed Anonymous within this rubric.[24] Had they done so it is likely that some mainstream media outfits would have followed by parroting and thus potentiating this dubious message.

Conclusion

On November 13, 2015, terrorists struck again in Paris. This ambush was even more brutal and grim than the *Hebdo* attacks: ISIS operatives murdered scores of people who were enjoying an evening out. In the aftermath Anonymous issued a declaration of war against ISIS. It wasn't the first time; ten months earlier some Anons had begun fighting back against the organization under the guise of OpIsis. But it prompted those involved with the op to redouble their efforts and an Italian wing of Anonymous to initiate a distinct endeavor, fittingly dubbed OpParis. Both ops aimed to monkey-wrench the well-oiled ISIS online propaganda machine by taking down websites, flagging social media sites for removal, and, in rarer instances, gathering intelligence and channeling it directly to Western law enforcement.

A number of longtime Anonymous participants were thrown into an ethical tizzy over these two operations and the media attention they triggered. The largest Anonymous Twitter account, Your Anonymous News, posted a denunciation: "We think it's great if people want to hack ISIS and publish their secrets. But engaging in social media censorship campaigns and dealing with intelligence contractors and government agents is deeply stupid. The former will contribute to legitimize the spread of internet censorship and will lead to the increased censorship for everyone, including Anonymous."[25] A respected Anonymous hacker, blackplans, decried the moment in a tweet as a "media cheerleading frenzy."[26]

Yet even as the Anonymous offensive against ISIS was distinguishing itself as one of the most internally unpopular operations to date, the mainstream media bubbled over with giddiness about the entity's supposedly new direction. Some variation of the headline "Anonymous at Cyberwar with ISIS" crowned dozens of articles. As had been the case in previous instances where an Anonymous operation involved an antiterrorist mandate, cable news networks were quick to report—so quick in fact that participants in OpParis had yet to do anything beyond releasing a video.

It wasn't long before I was drowning in media requests. Keeping with recent tradition, most of the media professionals who approached me arrived well stocked with enough basic knowledge about the workings and logic of Anonymous to ask intelligent questions and modulate their subsequent queries. Yet, once again, the journalistic exception reared its head, this time in the form of a producer for a U.S. cable news network. Shortly after we began to chat she revealed her desire to feature the "leader" of Anonymous on her evening news show. Fortunately she proved less arrogant than the journalist I described earlier. Admitting her ignorance, she adjusted her expectations after I politely explained why this was impossible. (Nevertheless in instances like these I wonder whether under different circumstances—say, if I were a white male professor of political science working for the Harvard Kennedy School—I might have been invited to clarify this issue myself, on the air, as an expert.)

Yet this time the mainstream media's failure to capture the underlying reality of Anonymous's involvement in a situation ironically resulted in a positive outcome. While the coverage was largely premised on misunderstanding that a cyberwar could be waged on social media platforms and the bogus generalization of an unpopular, fringe sentiment to the entirety of Anonymous, the bulk of the mainstream media coverage nevertheless had the effect of positively boosting Anonymous's public image. Portrayed as a band of brave underdogs willing to courageously pit themselves against the most dastardly evil scourges of the Western world—the Islamic terrorists—Anonymous was now firmly slotted in the "good" category. It was all wins—except, of course, for the negative side effect of convincing millions of Americans that Anonymous is interested in or capable of engaging in cyberwar, when in fact the operatives were mostly involved in a propaganda battle that involved identifying social media accounts and asking the responsible authorities to take them down.

During this wave of Anonymous-related media requests, my mind invariably gravitated to other aspects of the story. Even if Anonymous had dodged accusations of complicity, there were many other actors in the hacker world who could be singled out for scapegoating. For days I obsessively tracked the coverage of the Paris terrorist attacks, wondering whether computer encryption experts would be implicated by the suggestion that the terrorists were using cryptography to communicate, or if Edward Snowden, the NSA whistleblower, would be blamed for publicizing information that some pundit would suggest had given the terrorists an edge. Almost immediately both of these anticipated accusations surfaced—and more forcefully and absurdly than I had imagined. The implication that these attacks would not have happened without the public availability of sophisticated encryption technologies was so delusional it bordered on media psychosis. Yet without a shred of evidence a loud chorus of media outlets, including the major cable news networks and (most disappointingly) the *New York Times*, suggested just that: the terrorists had relied on encrypted communications to coordinate the attacks. (As it later turned out, the terrorists had sent unencrypted text messages.)[27] A smaller number of outfits, mostly cable news networks, also aired the deeply dubious claim proffered by a former director of the CIA, James Woolsey: "I think Snowden has blood on his hands from these killings in

France."[28] A sentiment that should have simply been ignored was offered without even an attempt at substantiation.

During this period the media bubble I had happily inhabited for the past few years seemed suddenly to have been punctured. It was a stark reminder that the contemporary media field is so highly heterogeneous that, like Anonymous, it cannot be subject to any sweeping generalization. Contemporary reporting of such exceptional quality that some journalists have dubbed this period the golden age of journalism routinely appears today in the same newsfeeds as perhaps the most sloppy, lazy, sensationalist yellow journalism the world has ever known. As one proponent would have it, the journalistic present is cause for celebration: "In terms of journalism, of expression, of voice, of fine reporting and superb writing, of a range of news, thoughts, views, perspectives, and opinions about places, worlds, and phenomena that I wouldn't otherwise have known about, there has never been an experimental moment like this."[29] Yet even if this is the case, the mere availability of high-quality journalism does not guarantee its inclusion in the media diet of most consumers. The majority of Americans still imbibe most of their news from TV news sources, especially cable television,[30] far away from the epicenter of any journalistic golden age.

As the breathless sensationalism pumped into so many articles on the Paris attacks worked to temper my only recently discovered enthusiasm for the field of journalism, I felt a combination of shame, cynicism, and resignation. Perhaps all my media contributions of the past three years were in vain: So what if *Mother Jones* and the *Motherboard* got it right when CNN and ABC got it so wrong? In my sudden drive to track the breadth of the coverage, it was as if figures like Noam Chomsky and Bob McChesney—longtime critics of media consolidation and propagandizing—had suddenly paid me a visit, sat me down, and castigated me for generalizing my local, personal experiences to larger, broader societal trends.

Ultimately, however, I was pleased to see that I was not the only one who had these opinions. A number of journalists, some employed by mainstream news establishments, became sufficiently frustrated by the reporting to levy trenchant autocritiques. "If government surveillance expands after Paris, the media will be partly to blame," proclaimed Brian Fung of the *Washington Post*. "In this case, the shootings have sparked a factually murky debate over what technology the terrorists used to communicate to each other and whether governments have enough power to monitor those channel[s]."[31] As could be expected, the great majority of journalists covering civil liberties, technology, and national security were similarly incensed, and the resulting pieces and op-eds flagged the worst media offenders as they shredded the terrible reporting to pieces.

As the condemnation of erroneous reporting raged, I stumbled upon another survey that led me to once again reassess the contemporary state of journalism and a potential role outside experts could play in shaping the news for the better. If most Americans still receive their news from television news networks, a majority of them are also deeply skeptical of the accuracy and reliability of the information provided. According to a 2014 Gallup poll, "since 2007, the majority of Americans have had little or no trust in the mass media." Those under fifty reported the least amount of trust, and 2014 represented "an all-time low" in general trustworthiness.[32] While this information might at first seem to be utterly negative—describing utmost cynicism in our media establishments—it might also be cause for cautious and circumscribed optimism, for this study suggests that the bulk of news viewers, aware of the shoddy quality of mainstream news, may be actively seeking alternatives. Therefore, under conditions of relentless mistrust, the dominance of the mainstream media is not inevitable.

The contemporary moment is best thought of not as a golden age but as an interregnum, an in-between, transitional state composed of competing forces and parties. For those of us who can fruitfully contribute in some capacity, for those who care about having the truth told, it is our responsibility to embolden and support the large number of outlets and journalists who are implementing higher standards in their reporting. Indeed the value of having ethnography go public lies not in our ability to comment generally as might, say, a technology pundit, but in the "circumscribed as well as more qualified" nature of our knowledge and expertise as academics, to borrow phrasing from Didier Fassin.[33]

Still anthropologists face a particular set of challenges when entering the journalistic arena due to substantial differences in how these two professions treat their sources and how they view the very nature of knowledge production. If publicity might harm a source, an anthropologist usually proceeds in one of two ways: creating composite characters to protect subjects or simply forgoing publishing the material. These conventions, deployed fairly commonly, are meant to uphold a long-standing norm in operation among anthropologists, also ratified in the American Anthropological Association's Principles of Professional Responsibility, adopted in 1971. The first principle stipulates, "Anthropologists' paramount responsibility is to those we study."[34]

Increasingly we are expected to do even more than prevent harm and are obliged to contribute something to the communities we study during or after our research.[35]

Journalists' allegiance, however, tends not to lie with their sources but with the public, formulated in terms of the public interest. The media scholar Isabel Awad, who has thoughtfully laid out the major differences in the ethical treatment of sources between journalists and anthropologists, observes that in "journalism . . . 'ethical quality' is a matter of *getting it right* rather than treating the sources in the right way. The profession's take on ethics . . . is fundamentally related to the motto of 'the public's right to know'; the prevalence of a narrow definition of truth in terms of facticity In brief, it is an ethics constrained by the ideology of objectivity . . . consequently, a manipulative relationship with [a] source is as commonsensical to the profession as the paradigm of objectivity."[36] While my experience has been that most journalists rely on guile sparingly and as a last resort—after all, it is counterproductive to repeatedly burn or manipulate your sources—nevertheless the mere idea that a source can be instrumentalized in the service of a higher purpose points to a major point of contention between the two fields of endeavor.

As a close corollary, journalists may interpret as pernicious the proximity and intimacy of the sort that cultural anthropologists strive to achieve during the course of their research, as a corrosive force that seems to run counter to the imperative of objectivity that so thoroughly defines their craft. Although the status of objectivity in journalism has long been under debate, it remains foundational for a huge swath of contemporary journalism.[37] It is perhaps unavoidable, then, that when such an endeavor meets cultural anthropology—a discipline whose practitioners tend to be hypercommitted to empirical research but who are skeptical of knowledge purporting to be neutral and objective—there is bound to be misunderstanding and confusion about what we do. Journalists at times see anthropologists like myself as biased or complicit, while anthropologists see this as a misperception symptomatic of the way journalists and other publics can "confuse empathy with sympathy, understanding with promotion, and engagement with contamination," as the anthropologist Tom Boellstorff has aptly put it.[38]

This gulf of understanding helps to explain why a number of journalists who reviewed my book on Anonymous aligned in pointing to my "bias"— even journalists who otherwise stamped the book with a seal of approval. Never mind that I had been upfront about my methodology and reasons.

(Had I purported to be neutral, this might have been a different story.) It was frustrating—and tedious—to read indictments of proximity brandished over and over again, especially since it was that very intimacy that was of benefit to many journalists when they sought my advice.

My motivation to write a popular account of Anonymous also far exceeded a mere desire to make Anonymous intellectually sensible—although that was certainly a goal. I also sought to embolden the field of activism itself. Even though Anonymous is not perfect (far from it), a far greater political risk looms today from those who avoid imperfect activism in favor of doing nothing or approach political life through discourse alone: political inaction masquerading as democratic process, attached to the naïve belief that publicity alone can spark meaningful political change.[39] Even at its best, informed by thoughtful academic research and expertise, a politics of deliberation, whether taking the form of journalistic publication or citizen commentary on social media, is obviously limited in its capacity to spur political awareness, much less lead to meaningful societal change.

Nevertheless political activists do read the news. Political organizing without publicity—without hard-hitting journalism—would not get very far. It is undeniable that we would be worse off without the presence of an aggressive, honest, and ruthlessly investigative and critical field of journalism. There is a reason so many of us, from academics to journalists—most notably otherwise concerned citizens themselves—passionately decry the media when they fail to live up to basic standards. It is the same reason we are elated that change may be on the horizon when an outfit like the *Washington Post* finally publishes a story on the high levels of lead in Flint, Michigan's drinking water. And this is also why so many advocates and activists, past and present, have targeted the media as a site for radical reform, initiating a slew of alternative endeavors that have without a doubt shifted the contemporary journalism sphere in positive ways.[40]

My experience has led me to believe that journalists do their best work when they devote themselves to specialization in a certain area or are willing to rely on those who have dedicated themselves to a field of study. A mixture of the two is better yet. And, ideally, when they do tap those experts they might listen to what they have to say instead of stubbornly (or cynically) moving forward on false premises—whether out of an inflated belief in their own judgment or out of a cynical belief that all that matters is delivering an entertaining or sensational story. As for the persistent confusions and misconceptions regarding the nature of anthropological research, it is up to us to change minds and better relate our own intentions. And there is probably no better way to do this than direct experience and engagement—the anthropological imperative—with the journalist communities concerned to begin the process.

Notes

1 Anonymous 2015.
2 See Fassin (2013) on the difference between popularization and politicization in public anthropology.
3 I would like to thank Ben Wizner, who encouraged me to drop "social movement" to describe Anonymous for these reasons.
4 Deseriis 2015.
5 Coleman 2010, 2012; Coleman and Ralph 2011. Many of the problematic journalistic pieces are cited in the blog and op-ed critiques. In *Hacker, Hoaxer, Whistle-blower, Spy* (2015: 155–56) I also address the early journalistic quest to locate the single leader.
6 Helmreich 1998; Juris 2008; Scheper-Hughes 1995.
7 Ingold 2014: 383.
8 *On the Media* 2011.
9 See Geismar (2015) for a thoughtful discussion of my role as a trickster in both my dealings with Anonymous and my book's writing style.
10 Van Meijl 2005: 9.
11 See Coleman (2015: 173–76) for a discussion of the diverse composition of Anonymous: while the hackers were exclusively male, a number were people of color and came from more diverse class backgrounds as well. Among the nontechnical participants—the great majority of Anons—the diversity is even more apparent and includes gender, sexuality, class, profession, and national diversity. Since participants are cloaked and since Anonymous's ideology is ill defined, it scrambles the human tendency to seek and find like-minded people.
12 Pangburn 2011.
13 Wood 2012. The Stop Online Piracy Act (SOPA) and the PROTECT IP Act (PIPA), two copyright and internet regulation laws proposed by the US Congress, were shelved after a massive wave of internet-based protest against them in 2012.
14 Bazelon 2014; Knafo 2012; Reitman 2012.
15 See Kushner 2013, 2014.
16 Carr 2013; Horne 2015; Humphreys 2014; Reitman 2012; Zaitchik 2013. To be sure, some of these pieces, especially the two in *Rolling Stone*, were called out for some inaccuracies and problematic representation; nevertheless they are quite sympathetic and generally accurate. In contrast, as far as I saw, Anonymous advocates universally praised the piece by Adrian Humphreys in the *National Post*, which was

exceptional in its accuracy and depth; it totaled 15,000 words and was published in four parts. It also won the silver award for best article, granted by the Canadian Online Publishing Awards.

17 Klein 2015.

18 Ettema and Glasser 1998.

19 Duncombe 2007.

20 See, for instance, the television series *House of Cards*, whose technical consultant for the show was Gregg Housh, an ex-Anonymous participant; the comic book *Hacktivist* (2014), which was inspired in part by all the hacktivist interventions of 2011; and the German Hollywood film released by Sony Pictures, *Who Am I* (2014), which explicitly references an affiliated Anonymous group, Lulzsec.

21 Downing 2000; Gitlin 2003.

22 Coleman 2015.

23 Coleman 2016. While Anonymous has until now managed to avoid being framed as cyber extremists it may become harder to dodge this designation in the future. The cyber warfare pump has been so primed for so long that all it will take is one major hacking attack on infrastructure to potentially demonize the entire field of direct action hacktivism. And while there is no evidence that progressive hacktivists want to target critical systems, these systems are vulnerable to attack. The U.S. government spends far more money propagating fear-mongering machines and surveillance apparatuses than investing in securing critical infrastructure (Masco 2014). Since the forensics of hacking attribution is a notoriously difficult and politically malleable science, it is also conceivable that any attack on infrastructure could be pinned to hacktivists even in the absence of credible information (Rid and Buchanan 2014: 4).

24 Potter 2011; Stampnitzky 2014.

25 This Anonymous Twitter feed is available at https://twitter.com/YourAnonNews /status/676111595009925122?ref_src=twsrc%5Etfw.

26 https://twitter.com/blackplans/status/667368507357528065. No longer available.

27 Bode 2015.

28 Nakashima and Miller 2015.

29 Engelhardt 2014.

30 According to a 2013 Pew Study on the new habits of Americans, "cable news handily wins the competition for the time and attention of news consumers at home" (Olmstead et al. 2013).

31 Fung 2015.

32 See Riffkin 2015.

33 Fassin 2013: 23.

34 American Anthropological Association (1971) 1986.

35 See Rutherford (2012) for an excellent discussion of these expectations of obligatory entanglement.

36 Awad 2006: 935.

37 Shudson 1981.

38 Boellstorff 2015.
39 Barney 2013.
40 Pickard 2014; Wolfson 2014.

References

American Anthropological Association. (1971) 1986. Principles of Professional Responsibility. November. http://www.americananthro.org/ParticipateAnd Advocate/Content.aspx?ItemNumber=1656.

Anonymous. 2015. "ANONYMOUS #OpCharlieHebdo." Posted by Anonymous Operation News. YouTube, January 10. https://www.youtube.com/watch?v=1yCRA6cBZnQ.

Awad, Isabel. 2006. "Journalists and Their Sources: Lessons from Anthropology." *Journalism Studies* 7.6: 922–39.

Barney, Darin. 2013. "Publics without Politics: Surplus Publicity as Depoliticization." In *Publicity and the Canadian State: Critical Communications Approaches*, edited by Kirsten Kozolanka, 72–88. Toronto: University of Toronto Press.

Bazelon, Emily. 2014. "The Online Avengers." *New York Times Magazine*, January 15. http://www.nytimes.com/2014/01/19/magazine/the-online-avengers.html.

Bode, Karl. 2015. "After Endless Demonization of Encryption, Police Find Paris Attackers Coordinated via Unencrypted SMS." *Techdirt,* November 18. https://www.techdirt.com/articles/20151118/08474732854/after-endless-demonization-encryption-police-find-paris-attackers-coordinated-via-unencrypted-sms.shtml.

Boellstorff, Tom. 2015. "Audience, Genre, Method, Theory." *Hau: Journal of Ethnographic Theory* 5.2. http://www.haujournal.org/index.php/hau/article/view/hau5.2.023.

Carr, David. 2013. "A Journalist-Agitator Facing Prison over a Link." *New York Times*, September 9. http://www.nytimes.com/2013/09/09/business/media/a-journalist-agitator-facing-prison-over-a-link.html.

Coleman, Gabriella. 2010. "Anonymous vs. the Guardian." *Savage Minds*, December 16. http://savageminds.org/2010/12/16/anonymous-vs-the-guardian.

———. 2012. "Everything You Know about Anonymous Is Wrong." *Al Jazeera*, May 8. http://www.aljazeera.com/indepth/opinion/2012/05/201255152158991826.html.

———. 2015. *Hacker Hoaxer Whistleblower Spy: The Many Faces of Anonymous*. New York: Verso.

———. 2016. "How Anonymous Narrowly Evaded Being Framed as Cyberterrorists." Posted by the Internet Society/Hackers on Planet Earth. July 20. http://livestream.com/internetsociety/hopeconf/videos/130645379.

Coleman, Gabriella, and Michael Ralph. 2011. "Is It a Crime? The Transgressive Politics of Hacking in Anonymous." *Social Text* 28 (September).

Deseriis, Marco. 2015. *Improper Names: Collective Pseudonyms from the Luddites to Anonymous*. Minneapolis: University of Minnesota Press.

Downing, John. 2000. *Radical Media: Rebellious Communication and Social Movements*. Thousand Oaks, CA: Sage.

Duncombe, Stephen. 2007. *Dream: Re-imagining Progressive Politics in an Age of Fantasy*. New York: New Press.

Engelhardt, Tom. 2014. "The Rise of the Reader." TomDispatch.com, January 21. http://www.tomdispatch.com/blog/175796/tomgram%3A_engelhardt,_the_rise _of_the_reader/.

Ettema, James, and Theodore Glasser. 1998. *Custodians of Conscience: Investigative Journalism and Public Virtue*. New York: Columbia University Press.

Fassin, Didier. 2013. "Why Ethnography Matters: On Anthropology and Its Publics." *Cultural Anthropology* 28.4: 621–46.

Fung, Brian. 2015. "If Government Surveillance Expands after Paris, the Media Will Be Partly to Blame." *Washington Post*, November 19. https://www.washingtonpost .com/news/the-switch/wp/2015/11/19/if-government-surveillance-expands-after -paris-the-press-will-be-partly-to-blame/.

Geismar, Haidy. 2015. "Tricksters Everywhere." *Hau: Journal of Ethnographic Theory* 5.2: 376–81. http://www.haujournal.org/index.php/hau/article/view/hau5.2.021/2032.

Gitlin, Todd. 2003. *The Whole World Is Watching: Mass Media in the Making and Unmaking of the New Left*. Berkeley: University of California Press.

Hebdige, Dick. 1979. *Subculture: The Meaning of Style*. London: Routledge.

Helmreich, Stefan. 1998. *Silicon Second Nature: Culturing Artificial Life in a Digital World*. Berkeley: University of California Press.

Horne, Bethany. 2015. "The Case against Matt DeHart." *Newsweek*, May 20. http:// www.newsweek.com/2015/05/29/porn-run-333599.html.

Humphreys, Adrian. 2014. "Hacker, Creeper, Soldier, Spy." *National Post*, May 24. http://news.nationalpost.com/matt-dehart-claims-hes-wanted-for-working-with -anonymous.

Ingold, Tim. 2014. "That's Enough about Ethnography!" *Hau: Journal of Ethnographic Theory* 4.1: 383–95.

Juris, Jeff. 2008. *Networking Futures: The Movements against Corporate Globalization*. Durham: Duke University Press.

Klein, Adam. 2015. "Vigilante Media: Unveiling Anonymous and the Hacktivist Persona in the Global Press." *Communication Monographs* 82.3: 379–401.

Knafo, Saki. 2012. "Anonymous and the War over the Internet." *Huffington Post*, January 30. http://www.huffingtonpost.com/2012/01/30/anonymous-internet -war_n_1233977.html.

Kushner, David. 2013. "Anonymous vs. Steubenville." *Rolling Stone*, November 27. http://www.rollingstone.com/culture/news/anonymous-vs-steubenville -20131127.

———. 2014. "The Masked Avengers." *The New Yorker*, September 8. http://www. newyorker.com/magazine/2014/09/08/masked-avengers.

Masco, Joe. 2014. *The Theater of Operations: National Security Affect from the Cold War to the War on Terror*. Durham: Duke University Press.

Nakashima, Ellen, and Greg Miller. 2015. "Does Edward Snowden Really Have Blood on His Hands over Paris?" *Independent*, November 11. http://www.independent

.co.uk/news/world/europe/does-edward-snowden-really-have-blood-on-his
-hands-over-paris-a6740626.html.

Olmstead, Kenneth, Mark Jurkowitz, Amy Mitchell, and Jodi Enda. 2013. "How Americans
Get TV News at Home." Pew Research Center: Journalism and Media, October 11.
http://www.journalism.org/2013/10/11/how-americans-get-tv-news-at-home/.

On the Media. 2011. "The Many Moods of Anonymous." WNYC, March 4. http://www
.onthemedia.org/story/133097-the-many-moods-of-anonymous/transcript/.

Pangburn, D. J. 2011. "Digital Activism from Anonymous to Occupy Wall Street: A
Conversation with Gabriella Coleman." *Death and Taxes*, November 8. http://
www.deathandtaxesmag.com/157192/digital-activism-from-anonymous-to-occupy
-wall-street-a-conversation-with-gabriella-coleman/.

Pickard, Victor. 2014. *America's Battle for Media Democracy: The Triumph of Corporate
Libertarianism and the Future of Media Reform.* New York: Cambridge University
Press.

Potter, Will. 2011. *Green Is the New Red: An Insider's Account of a Social Movement
under Siege.* San Francisco: City Lights Books.

Reitman, Janet. 2012. "The Rise and Fall of Jeremy Hammond: Enemy of the State."
Rolling Stone, December 7. http://www.rollingstone.com/culture/news/the
-rise-and-fall-of-jeremy-hammond-enemy-of-the-state-20121207.

Rid, Thomas, and Ben Buchanan. 2015. "Attributing Cyber Attacks." *Journal of
Strategic Studies* 38.1–2: 4–37.

Riffkin, Rebecca. 2015. "Americans' Trust in Media Remains at Historical Low."
Gallup, September 28. http://www.gallup.com/poll/185927/americans-trust
-media-remains-historical-low.aspx.

Rutherford, Danilyn. 2012. "Kinky Empiricism." *Cultural Anthropology* 27.3: 465–79.

Scheper-Hughes, Nancy. 1995. "The Primacy of the Ethical: Propositions for a Militant
Anthropology." *Current Anthropology* 36.3: 409–40.

Shudson, Michael. 1981. *Discovering the News: A Social History of American Newspapers.*
New York: Basic Books.

Stampnitzky, Lisa. 2014. *Disciplining Terror: How Experts Invented "Terrorism."*
Cambridge: Cambridge University Press.

van Meijl, Toon. 2005. "The Critical Ethnographer as Trickster." *Anthropological
Forum* 15.3: 235–45.

Wolfson, Todd. 2014. *Digital Rebellion: The Birth of the Cyber Left.* Urbana: University of Illinois Press.

Wood, Molly. 2012. "Anonymous Goes Nuclear: Everybody Loses?" CNET, January 19.
http://www.cnet.com/news/anonymous-goes-nuclear-everybody-loses/.

Zaitchik, Alexander. 2013. "Barrett Brown Faces 105 Years in Jail." *Rolling Stone*,
September 5. http://www.rollingstone.com/culture/news/barrett-brown-faces
-105-years-in-jail-20130905.

2

What Is a Public Intervention?

Speaking Truth to the Oppressed

GHASSAN HAGE

In early 2013 I was invited by the Ibrahim Abu-Lughod Institute of International Studies at Birzeit University in Ramallah to deliver a keynote address for a conference titled "Between Dependence and Independence: What Future for Palestine?" As my writings and public activism and interventions clearly show, Palestine is not just a marginal academic or intellectual space to me. I have carefully examined the way the Arab diaspora experiences Palestine, and I have analyzed various features of Zionism as a colonial settler movement from a comparative perspective. Last but not least, I am interested in thinking through ways of ending the conflict and have written and made a number of public interventions on the subject. All in all I invest a lot of political affect in the Israeli-Palestinian conflict and think of the struggle for the decolonization of Israeli-Palestinian relations as one of the, if not *the*, defining political struggles of our time. I am prepared to accept that giving so much centrality to this conflict has something to do with my own background; some of those who know that I grew up in a very anti-Palestinian and pro-Israeli Maronite Lebanese family have even hinted that my Palestinian interests have compensatory dimensions. Nonetheless I think this centrality and global pervasiveness is far beyond the particularity of my experience. While all localized political conflicts have a global existence, as I explain later, no conflict exists as a global reality the way the Israeli-Palestinian conflict does, and in my work I have always seen myself as an anthropologist of the conflict in its global dimension. I have applied for and obtained research grants specifically to analyze this question. I do not have a total empirical sense of something as enormous as a global reality, any more than an anthropologist has a total empirical sense of any space he or she is researching. But I have engaged in what can be referred to as multisite ethnography and experienced enough spaces where the conflict is unfolding to have a good sense of the totality as a global field, the issues that animate it, the tendencies that shape it, and the political forces that are active within it. This has included participant observation in mainly global solidarity events, demonstrations, cultural festivals, discussions, and meetings with Palestinians, pro-Palestinian activists, and sometimes even anti-Palestinian activists in Lebanon, Jordan, Turkey, France, Belgium, the Philippines, Australia, Canada, the United States, and the United Kingdom.

But global as the conflict may be, it remains a Palestinian-Israeli conflict, and to know that some people in Palestine itself were reading my work and were keen to hear what I have to say was significant to me. I experienced this as recognition of a certain intellectual authority to speak with relevance about the subject by the people who are most concerned by it. As such it was a particularly validating recognition. Nonetheless it was also a recognition that filled me with dread. Indeed at the time I was somewhat surprised to be the one asked to deliver a keynote on such a topic. I checked on the center that invited me, and it didn't seem to me to be associated with the kind of anthropology, cultural studies, and social theory space where I usually operate. It seemed more like a straightforward social and political science center interested in producing positive empirical knowledge about Palestine. So I worried that maybe I could not deliver what they wanted. After all, even though I am totally immersed in the conflict empirically and affectively and follow its macro and micro manifestations very closely, I have not done any ethnography of Palestinian living conditions in Israel or Palestine as such. My knowledge of this is based on extensive reading of secondary journalistic and academic sources. I could think of so many other colleagues whose work was more directly grounded in the terrain of the conflict and who would do a far better job than I. So I contacted the director of the center, who had sent me the invitation, and expressed my concerns. He told me that I had the reputation of making people think differently. He suggested that I treat this event more like a public talk as there would be activists, NGO workers, and other non-university people who would be attending, including officials of the Palestinian Authority. With this quest for making people think differently and for addressing a variety of publics in mind, I proceeded to think about my keynote address.

In this essay I consider auto-ethnographically the various factors that came into play as I conceived of and delivered my intervention. I reflect on and problematize the way I was making my own ethnographic knowledge public and the imaginary and concrete publics that I saw myself engaging with in the process of writing and presenting my lecture. I end by highlighting how my conception and execution of this public engagement changed, in content and form, when I arrived in Palestine to deliver the lecture. But to begin with, and to make the above clearer, I will situate my experience in relation to various conceptions of public intellectuals and their function.

On Intellectuals and Their Public

Having begun my academic research writing a dissertation about the Lebanese Civil War while it was still raging and continuously in the news, I have always had to come to grips with the way my work circulated outside the academy: I was often asked then, and just as often I volunteered, to write opinion pieces for newspapers and likewise to participate in public debates about various aspects of the war. But it was not until I began writing about racism, multiculturalism, and ethnic relations in Australia that the term *public intellectual* was used to refer to me.

For my first sole-authored book, *White Nation*, I consciously attempted to write a work that was both uncompromisingly academic and theoretical and yet was publicly accessible and politically useful for the antiracist activists and community workers who were my central public at the time.[1] And the book was taken up by activists as well as discussed in the mainstream media. I was increasingly being asked to appear as a media commentator on questions of racism, multiculturalism, and interethnic relations, particularly when it was a question of Arab immigrant communities, which made me reasonably versed in the art of coexisting and working in both the public and the academic domain. This is when I started to be explicitly referred to as a public intellectual,[2] which made me reflect on the significance of the term and its application.

As a PhD student who considered himself a Marxist, I was attracted to Gramsci's concept of the organic intellectual.[3] However, my thesis was centered on the Lebanese Christian right, my own community as it were, which in terms of neither political affinity nor ethos was the kind of "suffering subject" I could fantasize being organically connected to.[4] This continued with *White Nation*, which was an exploration of the white Australian experience of multiculturalism rather than, as is more common in the literature on racism, an investigation of racialized subjects. By that time, however, I had become more sympathetic to Bourdieu's conception of intellectual labor as involving both the very Marxist idea that sociological activism entailed the unmasking of relations of power and the very anti-Marxist idea of the need for intellectuals to struggle to establish their autonomy from politics since, as he often put it, good politics do not necessary lead to good social science.[5] Indeed as I became associated, first as a post-doc and later as a visiting professor, with Bourdieu's Centre de Sociologie in Paris, my thinking at the time about what it means to be a public intellectual was an extended conversation with his many works on the subject.[6] This was at the height of Bourdieu's political activism. At the time it did not escape me, or anybody else at the Center, that despite his attempts at differentiating himself Bourdieu was increasingly taking public positions similar in style to those taken by Sartre before him—the very positions he spent a considerable amount of time criticizing, using Weber's concept of the "proletaroid."[7] I was also involved in many debates on the notion of public intellectuals in Australian and U.S. cultural studies circles centered on the work of Edward Said, Fredric Jameson, Meaghan Morris, Bruce Robbins, and Larry Grossberg.[8]

Some of the discussions and developments on the classical ideas of speaking truth to power and unmasking relations of power that happened then helped me define the way I saw my practice and my aspirations. At the same time, however, my experience also led me to question some explicitly and implicitly held assumptions that were circulating about the nature of public engagement. I want to highlight here the ones that had a bearing on my presentation in Palestine.

The first of these is the imagined separation between the academic and the public domain that is behind the notion of the "public." I don't want to argue, of course, that there are no differences between the academic and the nonacademic fields; my concern is more how this difference is constructed and what function it has for those constructing it. Bourdieu, for instance, for sociological purposes, argues that every process of cultural production occurs in a restricted and an extended field: a musician produces both for other musicians (restricted field) and for a wider field of listeners (extended field). For Bourdieu the accumulation of capital in one of the fields is not straightforwardly convertible into capital in the other. To stay with musicians, we can say that if one writes difficult music that can only be appreciated by and have an impact on other musicians and a restricted number of connoisseurs, this shrinks one's capacity to reach and affect a wider audience that lacks the musical literacy required to understand such specialized production. It limits one's capacity to accumulate wider public recognition. On the other hand, if a musician opts to produce relatively easy music that can be understood by and have an impact on a much wider audience, this diminishes one's capacity to accumulate "serious musician"–related forms of capital, the ones required to earn the respect of others in the restricted field of musicians. Furthermore having an impact and being appreciated can be achieved by nonmusical means. Your peers can resent it if you become famous not only because your music is populist but because you are good at packaging it and distributing it to the media. Consequently there are many tensions associated with gaining recognition and impact in both the restricted and the extended (public) field, and the capacity to navigate those tensions and to operate and be successful in both fields requires special skills. The same can be said of academic production: Margaret Mead is a classic example of someone whose way of making her ethnography public was seen by academic anthropologists (far from being free of sexism and elitism) as involving an unacceptable degree of vulgarization of ethnographic knowledge. This ultimately led to the work's academic devalorization at the very same time it was being publicly celebrated.

Despite this, the divide between the academic and the public domain and the kind of intellectual labor needed to have an impact in each is not always as neatly experienced as some would make it out to be. Though not often recognized in discussions of public intellectuals, there is something specific to the academic field that softens considerably the divide between the academic and the public domain. It is the academic function of teaching. When it comes to thinking about public intellectuals, it can be said that the idea of an academic domain so distinct from the public domain is more often than not reproduced by the dominant, masculinist imagination of the academic as an original researcher, thinker, and writer rather than as a teacher, and particularly as a teacher of first-year university students.[9] When the figure of the teacher is present in discussions of public intellectuals it is as a teacher of senior students discussing difficult articles and concepts in a small workshop, conjuring images of depth and complexity.

If one begins with the academic as a teacher of first-year students and of teaching as one process of making knowledge enter the public domain, especially when it takes the form of addressing hundreds of first-year students crammed in a huge lecture theater, then public intellectual practices do not need to be perceived as requiring a radical break from academic practices. Instead they mark a continuity: a public intellectual expands the process of making knowledge public that begins in such university situations by taking it elsewhere in society. One important definition of good teaching in the humanities and social sciences is to make the theoretical and empirical questions one is confronting as a researcher relevant, that is, to allow students to feel that what is being conveyed is useful in helping them formulate and think through social issues they are already intuitively confronting. Another important definition is the capacity to speak, sometimes simultaneously, to a multiplicity of audiences with various degrees of intellectual sophistication. A public intellectual is often someone who is capable of transposing both of those skills outside the university. It is important to note here that those skills require good knowledge of the sociocultural milieu one is addressing. This is where the ethnographic question becomes important when dealing with public spaces. It is impossible to produce high-quality public knowledge in an environment where one is not familiar with most of the key social and political issues that animate that environment and also, and as important, with the different ways various sociologically pertinent sections of the population experience them intellectually and affectively. This leads me to the second important divergence from commonly accepted accounts of engaging in public intellectual practice. It is related to the public status, authority, and function of ethnographic knowledge.

As I have already pointed out, I could relate to being someone who through his research is uncovering relations of power and speaking truth to power, yet I found this rather limiting or even ineffectual when it came to working in situations of interethnic conflict or in the context of colonial settler societies such as Australia and Israel-Palestine. This is because the idea of speaking truth to power always assumes a model where there is a general population facing *power*, a term usually acting as a signifier of a political or economic elite. In intercommunal conflictual situations, however, one always finds two groups or social formations, each with its own elites and power structure facing each other. One group dominates the other, such as in a colonizer-colonized relationship, but there are also dominant and dominated within each side of the relation. In such circumstances it is easy to speak truth to power, for instance, by ethnographically detailing the micromechanisms of the ongoing nature of colonial settler realities that the colonizers are trying to evade, to end up being recuperated by the elite of the colonized. I often faced situations when discussing the racialization of ethnic minorities in Australia where I felt I was speaking truth to power by minutely describing the way relations of white racist domination operated even in the midst of multicultural realities to find myself in the lap of community leaders with normative cultural agendas about what Greek or Lebanese or Vietnamese culture entails. I quickly learned that speaking truth to power needs to be continual and not fixated on one power and one process of domination if a public intellectual wishes to maintain some autonomy from the political forces that are aiming to invest in his or her knowledge to shore up their own power. This became, as I explain below, even more important when dealing with Palestinian questions.

There is another important dimension of reality that an ethnographer making his or her findings public has to face in situations of intercommunal conflicts. This is something that became very clear to me working in the midst of the Lebanese Civil War, and it was confirmed in other conflicts. In such situations each community lives its truth. That is, each community inhabits the world in an entirely unique manner and produces its truth from the particular form of inhabitance that dominates within it. The differences between communities are often more ontological than epistemological; they inhabit reality in different ways and often disagree about what they are disagreeing about. It is not a situation where community A believes A and community B believes B and the ethnographer can come and say, "Let me tell you the truth: the situation is actually C," or even "a little bit of A and a little bit of B." Community A lives its truth A, and community B lives its truth B, and each finds plenty of evidence in its experiential reality to support its views. Furthermore, because each side feels its reality and truth threatened, people on either side of the divide grow up learning and creating a multiplicity of ways and strategies of being protective of their truth and their reality.

In such situations intellectuals at public forums always find themselves in front of audiences of people who always come as judges, as subjects who already know what there is to know, rather than as students. Each communal public learns to determine a priori, and with a reasonable degree of precision, whether an intellectual is on their side or the side of the enemy. If they determine an intellectual to be on the side of the enemy, they either ignore him or her or try to make him or her hear their truth. They never come to learn something new. They are predisposed to treat whatever challenging position such an intellectual has as predictable and motivated by enmity.

It is not better when the public classifies intellectuals as being on their side. Here also the public does not tend to listen to learn anything new. On the whole, people attend forums to have their vision of the world confirmed by an intellectual authority. Communities that are in conflict and feel threatened celebrate their intellectuals insofar as they are confirmationist intellectuals. When they applaud the public is telling these intellectuals, "Very good. You have worked for ten years to know what we already know, but you say it so well." Someone will even come along and say, "I couldn't have put it better myself."

Such situations not only challenge the idea of the intellectual as a possessor of a scientific truth that is more objective or with a higher truth-value than that produced by the publics of the conflicting communities. They also challenge another divide that is often posited in discussing public intellectuals: the divide between the academic as an active human subject and dispenser of scientific knowledge and his or her public as passive recipients of such knowledge. This separation is less present in the Gramscian and Foucauldian traditions than in the Sartrian and Bourdieusian ones.[10] Traces of it can be seen in some overly extreme versions of the anthropological differentiation between the etic and the emic. It is also present in the American tradition, which conceives of the public intellectual as a translator of academic knowledge into accessible public discourse.[11]

To be sure, the fact that, as I've described, these separations are challenged in situations of intercommunal conflict does not mean there is no room for public intellectual labor in such circumstances. Rather it is always an invitation for thinking it along lines other than, though not necessarily in opposition to, the standard speaking-truth-to-power approach. The most common statements I hear from people from ethnic minorities in Australia who have read *White Nation* are "You've put in words what I have always felt but couldn't say," "You've said something I've always wanted to say but I didn't know how to say it," "This was really waiting to be said," and many variations along the same theme. This has made my public intellectual labor a rewarding experience. I came to see it as a process akin to psychoanalysis, in which a high point of a long-term analytical and interactive relation with a social space is to gain sophisticated knowledge of various groups of people's experiences of their environment to be able to facilitate the signification of what they themselves are struggling to signify. In this process, rather than seeing the public and the academic, the emic and the etic, as opposite categories, one can say that the role of the public intellectual is to create etic categories that aspire to be, and are already on the way to becoming, emic. This was a crucial experience that I transposed into the field when I began working on the Israeli-Palestinian conflict.

Before examining the way the question of the public was played out in particular when I began work on my Palestinian presentation, I want to highlight one last experience that has also been of considerable importance for me and that I also transposed into the Palestinian field. This has to do with the very separation between the intellectual or ethnographer as an individual and his or her public as a kind of reality out there. I maintain that in reflecting on public intellectual labor one is automatically dealing with more than the intellectual as a person with a particular history and particular inclinations. What needs to be brought to the fore is that public intellectuals are always an articulation of a variety of assemblages made out of themselves and the various publics they see themselves as addressing. This is because public intellectuals by necessity are always thinking with or writing for a variety of publics that constitute their imaginary of those they are addressing. It is perhaps useful to think of them, like Marilyn Strathern's dividuals, as the nodal space where a multiplicity of intellectual-public relations interact. Thus this multiplicity of publics do not come after the act of writing or talking; rather they have already participated in its very production. This is why, when an intellectual is speaking at a particular event and addressing a particular public at an equally particular conjuncture, these other publics will not simply disappear but are always present as part of a wider audience and readership. As I will show, in preparing and presenting my talk, in the issues I developed, in the way I invest in my ethnographic knowledge to create particular public effects, the concrete public I was speaking to in Palestine was always shadowed by a variety of other publics who are always part of my imaginary public space. At the same time this concrete Palestinian public also disrupted the familiar imaginary of a public to which I was more habituated.

Preparing a Public Intervention: Resisting Resistance and Its Imaginary Public

As I stated earlier, since I began working formally on the way the Arab-Israeli conflict is played out among the Arab diaspora, I inexorably moved from being merely politically interested in the conflict to being a researcher of its global dimension. My initial entry into the field was an interest in the way Arab youth in Australia gave affective primacy in their lives to the Palestinian question. I rhetorically asked many, "You complain about the Australian government not doing enough about combating racism and Islamophobia, and you complain about it being too pro-Israeli. If the government says to you 'I can't satisfy both your demands. You have to choose one,' which would you prefer to see it acting on first: introducing more efficient antiracist legislation or becoming less supportive of Israel?" By far the great majority wished that the government would stop supporting Israel.

Well before that time the global pervasiveness of the Palestinian conflict was something I had to deal with throughout my research career regardless of whether or not I was interested in Palestine as such. This pervasiveness was way beyond a mere generalized foreign policy interest in the conflict by governments around the world. Along with its centrality to the general population everywhere in the Middle East, the conflict had an independent circulation among people everywhere, including in Europe, Australia, and the Americas. Given the substantial inflow of Palestinian refugees to Lebanon since 1948, the particularities of Lebanese society, and the country's geographic location, the Palestinian question was inexorably articulated to Lebanese politics. It was, for obvious reasons, inescapable when I was writing my PhD on the Lebanese Civil War. But, less obviously, it remained inescapable as I began researching racism and Islamophobia in the West, not least when examining the difficult intersections of Islamophobia with anti-Semitism. The ubiquitous global presence of Jewish and Arab diasporas has been one crucial factor in making the conflict an integral part of many national political realities around the world. It is impossible, for example, to think Western, and particularly U.S., domestic, let alone foreign, policy debates without understanding the way they are articulated to the Israeli-Palestinian conflict.

But like many other globalized cultural forms today, from particular ethnic cuisines to yoga and Zen Buddhism, its globalization takes a dual form: one globalized form, often more parochial in its origins and concerns, circulates in the diaspora, carried along by the practices and interests of migrants as they settle around the world, while another circulates independently of particular migrant subjects, through various global media, as a more universal and cosmopolitan cultural form.[12] Thus, besides its circulation by Arab, Muslim, and Jewish diasporic interests, the Israeli-Palestinian conflict also circulates globally as a universal political frame independent of these diasporas. It operates as a global space of political investment, working like an emotional magnet on which many other politics have become articulated.

It is this form of globalization that helps us understand peculiar phenomena such the usage of Palestinian and Israeli flags by the Republicans and Loyalists, respectively, in Northern Ireland, observed by a number of ethnographers and journalists. As Conor Humphries has explained, "In the complex web of alliances that underpins the British province's flag-obsessed politics, the Star of David has been adopted by pro-British Loyalists, mainly Protestants, many of whom sympathize with Israel. Flying the green, black, red and white flag of the Palestinian territories, meanwhile, is a sign of support for Catholic Irish Republicans and their aspiration for a united Ireland against what they see as British occupation."[13]

There are many explanations for the conflict becoming a symbolic device for the marking of positions within other colonially framed conflicts. These cannot be dealt with here, but they all converge on affirming the extent of the global existence of the conflict. As Jared Cohen asks in an editorial in the *World Post*:

> What is it about the Arab-Israeli conflict that makes it evoke emotion on such a global scale across such a diverse set of populations? I don't dispute that for Muslims, Jews and concerned citizens of the world, the Arab-Israeli conflict genuinely induces powerful reactions. But I often wonder about the magnitude and scope of this global outcry and why it seems to dominate other more local grievances like unemployment, restrictions on civil liberties, and corruption. . . . There are aspects of the global reaction I find perplexing. At times, I have remarked to friends that the further one goes from the epicenter of the Arab-Israeli conflict, the angrier people seem to be about it. Why do young people in Algeria, unemployed and living in poverty, tell me that their primary grievance in life is the fact that the Palestinians do not have a state?[14]

This has meant that the conflict is present in a variety of forms across the globe. It has also meant that it is of interest to a variety of sections of any given local population. Thus I was not surprised when the director of the Birzeit Institute mentioned that nonacademics would be present at the talk. This has been my experience when I have attended Palestine-related conferences and workshops. In all of these locations academic events, in the sense of featuring academic speakers and being organized by universities, never end up being purely academic. There are always many others beside academics and Arabs, Muslims, Israelis, and Jews attending: unionists, members of local left-wing and radical political parties, radical anti-imperialist student organizations, as well as municipal and parliamentary political figures regularly attend related conferences. In non-Arab countries the list always inevitably includes Arab ethnic community leaders. What's more, such people do not merely sit in the background to passively hear the academics present and interact. They expect to understand what is being said, and more often than not they eagerly participate in discussions and debates.

Even when they do not have a background in being public intellectuals, many academics presenting at such conferences have learned to speak in a way that caters to such a multiplicity of backgrounds in their audience. This does not mean seeking some kind of condescending lowest common denominator but a far more artful and difficult capacity to make one's work incorporate a variety of narratives so as to have an impact on as many people as one wishes to. This involves mastering a plurality of forms of presentation as well as a plurality of content, for example learning to combine suggestive anecdotal empirical details alongside broader ethnographic information and alongside theoretical elements with differing degrees of abstraction. The degrees of skillfulness and sophistication at engaging in such combinations vary, of course, but there remains a generalized sense that the addressees are a multiplicity of publics, not just a general division between an academic public and a public at large but an even finer subdivision: empirical public, theoretical public, policy-oriented public, grassroots activist public, and so on. As important, however, and as mentioned earlier, the more one does this, the more this multiplicity of publics becomes part of oneself as a writer and presenter.

If truth be told, no sooner had I looked at the conference topic and begun to seriously contemplate how to tackle it than I knew the issue I wanted to address. The opposition between *dependence* and *independence* in the title immediately spoke to an ongoing intellectual-political concern that was part of a continual conversation, sometimes imaginary and sometimes concrete, that I have with one particular public: the Palestinian and pro-Palestinian groups looking for secular alternatives to the Islamicist opposition to Israel and the passivity and quietism of the Palestinian Authority. Chief among those are the activists inside and outside the academic domain arguing for an economic, cultural, and academic boycott of Israel, the Boycott, Divestment and Sanctions (BDS) movement. The centrality of my relation with this public is based on shared political goals, but at the same time my work has aimed to counter a tendency in the BDS movement to continue an unhealthy antirelational narcissism that pervades antiracist and anticolonial politics. This antirelationality arises when those disempowered by colonial domination and exploitation see their aim solely in terms of how to empower themselves. This, I have argued, comes at the expense of seeing racism and colonialism as "bad relations" that need to be transformed into "good relations." In the first narcissistic mode all the oppressed care about is to empower themselves. In the second their desire to empower themselves is only the means toward reconceiving of the previous racist or colonial relation. One politics is centered on the self; the other is relational.

This was an issue I felt I could address in my talk since I was certain that the particular public I wanted to raise it with would be present at the conference. I thought I could do so by questioning the opposition between dependence and independence and by critiquing the way the notion of independence features as a core value of anticolonial politics. What's more, to my mind, the Zionist appropriation of the Holocaust is a prime example of the narcissistic politics of independence: we Jews need to be strong and independent, and we don't care how people relate to us while doing so, for what is crucial to us is that no one is going to oppress us ever again. Thus I considered it particularly important to convey to my Palestinian public that in resisting Zionism it is crucial not to end up reproducing its core psychosocial structures. To me this was all the more critical since I saw the rise of Islamic fundamentalism, in Palestine as elsewhere in the Arab world, as precisely entailing the reproduction of this kind of narrow narcissism. I am trying to make explicit here that even in the very process of addressing my imaginary public of activists, I am also trying to speak truth to Zionist power as well as speak critically to Islamic fundamentalist publics. It is a result of the depth of my engagement in this field that I don't need much to conjure up such publics; they are present the very moment I start writing about Palestine.

But there were many other issues and their public that came to mind as I was writing, including, of course, academic publics. For the issues I wanted to explore were part of a wider problem that I have also been thinking through at a more theoretical level and not just in relation to Palestine. These issues have to do with what I have called the "anti" and the "alter" moments of anticolonial and antiracist politics. My thinking was based on "an increased realization that an 'anti-politics' concerned with the overthrow of existing orders needed to be supplemented with an equally vibrant 'alter-political' thought capable of capturing the possibilities and laying the grounds for new modes of existence."[15]

Nowhere was this more true than in the Arab world, where resistance to colonialism and Zionism produced all kinds of authoritarian regimes that ended up defining the very nature of the Arab postcolonial moment. But this was not only a historical problematic of a tendency that has emerged in the era of anticolonial struggles. It was a burning issue manifesting with particular urgency in Syria and Lebanon at the time I was writing (and it continues to do so today). Indeed as I conceived of the initial title I gave to my talk, "Resisting Resistance," the events in Syria and Lebanon and their significance to Palestinian political trends were foremost on my mind. It was born of an acute sense of how the Syrian and Lebanese scenes were intimately articulated to the Palestinian scene and the way they are central to my Palestinian public.

In Syria we have a dictatorial regime that has used resistance as an ideology of legitimacy. In a kind of tyranny of geopolitical reasoning, Syria, meaning the Syria of the Assad regime, is understood to be the bastion of opposition and resistance to Zionism and U.S. imperialism. Consequently all internal dissent and all attempts at fighting Syrian authoritarianism are portrayed as an attack on the resistance. Those demanding social change are portrayed as tools of Zionism and U.S. imperialism and crushed in the name of protecting the resistance. What this resistance is actually resisting and what it has achieved since it began doing so are not questions that can even be asked.

In wanting to use my intervention to criticize this kind of resistance, I was well aware that similar tendencies animated the Palestinian Authority, where, paradoxically, the worst kind of complicit passivism in the struggle against Zionism flourished under the banner of resistance. What made this critique even more imperative was a similar and tragic transformation of the discourse of resistance in the ideology of Hezbollah in Lebanon, for here was a movement with a well-proven heroic resistance against Zionism. It has efficaciously resisted the Israeli occupation of southern Lebanon and managed to actually defeat it, successfully liberating the region. It also withstood a massive Israeli attack in 2006, carried out by the Israeli Army but with the clear blessing of the United States and many conservative Arab regimes worried about Iranian influence in the region. Yet almost inexorably its concept of resistance was before our very eyes being emptied of any national or regional transformative significance and turned into an ideology of ethnoreligious self-reproduction articulated to and fully embracing what I have called the tyranny of the geopolitical.

It was with a keen awareness of the importance of these questions to the many publics I was soon to meet in Palestine that I began writing my critique of the politics of resistance insofar as it constitutes a governmental mode of domination. This was not an easy critique, for I knew that it had to be tempered by an awareness that my Palestinian and, generally speaking, my anti-Israeli public has invested, still invests, and indeed should invest a lot in resistance. I did not see my job as simply providing knowledge of the way resistance works as a mode of domination. Indeed I didn't feel anyone reading me or listening to me needed any lecturing from me in this regard: most people knew this all too well. I felt my task was to put in words the difficult, ambivalent situation that everyone was in as they tried to negotiate the need for resistance and the respect for those who engaged in it and the noble tradition they represent and, at the same time, the need to resist resistance and its transformation into an ideology of domination. Such a role was in line with the public intellectual's capacity to express a certain truth that everyone was feeling but was finding hard to express. Needless to say being an anthropologist in this field was crucial to performing such a task; speaking to the rather subtle experience of being cornered by contradictory choices is possible only after a long engagement with a particular environment of the type fieldwork makes possible.

In this sense the introduction to my talk, which I reproduce in an edited form below and which I had written before arriving in Palestine, was a direct product of my ethnographic engagement with the global dimension of the Palestinian-Israeli conflict.[16] It allowed me to create the concept of the unoccupied, which I saw as a lived space where one can escape being captured by resistance while continuing to resist the occupation. As I saw it, I was speaking truth to the power of the occupation as well as speaking truth to the power of resistance, critiquing resistance while not dismissing it as a practice or a tradition.

> Given the totalising nature of Israeli colonial domination and the way the occupation saturates Palestinian society in its most intimate details, one can legitimately ask whether there is, anywhere in Palestine, any such thing as an "independent" space for the formulation "between dependence and independence" to be meaningful. Nonetheless . . . there is still a vital force and a will for resistance and self-affirmation that permeates Palestinian society despite the occupation. Such vital force is enough to indicate that there is a Palestinian mode of existence that remains free and autonomous from the occupation. It is an "independent" mode of existence or what I will call here—for reasons that will become clear soon—an "unoccupied space," or simply "the unoccupied," since this independent, unoccupied mode of existence is not just a space but also a dimension of life. . . . [Here] we are immediately faced with the task of engaging critically with another facile tendency when it comes to discussing questions of independence: that of equating the unoccupied with the space of resistance. Indeed, some of those who consciously or unconsciously advocate this equation might feel offended by the very idea that spaces of independence are not so easy to locate in Palestine. Is that not disrespecting and dismissing the long and ongoing history of Palestinian resistance, which has continued to protect and foster various forms of Palestinian autonomous decision-making since 1948—both the organised political resistance that has happened and continues to happen through the PLO or Hamas, and the individual and communal grassroots resistance that Palestinians are continuously engaging in against the various forms of Israeli apartheid? I, of course, hope to show

that this is not the case at all. Indeed, as the question above implies, it is useful to differentiate between resistance and the autonomy that one is struggling to create or preserve through resistance. Ensuring that the two are clearly demarcated has both analytical and political ramifications. In theorising his concept of *illusio* Pierre Bourdieu establishes a highly evocative relation between "occupation," in the sense of occupying or assuming a position in social space, and "pre-occupation." . . . Although "occupation" when speaking of Israel's colonial occupation of Palestine has a different meaning from that highlighted by Bourdieu, what interests me here is more the nature of resistance as an "occupation"; that is, resistance as a *raison d'être* that gives Palestinian life a meaning. By resisting Israeli occupation Palestinians give meaning and direction to their lives. But it is precisely because of this that, despite resistance exemplifying a form of agency that is independent of and antagonistic to colonial occupation, it can nonetheless hardly be described as an "unoccupied" mode of existence. For resistance is a mode of being that is by definition entirely preoccupied by the occupation, as it were.

When I wrote this, and while I was confident of the existence of the unoccupied as a lived space, I was still finding it hard to exemplify empirically and anecdotally what it meant. Paradoxically it was the two days I spent in Palestine that provided me with a concrete exemplification. I say paradoxically because, in some important ways, my fear and ambivalence about speaking in Palestine proved to be more than justified. At the very time the occasion provided me with ammunition for thinking the unoccupied it also made me realize that any continuity I expected between the global field of Israeli-Palestinian conflict and Palestine itself as an occupied land was, while existing, less than I had hoped for.

Resistance, Resilience, and the Unoccupied

While I was confident that the interconnection of the local, the regional, and the international dimensions of the struggle is a salient feature of Palestinian politics, the two days I spent experiencing Palestinian everyday life before I was to give my talk made me see that being ethnographically connected to the way the Palestinian-Israeli conflict is lived in the diaspora and pursuing its evolution by reading the daily English and Arabic papers and social media is no substitute for the local ethnographic engagement that I lacked. I quickly became aware that some of the notes I had written about how to resist resistance had all the hallmarks of this form of pontificating from above that only those who are detached from the everyday realities they are speaking about can produce. I was somewhat panic-stricken. I often use Facebook as a public diary; here is my entry the night before I was to give my talk:

> I did tell the organiser of this conference that I don't feel I should be giving a keynote on "Palestine between dependence and independence," that I am hardly the most empirically knowledgeable person in this field. But he insisted. "Everyone says you make people think outside the box. That's what we need," he said. I was flattered. But one day of experiencing the "settlements" and the wall has already so fundamentally disturbed me. I've read all that can be read about the Wall and the settlements and I was still fundamentally shocked. . . . How is this possible today? It is like a colonialism running amok with power. Walling people as they please, mistreating them as they please, building colonies high up on the hills and literally shitting on those living down the hill by letting their sewer come out outside the settlements for others to cope with it. How heroic is it that the Palestinian people are still managing to squeeze a bit of life in the midst of this? And what is there more to say that does not sound cheap? I seriously am not enjoying the prospect of presenting this keynote.

I spent a very late night and many morning hours the next day rethinking my paper, trying to draw on the experiences and the conversations I'd had. In retrospect it would not have been possible to come up with and develop so quickly the connection between resilience and the unoccupied that I ended up with in the paper had I not been so engaged in the Palestinian question to begin with. And it would have been impossible to think without the shock of the local experience, brief as it was.

What really affected me during my short stay prior to the talk and what became metonymic to the colonial monstrosity of Zionism was the way some of the settlements discharged their sewage on Palestinian villages, whose inhabitants had to live continuously exposed to the smell. Twice we were driving through a Palestinian village when the smell of the Israeli shit landing nearby suddenly invaded the car. I kept thinking that a historical and ethical line was being crossed: *You colonize and you oppress. Okay, it's been done before, but to also literally shit on the people you are colonizing takes colonization into a different realm.* It struck me that in fact the Israeli colonists probably saw a classificatory affinity between shit, waste, and refuse and the Palestinians. I have often noted that what differentiates Israeli apartheid from South

African apartheid is that white South Africans actually needed black South Africans as cheap labor, whereas the Israelis have no need for Palestinian labor. Indeed they have no need for the Palestinians full stop. And so, in the colonists' eyes, Palestinian space is always already a kind of social rubbish dump suitable for disposing of one's sewage.

The historians of slavery have often pointed out that, despite the vile racism that characterized slavery, slave owners had an interest in the well-being of their slaves. After all, slaves were their property, and they were useful. I could see that this was not so in the case of the Israeli relation to the Palestinians. But what grabbed my attention even more and what I hinted at in my Facebook entry was the striking capacity of the Palestinians to endure this and still snatch for themselves various forms of dignified life that clearly no one was in a rush to offer them. It was this that led the concept of resilience to fill and make more concrete the empirically hazy space of the unoccupied, allowing me to offer it as an actual everyday Palestinian mode of existence, albeit one among many.[17] As I defined it in my talk:

> Resilience in physics, such as when we speak of a resilient substance, is defined in an interesting way. The word has no exact equivalent in Arabic. The dictionary translates it as *murunah*, although *murunah* is a better translation of "malleability" than resilience. Yet I particularly liked one Arabic definition of this *murunah*/resilience, which I found very evocative. The definition speaks of resilience as the capacity of a substance to absorb a deforming force without being deformed. This seems to me a crucial dimension of the "practices of resilience." . . . We can say that occupation is a deforming force in Palestinian society and resistance is the point where Palestinian society and Palestinian individuals try to counter this deforming force. But no matter what one thinks of the importance, sacredness and so on of resistance, one cannot say that the subject of resistance is not deformed by the deforming force it is resisting. Resistance, as we have already pointed out, entails durable damage to the people and the social fabric that are engaging in it. Indeed it could be said that this is the tragic dimension of resistance. It is heroic, it is indispensable, a viable life is impossible to think without it, yet it damages the viability of life. Resilience is in a sense the carving of a space that minimises this damage.

It was at this point that I was able to use my Palestinian experience of the past two days to forcefully exemplify what I was talking about:

In the household of a recently deceased Palestinian male martyr, his widow had to make some choices in terms of how much to remember him and to make her children remember him, which, of course, has changed with time. Putting his photo on the wall is an act of remembrance, but is also a celebration of his resistance and thereby an act of resistance in itself. There is a kind of shrine for him in the house ensuring that the children always remember the heroism of their father, inherit it, and participate in the culture of resistance he has been part of. Nonetheless, at night the widow always reads the children some relatively apolitical children's books and tucks them in, wishing them goodnight with a warm kiss that allows them to experience a sense of existence that is not subjectively governed by the death of their father; a sense of existence that is neither governed by colonialism, nor governed by resistance to colonialism. That is, she makes them experience a form of normality that children who are not subjected to colonialism and who do not have a martyred father also experience. This is what constitutes an act of resilience.

One can call resilience a space of heroic normality. It is heroic because it is not easy to snatch a bit of normality in the midst of such an abnormal situation. It goes without saying that it has a dimension of resistance built into it. One can capture ethnographically a whole domain of resilient practices that partake in the making of the unoccupied. When I was being driven around the West Bank and shown the settlements, the separation wall and the checkpoints, I noted that my young colleague who was showing me around and who had only been living in Palestine for a few years was capable of pinpointing to me in great detail all the outrageous things that the Israeli colonialists were doing. Just as importantly, he was clearly very affected by it. I could not help thinking that the Palestinians who have lived all their lives under the occupation, and who unlike my colleague did not have the luxury of leaving Palestine if they wished, must be even more strongly disturbed by what they are subjected to. Yet, at the same time, when observing them, they appeared far less concerned and affected. I asked the uncle of another colleague who had invited us to his house about this. The uncle's reply was very lucid and telling. He said, "We have families to feed and look after. We cannot spend our time thinking about nothing but the wall. We have to try and forget." He stopped for a second, then he said, "We have to forget and we have to never forget." He stopped again, then quickly added, "In any case, they [the Israelis] never let us forget."

Conclusion

Of all the places I visited in Palestine it was when I stood before my audience at the university that I felt most surely on familiar grounds. Everywhere I looked I could see people who metonymically made me face my variety of imaginary publics: the radical activist, the theoretically or philosophically inclined students and staff, the community researchers and workers, and the variety of university and nonuniversity officials, and everyone engaged with me in ways that were familiar to me such that I felt again that I was in a space that was part of the global Israeli-Palestinian struggle.

However, the moment I finished presenting my paper I experienced a type of interaction I was not accustomed to. A man in a gray suit—it was confirmed to me later that he was from the Palestinian Authority—told me, "What you are saying is dangerous." All my effort to avoid creating a polarity between resistance and resilience had clearly not worked on him. I looked at him and said, "Of all the things you Palestinians are confronting there must be more dangerous things to worry about than what an academic from Australia is saying at a little conference like this." He looked at me with a hint of a smile and replied, "People probably said this about Zionism once." This made me stop and think more than I thought it would, but I also felt that his reaction was confirmation that I was successfully exploring and allowing a more public exploration of an important tension at the heart of the Palestinian struggle.

Notes

1 See Hage 2000.
2 I was also quasi-officially ranked twenty-seventh in a list of "Australia's top 100 public intellectuals" compiled by an Australian mainstream newspaper (Visontay 2005).
3 Gramsci 1971: 6.
4 See Robbins 2013.
5 See, for example, Bourdieu 1993: 52.
6 Bourdieu 2008.
7 Bourdieu 1990: 45.
8 See Said 1996; Jameson 1991; Morris 1992; Robbins 1993; Grossberg 2010.
9 See Said 2002: 24.
10 A critique of this conception of the public intellectual as represented in the work of Bourdieu is present in Rancière's work *The Intellectual and His People* (2012).
11 Posner 2003: 46.

12 In the case of Buddhism see Rocha 2006.

13 Humphries 2014.

14 Cohen 2009.

15 Hage 2015: 2.

16 The talk is included in Hage 2015.

17 While I don't have the space to develop this here, my attempt at thinking Palestinian life as a multiplicity of modes of existence was an attempt to think productively with the concept of multiple realities offered by Eduardo Viveiros de Castro (2004) and is part of another dialogue with my anthropological public about the value of the ontological turn. In my instrumentalization of the notion of multiple reality is also a critique of those who see theory in religious terms as a mode of totalizing adherence.

References

Bourdieu, Pierre. 1990. *In Other Words: Essays towards a Reflexive Sociology*. Stanford: Stanford University Press.

———. 1993. *Sociology in Question*. London: Sage.

———. 2000. *Pascalian Meditations*. Stanford: Stanford University Press.

———. 2008. *Political Interventions: Social Science and Political Action*. London: Verso.

Cohen, Jared. 2009. "The Arab-Israeli Conflict: Why So Global?" Huffington Post, February 14. http://www.huffingtonpost.com/jared-cohen/the-arab-israeli -conflict_b_157989.html.

Gramsci, Antonio. 1971. *Selections from the Prison Notebooks*. Edited by Quentin Hoare and Geoffrey Nowell Smith. New York: International.

Grossberg, Lawrence. 2010. *Cultural Studies in the Future Tense*. Durham: Duke University Press.

Hage, Ghassan. 2000. *White Nation: Fantasies of White Supremacy in a Multicultural Society*. New York: Routledge.

———. 2015. *Alter-Politics: Critical Anthropological Thought and the Radical Imagination*. Melbourne: Melbourne University Press.

Humphries, Conor. 2014. "Northern Ireland's Protestants and Catholics Adopt Israeli, Palestinian Flags as Symbols." *Haaretz*, September 4.

Jameson, Fredric. 1991. *Postmodernism, or, The Cultural Logic of Late Capitalism*. Durham: Duke University Press.

Morris, Meaghan. 1992. "On the Beach." In *Ecstasy and Economics: American Essays for John Forbes*. Sydney: EMPress.

Posner, Richard A. 2003. *Public Intellectuals: A Study of Decline*. Cambridge, MA: Harvard University Press.

Rancière, Jacques. 2012. *The Intellectual and His People: Staging the People*. London: Verso.

Robbins, Bruce. 1993. *Secular Vocations: Intellectuals, Professionalism, Culture.* London: Verso.

Robbins, Joel. 2013. "Beyond the Suffering Subject: Toward an Anthropology of the Good." *Journal of the Royal Anthropological Institute* 19.3: 447–62.

Rocha, Cristina. 2006. *Zen in Brazil: The Quest for Cosmopolitan Modernity.* Honolulu: University of Hawai'i Press.

Said, Edward W. 1996. *Representations of the Intellectual: The 1993 Reith Lectures.* New York: Vintage Books.

———. 2002. "The Public Role of Writers and Intellectuals." In *The Public Intellectual,* edited by Helen Small, 19–39. Oxford: Blackwell.

Visontay, Michael. 2005. "Australia's Top 100 Public Intellectuals." *Sydney Morning Herald,* March 12.

Viveiros de Castro, Eduardo. 2004. "Perspectival Anthropology and the Method of Controlled Equivocation." *Tipiti: Journal of the Society for the Anthropology of Lowland South America* 2.1: 2–20.

3

Before the Commission

Ethnography as Public Testimony

KELLY GILLESPIE

What kind of information is ethnography? Is it possible for the information to be used well for purposes other than ethnographic writing? What are the stakes of the translation of ethnographic data and method into different contexts, in which information is managed and negotiated in different ways and for different ends? How might ethnographers engage with these moments of translation, of transposition, in ways that allow ethnography to claim a generative role in public life? How does the constitution of an ethnographic object differ or coincide with the constitution of other kinds of objects? These are questions that have been with me since I somewhat reluctantly agreed to write a report and testify for a commission of inquiry into policing in South Africa in 2014. Officially titled the Khayelitsha Commission of Inquiry into Allegations of Police Inefficiency in Khayelitsha and a Breakdown in Relations between the Community and Police in Khayelitsha, it requested testimony from me because of ethnographic research I had been conducting in Khayelitsha, the largest and poorest black township of Cape Town, on matters broadly concerning violence and policing.[1] This essay is an attempt to work through the meaning of my reluctance to testify before the Commission and to understand what that reluctance implies about the nature of ethnography and about its relationship to commissions as institutions of governance.

I make the argument that ethnography's most important methodological and analytical work is *contextualization*: the explanation of worldly events by means of careful framing, layering, scaling, and all of the acts of translation that attend these moves. I read ethnography's critical potential along the range and levels of social form that bear on any contemporary moment. The best ethnography, I argue, is a composition of this complexity of social life, paying careful attention to the passage between social scenes, between intersecting layers and frames, always with the understanding that the specific elaboration of context is crucial to any useful understanding of the social. What makes ethnography different from other kinds of writing that dwell on the daily, lived experience of people and places—like journalism or realist novels—is that it insists on the question of how to read the everyday in terms of the edifice of its own context. I arrive at this reflection by virtue of a moment of public ethnography in which data from fieldwork I had conducted were put before a public commission of inquiry and subjected to the framing questions of the commission's mandate. My loss of authorship over how the data of everyday urban life were construed and framed brought home that it is not so much the gathering of information about the everyday that defines ethnography as it is the emplacing of that information into a carefully wrought context that gives ethnography its critical purchase.

Although I would argue strongly for the importance of expanding the reach of our audiences, of articulating the rarified spaces of academic practice with their contexts, of making scholarly knowledge public, and of bringing our research closer to the social conversations that happen in and around our field sites, there are risks in these moves, and it is my task here to elaborate one such risk. In this essay I track the way I struggled with and against the mandate of the Commission, trying to find a way to interrupt and query its contextualizing frame. In particular I show how the Commission's primary object of police inefficiency is one that any decent ethnography should doubt, if not outright reject. In order to convey this risk to ethnography—the loss of control over how data of everyday life are contextualized—I trace the history and politics of the Commission before which I gave testimony, think through police inefficiency as its object, and analyze the difficulty of testifying while wrestling with the limits of the Commission's mandate.

In late 2013 I was contacted by the secretary of the Khayelitsha Commission of Inquiry into Allegations of Police Inefficiency to write an expert report on new research I had begun conducting in Khayelitsha. My ethnographic research was on a spate of murders of alleged criminals by township residents that took place in 2012 in Khayelitsha. In these attacks fourteen young black men had been beaten or burned to death by Khayelitsha residents for their alleged criminal activity, mostly involving theft and housebreaking. The attacks, often referred to as "vigilante justice" or "mob justice," are forms of nonstate popular punishment that have been growing in frequency in South Africa, and I was researching them as part of a book project on postapartheid crime and punishment. I had spent the preceding thirteen years intermittently conducting ethnographic research on various parts of the criminal justice system in and around Cape Town, and this was my final piece of research for the book. Importantly the spate of killings had also provided the impetus for the establishment of the Commission. The vigilante killings in Khayelitsha were cited as the clearest indication that the criminal justice system was in crisis and that the Commission should be set up with urgency.

The Commission was explicit in its framing of vigilante killings as a symptom of the failure of policing in the township. My anxiety and reluctance at having to testify before the Commission emerged from the fact that my ethnographic analysis of the murders did not hinge on the problem of policing. The Commission's argument was that people take the law into their own hands because police fail to effectively carry out their duty of public protection. But even as residents of Khayelitsha indeed argued that the police did not do their work properly and that the police could not be relied upon, it seemed clear to me from the research that policing was neither the source nor the answer to the problem of township crime and violence. It seemed to me that the precise responsibility of ethnography was to take seriously what people in Khayelitsha were saying about police but to insist that this discourse had to be read in its complex relation to other discourses and practices, other structures, other places, and other times. In writing my report for the Commission I was at pains to draw on examples of vigilante violence from elsewhere, to show the long history of alternative justice practices in the township, to make the argument that much of the violence and counterviolence in Khayelitsha, as elsewhere, must be explained in multiple ways and not reduced to the question of policing and its efficiencies. I quote my report:

> There is . . . evidence that [the] increase in popular justice is not limited to South Africa. There now exists a substantial body of journalism and scholarly literature on popular justice in Kenya, Tanzania, Uganda, Nigeria, Bolivia, Guatemala, Mexico, Nicaragua, Brazil, Indonesia, India, and elsewhere. As two leading scholars have shown in their 2008 book *Global Vigilantes*,[2] vigilante movements and practices are gaining ground all over the world, particularly in poor, peripheral urban neighbourhoods of countries in the global South that have high rates of resource inequality. There

are various explanations that have been offered for this global rise in popular justice methods. Many show how the rise in popular justice reflects the failure of states and economies to provide for their poorest citizens, not only in terms of a formal criminal justice system that protects and serves the poor, but mostly in terms of the provision of basic services and the means of life. The global increase in micro-level violence associated with underground economies and their corrupt officials, the withdrawal, or insufficient provision, of welfare-state support for citizens, and the increase in poverty and inequality brought on by structural adjustment programmes have created conditions in which urban residents in expanding, under-resourced neighbourhoods are acting in anger and desperation to contain the levels of violence in their communities. The literature also points to "mob justice" as a form of moral action by the politically and economically marginalised that, much like the fundamentalist religions that have also been on the rise in similar neighbourhoods, seeks solutions beyond state structures to put right a world that seems immoral, where the poor are consistently alienated from safety, wealth and basic rights, even as other residents of the same cities live in luxury.

I had written my report in the genre of ethnography, quoting verbatim from residents with whom I had spoken, describing interactions, accounting for patterns in popular justice that I had recorded in field notes, and then contextualizing this information with recourse to international literature, the history of vigilante violence in South African townships, and a broad general knowledge of the urban and national contexts. I had left out much of the theorization that I would have included in academic writing, but none of the analysis. In short, the labor of the report was in explication and interpretation, making a case for the multiple valences of the Khayelitsha killings, from the very particular context of residents' words and terms to the global structural condition of violence and inequality. After my report was submitted along with reports from other researchers and stakeholders, the Commission's staff sent it back to me to ask me to insert a description of the methodology used to generate the report. The request seemed to treat my report as somewhat suspicious. When read against the other reports, mine was remarkably less statistical, less quantitative, and less "verifiable" in the epistemological terms of the Commission. The difficulty of bringing ethnography to the Commission was only heightened when I was asked to give oral testimony in person before the Commission. Even after writing a report and thinking at length about how I would give my testimony, I still did not know how to translate my research into a form of information that would be appropriate for the Commission or how to approach the Commission in a way that would be appropriate for my research. I was clear that my research overlapped significantly with the themes and information that the Commission sought to collate. But it was also clear to me that my research did not follow in any easy way the mandate of the Commission.

I began to have fantasies of using my testimony to perform a tactical attack on the core mandate of the Commission, breaking frame by interrupting the commissioners and the formal proceedings and by using an entirely different kind of language of analysis from the technolegal language of the Commission. And yet I also felt obliged by professionalism and the task of representing the academy to display respectability to the commissioners and the plethora of legal practitioners and other professionals who attended them. I wanted to inhabit the category of expert to try to open more space for understanding township violence and its viable remedy, and yet I wanted to refuse the technical trappings that the category of the testifying expert seemed to impose on what was possible to say and argue before the Commission. Compared to the other experts, who brought hard currencies like statistics laid out in Power-Point presentations, or historians who could draw on recognizable historiographic tropes to tell the settled story of the township's earlier formation, or even Khayelitsha residents who brought "real-life experience" before the Commission, ethnography in this quasi-legal context was difficult to present.[3] In particular it seemed difficult to do precisely what ethnography is good at and *should* do, which is to question interpretive frames, to unsettle normativities by defining them, to reframe them through recourse to other times and places and concerns. But how does one choose a register, a set of information, that can do this work in the midst of a commission with a settled political and informational mandate?

The History and Politics of the Khayelitsha Commission

The Khayelitsha Commission of Inquiry into Allegations of Police Inefficiency in Khayelitsha and a Breakdown in Relations between the Community and Police in Khayelitsha originated as a formal complaint sent by a cluster of social justice organizations working in and around Khayelitsha in October 2013.[4] The complaint called for the premier of the Western Cape province of South Africa to create a provincial-level commission to inquire into the state of policing in the township of Khayelitsha, a part of the city marked by

high levels of violence and poverty, large sections of informal housing, struggles over basic services such as sanitation and heath care, and little status in
the politics of Cape Town.[5] In their joint press statement announcing the
complaint the organizations wrote:

> Since 2003 our organisations have held more than one hundred demonstra-
> tions, pickets, marches and other forms of protest against the continued
> failures of the Khayelitsha police and greater criminal justice system. We
> have submitted numerous petitions and memorandums to various levels
> of government in this regard. There have been sustained and coordinated
> efforts from various sectors of the Khayelitsha community for action to
> be taken by government agencies, including the police, to improve the
> situation. . . . A Commission of Inquiry will identify the true extent and
> scope of the problems and be able to make recommendations that will re-
> sult in Khayelitsha becoming a safer area to live, and one in which access
> to justice is a right, not a privilege.[6]

The call for a commission from progressive social justice organizations
whose method is normally the march and demonstration against the government was highly unusual and lent the Commission early on the quality of a
tactical intervention into the politics of governance over conditions of social
inequality. The legal provisions the organizations used to call for a commission were drawn from the national and provincial constitutions, exploiting
the possibility for the provincial government to call a commission on policing
without the approval of the national government.[7] The attempt to open political space by claiming the right for a provincial-level commission produced
difficult political tensions. The Western Cape is governed by the Democratic
Alliance, the center-right, pro-business political party that is associated with
the white vote and serves as the official opposition to the African National
Congress (ANC) in Parliament. Thus the Commission immediately took on
the character of a contestation between the two political parties and set up a
controversy over who had the political right to adjudicate the performance of
the national police force. What complicated the politics of the Commission
was the fact that the more conservative Democratic Alliance was being as-
sisted in an implicit critique of the ANC by progressive social justice organizations that occupy a space to the left of the ANC. In almost a year of legal
battles the national government tried to close down the provincial Commission for fear that the Democratic Alliance would score political points from
hosting a commission that would criticize the nationally governed police ser-

vices. Thus the social justice organizations found themselves in a strange alliance with the center-right political party with which they had been in a long political struggle over its antipoor policies in the Western Cape. In the end the High Court in Cape Town ruled that it was within the jurisdiction of the Western Cape premier to host a commission on policing in the province, scoring a political victory for the Democratic Alliance and for the social justice organizations at the same time. The Commission thus became the site of a complicated political conjuncture, and quite what it meant in the landscape of political action in South Africa was unclear. In short, the Commission joined together strange bedfellows and had an unfamiliar political character.

The gamble the social justice organizations took in calling for a commission could easily have failed if the commission was reduced to a point-scoring battle between the two political parties; or if it became—much like the Truth and Reconciliation Commission and the Marikana Commission, the two most important postapartheid commissions—a sophisticated technique for the state to acknowledge serious social and political problems while deflating political energy and deferring accountability.[8] Indeed more and more commissions have been dismissed by other social justice actors in the postapartheid period for being complicit in the quieting of critique and the reinstatement of the status quo. However, the activists who called for the commission maintained the hope that it could be a way to force onto a public and government agenda the lives of poor, black, and repeatedly peripheralized residents of Cape Town, to insist that the experience of life in Khayelitsha needed to be taken seriously through the creation of an institutional spectacle that brought into public view information about those lives and experiences. The hope, therefore, was that this commission could be mobilized for purposes of progressive struggle rather than fulfill the standard historical function of commissions as "reckoning schemes of legitimation" through which states elaborate themselves and bureaucratize conflict.[9] If, as Matthew Keller argues, "commissions are a concrete form of governance that mediate between structures of state/elite power and the popular legitimacy necessary to maintain power in democratic forms of governance," then the social justice organizations were trying to reconfigure that mediation in the interests of forcing elite state power to acknowledge the realities of the lives of the poor and black residents of the township.[10]

The Commission set up its offices and venue at Lookout Hill in Khayelitsha, one of the few public buildings in the township that could accommodate its proceedings. The choice to host the Commission in Khayelitsha, far away from the center of Cape Town, where the political and economic power of the city lies, meant that the Commission's public proceedings always had an audience drawn from residents of Khayelitsha and that the middle-class journalists and experts covering and participating in the Commission had to travel daily to the periphery of the city. The Commission was presided over by two well-respected and experienced commissioners, Justice Kate O'Regan, who had been a professor of law at the University of Cape Town before serving for fifteen years as a judge in the Constitutional Court, and Advocate Vusi Pikoli, a former special advisor to the minister of justice and former head of the National Prosecuting Authority. When I first arrived at Lookout Hill I was struck by the number of Khayelitsha residents sitting in the main hall listening to proceedings, many of them with headphones, receiving live translation from English to isiXhosa; that the social justice organizations were present at the Commission and engaging with its work and proceedings; and how makeshift, provisional, and nonelitist the quasi-legal structure of the Commission seemed in the township hall, with its large windows and rows of plastic chairs.

On the day of my testimony, at the front of the hall giving evidence behind a simple table was a friend of mine, a feminist activist who had worked for many years doing important work in the intersection of policy, law, feminist theory, and activist training in South Africa. As I listened to her I was in awe of the ease with which she was able to mobilize her information on criminal justice in Khayelitsha for the Commission's findings. She had meticulously combed through the records of the three police stations in Khayelitsha for evidence of police incompetency in the management of domestic violence in the township. She was able to show in stark terms how inadequate recording of information about domestic violence, the lack of implementation of victim protection practices, and lack of further investigation and prosecution proved the failure of policing as a protective service for women living in the township. I found myself becoming increasingly anxious as I listened to her eloquent intervention. She was, if you like, the perfect witness, giving the Commission evidence it could use to directly answer the question that had been legally provided for it. Her information, and its framing, fit directly into the terms of the Commission's mandate.

According to both the request from the social justice organizations and its legal inauguration by the premier, the Commission was explicitly established to answer whether the police in Khayelitsha were "inefficient" in their duties and whether there had been a "breakdown in relations between the Khayelitsha community and members of the South African Police Service."[11] As I tried to understand my rising anxiety, I realized that my friend's evidence seemed so exquisite, so precise, not only because of her particular intelligence but mostly because she kept her informational purview strictly internal to criminal justice processes. In other words, she took the categories, the policies, the logics of police work on their own terms and assessed the performance of police from within the expectations that policing best practices laid out for it. She was such a good witness for the Commission because she could easily assume the validity of policy and legal frameworks so that her work became a project of fact-finding on the specificities of compliance with the Domestic Violence Act in terms of its formal application and procedure. This assumption of the righteousness of the legal and policy framework was her compelling way of making a strategic intervention to improve protection of the lives of women in Khayelitsha.[12]

On Policing as a Political Object

One of the two advocates working as evidence leaders for the Commission sat me down at a table in the restaurant at Lookout Hill, a few meters away from the hall where the Commission was hearing proceedings, to prepare me. We sat for over an hour in conversation about my report and how he would lead me in my testimony. He had read through my report and highlighted sections that seemed most clearly to suggest that there was a problem with policing in Khayelitsha. When I tried to point out that my report was explicitly trying to place policing in Khayelitsha in a much broader context of the history of Khayelitsha and South African criminal justice, as well as of policing elsewhere and its symptomatic relationship to broader social relations, he cut me short. The Commission, he countered, had already amassed a great deal of testimony from residents and other researchers about the failure of police in the township. "It is clear from the evidence," he told me, "that there is a serious problem with the police." Already, he said, the Commission had proved without a doubt that the police are inefficient in Khayelitsha; now they just want the Commission to end as quickly as possible because the evidence has been so damning of their performance. When I offered that my research was making a very clear argument that the social and economic conditions of inequality in the city and the country were the major drivers of violence and that it was not at all evident that more "efficient" police would have any major impact on crime reduction over the long term, he disagreed. He told me that "changing the socioeconomic conditions will change crime one or two percent, but changing policing will dramatically change the crime rate," leading me strongly away from the core arguments emerging from my research and pushing me into the terms of reference for the Commission. It was a move that I had been expecting but was trying to avoid making; I did not want the broad terms of my research to be constrained and instrumentalized by the specificity of the Commission's own questions.

In somewhat of a panic I quickly made some notes for myself before the hearing so that I could frame my testimony explicitly in terms of my own intellectual work and project in order to resist being led toward the particular perspective on policing that the Commission seemed eager to produce. I wanted to undercut the sufficiency of the Commission's terms of reference, to try to expose how its limited mandate shrank the possibility for serious discussion about the criminal justice system and how it functions in the social reproduction of the city. As Adam Ashforth explains about the function of commissions, "to name a problem and to seek causes from which to reason solutions, that is, ways of producing desired effects, is also to specify ways in which these matters may be properly spoken of."[13] The transcript of the introduction to my testimony reads:

> First let me say thank you very much for having me here, and also just to say that sometimes it is quite difficult for a social scientist to fit into the terms of a Commission of Inquiry. I've studied some of the history of Commissions in South Africa and Commissions themselves are often delineated and mandated in ways that can often constrain general critique so I hope that I will be of help. I also want to say something about my work on the criminal justice system, which has predominantly focused on the Western Cape. I started working about thirteen years ago on the prison system and since then I have been doing more and more work on what is called "popular punishment" because increasingly more and more forms of punishment in this country as elsewhere but particularly in this country are falling outside of the formal criminal justice system so what I think we have seen recently across the country including in Khayelitsha is a surge in forms of popular punishment. And after many years of working on criminal justice in this region I am now part of a critical tradition that really questions whether the use of criminal justice, of the criminal justice system, can fix problems that are essentially social in nature. I worry that any easy call for the escalation of criminal justice measures particularly in a country like ours will be of service to the project of transforming the social

problems that we have. So I want to just say up front that I work particularly in prison contexts which are deeply violent institutions that are predominantly full of poor black South Africans whose contexts have entailed them at vastly higher rates than their white middle class counterparts into the criminal justice system. And I want to say up front that I am politically and intellectually obliged before I talk about the research that I did on Khayelitsha to say that I would hope that our work here on the criminal justice system should not be an extension of the criminal justice system more unfairly into the lives of poor black South Africans; the incarceration of more and more people. Because what kind of democratic project is that? I would hope that what I have to say would contribute to the work of the prevention of crime and violence and that if we are working here in service of making the police more efficient it would not be in service of the further incursion of a violent criminal justice system into the lives of poor black South Africans. I would like to say that up front.[14]

Of the social justice organizations that campaigned for the Commission, four of them, including the leading organization, the Social Justice Coalition (SJC), were social movement-NGO hybrids broadly led by the well-known South African activist Zackie Achmat. Achmat was a founder of the Treatment Action Campaign (TAC), the movement that successfully campaigned for universal access to antiretroviral medication in the midst of the AIDS pandemic in South Africa in the late 1990s and early 2000s. The SJC draws its inspiration from the TAC's successful campaign, which remains the most important social justice victory in postapartheid history. Crucial to the TAC's success was its focus on a *single-issue campaign* around a specific political object: antiretroviral drugs. It is a method of constraining political claims into particular forms in order to win specific battles over resources for the poor. Choosing one specific object that is important in the everyday lives of the poor, one fights strategic campaigns in order for a discernible and measurable victory to be made in service provision.[15] It has been an extremely important method in postapartheid politics, one that has used a panoply of tactics and strategies around single political objects to cunningly force the state to confront its responsibilities to those most disenfranchised by apartheid. At the time of the Commission the SJC had been working in Khayelitsha for a number of years, focusing on campaigning for the provision of basic services to the poor. They began their work on the lack of adequate sanitation in the township, leveraging the provision of running water, sewage systems, and toilets as a kind of threshold service to force the state to be accountable to the residents of the township. When I first walked into the SJC offices in Khayelitsha, what struck me most immediately were the images of toilets that were pasted on the walls of their office. Porcelain bowls of various sizes in various states of repair, different types of cisterns, in color and black and white, and alongside them newspaper articles about toilets. This wallpapering starkly indicated that the SJC, reading the context and conversations of Khayelitsha, had chosen the toilet as their object. Indeed the organization has been involved in a veritable shitstorm of local toilet politics. It has organized long "toilet queues" outside of Parliament, busing in township residents in acts of toilet spectacle. It helped township residents take their toilet buckets full of excrement to the offices of government leaders, forcing government officials and middle-class residents of Cape Town to confront the stink and degradation of living without toilets. The SJC had even named their broadsheet periodical *The Toilet Paper*, punning on an alternative use of newspaper in poor households.

It is this strategy of identifying the key political objects emerging out of the everyday life of poor neighborhoods that led the SJC to call for an inquiry into *policing* in Khayelitsha. Rising levels of violence and crime in the township is present in the everyday talk of Khayelitsha residents, who are scared their children will join the gangs that are transforming the social landscape of young people's lives, scared their homes will be broken into at night or they will be mugged on the way home from work. Listening to these fears, the SJC began to identify crime and safety as the second prong in their Khayelitsha campaigning. They argued that the inefficiency of police in Khayelitsha, their unwillingness to be responsive to the needs of residents, created a context wherein people were taking the law into their own hands. They read policing as the best strategy for helping meet the specific demand for a reduction in levels of crime in the township. The manner in which the SJC constituted *the police* as a single-issue campaign rubbed against the grain of my political and research sensibilities. Could the police be called for in the same way that antiretrovirals and toilets could be called for? *Should* the police be summoned as a threshold issue in social justice campaigning? What does it mean that, twenty years after the end of apartheid's police state and under conditions of sustained racialized inequality, black townships should be calling for police efficiency as a key strategy in improving the lives of the poor?

There is no doubt that policing has become a flashpoint in the negotiation of contemporary social inequalities. The proliferation of media reports on police brutality, in particular from the United States but also from Latin America, Europe, and beyond, indicate that policing has become an important contemporary social sign. The alarming series of racist events that have recently shaped a global political imagination spanning Ferguson, Marikana, Brazilian flash mobs, European immigration camps, and elsewhere have all involved police violence as a key vector for and diagnosis of social relations. As the Khayelitsha Commission was proceeding in Cape Town, the Marikana Commission on the police killing of thirty-four striking mineworkers in the north of the country was ongoing. There is no doubt that there is much to be improved about the state of policing, but while better training in crowd control, more disciplined investigative work, the use of body cameras for oversight, the inclusion of ethics and antiracism training in police colleges would make police less violent and more accountable to democratic rules, to imagine policing as a threshold for the creation of social justice ignores the entire critical history of policing. The use of policing and criminal justice to improve social conditions and make cities safer has historically relied heavily on existing registers of exclusion and social inequality, in particular the mobilization of antiblack, antipoor, and anti-immigrant control.[16] To quote one critic, "We must stress the fact that, far from being a solution, police surveillance and imprisonment typically aggravate and amplify the problems they are supposed to resolve."[17] To imagine that the police can have an active role in the production of social equality ignores the role that policing plays in societies premised on inequality. It fails to recognize the epiphenomenal character of policing, its primarily reactive social form that conserves rather than transforms social relations.

There are a series of political tensions in South African left politics around the use of single-issue politics. The tacticians at TAC and SJC argue that the congealing of a political vision into small objects, and the deployment of a bricolage of activisms around them, is the only way in this current dispensation and in this current global order to improve the daily lives of the poor. It is a politics of strategic essentialisms. Scholars and activists aligned with trade unions and other left alliances criticize this style of politics for how easily it can slip into a reformist politics of gradual improvement. Particular objects, they argue, are symptoms of systemic problems, and unless those systemic issues are addressed, equal access to anything will remain elusive. Although toilets in townships are important, if the structure of the ghettoized black township in relation to the white settler town remains in place, toilet activism falters into a kind of minimalist welfarism. The SJC activists retort that because of the diminishing amount of space afforded left activists under conditions of contemporary capitalism, radical critiques of systemic inequality are not much more than rhetorical flourishes that alienate those the left is trying to serve. What is needed are concrete manifestations of broader political goals that are meaningful in the lives of township residents. What is significant here are the stakes of creating what we might call *political objects*: the terms, both material and conceptual, that we identify as the grounds for being able to contest and transform our worlds.

Ethnography, it seems to me, offers precisely the kind of method that refuses this stand-off between specificity and generality. It strives always to link the specificities of everyday objects with their broader social and political context. It is our task not to choose between these registers and levels of analysis but exactly to show their complex relation in all of its depth. Ethnography must ask what kind of object is being made of policing in the contemporary social context. It must weigh the grounds for positioning policing as a project of social transformation, the social claim that policing as an idea or as a practice can perform useful work in the critique of the inequality of the city. It must ask how more efficient policing is being imagined as an opening onto a politics of equality. Ethnography must attend to political objects as social forms, carefully tracing their layered manifestation.

On Ethnography and Its Objects

Ethnography has become—perhaps always has been, at its best—a project of understanding context. Its place within the pantheon of methodologies is secured not simply by the detailed and prolonged recording of everyday life but also by the positioning of that record into a complex and considered context. The labor of ethnography is this careful work of stitching a host of everyday details to its context. The origins of our method lie famously in the first serious attempts at producing the idea of cultural relativism as method, which was an exercise in understanding the relationship between everyday objects and their particular cultural context. Malinowski's historic intervention in 1922 was to insist that anthropology's disciplinary claim rested on explaining the "imponderable yet all important facts of actual life" not in terms of the cultural prescriptions of Victorian England but in terms of the cultural context in which they were observed.[18] It was an intervention into the practice of contextualization and the politics of framing. I would venture that the history of anthropology could be told as a history of the question of contextualization: In relation to *what*, against what, through what, does one read a social fact in order to understand and explain it? Contextualization has taken different turns over the history of anthropology; in each moment in that history it has never been enough to use ethnography to provide a "thick description" of everyday life, much as Geertz is valorized today.[19] While description remains a critical starting point for ethnography, particularly in the early phases of writing, the major obligation in ethnography is to build a deep scaffold of context around the description such that our evocation of specific places and times is always explained and translated through access to other places and other times, whether they be in the register of history, theory, or concurrent events. We are experts in crafting context.

What we have lost as we abandoned the grand tradition of comparativism in the mid-twentieth century we have found in our grand scaling between the everyday and the global. What anthropologists specialize in is the capacity to move between incredibly precise descriptions of specific forms and practices, what we call the "local" or the "everyday," and telescoped framings thereof that insist on reading the specific always in relation to its multiple contexts and in ever broader perspective. Ethnographic writing has become a gesture in *scale*. Its scalar practice attunes us to the complexity of framing, the inseparability of visible and invisible forms, and the difficult conceptual work of articulating, convincingly, the presence of one thing in another. There are better and worse ways of negotiating this scale of course. Good ethnography never moves too quickly between, for example, a description of a protest in a township in South Africa and a too easy invocation of global capital and neoliberalism. It is precisely the demand to move carefully and precisely, explaining the spatial and historical gradations of the scale, between these phenomena that is the burden of ethnographic research and writing. Equally, heavy-handed descriptions of local scenes that do not invoke world histories, forms, and concepts are wholly insufficient for the world we research, especially after the critiques of anthropology since the Second World War, when the project of positivist description was roundly and rightly dismissed as being complicit with projects of imperial power.[20] Various methods of structuring context in ethnography have been proposed, most eventfully perhaps by the Manchester School, by the carefully graded anthropologies of global capitalism by the Marxist anthropologists Sydney Mintz and Eric Wolf, by anthropologies of colonialism that paid attention to the dialogic or dialectical or discursive encounters in the colonial world, by anthropologies of globalization interested in flows or transformations or frictions.[21] It is in this space of the scalar that ethnography tests the worth of large abstractions for the contemporary world and reckons the world in terms of a critical project. All to argue that we have been having an extended debate about the problematic of context for quite some time.

Critical contextualization as a method for intellectual labor requires ethnographers to be skilled translators across masses of information operating at vastly different registers. The complexity of the contemporary ethnographic project is to be able to move across scale and register with intellectual integrity, translating and transposing between languages, between events, across time frames, from lived experience to text, often across disciplines, between theory and practice, mindful of the need for description, while testing and building abstractions. Each ethnographer will treat the composition of these registers differently, weighting them according to individual persuasion as well as the material of the project being worked on. Many contemporary anthropologists remain invested in the writing of thick description into ethnographic texts as an ethical duty to research participants and readers who should have access to the research data. Others argue that anthropology needs to lean more heavily on theoretical writing or history in order to undercut the discipline's problematic historical relationship to description as a form of capture.[22]

Michel-Rolph Trouillot in his critique of the construction of "the field" in relation to anthropological knowledge parses the ethnographic project by arguing that "objects of observation" and "objects of study" are not at all the same thing. The objects we write about in our field notes are a fraction of the objects they need to become if we want to understand them and write about them well in our ethnographic texts.[23] To observe the world without making a study of the many other forms and histories congealed into every observable object, as well as into our very modes of seeing, is to settle for a naïve and positivist project. The task of scaffolding context in ethnography is precisely to inherit the challenge of transforming the observable world into an object of study.

And so to think that the observations from ethnographic fieldwork, necessarily attentive as they are to the lived experience of social life among those with whom we conduct our research, can in any simple way be put to use in a context other than ethnographic writing carries substantial epistemological and political risks. To simply display knowledge of the everyday to whoever requests it and into whatever context it is required abdicates responsibility not only for the ethics and politics of knowledge production and the ways in which information can be used for quite different ends but also for the deep and precise work of contextualization that the ethnographic project requires. Ethnography is particularly obliged in this regard precisely because of the amount of information it sustains about people's lives, particularly the lives of people who are already caught up in the violent end of histories of oppression and marginalization. The intellectual and political demands on how one records that life—in itself, I would claim, an important project precisely because that life would otherwise go unrecorded—and how one disseminates and negotiates information thereof are fierce, and should be so.

I think the stakes of these political demands only increase in ethnography on township violence in South Africa, as with research on violence in any ghettoized, socially marginalized, usually black social space. I think the ethnographer has a primary obligation to not fetishize that violence, to not read it as a thing-in-itself; and to work very hard against long-standing tropes that treat such violence with immediacy, that is, gratuitously.[24] There has been a deeply offensive and racist characterization of township and ghetto violence as "black-on-black violence," a trope that persists in obfuscating the long white supremacist and class projects in its analysis. And nothing fits the characterization of black-on-black violence better than the deployment of police and prisons as its response. Both are gestures in truncation of the deeper social relations and fields that persist in this violence and in its response. Ethnography, working at scales beyond other methods, should be able to work systematically against this truncation, both in terms of the long histories of the present and in terms of its multiply layered contemporary context.[25]

So even as township residents gloss the police as a problem, it is the ethnographer's job to not stop at this emic problematization. Indeed figuring out what the problem in fact is, is the work of contextualizing emic propositions, local social forms—in short, symptoms. The police certainly are problematic in all kinds of demonstrable ways. The police in contemporary South Africa are a significant apparatus in the emergence of "violent democracy."[26] Police officers are invested in the corrupt project of their own bellies.[27] Police departments are shot through with private domains and claims and are full of imposters.[28] The desire at the heart of the Commission, to make the police coherent, to domesticate them, to make them simply act as police *should* do in service of the urban public, skips over a multitude of huge questions that have to be taken seriously if we are to address with any sincerity the problem of violence. As Taussig has shown in Colombia, the threat of "lawlessness" makes for a compelling reason to strengthen the police as a state institution.[29] Yet the attempts to stabilize and extend the police in a postcolonial, postauthoritarian place like South Africa, in which the meaning of the police is deeply volatile, cannot begin from the assumption that the police can be reclaimed as any simple public good. The police force is itself a symptom of a complex and violent social system.

Since the very creation of townships there has been a racialized history of unequal policing in South Africa such that the township has been underpoliced in the everyday and overpoliced in times of protest.[30] But in the current context of the rise of the securitized state under conditions of growing inequality and urban slums it is not at all clear that the extension of police activity into the lives of township residents will be of benefit to those most marginalized by a national and global system.[31] Even as law has been instantiated as an important arbiter of the transition out of apartheid and coloniality more generally,[32] this "lawfare" is part of a complex set of social and historical terms that must be considered part of our context for making interventions. The work of good ethnography is to diagnose this condition, not to capitulate to it. Otherwise public ethnography becomes a repetition of the social it studies rather than its critical counterpoint.[33] Even as the call to public ethnography invites a more rigorous engagement with the political impact of the knowledge we create, the importance of remaining at a critical distance from the context we seek to affect is crucial.

Anthropology and Commissions of Inquiry

In the history of anthropology commissions of inquiry have provided a primary interface between ethnography and public affairs. Anthropologists across the colonial world used the public platform of commissions to give their ethnographic work political significance. Commissions of inquiry were consolidated as a mode of governance in nineteenth-century England as an integral component of the British imperial project and widely used in British colonies, especially in the management of race and labor.[34] In southern Africa a slew of commissions throughout the first half of the twentieth century fill the archives with masses of information about the lives of Africans and how to manage them. In particular, commissions have been central to defining social "crisis" and providing sets of epistemological and political ideas for its management.[35] Commissions were central in forging the relationship between knowledge production and colonial governance, granting the colonizers a space to define with more precision their terms of rule. Ann Laura Stoler remarks on the colonial archive of commissions, "If statistics help 'determine the character of social facts' . . . it is commissions that provide their interpretive, historical, and epistemic frames."[36]

Under conditions of colonial rule in which the colonized were seldom given the chance to represent themselves in commissions, anthropologists quickly came to be seen as experts on, and indeed often as representatives of, the colonized people they studied. Much of this historical relationship between anthropology and commissions of inquiry has not yet been written, but a review of existing literature shows a host of anthropologists participating actively in colonial commissions. In southern Africa we find Gèrard Lestrade in the 1931 Native Economic Commission; Alfred Radcliffe-Brown, Monica Wilson, and Z. K. Matthews in the 1946–48 Native Laws Commission; Winifred Hoernlé in the 1947 Penal and Prisons Reform Commission; P. J. Schoeman in the 1949 Commission for the Preservation of the Bushmen; W. W. M. Eiselin, who chaired the 1949–51 Native Education Commission; J. P. van Schalkwyk Bruwer and others in the 1964 Commission of Enquiry into South West African Affairs; and possibly Max Gluckman through his work at the Rhodes-Livingstone Institute.[37]

All except one of these are instances of white professional anthropologists providing expert evidence on the lives of black Africans, much like myself, a white anthropologist before the Khayelitsha Commission. They are, however, of quite different political and intellectual persuasions, some working as state ethnographers and explicitly invested in producing systems of apartheid rule, others using commissions as a way that "anthropological expertise might help to mitigate some of the . . . evils of colonialism."[38] Of the latter, anthropologists like Malinowski, Radcliffe-Brown, Wilson, and Hoernlé, all deeply invested in British social anthropology, accepted the obligation to bring "scientific" information about the cultural systems of black southern Africans to commissions as a way of proving the validity of African modes of life and making an argument against the wholesale incursion of settler colonialism into that life.

Taken as a whole, though, and with hindsight, it becomes clear that despite the best anticolonial intentions of anthropologists like Radcliffe-Brown, commissions were seldom venues for progressive social change. At their best they were venues for colonial liberalism, negotiating a softening of the hard edge of colonization. Ultimately they were sophisticated tools in the governance of native affairs and the conservation of rule. As Gordon describes them, "commissions of Inquiry are notorious 'anti-politics' machines, to use

Jim Ferguson's fortuitous phrase, that systematically mis-recognize and de-politicize understandings of the lives and problems of local people through the use of the patina of 'objectivity' and 'science'; ostensibly for neutral commonly agreed purposes, but in reality, simply a means of political bush encroachment."[39]

In other words, it was very difficult for those anthropologists wanting to use their ethnography in the context of commissions as a way to argue against colonial rule to be positioned as anything other than complicit in the general project of rule. True, they may have in some ways softened the presiding attitudes and practices of racism and settler domination, and perhaps this is enough to have done under those historical conditions, but there was little space in the commissions to do anything more than make tactical maneuvers in the midst of the colonial commissions' major terms. The robust survival of commissions of inquiry in postcolonial contexts raises interesting questions about how a political form so roundly associated with developing the knowledge and techniques of "the native problem" might be differently deployed in a new political era. Can the modes of colonial knowledge lying deep in the history of commissions be dismantled to the extent that the "problems" animating commissions do not draw on the trope of the native problem in fashioning a contemporary politics? And what could be the role for a contemporary anthropologist in this institutional milieu?

Conclusion

If we are to use our ethnographies to enter meaningfully into public debates and institutions, we must be mindful that one of our core tasks is to consider how the framing of those debates might be put into relief by an ethnographic insistence on the importance of contextualization. How might one escape the conditions of mandate, the framing that commissions suggest in order to bring ethnographic scale to bear on proceedings? How might one engage them as a way to force open some of their own terms and to create space for larger histories and social questions within the commission, or any other public institution for that matter? When does one intervene into political and institutional debates, and when does one see their terms as too conservative or framed in ways too complicit with presiding orders to lend one's work and opinion to them?

The 2014 Khayelitsha Commission of Inquiry into Allegations of Police Inefficiency in Khayelitsha and a Breakdown in Relations between the Community and Police in Khayelitsha included experts from a host of disciplines—historians, sociologists, criminologists, gender studies specialists—as well as a range of people with specialized knowledge in the working of the police and the criminal justice system. It also included testimony from many residents of Khayelitsha on the life of the township and its relationship to policing. The strength of the Commission was in its capacity to be expansive about the information it gathered about Khayelitsha. The commissioners were interested in the history of the township, for example, and wanted testimony from historians in order to understand the context for policing. The strength of the social justice organizations was that they were constantly at work disseminating the information from the commission to websites and news channels, into activist networks, and to local journalists. The information generated by the Commission will not simply sit idle until a future historian wants to study it. It has been made into an available archive that has been widely publicized both by the Commission itself on its website and by the social justice organizations. If one of their key tactics was to get people talking about Khayelitsha and its demands, they were successful in that task.

In the end the Commission did find that the Khayelitsha police were "inefficient" and that relations between police and residents warranted intervention. In its final report the Commission made twenty recommendations for the improvement of policing in the township, including the adoption of a community policing approach at all stations; the establishment of better monitoring systems, visible policing, and CCTV cameras; an increase in numbers of police in the township; and the streamlining and better management of complaints and investigations. In other words, the recommendations of the Commission read the problem of policing not as a potent international symptom of structural volatility around safety, security, and inequality but rather as a management and infrastructure problem to be corrected by means of interventions internal to policing practice. At the time this book went to press very few of the recommendations had been adopted, and the social justice organizations that mobilized for the Commission had begun to mobilize again for the implementation of its recommendations.

What made me so anxious to appear before the Commission was that I wanted to resist the ease with which the police as an instance of single-issue politics could be used to account for the violence of township life. I wanted to force open the terms of the discussion while still contributing to the political work of forcing the state's attention onto the lives of Khayelitsha residents. I wanted to try to pry open the question of the township, of the relationship of this township to the rest of the city, to the continued politics of inequality.

I wanted to read the history of policing not in any simple relationship to the problem of violence but as itself a historical function caught up in long trajectories of violent state practice. This was the important role I saw for the critical ethnographer to play before the Commission: to try reflect on and contextualize the mandate of the Commission within a politics of scale that troubled the positivist reading of policing as understandable from within its own terms.

If we bring our knowledge of the lives of people and places to bear on public conversations and institutions, we must find a way too to bring our knowledge of how we frame and contextualize those lives and places. It is not good enough to simply hand over our data, as much as it might be wanted. Our responsibility is to challenge the very ways in which that information is construed and understood. It is in this way that we might have the kind of impact we want in public conversation. We have to figure out ways to interrupt the framing, to assert a kind of authorship over the mapping of context such that we do not simply repeat problematic framings. In short, we must find ways to make public too the work of contextualization and recontextualization that is and should be ethnography's mandate.

At the end of my testimony at the Khayelitsha Commission, Advocate Pikoli seemed troubled by my attempts to exit the frame of the Commission, reflecting on the difficulty of making criminal justice policy in the context of such high levels of social inequality. I responded with this challenge to the commissioners: "I would hope that one of the recommendations of the Commission would be that the problem of violence in Khayelitsha cannot be read simply as a problem of one fact of service provision, that it is a deep systemic issue that needs dramatic political attention." On my way out the door the Commission's secretary thanked me for my time and research. I told her I hoped I had been useful, and she responded, in passing, "We got what we needed from you. You said enough in your testimony about the incompetence of the police to prove our case." Perhaps, I thought, I'd best return to writing my book.

Notes

1   In South Africa the word *township* (sometimes also *location*) refers to urban areas reserved for blacks under the colonial and apartheid policies of urban racial segregation. Townships were planned on the peripheries of South African cities as spaces to house black workers, who were seldom entitled to reside permanently in the city. Townships have remained a central feature of South African cities in the postapart-

heid period, despite the scrapping of apartheid laws that systematically regulated black life. They have largely remained places for poor and black urban residents, even as their class and racial character has marginally transformed under postapartheid conditions. See, for example, Alexander et al. 2013.

2   Pratten and Sen 2008.

3   There is literature on anthropologists and legal testimony that gives interesting insight to this predicament. See, for example, Burke 2011; Good 2004; Goodwin 2009; Hopper 1990; Rosen 1977; Scarce 1994.

4   The organizations were Social Justice Coalition, Treatment Action Campaign, Free Gender, Triangle Project, Ndifuna Ukwazi, and Equal Education, all reputable and important actors in progressive politics in Cape Town and beyond.

5   See Gillespie 2014. The position of premier is roughly equivalent to the governor of a state in the United States.

6   For the press statement and a copy of the full official complaint document, see Social Justice Coalition et al. 2011.

7   The call for the Commission was made in terms of section 206(5)(a) of the Constitution of the Republic of South Africa and section 66(2)(a) of the Constitution of the Western Cape.

8   See Mamdani 2002; McKinley 2015.

9   Ashforth 1990: 6; Keller 2014: 207.

10 Keller 2014: 208. Steven Robins (2014), an anthropologist working with the SJC and TAC on understanding social movement politics, seems to see the potential for this effect in his early assessment of the Commission.

11 Khayelitsha Commission 2014b.

12 Transcripts of the referenced testimonies can be found at Khayelitsha Commission 2014a.

13 Ashforth 1990: 17.

14 Khayelitsha Commission 2014a.

15 See Robins 2008.

16 See, for example, Blomberg and Cohen 2003; Chanock 2001; Davis 1977; Garland 2002; Hall et al. 1978; Linebaugh 2003.

17 Wacquant 2001: 410.

18 Malinowski (1922) 2014: 21.

19 Geertz 1973.

20 Said 1979. See, however, the important critique by Clifford 1988.

21 Appadurai 1996; Comaroff and Comaroff 1997; Mintz 1986; Trouillot 2003; Tsing 2004; Wolf 1982.

22 See Povinelli's (2011) account of "ethnography light"; Rolph-Trouillot's (2003) critique of fieldwork.

23 Trouillot 2003, especially 125.

24 For an excellent critical review of Alice Goffman's ethnography of the policing and surveillance of young black residents of Philadelphia, *On the Run: Fugitive Life in an American City*, see Sharpe 2014.

25 Comaroff and Comaroff 2003.
26 Von Holdt 2013.
27 Hornberger 2015.
28 Comaroff and Comaroff 2014; Hornberger 2014.
29 Taussig 2003.
30 Minaar 2010; Steinberg 2009.
31 See Davis 2007.
32 Comaroff and Comaroff 2008.
33 Gillespie and Dubbeld 2007.
34 Ashforth 1990.
35 Gilligan 2002.
36 Stoler 2009: 169.
37 Bank and Bank 2013; Brown 1979; Gillespie 2011; Gordon 2007, n.d.; Kuper 1999.
38 Radcliffe-Brown and Kuper (1924) 1986: 18
39 Gordon n.d.: 25.

References

Alexander, Peter, Claire Ceruti, Keke Motseke, Mosa Phadi, and Kim Wale. 2013. *Class in Soweto*. Durban: University of KwaZulu-Natal Press.

Appadurai, Arjun. 1996. *Modernity at Large: Cultural Dimensions of Globalisation*. Minneapolis: University of Minnesota Press.

Ashforth, Adam. 1990. "Reckoning Schemes of Legitimation: On Commissions of Inquiry as Power/Knowledge Forms." *Journal of Historical Sociology* 3.1: 1–22.

Bank, Andrew, and Leslie Bank. 2013. *Inside African Anthropology: Monica Wilson and Her Interpreters*. Cambridge: Cambridge University Press.

Brown, Richard. 1979. "Passages in the Life of a White Anthropologist: Max Gluckman in Northern Rhodesia." *Journal of African History* 20.4: 525–41.

Burke, Paul. 2011. *Law's Anthropology: From Ethnography to Expert Testimony in Native Title*. Canberra: ANUE Press.

Chanock, Martin. 2001. *The Making of South African Legal Culture 1902–1936: Fear, Favour and Prejudice*. Cambridge: Cambridge University Press.

Clifford, James. 1988. "On Orientalism." In *The Predicament of Power: Twentieth Century Ethnography, Literature, and Art*. Cambridge, MA: Harvard University Press.

Cohen, Stanley, and Thomas G. Blomberg, eds. 2003. *Punishment and Social Control*. New York: Aldine Transaction.

Comaroff, John L., and Jean Comaroff. 1997. *Of Revelation and Revolution: The Dialectics of Modernity on a South African Frontier*. Vol. 2. Chicago: University of Chicago Press.

———. 2003. "Ethnography on an Awkward Scale: Postcolonial Anthropology and the Violence of Abstraction." *Ethnography* 4.2: 147–79.

———. 2014. "The Return of Khulekani Khumalo, Zombie Captive: Imposture, Law and Paradoxes of Personhood in the Postcolony." *Significação* 41.42: 186–211 (in Portuguese).

———, eds. 2008. *Law and Disorder in the Postcolony*. Chicago: University of Chicago Press.

Davis, Angela Y. 1997. "Race, Cops and Traffic Stops." *University of Miami Law Review*, 424–43.

Davis, Mike. 2007. *Planet of Slums*. New York: Verso.

Garland, David. 2002. *The Culture of Control: Crime and Social Order in Contemporary Society*. Oxford: Oxford University Press.

Geertz, Clifford. 1973. *The Interpretation of Cultures*. New York: Basic Books.

Gillespie, Kelly. 2011. "Containing the 'Wandering Native': Racial Jurisdiction and the Liberal Politics of Prison Reform in 1940s South Africa." *Journal of Southern African Studies* 37.3: 499–515.

———. 2014. "Murder and the Whole City." *Anthropology Southern Africa* 37.3–4: 203–12.

Gillespie, Kelly, and Bernard Dubbeld. 2007. "The Possibility of a Critical Anthropology after Apartheid: Relevance, Intervention, Politics." *Anthropology Southern Africa* 30.3–4: 129–34.

Gilligan, George. 2002. "Royal Commissions of Inquiry." *Australian and New Zealand Journal of Criminology* 35.3: 289–307.

Good, Anthony. 2004. "'Undoubtedly an Expert'? Anthropologists in British Asylum Courts." *Journal of the Royal Anthropological Institute* 10.1: 113–33.

Goodwin, Charles. 2009. "Professional Vision." *American Anthropologist* 96.3: 606–33.

Gordon, Robert. 2007. "'Tracks Which Cannot Be Covered': P. J. Schoeman and Public Intellectuals in South Africa." *Historia* 52.1: 98–126.

———. N.d. "The Strange Career of J. P. van S. Bruwer, the Making of Namibian Grand Apartheid and the Decline of *Volkekunde*." Unpublished manuscript.

Hall, Stuart, et al. 1978. *Policing the Crisis: Mugging, the State and Law and Order*. London: Macmillan.

Hopper, Kim. 1990. "Research Findings as Testimony: A Note on the Ethnographer as Expert Witness." *Human Organization* 49.2: 110–13.

Hornberger, Julia. 2014. *Policing and Human Rights: The Meaning of Violence and Justice in the Everyday Policing of Johannesburg*. New York: Routledge.

———. 2015. "The Belly of the Police." In *Police in Africa: The Street Level View*, edited by Oliver Owen and Jonny Steinberg. London: Hurst.

Keller, Matthew. 2014. "When Is the State's Gaze Focused? British Royal Commissions and the Bureaucratization of Conflict." *Journal of Historical Sociology* 27.2: 204–35.

Khayelitsha Commission. 2014a. "Phase One Hearings." January–April. http://www.khayelitshacommission.org.za/2013-11-10-19-36-33/hearing-transcriptions/phase-one-hearings.html.

————. 2014b. *Towards a Safer Khayelitsha: Report of the Commission of Inquiry into Allegations of Police Inefficiency and a Breakdown in Relations between SAPS and the Community of Khayelitsha*. August 15. http://www.khayelitshacommission.org.za /final-report.html.

Kuper, Adam. 1999. "South African Anthropology: An Inside Job." *Paideuma* 45: 83–101.

Linebaugh, Peter. 2003. *The London Hanged: Crime and Civil Society in the Eighteenth Century*. New York: Verso.

Malinowski, Bronislaw. (1922) 2014. *Argonauts of the Western Pacific*. New York: Routledge.

Mamdani, Mahmood. 2002. "Amnesty or Impunity? A Preliminary Critique of the Report of the Truth and Reconciliation Commission of South Africa (TRC)." *Diacritics* 2.3–4: 33–59.

McKinley, Dale. 2015. "Commissions of Inquiry or Omission?" South African Civil Society Information Service.

Minaar, Anthony. 2010. "The Changing Face of 'Community Policing' in South Africa." "CRIMSA Conference," special edition of *Acta Criminologica* 2: 189–210.

Mintz, Sidney. 1986. *Sweetness and Power: The Place of Sugar in Modern History*. New York: Penguin.

Povinelli, Elizabeth. 2011. *Economies of Abandonment: Social Belonging and Endurance in Late Liberalism*. Durham: Duke University Press.

Pratten, David, and Atreyee Sen. 2008. *Global Vigilantes*. New York: Columbia University Press.

Radcliffe-Brown, A. R., and Adam Kuper. (1924) 1986. Introduction to "Science and Native Problems: How to Understand the Bantu." *Anthropology Today* 2.4: 17–21.

Robins, Steven. 2008. *From Revolution to Rights in South Africa: Social Movements, NGOs and Popular Politics after Apartheid*. New York: James Curry.

————. 2014. "Making Room for Other Voices." *Cape Times*, March 28.

Rosen, Lawrence. 1977. "The Anthropologist as Expert Witness." *American Anthropologist* 79.3: 555–78.

Said, Edward. 1979. *Orientalism*. New York: Vintage.

Scarce, Rick. 1994. "(No) Trial (but) Tribulations: When Courts and Ethnography Conflict." *Journal of Contemporary Ethnography* 23.2: 123–49.

Sharpe, Christina. 2014. "Black Life, Annotated." *New Inquiry*, August 8. http:// thenewinquiry.com/essays/black-life-annotated/.

Social Justice Coalition et al. 2011. "Zille Must Appoint Inquiry into Khayelitsha Policing: SJC." Politicsweb, November 30. http://www.politicsweb.co.za /politicsweb/view/politicsweb/en/page71619?oid=269638&sn=Detail&pid =71619.

Steinberg, Jonny. 2009. *Thin Blue: The Unwritten Rules of South African Policing*. Cape Town: Jonathan Ball.

Stoler, Ann Laura. 2009. *Along the Archival Grain: Epistemic Anxieties and Colonial Common Sense*. Princeton: Princeton University Press.

Taussig, Michael. 2003. *Law in a Lawless Land: Diary of a Limpieza in Colombia.* Chicago: University of Chicago Press.

Trouillot, Michel-Rolph. 2003. *Global Transformations: Anthropology and the Modern World.* New York: Palgrave Macmillan.

Tsing, Anna. 2004. *Friction: An Ethnography of Global Connection.* Princeton: Princeton University Press.

Von Holdt, Karl. 2013. "South Africa: The Transition to Violent Democracy." *Review of African Political Economy* 40.138: 589–604.

Wacquant, Loïc. 2001. 'The Penalisation of Poverty and the Rise of Neoliberalism." *European Journal on Criminal Policy and Research* 9: 401–12.

Wolf, Eric. 1982. *Europe and the People without History.* Berkeley: University of California Press.

4

Addressing Policy-Oriented Audiences

Relevance and Persuasiveness

MANUELA IVONE CUNHA

How do ethnographers working on social issues engage with policy-oriented audiences? Can they productively publicize their research without fitting into these audiences' particular frames of expectation and communication? Can ethnographic research not designed for policy be perceived as relevant for policymaking purposes? What possible impacts can be expected from research offering these audiences in-depth, complex depictions rather than direct, itemized recommendations?

This chapter is about communicating ethnographic findings to publics mediating between research and policymaking.[1] The ethnographer's interlocutors and the ethnography's recipients mentioned here are not therefore policymakers themselves or the general public but specialized audiences oriented to policy definition.[2]

The ethnographic inquiries I discuss were not policy-driven, although they were not without policy implications. Moreover, although they were far from matching these audiences' dominant frames of expectations, they produced a particular kind of impact, a form of ethnographic sensitization relevant to policy. I explore in two steps the nature of this sensitization and the potential of ethnography as a comprehensive resource for reasoning about social problems. In order to do so I start by taking stock of my experience of communicating ethnography within the criminal justice system in Portugal and by centering on the circumstances surrounding the receptiveness of an ethnographic inquiry on penal confinement whose findings were taken into account in a report produced by my interlocutors for policymakers.

In a second step, not intended as a full comparative case but as a short complement merely aimed at putting this main experience into perspective and at calibrating the conclusions to be drawn from it, I briefly describe the outcome of an entirely different ethnographic inquiry, on vaccine social acceptability and nonimmunization. Its findings were likewise communicated to specialized policy-oriented audiences. The communication of these results did not benefit from the uniquely favorable conditions of reception that were met at the onset in the research on penal confinement. However, despite the different context of communication and reception, the results of this inquiry also ended up being productively integrated in a report intended for policy-making purposes. Both experiences provide material for a reflection on ethnographic relevance and on the ingredients (extrinsic *and* intrinsic to ethnography) that can render ethnographic accounts valuable and persuasive to policy-oriented publics.

Prison Ethnography and a Report for Policy
Securing Access, Reshaping Expectations, Establishing Credibility

My ethnographic experience on prisons and penal confinement in Portugal since the 1980s has led me to interact with publics involved in policy at different levels. I have also interacted with a variety of institutional agents and front-line personnel who, directly or indirectly, act on what they generally define as a "social problem." From policy officials to prison-reform commissions, members of the judicial system, national and local prison directors, and social workers and other actors, these have always been, in general, policy-oriented audiences, regardless of the nature or degree of their power to intervene in the problem. Their expectations in relation to prison research and its outcomes are usually formed within particular frames, such as the exposure or denunciation of prison deficiencies and the production of recommendations to remedy them.

I started by participating in 1987 in a multidisciplinary research project on "total institutions," such as prisons, youth correctional facilities, psychiatric hospitals, and asylums, commissioned by the Portuguese Ministry of Justice.[3] A team of ethnographers was set to produce a ground-level interrelated view of these institutions. Long-term fieldwork and direct observation were expected to capture the concrete workings of institutional regimes and how they combine with particular social and moral worlds that statistical surveys alone were unable to illuminate. The researchers were given complete autonomy at every stage. The funding agency's policy agenda did not define the research scope or design or even require that its outcomes assume the form of policy recommendations. It also abstained from redirecting the course of research toward other aspects than the ones intended or subordinating research choices to its own criteria of relevance. Thus the political conditions of ethnographic production left little room for tension, let alone conflict, between research agendas and policy agendas. The very terms under which the research project was commissioned, being themselves broadly defined, also suited ethnographic research well: although question-driven, ethnographic studies tend to adopt a broad focus that does not fit easily into narrowly predetermined approaches.

The fact that the project was launched by a public agency indirectly overseeing some of the institutions in question and vouching for others opened doors that would have otherwise remained closed. This explains the exceptional practical conditions we obtained for the production of in-depth ethnographic research. Benefiting from full, unrestricted, and unconditioned access to the premises of secluded and, for the most part, coercive environments, we did not have to struggle with the issue of accessibility and with institutional barriers that usually allow for no more than a "quasi-ethnography."[4] Such were the conditions under which I carried out two years of fieldwork in a women's prison after a two-year period of field research in a psychiatric institution.

Producing ethnographic knowledge in these terms was one thing. Communicating it was an altogether different exercise. Although the main motivation of the funding body was to generate knowledge on previously little known worlds and to contribute to an understanding of trajectories under its rule or in its orbit, the specialized publics for whom it was primarily intended held different expectations. These expectations were not entirely alien to those framing the public debate (e.g., Are psychiatric hospitals "warehouses"? Are prisons "schools of crime"?) that labeled such institutions "social problems," which, by definition, need intervention. But the fact that we had unprecedented access to these worlds also produced additional types of assumptions: the detection, exposure, and denunciation of institutions' flaws and deficiencies, whether in terms of their facilities, professionals' conduct, local governance, or other elements. The role imputed to social research was thus aligned with an auditing role, and ethnographers with inspectors.

In the formal and informal meetings held to present research results to several institutional actors from national to local levels, every description was thus bound to be reinterpreted as a positive or negative judgment. Given these conditions of reception, our audiences tried to read into those accounts a subtext conveying criticism or approval or assessing responsibilities, and eventually validating or denigrating their own performance. In the process minor aspects in the research were sometimes amplified and given new meaning; for instance, a high-ranking prison official interpreted a brief reference to the fact that prisoners' sociality was seldom governed by a "convict ethos" as evidence that prisons are not deleterious environments and do not hinder social reintegration and that in general Portuguese prisons were doing well. Although these expectations were sometimes disconcerting, eventually we learned to navigate and manage them, to anticipate potential divergences between our texts and the subtexts most likely to be superimposed by our interlocutors in light of their different social positions in the prison field. We learned to minimize inevitable distortions, either by clarifying those points most prone to misconstruction or by being more explicit on what could and could not be inferred from them.[5]

On the whole this experience is not uncommon among ethnographers communicating their research to particular publics. I mention it here only in order to portray the context in which a subsequent experience is to be understood a decade later. These first ethnographic inquiries—in a prison and in a psychiatric hospital—and the publications resulting from them,[6] established me as a credible researcher in the eyes of those publics. Moreover both the published materials and the meetings mentioned earlier contributed to reshape the expectations of those publics and to render them more attuned to what an ethnographic inquiry entails or has to offer. If nothing else, these studies gave them a chance to find that this sort of inquiry is not about the superficial and piecemeal denunciations they had anticipated or feared, that although institutions' deficiencies became visible in ethnographic descriptions, our unprecedented access to these institutions was intended to provide comprehensive views on the structure of different problems.

Two Policy-Building Processes

Ten years later I returned to the same prison for a new ethnographic inquiry, funded by the Wenner-Gren Foundation for Anthropological Research. Even though this time it was an entirely university-based research, thus independent of the Ministry of Justice, my work was already known in the milieu and I could now easily secure the same unrestricted access I was granted under the Ministry's sponsorship of the previous study. Although initially intended as a restudy, the scope and scale of the transformations that had affected this universe in the meantime were such that I was led to radically change the questions that had guided the previous research and to reconsider its focus entirely.[7] During the 1990s, a period that coincided approximately with the ten-year interval between my two prison ethnographic studies, the country's correctional stock nearly doubled, climbing from 7,965 prisoners to 14,236, to post the highest incarceration rate in the European Union, with 145 inmates per 100,000 in 2000, while the proportion of women among inmates rose from 6 to 10 percent—also the highest in the European Union.[8] Drug-related offenses (mostly drug trafficking) were the main factor in the rapid growth of the number of remand prisoners and became the top cause of incarceration, which in the case of women reached a proportion of approximately 70 percent. This hyperincarceration occurred especially in a handful of destitute urban territories, for reasons explained below. This caused the prison and the neighborhood to become inextricable realities that could not be understood separately: prisons were now extensions of these neighborhoods. The nature and experience of confinement changed since prisoners were no longer cut from their previous social and moral world and since they were imprisoned with relatives and neighbors. Moreover the branching networks connecting both worlds brought a translocal dimension to prison sociality and everyday life.

These transformations—their causes, context, and implications within and outside prison—were the topic of my presentation when in the aftermath of this research I was asked to participate in a meeting organized by the recently appointed national Commission for Prison Reform.[9] The mission of this government-appointed commission was twofold. First, it was mandated to make a comprehensive analysis of the present situation of the prison system in Portugal as well as of the central aspects of the legal structure and external environment framing that situation. It was instructed to seek cooperation from universities and civil society to promote a debate on the most important issues for the future definition of the prison system. Second, the Commission was expected to produce a report with the conclusions of that joint reflection, followed by recommendations. These meetings were held in the universities that hosted researchers conducting relevant research on prison-related issues. The fact that a five-member commission of high state officials had gone to the trouble of traveling throughout the country to listen to what researchers had to say on such matters seemed in itself to suggest a willingness to build a research-informed policy. This willingness did not, in any case, appear to be incidental since it also transpired in another policy-building process almost contemporary to this one but developed by a different government, to which I return later.

In the meeting I addressed some of the topics included in the script previously sent by the Commission with the intention of setting a framework for the discussion. But in the same way that I had had to revise my own research script in the face of transformations that had rendered the prison I knew unrecognizable (both the one I had studied a decade before and the institution theorized in prison studies), I also tried to elaborate on some of the terms of the Commission's script in order to match the penal landscape revealed by the ethnographic inquiry and to enable a more comprehensive assessment. In line with this elaboration my presentation focused less on prison itself than on its present close intertwinement with a few neighborhoods increasingly affected by concentrated incarceration. I described the effects of these transformations in prison life and on prison governance and suggested that if ethnographic data contributed to change our reasoning about prisons, by decentering our perspective from these institutions and by leading us to adopt a more comprehensive one, they were also not without implications for social intervention on prison issues.

I tried to depict the context in which these transformations came about during the 1990s. The Commission was aware of the alarming growth of incarceration rates, including the one of remand prisoners, as well as of its visible overall effects in prisons, such as overcrowding. What eluded the Commission were the processes behind these numbers, the connections between them, and some of the concrete circumstances occluded by these figures. Unless the numbers were triangulated with ethnographic data, they might be misconstrued in policy assessments. A crucial aspect consisted in the specific policies of penal repression aimed at retail drug trafficking during that decade. First, drug control fostered a proactive style of law enforcement that increased the potential for sociospatial selectivity and bias. Police interventions were increasingly aimed at poor urban neighborhoods and housing projects, which became routine targets of intensive surveillance and indiscriminate sweeps. These stigmatized territories were massive suppliers of inmates (both detainees awaiting trial and convicted prisoners). This was not the case in Portugal until the 1990s, with the exception of Gypsies, a stigmatized minority that had already experienced a similar kind of collective targeting in rural areas.[10]

Second, and compounding the effects of this particular type of law enforcement, the penal management of drugs fostered a procedural massification unparalleled in other forms of crime control. Not only did the courts deliver harsh sentences and delayed probation in drug matters in general, but they also tended to amalgamate several individual drug cases into a single case based on the slightest indication of an existing connection between some of them.[11] This form of judicial construction could thereby produce otherwise inexistent continuities between two or three dozen people. Represented thus as a trafficking network, such cases became additionally more vulnerable to aggravating charges of conspiracy, which had serious repercussions not only in sentencing (by increasing their severity) but also in the adoption of exceptional criminal proceedings, such as the extension of remand custody up to three years—as, for example, in cases of terrorism. However, drug-trafficking networks reported by the courts often had little sociological consistency and were a mere artificial outcome of the way individual cases were handled and juxtaposed by the criminal justice system. The retail drug economy in Portugal was not organized in the form of extensive networks. On the contrary: it revolved around small, variable circles of associates (kin or neighbors) that had flexible structures and worked autonomously.

Nonetheless small-scale drug trafficking did bring to impoverished urban areas a booming structure of illegal opportunities in which all of the residents could participate, regardless of age, gender, or ethnicity. These retail markets were very weakly stratified along these lines; the very fluidity of their freelance profile, as opposed to a business structure (prevalent, for example, in the United States) makes existing ideological barriers to entry more permeable and ineffective.[12] With relative ease women could get started on their own in dealing as freelancers, obtaining drugs through a neighborhood's traditional forms of interest-free informal loans that facilitate the circulation of both legal and illegal goods; they could borrow from a neighbor small quantities of heroin or hashish for resale in the same way that they would borrow groceries or money on other occasions.

In sum, the cause of the large clusters of prisoners incarcerated for drug crimes who knew each other before imprisonment, especially in women's prisons, was not the supposed existence of a "new female [drug] criminal" or of extensive, highly structured criminal organizations operating in these neighborhoods.[13] It resulted instead from the severe repression exerted by law enforcement and the courts on a small-scale drug economy in which residents from the same neighborhoods participated irregularly and independently. During and after my second fieldwork some prosecutors, judges, and prison officials had confided in me that they were often intrigued by the striking discrepancy between the noticeable small-time petty offenders they encountered and the harshness of their penal management. It also surprised the Commission during our meeting, as it showed that this discrepancy might not merely have been designed and might be the result of unintended cumulative effects of criminal justice proceedings and sentencing practices for drug crimes.

Ethnography thus provided a comprehensive, systematic description of processes affecting prisons as they emerged interrelated in concrete lives and trajectories inside and outside prison. This comprehensive view made apparent at the same time both the reasons for and the effects of the present intertwinement between prisons and destitute social spaces. It suggested that a focus on the prison system alone would be inadequate. In the same vein it implied that it would have been more than ever paradoxical to center policies of social intervention entirely on in-prison cognitive behavioral programs, oblivious not only to prisoners' multiple disadvantages and deprivations but also to their social backgrounds and life contexts.[14]

A few weeks after this meeting I received a written message from the Commission chairman stating that he had been struck by my presentation and was overwhelmed by what it conveyed. He was interested in knowing more, so I sent him the book I had published on this second research, which had recently received a high-profile social sciences award and as a result had attracted some attention from the print media.[15]

The final report, produced months later by the Commission, explicitly acknowledged each meeting's contribution and took them into account in its assessment of the prison system situation. The ethnographic findings resonated with the legal scholars', professionals', and NGOs' contributions to the debate and converged with their views regarding the prevailing penal severity. The report mentioned having identified certain causes prior to the prison system that had negative repercussions in the system itself (e.g., overcrowding, an excessive amount of remand prisoners, an excessive rigidity in implementing measures of flexibility in custodial sentences such as parole). It argued that such causes rested with criminal law, criminal justice proceedings, and their deficient interpretation and implementation. In line with this assessment the report produced several recommendations. In order to prevent the prevailing situation regarding drug charges—in which insufficient judicial differentiation between serious and less serious offenses was often conducive to the imprisonment of petty offenders, added to the courts' tendency to overuse the category "major trafficking" and underuse other categories available in drug law such as "minor trafficking" and "user-trafficker"—the

Commission recommended specific changes aimed at a clearer definition and application of the different legal types according to the severity of drug offenses. Furthermore it issued specific recommendations for a more precise revision and characterization of the aggravating circumstances enumerated in drug law—again in order to distinguish clearly between minor offenses connected with drug use and the organized, large-scale drug trade. Finally it recommended lower minimum sentences for drug trafficking and related activities, a revision of the restrictions on parole eligibility affecting important proportions of drug offenders, and a revision of the legal regime and judicial practices on remand custody in order to effectively limit its use to exceptional cases.[16]

Other sections of the report were dedicated to recommendations aimed to improve prisoners' living conditions and the implementation of prisoner's rights concerning access to legal counsel, education, health, training, and voting rights.[17] This set of recommendations stemmed mostly from supranational guidelines such as the European Prison Rules and the most recent resolutions and recommendations emanating from the European Council.[18] In general, therefore, these other sections stemmed from the same human rights framework that had inspired previous prison reforms.

It is difficult to gauge the recommendations' direct impact on judicial practices, even though it is reasonable to assume they were not ignored given the Commission's high profile and influential position with the judiciary and policymakers, as well as the nationwide publicity received by the report itself. But the patterns of drug sentencing did change drastically. Between 2003 and 2012 the number of imprisoned drug offenders dropped by nearly half, accompanied by the same steep drop in the amount of firm prison sentences applied to drug trafficking, which were partly replaced by suspended sentences. Overall the amount of remand prisoners decreased, and courts applied shorter sentences to drug-trafficking cases, ceased to systematically characterize them as "major trafficking," and resorted more frequently to the category "minor trafficking" instead.[19]

Whatever impact—if any—the knowledge conveyed by the researchers, scholars, and professionals invited by the Commission, and translated into recommendations, may have had on this change of practices, the conditions of the commission and the reception of such knowledge should in any case be considered in conjunction with those underlying another, much more visible drug policy, adopted in the country three years earlier: the decriminalization of drug use and possession.[20] Opting for a treatment model and a pragmatic public health approach backed by the possibility of administrative sanctions,[21] this policy attracted wide international attention due to some of the unique features it brought to the existing landscape of drug regulation. Besides explicitly linking decriminalization to dissuasion, treatment, and integration,[22] it decriminalized the use of all illicit drugs—and not just cannabis—while not legalizing them. Drug use remained prohibited (as a public order or administrative offense) but ceased to be a crime (sanctions under criminal law were removed).

This policy also dejudicialized drug use and possession. Cases detected by the police were no longer handled by the courts but referred to specially devised regional multidisciplinary commissions for the dissuasion of drug addiction, whose mission was to discourage further use, encourage treatment, and promote risk and harm reduction. Minor drug offenders were thus diverted from the criminal justice system and channeled to the drug treatment system. Although decriminalization had a negligible impact on imprisonment rates per se (drug use was previously dealt with by the courts mostly with fines or suspended sentences), it unburdened the criminal justice system while not leading to a major rise in drug use. On the contrary, the evidence indicates reductions in problematic use and in drug-related harms such as infectious diseases and drug-related deaths.[23]

I summon this experiment in alternative forms of legal regulation of drugs in order to outline the intellectual and political context in which two independent but close policymaking processes developed. Both of these processes, even though launched by different governments, showed a common willingness to build a research-informed policy. The drug policy reform was almost entirely based on the assessment and recommendations of a government-appointed multidisciplinary expert commission (Commission for a National Anti-Drug Strategy).[24] The willingness to rely on expert knowledge, shown by policymakers in prison reform, was boldly anticipated in this case, insofar as it tested the limits of United Nations conventions on illicit drugs, which require that nation-states repress drug trafficking as well as possession.[25] Considering the international landscape, Portuguese policymakers nevertheless went the furthest, within these limitations, in the development of an antidrug strategy that relied on treatment rather than prosecution.

Second, the Portuguese policy in the first decade of this century contrasts with the punitive turn in contemporary penality, thereby challenging hasty generalizations about the universal appeal of neoliberal governance, since it both reduced the penalization of drug users and extended the welfare infrastructure;

moreover its use for political-electoral purposes has been pointed out as a counterexample of penal populism.[26]

This was perhaps a unique juncture, for the present decade is already showing different signs. Even though the right-wing political majority that followed has not reversed the drug policy implemented by previous governments, it has drastically cut back on social services and the welfare structure, thus shaking central pillars of the reforms. It also proposed several measures ideologically aligned with neoliberal governance,[27] for instance making the registry of child sex offenders universally available to parents rather than law enforcement agencies alone. The social sciences were particularly hit by the retrenchment in science funding. Furthermore the room left for ethnography in government-commissioned projects was, at best, residual, and commissioned research predefined policies in such narrow, rigid frames that it rendered them impervious to ethnography's critical potential.[28]

The receptiveness involving my ethnographic research on imprisonment—insofar as it contributed to inform, together with other contributions, a report for policymaking purposes—is thus likely to have benefited from a convergence of several favorable aspects: a unique political and intellectual juncture; the authority and reliability obtained from the institutional sponsorship of a previous ethnographic inquiry and the results of the research itself, which a high-profile award for a subsequent inquiry later reinforced; and the continued interaction and different forms of engagement with several relevant actors, including the participation in training programs for the Portuguese judiciary (judges, prosecutors, and trainees) and the presentation of research results to prison agents.[29]

Although of a different sort, the interest shown by prison actors, which included some of my research interlocutors (among officials, frontline personnel, and prisoners), is also worth mentioning. They recognized themselves in the ethnographic account I had provided. But in addition, according to them this account enabled the recognition of patterns, structures, and relations as well as a comprehensive understanding of transformations they had perceived but could not make sense of. This opened up new, more contextualized perspectives for thinking about situations and behaviors that were usually made sense of with other instruments—for example, by resorting to ready-made psychological or culturalist categories such as "low resistance to frustration," "inability to defer gratification," and "present-time orientation."[30] One prison official used the image of a puzzle that this ethnography had helped her put together but that had also changed her previous fragmentary perception of each piece. I cannot ascertain whether this new understanding or awareness in any way affected professional practices that are deeply shaped by a variety of specific constraints, occupational cultures, and moral configurations. I did learn, however, that my second book on prisons was foisted on interns upon arrival by social workers, psychiatrists, and other prison personnel, leading me to assume that at this level they agreed ethnography provided a perspective relevant to their practice.

Ethnography of Vaccine Acceptability and a Report for Policy: Counterpoints

Returning to the level of policymaking, the receptiveness surrounding this ethnographic research was perhaps not detached from the unique set of circumstances I have described. That is why a brief comparison with a subsequent experience of communicating ethnography to an entirely different policy-oriented audience, one that occurred abroad, in an international context, and that benefited from none of those favorable circumstances, may add perspective to a reflection on aspects of ethnographic relevance and persuasiveness.

In the aftermath of ethnographic research coordinated by myself and Jean-Yves Durand on contemporary forms of vaccine refusal in Portugal and France, we were invited to participate in a project based in the Netherlands and funded by the European Union. This project was already in motion when we were taken on board, so we did not participate in its original design. Its aim was twofold: first, to identify *unvaccinated groups* in Europe, their *beliefs*, and the *determinants* of their decision to refuse vaccination; and second—and based on these determinants—to develop an effective communication strategy to be used by health professionals and public health agencies in case of major epidemic outbreaks of vaccine-preventable diseases. We were thus called to take part in a policy-oriented project whose frame and terms were already settled. We were supposed to provide a portrait of unvaccinated groups in Portugal and to contribute to a collective report and a communication package at the European scale.[31]

We had meetings with colleagues from epidemiology and surveillance, preparedness and response units of national agencies for public health and health protection from various European countries and from the European Centre for Disease Prevention and Control. Other meetings involved experts in world health communication, persuasive communication, and strategic social marketing. In this context all of these actors can also be considered a public with a policy agenda, or an audience brought together around a specific policy-driven task, before whom we were expected to convey the results of our ethnographic research. This experience was not without difficulties, some of which were inherent in an interdisciplinary dialogue involving different vocabularies and methodological instruments, while others involved different assumptions and categories of understanding. How did ethnography fit in this exchange, and what was its contribution?

Although our previous ethnographic approach had included the issue of vaccine opting-out and unvaccinated groups, it was intentionally more comprehensive and was framed otherwise. We had sought to identify the key themes, meanings, and experiences that bear upon the acceptability of vaccination as they emerge in routine vaccination and from parents' points of view. The term *acceptability* implies a perspective that considers acceptance and nonacceptance, or compliance and noncompliance, as aspects of the same research question rather than as separate problems. As they required a unified approach, we thus tried to grasp the scope of variation in current engagements with vaccination. It *is* true that certain forms of vaccine dissent are associated with particular communities or religious views (e.g., with some Roma communities and Dutch Orthodox Protestants) or with "alternativist" systems of ideas (e.g., anthroposophists, New Agers, and practitioners of particular dietary systems such as macrobiotics). Our research team had also studied these varieties in Portugal and France, and this provided an important comparative background for characterizing the specific properties of different varieties of vaccine acceptance and refusal.

But our ethnographic approach, oriented by the theoretical framework of acceptability rather than that of noncompliance or unvaccinated groups, tried to avoid exoticizing dissent and identifying it from the start with cultural *others*, or looking for it entirely within specific groups, particular communities, or cultural locations. This perspective allowed us to identify and characterize a distinct and more diffuse tendency of vaccine questioning (whether expressed in reticence, hesitation, ambivalence, or active rejection) that is not confined to a particular social scene or predicated on a given philosophy, religious view, or alternativist lifestyle. On the other hand, it would also be too narrow to frame these parents' views in terms of mere episodic vaccine scares caused by a few high-profile vaccine-science public controversies.[32] The form of critical acceptability we identified was broader, more pervading— and understudied.

The fact that our ethnographic interviews with parents adopted a conversational focus not restricted to health matters allowed parents to articulate their experiences in multiple spheres of life, from health to schooling and care. This broad focus enabled us to connect these seemingly disparate domains into common patterns. Whether reticent vaccine acceptors or vaccine decliners, parents claimed more leeway for participation and negotiated decision making—vis-à-vis not only vaccines but also other health matters, education, and care. This kind of comprehensive, flexible approach gave access to the *context* in which important differences in relation to other forms of vaccine acceptability could be identified. Unlike alternativist varieties of dissent, in which opposition to vaccination tends to be part of an identitarian adherence to a coherent ideological package on health and disease and in which seeking information on particular vaccines and vaccination is not so much a matter of finding a basis on which to *form* a decision as a means to gather evidence to *justify* a decision that has already been taken on a more general philosophical basis, in this case parents show an information-seeking attitude consistent with their more provisional views on vaccine issues.

In addition the ethnographic approach allowed us to understand decision making as an ongoing event, a *process*. This process is shaped by Internet-based knowledge and contact with friends, peers, and health care providers. Ethnography is well suited to show how the self-management of information flows is actually not self-sufficient but *relational*. As this information exposes parents to potential contradictory messages, they seek advice from doctors and pediatricians. However, these parents do not relate passively to biomedical authority—or to any authority from other spheres of activity. They try to obtain and discuss information as active interlocutors who expect to be informed about the available options. Some of the parents we interviewed reported a type of interaction in which doctors adopted a collaborative role typical of shared decision making; that is, they tried to combine patients' questioning with the promotion of decisions that refer to research-based knowledge. These parents ended up opting for vaccinating their children after a long process of reflection and hesitation about several vaccines, or they reversed previous decisions not to vaccinate. Other health care practitioners were not open to that type of communication. Parents who were unable to find in them a communication channel capable of contextualizing, mediating, and providing assistance in navigating the information they had or to cope with their questions and concerns eventually looked for support on their own. They found it in the only channels left available to them: antivaccination leagues and vaccinophobic sites. What had started as a negotiated convergence with biomedical views gave way to a general alienation from them. Vaccination dissent was thus more the outcome of a *pattern of interaction* and institutional environment than the expression of an individual decision grounded in a static, deep-seated belief. It was less a stance than the result of a process. And it could not simply be reduced to free-floating beliefs of unvaccinated groups.

Ethnography thus provided the sense of *context*, of *complexity*, and of *process* that was necessary to understand these emerging forms of dissent. The final European report ended up including several ethnography-based insights in its overall structure and recommendations—that is, besides the specific section dedicated to Portugal. To some extent the angle of acceptability made its way into a report that was supposed to be about unvaccinated groups; this report used a curious phraseology that ended up even including the notion of a "nongroup" in order to incorporate our findings.[33] An attention to *context and processes* of communication rather than *information* alone or *beliefs* seemed also to be accounted for in the general report, since communication with health care providers was understood to be a possible turning point in parents' decision-making processes. The report thus mentioned "the deficiencies in health authorities' ability to communicate . . . in a trustworthy manner."[34] Ethnography contributed therefore in some way to inform a report produced for policy-making purposes. We don't know yet if and how the report itself will impact policies, and if these policies will in turn shape the realities they are aimed at.

Conclusion

Tempting as it may be, it is risky to ascribe changes in policy, or their effects, to the simple causal impacts of any particular research, let alone to the influence of presentations of research results to policy-oriented audiences. Both the changes in policy and the responsiveness to these depictions occur in particular contexts involving numerous aspects, from political-intellectual circumstances to audiences' frames of expectation and the perceived legitimacy regarding the research and its authors. None of the circumstances favoring the receptiveness of my work on penal confinement bore upon the reception of the later research on vaccine acceptability. But despite these different circumstances, the fact that the ethnographic inputs of both were incorporated by specific audiences in the final reports produced by them for policymaking purposes allows us to presume that said inputs were deemed relevant and persuasive enough to induce these audiences to consider the subject differently or partly reorient their perspective on that issue. Ingredients intrinsic to ethnography were important to account for the receptiveness of these publics.

As in the penal confinement case, in which ethnographic knowledge may have played some part in the circumstances that brought about changes in legislation and judiciary practices, as well as widening the focus of in-prison policies of reintegration and their pervasive psychological vocabularies, in the case of reticent immunizers this knowledge might contribute to influence aspects of policy definition or policymaking on nonvaccination. However, I did not see my task as a matter of advising policymakers on how to "soften the natives" into vaccine uptake—any more than I had sought to advise them on how to turn felons into law-abiding citizens. Instead I believe my role was to put contemporary forms of nonvaccination and penal confinement in context and to shape new ways of thinking about them—within the alternative frame of vaccine acceptability, in the first case, and the prison-neighborhood nexus, in the second. Ethnographic knowledge was intended not as a problem-solving tool but as a more comprehensive resource for reasoning about a problem. And although it has perhaps contributed to some answers to a question, it was only through ethnographically assessing and elaborating on the terms of the question itself.[35] In other cases, however, policy agents may leave little room for reframing the issues in which they have sought to intervene, especially when this intervention is formatted by global agencies and patterned by transnational agendas.[36]

Ethnographic knowledge can be a powerful sensitizing resource for policy-oriented audiences. In hindsight I believe this sensitization in my encounters with these publics was of a particular kind. As I stated earlier, context, complexity, and process are among the main ingredients to make ethnographic accounts valuable and persuasive to those audiences. It is worth mentioning that, contrary to what I had anticipated, given the public perception of the scant scientificity of qualitative findings compared to quantitative results, my interlocutors never raised the issue of representativeness, let alone representativeness defined by statistical criteria. Context, complexity, and process can, no doubt, be conveyed using stories, narratives, and vignettes. But unlike journalistic stories and narratives, the persuasiveness induced by those ingredients is derived from the theory ethnographers embed in those stories. In other words, fine-grained accounts of the views and experiences of people affected by policies can be effective in exposing the inadequacy of policy categories, procedures, and conventional views. However, an ethnographic account is rendered more convincing to those specific audiences by making explicit the angles it proposes—by suggesting, for example, how potential insightful data emerge by framing the problem in a certain way instead of another that eludes them or by making not only evocative but also systematic descriptions whereby connections and patterns become visible and intelligible. Ethnographic sensitization can be all the more compelling the more theoretically informed it is. Theory, in this case, is called into play mostly as an explicit *mode of reasoning* rather than as a specialized vocabulary not always easily apprehended by circles of specialists besides our own.

Notes

1   The support of Fundação para a Ciência e Tecnologia, UID/ANT/04038/2013, is gratefully acknowledged.
2   For a critical reflection on ethnography, publics, and policies, see, among others, Cunha and Lima 2010; Dubois forthcoming; Fassin 2013.
3   Goffman 1961; Portuguese Ministry of Justice, Centro de Estudos Judiciários 1985–89.
4   See Cunha 2014; Rhodes 2001; Wacquant 2002; Waldram 2009.
5   Cunha 2011.
6   For example, Cunha 1990, 1994.
7   Cunha 2002, 2008.
8   Portugal has led the European Union throughout the 1990s with an incarceration rate ranging between 128 and 145 per 100,000 inhabitants (Ministério da Justiça 1987–2000).
9   Comissão de Estudo e Debate da Reforma do Sistema Prisional, appointed by the Ministry of Justice in 2003. Chaired by a former prime minister and president of the United Nations General Assembly, the Commission included the director general of the Portuguese Prison Service, the president of the Portuguese Institute for Social Reintegration, and the director of the Cabinet for Legislative Policy and Planning of the Ministry of Justice. Besides these officials there was a representative of the Permanent Observatory of Portuguese Justice. Although appointed by a center-right government, this was a consensual committee. There has been a broad consensus among political elites across the political spectrum regarding humanistic, progressive principles in criminal law and the criminal justice system. It was only in the second decade of the twenty-first century that punitive populist perspectives were echoed by right-wing parties' legislative initiatives.
10 Cunha 1994. *Gypsy* is the closest translation for the ethnonym used in Portugal by the people who call themselves *ciganos*. They do not use the term *Roma* and sometimes actively resist it.

11 Maia Costa 1998.

12 See Johnson et al. 1992; Cunha 2005.

13 The theme of the new female criminal, articulated in this period by judges and prosecutors, echoed a controversial view sustained by some scholars in the 1970s, according to which feminism had the collateral effect of also emancipating women into crime. See Adler 1975; Simon 1975.

14 In this respect see the growing influence of these programs, fueled by the revival of psychological perspectives on crime, on the global market of penal reintegration products described by Carlen and Tombs 2006. See also Kendall and Pollack 2003; Hanna-Moffat 2001.

15 Cunha (2002) received the Prémio Sedas Nunes para as Ciências Sociais, a biannual prize awarded by an international panel of social scientists.

16 Ministério da Justiça 2004: 92–96.

17 Like most European countries, Portugal does not disenfranchise felons; prisoners continue to participate in the political system by exercising voting rights in all elections (local, national, and European levels).

18 Ministério da Justiça 2004: 73–74.

19 Serviço de Intervenção nos Comportamentos Aditivos e nas Dependências 2012; Instituto da Droga a da Toxicodependência 2002–11. See also the annual reports of the European Monitoring Centre for Drugs and Drug Addiction (2002–2012).

20 Law 30/2000 (implemented in July 2001). The decriminalization was, however, restricted to use or possession of a limited consumer amount (i.e., up to ten days' worth of a drug). This was a policy adopted by the center-left government in office at time.

21 These can include fines, community service, suspensions on professional licenses, and bans on attending designated places. They exist, however, as a mere possibility. Depending on whether or not users are considered dependent, they are the object of a recommendation for entering a treatment program or of a provisional suspension of proceedings.

22 Hughes and Stevens 2010.

23 Hughes and Stevens 2010. See also Greenwald 2009; Quintas 2011.

24 Comissão para a Estratégia Nacional de Combate à Droga 1998.

25 United Nations 1988.

26 Hughes and Stevens 2010.

27 Garland 2001; Simon 2007.

28 One example is the recent call launched by the Commission for Citizenship and Gender Equality (Comissão para a Cidadania e Igualdade de Género), together with the National Research Agency, for a study into the prevalence of female genital mutilation in Portugal and on the communities in which it is presumed to occur. The research should respond to a public policy instrument in the exact terms in which this instrument was devised, even if those terms might have benefited from a critical ethnographic assessment themselves. See Cunha 2013.

29 These are provided by the national judicial training school, the Centre of Judicial Studies (Centro de Estudos Judiciários).

30 These reifying notions were profusely employed by prison staff to define individual prisoners and their conduct and trajectories, but they were also part of a psychosocial talk activated to generally describe the "mentality" of the incarcerated poor (see Cunha 2002). Structurally imposed marginality disappears behind these particular categories, which essentialize socially vulnerable populations and seem to confer on them a specific problematic quality.

31 Effective Communication in Outbreak Management for Europe 2013. The project was led by the National Institute for Public Health and the Environment in the Netherlands (Jan Hendrik Richardus, Erasmus University, Rotterdam). See Cunha and Durand 2011, 2013.

32 For example the controversy in the United Kingdom on the MMR vaccine (suspected of inducing autism), or the one in France about the hepatitis B vaccine (suspected of inducing multiple sclerosis).

33 "The critical citizens who are critical vaccine acceptors or vaccine refusers are not organised as a group as defined in this report. However, they shared common ideas and are a '(non)group,' which is growing. Developing communication strategies on their determinants seemed very useful and interesting for Public Health Institutes, therefore we decided to include them as well" (Effective Communication in Outbreak Management for Europe 2013: 12).

34 Effective Communication in Outbreak Management for Europe 2013: 7.

35 Cunha and Lima 2010.

36 See Cunha 2013.

References

Adler, F. 1975. *Sisters in Crime.* New York: McGraw-Hill.

Carlen, P., and J. Tombs. 2006. "Reconfigurations of Penality: The Ongoing Case of the Women's Imprisonment and Reintegration Industries." *Theoretical Criminology* 10 (13): 337–60.

Centro de Estudos Judiciários. 1985–89. "Do 'desvio' à instituição total: Sub-culturas, estigma, trajectos" (From "Deviance" to Total Institutions: Subcultures, Stigma, Trajectories). Lisbon. Portuguese Ministry of Justice,

Comissão para a Estratégia Nacional de Combate à Droga. 1998. *Estratégia Nacional de Luta Contra a Droga.* Serviço de Intervenção nos Comportamentos Aditivos e Dependências. Lisbon.

Cunha, Manuela. 1990. "Caracterização das relações entre os universos sociais de uma 'instituição total' da cidade de Lisboa: O Hospital Júlio de Matos" (The Social World of a Mental Institution). *Cadernos do Centro de Estudos Judiciários* 2 (1): 118–45.

———. 1994. *Malhas que a reclusão tece: Questões de identidade numa prisão feminina* (The Fabric of Confinement: Identity and Sociality in a Women's Prison). Lisbon: CEJ.

———. 2002. *Entre o bairro e a prisão: Tráfico e trajectos* (The Prison and the Neighborhood: Trafficking and Trajectories). Lisbon: Fim de Século.

———. 2005. "From Neighborhood to Prison: Women and the War on Drugs in Portugal." In *Global Lockdown: Imprisoning Women, Engendering Resistance*, edited by J. Sudbury, 155–65. New York: Routledge.

———. 2008. "Closed Circuits: Kinship, Neighborhood and Imprisonment in Urban Portugal." *Ethnography* 9 (3): 325–50.

———. 2011. "Agendas públicas, agendas de investigação e a prisão como objecto etnográfico" (Public Agendas, Research Agendas, and Prison as an Object of Ethnographic Inquiry). In *Etnografia e intervenção social: Por uma praxis reflexiva*, edited by Pedro Silva, Octávio Sacramento, and José Portela, 49–60. Lisbon: Fernando Mão de Ferro.

———. 2013. "Género, cultura e justiça: A propósito dos cortes genitais femininos" (Gender, Culture and Criminal Justice: On Female Genital Cutting). *Análise Social* 209.4: 834–56.

———. 2014. "The Ethnography of Prisons and Penal Confinement." *Annual Review of Anthropology* 43.1: 217–33.

Cunha, Manuela, and Jean-Yves Durand. 2011. *Razões de saúde, poder e administração do corpo: Vacinas, alimentos, medicamentos* (Health Reasons, Power and the Body: Vaccines, Food and Medication). Lisbon: Fim de Século.

———. 2013. "Anti-Bodies: The Production of Dissent." *Ethnologia Europea* 43.1: 35–54.

Cunha, Manuela, and Antónia Lima, eds. 2010. *Ethnography and the Public Sphere.* Special issue of *Etnográfica* 14.1.

Dubois, Vincent. Forthcoming. "Doing Critical Policy Ethnography." In *Handbook of Critical Policy Studies*, edited by F. Fischer et al. Cheltenham-Northampton, UK: Edward Elgar.

Effective Communication in Outbreak Management for Europe. 2013. "Undervaccinated Groups in Europe: Who Are They and How to Communicate with Them Outbreak Situations?" Work Package 6. EU Project Effective Communication in Outbreak Management: Development of an Evidence-Based Tool for Europe. http://ecomeu.info/wp-content/uploads/2015/11/ECOM-Under-vaccinated -groups-in-Europe-WP6.pdf.

European Monitoring Centre for Drugs and Drug Addiction. 2002–2012. *Annual Report*. Lisbon.

Fassin, Didier. 2013. "Why Ethnography Matters: On Anthropology and Its Publics." *Cultural Anthropology* 28.4: 621–46.

Garland, D. 2001. *The Culture of Control: Crime and Social Order in Contemporary Society.* Oxford: Oxford University Press.

Goffman, Erving. 1961. *Asylums: Essays on the Social Situation of Mental Patients and Other Inmates.* Harmondsworth, UK: Penguin.

Greenwald, G. 2009. *Drug Decriminalization in Portugal: Lessons for Creating Fair and Successful Drug Policies.* Washington, DC: Cato Institute.

Hanna-Moffat, K. 2001. *Punishment in Disguise: Governance and Federal Imprisonment of Women in Canada*. Toronto: University of Toronto Press.

Hughes, E., and A. Stevens. 2010. "What Can We Learn from the Portuguese Decriminalization of Illicit Drugs?" *British Journal of Criminology* 50.6: 999–1022.

Instituto da Droga e da Toxicodependência. 2002–11. *Annual Report*. Lisbon.

Johnson, B., A. Hamid, and H. Sanabria. 1992. "Emerging Models of Crack Distribution." In *Drugs, Crime, and Social Policy: Research, Issues, and Concerns*, edited by T. Mieczkowski, 56–78. Boston: Allyn and Bacon.

Kendall, K., and S. Pollack. 2003. "Cognitive Behaviouralism in Women's Prisons: A Critical Analysis of Therapeutic Assumptions and Practices." In *Gendered Justice: Addressing Female Offenders*, edited by B. Bloom, 69–96. Durham, NC: Carolina Academic Press.

Maia Costa, E. 1998. "Direito penal da droga: Breve história de um fracasso." (Criminal Drug Law: A Brief History of Failure). *Revista do Ministério Público* 74: 103–20.

Ministério da Justiça. 1987–2000. *Estatísticas da Justiça*. Lisbon.

———. 2004. *Relatório Final da Comissão de Estudo e Reforma do Sistema Prisional*. Lisbon.

Quintas, J. 2011. *Regulação legal do uso de drogas: Impactos da experiência portuguesa de descriminalização*. Porto. Fronteira do Caos Editores.

Rhodes, Lorna. 2001. "Toward an Anthropology of Prisons." *Annual Review of Anthropology* 30: 65–87.

Serviço de Intervenção nos Comportamentos Aditivos e nas Dependências. 2012. *Annual Report*. Lisbon.

Simon, J. 2007. *Governing through Crime: How the War on Crime Transformed American Democracy and Created a Culture of Fear*. Oxford: Oxford University Press.

Simon, R. 1975. *Women and Crime*. Lexington, KY: Lexington Books.

United Nations. 1988. Convention against Illicit Traffic in Narcotic Drugs and Psychotropic Substances. https://www.unodc.org/pdf/convention_1988_en.pdf.

Wacquant, Loïc. 2002. "The Curious Eclipse of Prison Ethnography in the Age of Mass Incarceration." *Ethnography* 3.4: 371–97.

Waldram, J. B. 2009. "Challenges of Prison Ethnography." *Anthropology News* 50.1: 4–5.

Part II

—Engagements

5

Serendipitous Involvement

Making Peace in the Geto

FEDERICO NEIBURG

In December 2012 I returned to Rio de Janeiro from a period of fieldwork in Greater Bel Air, a group of *geto* (ghettos) situated in the central region of Port-au-Prince, the focal point of my fieldwork in Haiti since 2007.[1] A few days later Pedro Braum, then a PhD student under my supervision, Robert (Bob) Montinard, a good friend from Bel Air who had moved to Rio de Janeiro after the January 2010 earthquake, and I began to receive messages from Haiti telling us that a new war had broken out in the zone. Reports and images of violence and killings, fear and insecurity were spreading through the streets, provoking long- and short-term memories of earlier wars. The messages were asking for our help in mediating the conflicts and containing the spiral of violence. But what could or should our role in this process be? And how would it impact our future work in the area? Among our concerns were how our ethnographic expertise could be translated into brokering peace and what the intellectual outcome of this experience might be. How and by whom would any such engagement be legitimized? By our networks in Bel Air? The generic "people of the ghetto"? The other agents involved in governance of the area, besides the armed groups, like the Haitian National Police (PNH), the UN blue helmets, the nongovernmental organizations (NGOs) and the international aid agencies (IAAs), all of whom we would have to interact with? There was also the question of how our engagement would be ethically and politically evaluated in Brazil. The country's presence in Haiti had become a sensitive public issue ever since the United Nations Stabilization Mission in Haiti (MINUSTAH) was launched in 2004 under Brazilian military command.

The disposition to ask for help—and to intermediate and give help—is a vital part of the geto's social life, particularly of the relations with *blan* (whites, including, among many others, missionaries, expats, and anthropologists). Constructed over the decades, these relations became more intense after the fall of the Duvalier dictatorship in 1986 and with the "endemization" of an emergency regime fueled by each successive political crisis and natural disaster.[2] Any actions we might undertake could not be construed as heroic, therefore; helping out was an ordinary part of geto life, traversed by aid and emergency.[3] We could not be optimistic either; given the configuration of the peace-building apparatus, we knew that peace, even were it attainable, was unlikely to be sustainable. This left us in a classic ethnographic double-bind—the kind humanitarianism seems to reveal in exemplifying[4]—between an imperative to answer the appeal for help and an imperative to critique the mechanisms and configurations that generate the demand itself and the social conditions for its own autopoietic perpetuation. However, three motives persuaded us to respond positively to the appeals: our strong personal ties, built up from the beginning of our research in the area; our assessment of the cost to be paid should we fail to respond to the request, possibly jeopardizing the very future of our presence in the area; and a feeling that we were being given a unique opportunity to gain a deeper ethnographic insight into the dynamics of politics and violence, the forms and meanings of war and peace in the geto.

In this chapter I describe this personal and collective experience, stressing its intellectual and anthropological impacts and its implications for public ethnography. The text is divided into four sections. In the first two I describe how I landed in the zone and the proximity to peace and war issues from the outset of my research—observing and participating in the peacekeeping world, even though I was no expert in the area and even though I originally had no intention of taking this topic as my locus of inquiry. With a description of our multiple involvements in the field I show how the universe of peacekeeping and stabilization was imposed on us as an ethnographic space of observation and participation for various reasons, including its omnipresence in the geto's daily life, because my first interlocutors—some of whom would became close friends—had been involved in it previously, and because I was a Brazilian blan working in a region targeted by Brazilian international intervention.[5] In the third section I describe how this peacemaking experience led me and my research team to a unique understanding of the dynamics of peace and war in the geto. I focus on two core categories: the base (*baz*), a social form related to geographical spaces, multiple different scales, belongings, affinities, and hostilities; and frustration (*fristrasyon*), a word that indicates individual and collective feelings on the verge of explosion, expressing suffering and uncertainty, and simultaneously threatening or justifying violence. In the last section I discuss some of the implications of this experience for the questions raised by public ethnography, stressing the entanglements between ethnographic subjects and ethnographic publics, publicity and secrecy. After showing how the production of ethnographic knowledge is cumulative, I return to the vignette described in the first paragraph to illustrate how the comprehension of the dynamics of violence in the geto was the outcome of a lengthy research itinerary, progressively combining the production of ethnographic knowledge, brokerage, and public ethnography. Thus war and peace emerge as something more and more complex than the "simple" presence or absence of violence or the augmentation or diminution of murders caused by armed groups, which as we shall see includes a delicate balance between publicity and concealment.

Helping make peace in the geto—as we tried to do, albeit in a very modest fashion—entails navigating the public spaces where, because of the hybrid nature of our work as ethnographers and mediators, our experience was embedded, generating expectations, scrutiny, and judgment of ordinary people and of the agencies involved in the geto's public life and governance. Hence, as I also explore in the final section, this text is an outline too of the topography and modulations of (national and international) public and hidden spaces through which we steered as ethnographers and brokers and where our actions and work were evaluated. Multiple entanglements between ethnographic encounters and engagements, ethnographic subjects and problems, different publics, forms and platforms of publicity and secrecy—these are some of the issues I address in the following pages.

Field Entanglements

Greater Bel Air is located in the center of Port-au-Prince, close to the political and economic heart of the country, a short walk from the National Palace, the Champ de Mars, the port, and the main hub of the Haitian market system—connecting the interior of the country with Port-au-Prince and with the Haitian commercial capitals beyond the country's borders, including Miami, Panama, and Santo Domingo. Something like 120,000 people inhabit the zone. More than 60 percent of women are linked to commercial activities, while more than 70 percent of men find themselves outside any kind of formal labor market or wage economy.

Between 2004 and 2006 the region experienced a period of heightened violence. It was the setting for the heaviest fighting between supporters of President Jean-Bertrand Aristide, deposed by a military coup backed by the armed forces of the United States, Canada, and France, and their opponents. Aristide had been raised in Lower Bel Air. The local Salesian seminary was where he first made his name as a preacher and later as a political leader. And it was this region too that saw the spread of some of the main bases providing grassroots support for him, his political movement, and the resistance to the coup d'état.

Due to its central location in the geopolitics of the city, MINUSTAH's operations started precisely in Bel Air. And because of the geopolitics of humanitarianism—the division of the territory between different national UN contingents, NGOs, and IAAs—the region was Brazilianized: the UN blue helmets had a Brazilian chief commander; its main headquarters was established in the High Bel Air (where the Brazilian battalion was based); and the zone was transformed into a showcase for the Brazilian Army (which has the biggest national corps in the UN mission), for the Brazilian Embassy, and for the Brazilian NGO Viva Rio, which, after being asked to establish a peace-keeping consultancy in the zone, decided to concentrate its work there and was transforming into a key broker in the region.

At the time the UN mission arrived, violence was spreading through poor neighborhoods of Port-au-Prince like Bel Air, embroiling numerous relatively independent groups and multiplying the conflicts. This situation was viewed by experts as something rather different from supposedly classic postconflict situations between two opposing forces and as being closer instead to the situation in Rio de Janeiro's favelas, where sovereignty is likewise disputed by different armed factions and state security forces. This, some experts argued, was the reason for integrating Viva Rio into the stabilization process in Bel Air: created in 1993 the Brazilian NGO had developed its expertise by pioneering peacemaking and disarmament processes in Rio de Janeiro.[6]

I first arrived in Port-au-Prince to collaborate in the creation of a training and research center (the Inter-University Institute for Research and Development, INURED).[7] I was interested in studying the dynamics of the popular urban economy and its entanglements with markets and humanitarianism.[8] I was also attracted by the possibility of observing the Brazilian participation in the stabilization process directly in the field. Bel Air seemed an ideal place to begin my ethnographic research. Furthermore I was first invited to get to know the region by the director of Viva Rio, Rubem Cesar Fernandes, a well-known Brazilian anthropologist. He introduced me to Herold Saint Joie, who would become one of my closest friends. Herold was then linked to the National Committee for Disarmament, Demobilization and Reintegration (NCDDR). He was born and raised in a small shack situated in one of the poorest alleys of Lower Bel Air. He, his mother, and his sister left the zone in the mid-1970s, when he was an adolescent, but he always maintained and cultivated his connections and friendships in the area. He was part of a deeply politicized generation that lived through the end of the Duvalier dictatorship, suffered the political violence that followed, and supported and then became disenchanted with Aristide's leadership. He took a degree in social psychology and also became an actor, convinced—like many others—that art could provide a nonviolent way to transform social reality. In the process he met blan people for the first time, first as a teacher of Creole, later as a "professional of development and conflict mediation," as he used to call himself, employed in short-term contracts for international cooperation projects. Through Herold I met Bob, a young Rastafarian musician who was involved in Bel Air's pro-Aristide resistance to the coup d'état. After some experiences working for development projects handled by the UN Procurement Division and other IAAs, Bob was recruited by Viva Rio. Both Herold and Bob were among the founders of the *Tambou lapè* (Drums for Peace) project, a partnership between NCDDR and Viva Rio that sought to combine infrastructural improvements (water and health supplies, for example) with disarmament and peace building.

Bel Air was, and still is, one of the two zones within the metropolitan area of Port-au-Prince labeled "red zones" by the UN, areas of "heightened risk" due to the presence of armed gangs, which bars UN civil servants from entering without military escort.[9] Following the recommendations made by Herold and our first interlocutors in the field, our first steps in the zone were public self-presentations. In a way we can say that we began to be ethnographers in Bel Air by doing public ethnography: people wondered what we were doing and what consequences our presence there might have for them. This also allowed us to gauge the depth of territorialization in the geto's social and political life. Then, day by day, we had a series of somewhat ritualized meetings with individuals and collectives, people recognized as leaders and members of a seemingly infinite number of committees and associations, always territorially based (linked to a street, a sector, a zone, a *lakou*).[10] Some of these collectives were active, implementing projects in partnership with NGOs, IAAs, and government agencies for facilities such as cyber cafés, drugstores, and water distribution kiosks, or promoting sports and cultural activities like music, painting, and craftwork. Other collectives seemed to be dormant, ready to embark on a new project as soon as an opportunity surfaced.

The meetings took place in closed locations (such as a shack or the head office of an association or committee promoting development or the welfare of the zone, a place that might also double as a shop, a lottery house, or someone's home) or in more public venues such as a street, an alley, or a *peristil* (the ritual Vodou space). Sometimes we met small groups; at other times dozens of people attended, including members of the collectives concerned and curious outsiders. The meetings started and ended with a prayer, frequently holding hands, spoken in Creole and Christian in content, though on some occasions when Islamic Rastafarians were present, Arabic words might also be pronounced. The prayer would be followed by our presentation, explaining who we were and describing our objectives: researchers from a Brazilian university who, in partnership with the Haiti State University, INURED, and Viva Rio, were interested in learning about the area's social and economic dynamics. The meeting would continue with the presentation of the collective's leaders and history and with the formulation of demands—sometimes heated—relating to their needs and expressing their expectations for aid and partnerships since we were Brazilian blan in a Brazilian humanitarian zone. The meetings would end with our expressing our gratitude and also our regret that we lacked the means to help them since we were from the university and (at least at that moment) not directly involved in any development or humanitarian projects.

Obviously as time passed and our personal relations increased in density, we began to walk about freely and stay for long periods in the region, sharing daily life with local people and, in particular, the everyday life of the leaders and brokers to whom we had become close. Time and the growing intimacy and trust between us and our interlocutors allowed us to accompany the details involved in preparing the peace agreements that formed part of the *Tambou lapè* project. Meetings and more meetings, conversations and more conversations in which people like Herold and Bob measured the temperature of the geto, identified expectations and potential threats to disarmament expressed in the language of frustration, and mapped the relevant actors to be included or excluded from the process, like people more or less openly linked to the zone's armed bases (*baz ame*).

Herold used to say that he had two hats, two jobs he liked equally: that of a researcher, working with me and my team, and that of an *ajan lyezon* (broker) or peacemaker with NCDDR. The two activities were entangled for him, as they became increasingly entangled for us over the following years.

Learning about Peace and War

At the time of our first incursions into Bel Air, in May 2007, people linked to NCDDR and Viva Rio, like Herold and Bob, were working on the signing of the second peace agreement between community leaders from different zones of the geto. The first agreement had been signed a year earlier by twelve community leaders. This time they succeeded in obtaining more: the second agreement was signed by twenty-one leaders. The aim of the *Tambou lapè* project was to progressively expand the territory, identifying and forming new leaders and gradually involving people less directly linked to armed bases—as we shall see, a crucial aspect in terms of the public legitimacy of the process. This was an impulse of the project form itself, which had the effect of steadily amplifying the territory understood as Greater Bel Air, incorporating new signatories linked to other sectors of the geto.[11] The expansion of the territory covered by the agreements was simultaneously a demonstration of the brokers' capacity to the bases and people of the geto and a proof of the project's effectiveness to partners like MINUSTAH, the PNH, the Haitian government, and the donors who funded Viva Rio (with funds coming from Norwegian and Canadian cooperation agencies). In total six agreements were signed, the last, in 2012, by more than a hundred signatories.

The *Tambou lapè* project also aimed to significantly reduce the number of violent deaths in the zone. These were evaluated monthly by a group of leaders that included signatories of the agreements, representatives from the PNH and MINUSTAH, and the brokers linked to the NCDDR and Viva Rio, like Herold and Bob. If it was established that there were no violent deaths during the period, lots were drawn for a motorbike by the recognized leaders in the territory covered by the agreement, and a scholarship for young people from the region. Quantifying and qualifying the violent deaths appeared to be a crucial topic. What counted? Should a marital fight ending in death be taken as a violation of the peace agreement and lead to the suspension of the lottery prizes that month? Should a death attributed to magical causes or entities be identified as an indication of conflict between bases and render the agreement null and void? In what situations could facts like these "become a scandal" (*fé skandal*), leaving the intimate sphere of those directly involved and transforming into public conflicts that required the intervention of the mediators? Understanding the importance of quantifying and qualifying deaths (and the meanings of the very notion of violent death) would lead to one of the actions developed in response to the request for help received years later, in 2013, being precisely, as we shall see, the creation of the Biwo d'Analyz (Analysis Office), run by people from the area, in order to produce more and better data on violent deaths in the region.[12]

The architecture of the Pact to Reduce Violence, as the peace agreement was called, was built around respecting the territorial principles that organize the geopolitics of the geto. Each party signing the agreement was identified with a particular zone or sector: St. Martin, Delmas 2, Bel Air, Solino, Fort National, Bastia, La Saline, Fortouron, Pont Rouge, Fort Dimanche, and so on. The signatory parties were community leaders, also referred to as "conflict prevention and management agents." Their job was "to work towards the training, education and dynamization of the community groupings of the district's various families, and towards reducing violence in their zone of influence." They were "employees of the NCDDR who perform a civil and social activity in his or her district, who should be a native of the latter, a resident of the zone and enjoy the trust and respect of people from the area."[13]

The peace agreement was solemnly signed in the afternoon in the Place de Paix, in the heart of Bel Air. During the day various other performances were held, the ritual and public dimensions of which, we began to learn, were also crucial to making peace—along with the economic dimension of the ceremonies, which involved the channeling of resources and small amounts of money by brokers and leaders. The day began early with cultural and sporting events and ended at night when the *rara* bands linked to the baz who had been at war or were threatening to fight each other paraded through the region's streets and alleys in a festive mood, accompanied by hundreds of people singing and dancing—a demonstration just as important as or even more important than the signed agreements themselves, reflecting the fundamental role that moving about within the territory has (and the rara bands play) in the geopolitics of the geto as a show of strength, a menace, or even the start or continuation of a spiral of violence.[14]

Peacemaking meant relying on the support of the armed leaders. Without them the project's protagonists and sponsors would fail and the only option left would be repression and an uncertain outcome. This was precisely the aspect of peace agreements questioned by those opposed to them both inside and outside the geto. In street discussions, documents produced by international agencies, newspaper articles, and even the debates held back in Brazil on the paths taken by the peacemaking process in the Caribbean country, critics alleged that this kind of peacemaking strategy legitimized bandits and clientelist networks that oppressed the local populations through the threat or use of arms. For them the baz were synonymous with gangs, responsible for kidnappings, thefts, illegal trade, and other crimes. This narrative linked the baz to the militias that had supposedly been organized by President Aristide and, orphaned from the Palace after his overthrow, had revealed their true nature as armed bands that, furthermore, exploited the development aid projects.[15]

From the outset our proximity to the brokers and leaders involved in this peace-building project also made us potential targets for such accusations, a risk similar to the one we would face during our involvement with peacemaking after the request for aid received in 2013. On the other hand, as we gained better knowledge of the social configuration in which we were inserted, we were able to more clearly understand the complexities of the social forms involved in violence and the complexity and extension of the social constellations implied in peace and war, beyond the acts of violence themselves. We also began to comprehend the entanglements between the dynamics of war and peace and realize that these were not simply local affairs, limited to friendships and enmities between the zone's leaders and bases. The politics and economics of violence and peacemaking form a single configuration to which a variety of agencies and agents belong, including NGOs and IAAs, and blan brokers, as we ourselves were perceived and eventually became. The dynamics of peace and war, for their part, were entangled with the dynamics of aid and humanitarianism, with the expectations and threats relating to the flow of resources, and obviously to the fluctuations in the international cooperation agendas, which had a direct impact on life in the geto, on the leadership structures, and on the dynamics of violence—as we were able to ascertain in the process inaugurated after the devastating earthquake of January 12, 2010.

Dealing with Bases and Frustration

As well as the enormous cost in human lives and infrastructure, the earthquake dramatically affected the relations between people and the territory. It also produced changes in the priorities and flows of international aid, accentuated by the cholera epidemic that broke out shortly afterward, altered our embedding in the region, deepened our relations with people from the area, and finally refocused our own research agenda.

The main national prison collapsed with the earthquake. Armed leaders fled and took refuge in Lower Bel Air, near the highly sensitive zone of the Croix de Bossales markets, where, as people know all too well, wars originate and converge. The fugitives provoked the segmentation of some bases and the birth of new ones, altering the balance of forces between them and destabilizing the geto. The Place de Paix, where the peace agreements had been signed, was transformed into a refugee camp, epitomizing the changes brought about by the emergency. In a context where the flows of aid had already started drying up because of the 2008 financial crisis, a huge increase some months after the earthquake was followed by international aid funds flowing to other destinations: the resources diminished, provoking instability and frustration, disordering spaces and relations.

Some months after the tragedy Michel Martelly was elected president. His networks were hostile to the Bel Air bases. He dissolved the NCDDR, radically changing the policies toward the geto's stabilization. Some months later Samba Boukman was murdered; he was one of the best-known members of the NCDDR and one of the most important leaders still remaining from the Bel Air resistance to the coup d'état that had overthrown Aristide more than eight years earlier. Security policies changed tack; circuits once used to distribute resources were deactivated and new ones were tested, introducing more instability.

I had been due to arrive in Port-au-Prince the week after the earthquake. Pedro Braum, then my student, was in the field with two Haitian members of my team. When the earthquake struck he was at the headquarters of Viva Rio in Bel Air, which immediately began to receive thousands of homeless and injured. Pedro was at that moment the only blan in the locality and became involved in assisting the victims, collaborating with local leaders in organizing the response to the tragedy. Over the following weeks he also became involved with aid agencies, including the leaders and brokers linked to Viva Rio and the IAAs providing assistance during the emergency. Pedro's relations, my own, and those of other team members with our interlocutors in the zone acquired a different density thereafter, founded on a new sense of proximity.

At the same time, soon after the earthquake we focused our research on the dynamics of politics and aid.[16] For some months we participated in the day-to-day life of the leaders and bases in different zones of Bel Air, including the refugee camps. We observed people's everyday lives and through long interviews we reconstructed the trajectories of more than forty leaders. A report was published in Creole, English, French, and Portuguese. This was discussed in diverse spaces, including at the Viva Rio headquarters in the geto with dozens of leaders, at the Brazilian Culture Center, and at INURED and the State University with experts and academics. It proved polemical. Some welcomed our findings: the people closest to the geto and the baz, the brokers linked to the peace-building process and the peace agreements, like those working for NCDDR and Viva Rio. Others implicitly or explicitly criticized our text for providing a voice for "bandits" and legitimizing their political participation.

Hence by the time Pedro, Bob, and I received the appeals for help from our friends in Bel Air in December 2012 we too had become specialists in the eyes of the geto leaders themselves. And we also knew very well that the first thing to be done in response to the request for help had to be a project. This was called Carnival for Peace since its objective was to reduce tensions in the run-up to the most sensitive period in the geopolitics of the geto: the period of Lent between Carnival and Easter, when the rara bands take over the streets. In another sign that the priorities of humanitarianism had changed, Bob received news from Viva Rio that they lacked the funds at that moment to support the project. We therefore decided that Pedro and Bob should travel to Port-au-Prince with funds from our own research; I would join them a while later. This gave rise to the rumor that this time it was the University of Rio that was sponsoring peace.

The next steps of the script were also familiar to us: we had to track down more funds, start the frenetic work of talking to the key figures in the conflicts or those willing to back the pacification process, plan the festivals leading up to Carnival, which celebrated the end of war (complete with drink, food, music, dance, and rara bands), and coordinate the support of the Brazilian battalion of MINUSTAH, which had jurisdiction in the area, in order to provide security during the events. Despite moments of tension and violence,[17] the project fulfilled its objectives. The festivals commemorating peace were held, and, just as important as this, new projects emerged that reactivated past sources of support (like Viva Rio). Although a few months later the armed conflicts returned to the geto, our hybrid experience as ethnographers and agents of the peacemaking universe would continue with the creation of the Biwo d'Analyz, the objective of which was to produce better data on violent deaths that could compete with those produced by other agencies (like the PNH and the Joint Logistics Operations Center, supported by the U.S. Southern Command, the U.S. State Department, and USAID), which, according to our comrades in the endeavor, were partial and superficial due to the distance of the experts involved in their production from real life in the geto. Thus the tasks of measuring and qualifying murders are themselves part of war and peace, a single social world.

As would be expected, over the course of this experience we had to deal with intense expectations, frustrations, leaders, and bases, all of which provided us with a unique insight into the social and political dynamics of the geto. The use of the word *frustration* (*fristrasyon*) had already been present in our first encounters with leaders and collectives in Bel Air. It had also appeared in the requests received in Rio de Janeiro and later returned with more intensity in our conversations in the geto. This was a frustration born of having no one to turn to because the zone had been abandoned to the bandits, and having no alternative but to turn to guns and add to the violence. We learned that what makes frustration a category organizing relations between agents and agencies, especially those involving resources from outside and contacts with blan like ourselves, is its polysemy and instability. Frustration indicates a situation on the verge of explosion, expressing extreme needs and uncertainty, menacing or justifying violence; it is a sentiment that should be tamed to make or to maintain peace. But frustration also signals an expectation, or even a more or less explicit threat of what may happen should this expectation not be met. Brokers and leaders need to remain aware of such frustration because it may be a sign of weakness and losing respect. At the same time they can pressure donors by pointing out the potential consequences should their people become even further frustrated: frustration can lead to disorder (*desòd*), criminal activity, and war. It thus simultaneously evokes a diagnosis of the present, past memories of better times, and prospects for a peaceful or violent future.

Making peace also required grasping the equally polysemic and unstable meanings of the term *base* (*baz*), beginning with the realization that the bases are much more than the immediate agents of violence or the same thing as gangs, as they are so often described by experts. The base, we came to realize, is a moral and a geographical space of affects, belonging, and protection. It is where one can find friends, a bed, or a plate of food; it is a place of sociability, a concrete location within a territory, sometimes marked in the streets and on the walls by graffiti or designs; it is a headquarters, a house, a place, or a street corner, a crew. The boundaries and scales of bases are mobile and malleable—even a single person can be a base for someone (*li se baz mwen*). Bases may also be more or less formally linked, if not always publicly, to the armed bases. A base linked to development (an association for the promotion of the welfare of Bloc X, for example) might also work to promote culture, or be associated with rara bands, or be connected to politics or arms. Sometimes a base acts at different levels, accessing different resources. We also find different bases with the same people gravitating around them, linked to some bases more than others, depending on the situation or the specific period in their personal lives. Bases have a segmentary dynamics and are traversed by a tendency to equalize peers and hierarchize leaders (*boss, chef, kòmandan*, etc.).[18] The latter are held responsible for dealing with the frustrations and expectations of their bases and their soldiers and generating and distributing resources.[19] They should also have the capacity to make friends and master ways of dealing with (*jere*) uncertainty.

Conclusion: Topographies of Publicity and Concealment

A little while after the project's conclusion, a few weeks after Carnival 2013, Pedro and some of the leaders from Bel Air who had taken part directly in the peace process received a phone call from MINUSTAH's Brazilian command, inviting them to a public ceremony at the Brazilian UN headquarters to receive an award in recognition of their work for peace. Even today Pedro keeps his medal stored well out of sight, embarrassed to show it to anyone in Brazil. The public display of recognition from the UN military mission was awkward for both him and our research team; it was even implicitly prohibited in Brazil, where the public debate on the country's presence in Haiti had acquired considerable visibility and a political dimension, demanding our participation and imposing interdictions.[20]

Over our years of ethnographic experience in Bel Air we needed to learn to navigate in a sensitive topography that includes, at the same time, publicity—in the double sense of being popular and being politicized—and concealment.[21] Both publicity and secrecy shaped our life in the geto, the conversations, learning the parables and allusions, where to sit to talk (*chita palè*); inside and outside the geto, in a particular house or corridor; mastering the kinds and levels of visibility and invisibility, the expected and avoided public, the tensions between what should be shown, what should be hidden and unspoken, and what should be subtly alluded to in certain contexts to some people and not others. Making peace epitomized this game, intrinsic to all good diplomacy (and maybe to all good ethnography too), between public demonstrations (like the festivals and rara bands circulating through the territory) and concealments (deals, promises, agreements) that involve some people, are known by others, and are the subject of rumors, speculations, and judgments more widely.

The pragmatics of concealment and publicity that we have learned—and learned to master, albeit always in a partial way—shows that these are always entangled with each other and their frontiers porous, subject to negotiations and manipulations. It also shows that this interplay between publicity and secrecy performs ethnographic subjects—categories that allude to social forms like the baz, sentiments like frystrasion, projects, peace agreements, personal and collective trajectories, and so on—and performs ethnographers themselves as hybrids of brokers and knowledge producers. If truth be told, it is a risky road where almost all ethnographers meet, even if not all ethnographers make the fact explicit or incorporate their multiple entanglements in the field into their ethnographic objects.[22]

In a way the experience narrated in this chapter evokes a characteristic shared by many long-term ethnographies: a process of progressive involvement and accumulation of knowledge—from our first encounters in the field, narrated at the start of this text, to the project in which we became directly involved with peacemaking. The collective dimension of our experience contributes to the multiplication of engagements and ethnographic subjects. This was consistent with the fact that the social configuration under study forced us to expand our involvement, considering and becoming related to many people, in a social topography that was at once highly localized in the geto and—as our own presence and actions make clear—traversed and shaped by national and transitional fluxes, agencies, and publics.

Notes

I should like to acknowledge the members of my research team who participated in the stories spoken about in this text and with whom I have discussed many of the issues explored here, sharing fragments of our own lives: Pedro Braum, the late Herold Saint Joie, Robert (Bob) Montinard, Handerson Joseph, Jony Fontaine, and Jean Sergo Louis. I appreciate the generous comments on previous versions of the text by Didier Fassin and Lucas Bessire. Through them I also acknowledge the other colleagues from the workshop that gave birth to this volume. Finally I thank David Rodgers for his marvelous help with the English version.

1   I prefer the Creole term *geto* to other terms commonly used to describe the Haitian shantytowns. It better expresses the viewpoint of local people: they identify themselves as originating from (or having been "made" in) the *geto* (*moun geto* or *fèt nan geto*); they speak a singular form of Creole (*kreyòl geto*); and they give a political meaning to the term. See Braum 2014: chapter 3; and, for example, the Creole song "Geto Racine" (Ghetto Roots) by the renowned Haitian American musician Wyclef Jean.

2   On endemization of emergency regimes, see Pandolfi 2010. The Creole term *blan* encapsulates both racial and national elements, indexing white people and non-Haitians. The international military interventions (by the United States, France, Canada, and the UN) and the international blockades after the fall of the Duvalier regime in 1986 were extremely intense and had devastating consequences. The same applies to natural disasters that have repeatedly mobilized the humanitarian apparatus in Haiti over the past three decades (hurricanes in 1994, 1998, 2004, and 2008; earthquake and cholera epidemics in 2010). For a larger picture of this process, see Dubois 2012; Farmer 2012. For some analytic appraisals of humanitarianism in Haiti, see Beckett 2014; Braum 2014; James 2010; Kivland 2012; Marcelin 2011, 2015; Neiburg et al. 2011 Among the many examples of denunciatory narratives, see Schuller 2012.

3   I am unable to depict the collective nature of this ethnographic experience in the present narrative. Here the first and third person are therefore synonymous. When it is significant to the description, I shall be more specific, naming the people involved in the situations described. I return to the collective dimension of the experience and its consequences for public ethnography in the final section.

4   See Fassin 2012.

5   For a broader argument on the heuristic potentialities of multiple scales of involvement in the research process, see Elias 2007.

6   On Viva Rio's involvements in Bel Air, see Fernandes 2014: 194; Moestue and Muggah 2009. On the place of MINUSTAH in the creation of a new paradigm for UN Missions, linked to the consecration of the concept of stabilization, see Hamann 2009; Muggah 2013.

7   Headed by Louis Herns Marcelin, a comrade since our time as PhD students in the same Brazilian social anthropology postgraduate program.

8   See, for example, Neiburg 2016.

9   The other red zone is Boston, located in the nearby district of Cité Soleil.

10   *Lakou* are clusters of houses inhabited by kin groups, including ancestors. Identified in the literature as a central social unit in traditional rural Haiti, they also compose an important sociospatial category in contemporary popular urban districts like Bel Air.

11   On the project form, see Boltanski and Chiapello 1999: 135; Braum 2014: 25–26; Mosse 2005: 12. The introduction of the expression *Greater Bel Air*, which includes Bel Air itself and other districts, formed part of this expansive dynamic of humanitarian aid. Its coinage combined the interests of the IAAs and NGOs trying to extend their area of influence and the aims of local organizations, leaders, and brokers

wishing to territorially amplify their influence and prestige by mediating resources and projects.

12   The "connectivity" and "collapse" between scales in urban Haitian violence (Marcelin 2015) explains why the qualification and quantification of murder are always contextual and disputable.

13   The UN Disarmament, Demobilization and Reintegration program was created in 1989 and implemented for the first time in Haiti following the 1994 military intervention that returned Aristide to power after the first coup d'état had removed him from office in 1991. The program's objectives included the "dismantlement of armed groups, reintegration of hard core members and the identification and formation of community leaderships" (UN, Department of Peacekeeping Operations 2010: 5). The community leader, a central figure in such programs, has a long history in humanitarianism in Haiti. The first aid missions to the country, which aimed to identify and train community leaders, date back to at least the period of U.S. occupation, 1915–34 (Smith 2001). Though I cannot explore this question here, the figure of the community leader, in the context of humanitarianism, expresses the persistence of forms of indirect rule in postcolonial contexts. Elements for a comparison with the Brazilian case in Amazonia and urban Rio de Janeiro can be found in Pacheco de Oliveira 2009, 2014.

14   On rara bands, see McAlister 2002. On the relationship between rara bands and baz in Bel Air, see Braum 2014; Kivland 2014.

15   Some of the terms used in the press and the peacemaking literature in reference to Aristide's supporters in the geto (like chimè) stigmatized them as disordered and delinquent. The first commander of MINUSTAH—who would later become a polemical figure in Brazil, associating himself with right-wing causes and positions—publicly argued in favor of the NCDDR's policies at the time, valorizing the fact that he had personally negotiated with the bosses of armed baz. The tone of this account, which was positive concerning the inclusion of the armed factions in the NCDDR program framework, was echoed in the first self-congratulatory memoirs written by Brazilian military personnel in Haiti, published soon after the mission began (see Ruppenthal 2007, for instance).

16   In Braum 2014: chapter 1 Pedro describes how the earthquake and the research that we began together soon after also had the effect of radically changing the subject of his thesis, until then planned as an ethnography of a rural region in the southeast of Haiti.

17   Superbly described in Braum 2014: chapter 5.

18   See Braum 2014: chapter 2; Neiburg et al. 2011.

19   The creole term sòlda underlies hierarchy and proximity. It is also a polysemic term that generally refers to supporters and followers, not only to armed actions. It could also refer to a companion, someone on whom one can rely, including affective personal relations.

20   Brazilian public opinion focused on the nation's involvement in the Caribbean country more intensely after the earthquake and especially after the first wave of Haitian

immigrants arrived in Brazil in the wake of the disaster and after army forces, who had been trained in Haiti, intervened in Rio de Janeiro's favelas in 2012. When presenting our research to Brazilian audiences (in op-eds, TV interviews, and academic discussions) we invariably refused to position ourselves within the dichotomous terms in which the debate was conducted. Typically this was polarized between accusations concerning the Brazilian government's geopolitical aims (aligned or not with the United States, depending on whether the accusation came from the political right or left), the denunciation of the use of Brazil's military experience in Haiti in the repression of poor people in Brazil, and the celebration of the supposed goodwill of South-South cooperation being extolled by government authorities at the time.

21 On this double sense of publicity, see Fassin 2013. On the pragmatics of secrecy, see Herzfeld 2009. For an argument on the presence of secrecy (and the tension between secrecy and publicity) in ethnographic work, as a thematized topic and a permanent implicit motive, see Jones 2014. On the interplay between intimacy and publicity, see Neiburg 2003.

22 In other contexts (De L'Estoile et al. 2005) we comparatively analyzed the paradoxes of denunciation and engagement that traverse the debates on the social conditions of anthropological knowledge, always hybrid.

References

Beckett, Greg. 2014. "The Art of Not Governing Port-au-Prince." *Social and Economic Studies* 63.2: 31–57.

Boltanski, Luc, and Eve Chiapello. 1999. *Le Nouvel Esprit du Capitalisme*. Paris: Gallimard.

Braum, Pedro. 2014. "*Rat pa Kaka*: Política, violência e desenvolvimento no coração de Porto Príncipe." PhD dissertation, PPGAS, Museu Nacional, UFRJ, Rio de Janeiro.

Braum, Pedro, Flávia Dalmaso, and Federico Neiburg. 2014. "Gender Issues: Relations between Men and Women in the Low-Income Districts of Port-au-Prince." Viva Rio/NuCEC/UFRJ. http://vivario.org.br/wp-content/themes/vivario/biblio tecaepesquisa/estudosepesquisas/2014/gender_issues_2014_en.pdf.

Campbell, John K. 1973. *Honor, Family, and Patronage: A Study of Institutions and Moral Values in a Greek Mountain Community*. Oxford: Oxford University Press.

De L'Estoile, Benoit, Federico Neiburg, and Lygia Sigaud. 2005. "Introduction: Anthropology and the Government of 'Natives.' A Comparative Approach." In *Empires, Nations, and Natives: Anthropology and State-Making*, edited by Benoit De L'Estoile, Federico Neiburg, and Lygia Sigaud, 1–29. Durham: Duke University Press.

Dubois, Laurent. 2012. *Haiti: The Aftershocks of History*. New York: Metropolitan Books.

Elias, Norbert. 2007. "Problems of Involvement and Detachment." *British Journal of Sociology* 7.3: 226–52.

Farmer, Paul. 2012. *Haiti after the Earthquake*. New York: Public Affairs.

Fassin, Didier. 2012. *Humanitarian Reason: A Moral History of the Present*. Berkeley: University of California Press.

———. 2013. "Why Ethnography Matters: On Anthropology and Its Publics." *Cultural Anthropology* 28.4: 621–46.

Fernandes, Rubem Cesar. 2014. *Fora da Ordem: Viagens de Rubem César*. Rio de Janeiro: FGV.

Hamann, Eduarda, organizer. 2009. *Revisiting Borders between Civilians and Military: Security and Development in Peace Operations and Post-Conflict Situations*. Rio de Janeiro: Viva Rio.

Herzfeld, M. 2009. "The Performance of Secrecy: Domesticity and Privacy in Public Spaces." *Semiotica* 175: 135–62.

James, Erica Caple. 2010. *Democratic Insecurities: Violence, Trauma and Intervention in Haiti*. Berkeley: University of California Press.

Jones, Graham M. 2014. "Secrecy." *Annual Review of Anthropology* 43: 53–56.

Kivland, Chelsey. 2012. "Unmaking the State in 'Occupied' Haiti." *PoLAR: Political and Legal Anthropology Review* 35: 248–70.

———. 2014. "Becoming a Force in the Zone: Hedonopolitics, Masculinity, and the Quest for Respect on Haiti's Streets." *Cultural Anthropology* 29.4: 672–98.

Lewis, David, and David Mosse. 2006. *Development Brokers and Translators: The Ethnography of Aid and Agencies*. Boulder, CO: Kumarian Press.

Marcelin, Louis Herns. 2011. "Cooperation, Peace, and Reconstruction: A Tale from the Shanties." *Journal of Peacebuilding and Development* 6.3: 17–31.

———. 2015. "Violence, Human Insecurity and the Challenge of Rebuilding Haiti: A Study of a Shantytown in Port-au-Prince." *Current Anthropology* 56.2: 230–55.

McAlister, Elizabeth. 2002. *Rara: Vodou, Power and Performance in Haiti and Its Diaspora*. Berkeley: University of California Press.

Mintz, Sidney. 1959. "Internal Market Systems as Mechanisms of Social Articulation." In *Intermediate Societies, Social Mobility and Communication*, edited by Em V. F. Ray, 20–30. Seattle: University of Washington Press.

MINUSTAH/RVC. 2013. "Réduction de la violence communautaire." Accessed May 15, 2014. https://minustah.unmissions.org/r%C3%A9duction-de-la-violence -communautaire.

Moestue, Helen, and Robert Muggah. 2009. "Social Integration ergo Stabilization: Assessing Viva Rio's Security and Development Programme in Port-au-Prince." Geneva: Viva Rio.

Mosse, David. 2005. *Cultivating Development: An Ethnography of Aid Policy and Practice*. London: Pluto Press.

Muggah, Robert, ed. 2013. *Stabilization Operations, Security and Development: States of Fragility*. London: Routledge.

Neiburg, Federico. 2003. "Intimacy and the Public Sphere." *Social Anthropology* 11.1: 63–78.

———. 2014. "Foucault em chave Etnográfica: O Governo dos *gueto* de Porto Príncipe." *Análise Social* 44.3: 742–47.

———. 2016. "A True Coin of Their Dreams: Imaginary Monies in Haiti (The 2010 Sidney Mintz Lecture)." *Hau: Journal of Ethnographic Theory* 6.1: 75–93.

Neiburg, Federico, Natacha Nicaise, and Pedro Braum. 2011. "Leaders in Bel Air." Viva Rio. http://vivario.org.br/wp-content/themes/vivario/bibliotecaepesquisa /estudosepesquisas/2011/community_leaders_2011_en.pdf.

Pacheco de Oliveira, João. 2009. "Contemporary Indigenous Politics in Brazil: Three Modes of Indigenous Political Performance." In *Indigenous Identity and Activism*, edited by Priti Singh, 80–103. Delhi: Shipra.

———. 2014. "Pacificação e tutela militar na gestão de populações e territórios." *Mana Estudos de Antropologia Social* 20.1: 125–61.

Pandolfi, Mariella. 2010. "From the Paradox to the Paradigm: The Permanent States of Emergency on the Balkans." In *Contemporary States of Emergency: The Politics of Military and Humanitarian Interventions*, edited by D. Fassin and M. Pandolfi, 153–72. New York: Zone Press.

Ruppenthal, Tailon. 2007. *Um soldado brasileiro no Haiti*. Rio de Janeiro: Editora Globo.

Schuller, Mark. 2012. *Killing with Kindness: Haiti, International Aid, and NGOs*. New Brunswick, NJ: Rutgers University Press.

Smith, Jennie Marcelle. 2001. *When the Hands Are Many: Community Organization and Social Change in Rural Haiti*. Ithaca: Cornell University Press.

UN, Department of Peacekeeping Operations. 2010. "Second Generation Disarmament, Demobilization and Reintegration (DDR) Practices in Peace Operations: A Contribution to the New Horizon Discussion on Challenges and Opportunities for UN Peacekeeping." January 18. http://www.un.org/en/peacekeeping /documents/2GDDR_ENG_WITH_COVER.pdf.

Viva Rio. 2007. "Censo demográfico de Bel Air: Port-au-Prince, Haiti, 2007." http://vivario.org.br/wp-content/themes/vivario/bibliotecaepesquisa/estudo sepesquisas/2007/recensement_bel_air_2007/censo_demogr%C3%A1fico_bel _air_%202007_pt.pdf.

6

Tactical versus Critical

Indigenizing Public Ethnography

LUCAS BESSIRE

This essay is about those moments when the force of public ethnography surges from concealment and the colonizing powers such secrecy often sustains.[1] I question how the uneven distribution of effective ethnographic knowledge—in its various modes as a schematic of voice, aspirational horizon, sociopolitical field, late liberal metanarrative, or analytic corrective—may be related to its promise to unmask something that must remain masked and to reveal something that must remain knowable only in its concealment.[2] More specifically I explore how this revelatory promise is especially central to the ethnography of Indigenous lifeways, modes of being, and cosmologies: the expert revelations of which have long served as anthropology's central charter within empire and the fetishized appeal of which have long wed ethnographic representations so tightly to the pragmatics of exclusionary containment, the logics of extermination, and the celebration of difference known in advance.[3]

The following meditation takes as its evidence not an example of successful public intervention but a series of failed experiments in anthropological advocacy conducted among the so-called Ayoreo Indians, members of a small, "recently contacted," and severely marginalized Indigenous people native to the Gran Chaco region of southeastern Bolivia and northwestern Paraguay. To do so I draw on chronicles of these failures recently discovered in the diaries, papers, footage, and field notebooks of an unidentified North American anthropologist, who arrived in the Chaco at a very young age, apparently by accident. His records, spanning nearly a decade, reveal that the anonymous young Chronicler was almost compulsively drawn to the inequities that he was driven unsuccessfully to confront. Paradoxically his repeated failures, each greater than the last, did not diminish his fervor to intervene but seemed to intensify it. The result, we may presume, was a frustration that grew until his mysterious disappearance, sometime around 2009.

The observations of this vanished source, which of course should be approached with skepticism, are cited only because their peculiar spectrality introduces this essay's central concerns: how ethnography intervenes in the relations between secrecy, revelation, and power; how such interventions may be co-opted into the terms of the politics they aspire to protest; and thus the problems of writing effectively against the systematic and ongoing dispossession of certain Indigenous peoples.

Publicizing the Private, Privatizing the Public

The anonymous Chronicler's records contain many anecdotes; even a random selection may be enough to illustrate the dilemmas of public ethnography in the Gran Chaco. Consider, for instance, the highly redacted summary of events transpiring over a five-week period in October–November 2006.

The Chronicler is several months into what will become a two-year stay among the ABG Ayoreo subgroup of northern Paraguay. The ABG were already iconic as the "most traditional" of Ayoreo subgroups and "the last great hope for Ayoreo cultural revitalization" after a band of voluntarily isolated ABG made contact in recent years. It was widely known that there were at least two other bands of Ayoreo holdouts that strenuously maintained a life of nomadic concealment in the dwindling forests of the Bolivia-Paraguay borderlands. In response to what he had come to perceive as earlier mistakes, the Chronicler committed himself to a collaborative research project. As part of this he agreed to work as an ad hoc *asesor* or advisor to the first ABG tribal organization. At that time, this organization operated largely under the supervision of a local NGO.

By October 2006, however, his initial optimism for the potential of this partnership had already begun to dim. His unease derived from a series of conflictive encounters with the leadership of the NGO that was a long-term partner and acting legal representative of the ABG communities. The NGO was led by two Paraguayan *indigenistas* who had inherited their positions from a former mentor. They were based in the capital city and directed a small field office in the central Chaco. The Chronicler imagined this NGO as a key collaborator, yet he soon discovered that there were stark differences of opinion and method all around.

By November the rift was clear, and he was no longer privy to internal NGO discussions, although he continued to attend meetings with the ABG leaders over the course of the following year. Convinced that the tribal organization would benefit from being more independent, he sought to facilitate alliances between the ABG organization and other institutions. This led to a collaboration with an international Indigenous rights support group with extensive expertise in defending the rights of "voluntarily isolated" peoples. Due to this fledgling partnership the Chronicler received a rare invitation to participate in a closed regional seminar organized by the United Nations, which aimed to discuss the parameters for legislation around the rights of voluntarily isolated Indigenous groups. The NGO working with the ABG was not invited.

At first the Chronicler was delighted with the invitation and he arranged for two representatives of the ABG tribal organization to also attend. However, the NGO leadership interpreted this attendance as problematic. The NGO told the ABG not to go with the Chronicler. They said they had received news from a source they could not disclose that doing so would endanger the ABG legal case. By this time the NGO had also written several letters to the organizers of the seminar, protesting their own exclusion. Despite not being invited, NGO personnel went to the meeting and managed to gain entry.

Once inside, the NGO joined the Chronicler, the ABG leaders, the director of a rival NGO, and two additional Ayoreo leaders. This rival NGO was affiliated with a separate Ayoreo tribal organization, which it also managed as a subordinate part of the non-Native institution. The constituents of this rival Ayoreo tribal organization, in turn, were the ancestral enemies of the ABG and were personally involved in the violent capture of the ABG bands in 1979 and 1986. At the time, each NGO claimed to represent the rights of the "isolated" Ayoreo holdouts. They were also actively competing for funding, and each side saw the seminar as another opportunity to undermine their rivals. Thus the NGO partnered with the ABG tribal organization asked the ABG leaders to distribute packets of materials to the various officials present. Such tactics made it easy to discount the ABG leaders as NGO stooges and thus discredit the real legitimacy of their position. Meanwhile the rival NGO used the situation to further the impression that they were the more reasonable, more tolerant, and more responsible organization to partner with.

The Chronicler soon discovered that other participants were involved in equally problematic games, not least through the exclusion of actual Indigenous voices. Predictably, the actual outcome of the meeting was frustratingly vague. The two rival Ayoreo leaders presented convincing statements arguing in favor of protecting Ayoreo cultural traditions and defending the rights of the isolated Ayoreo. The ABG and their NGO partners were mostly ignored.

Antipublics

If his notes are to be believed, the young Chronicler did not desist after such experiences—surely the wiser course. Instead he redoubled efforts to forge alliances, to leverage new openings for the ABG leaders, to establish protocols for protecting the forest bands, to facilitate a claim in the Inter-American system, and more. He was profoundly aided in these efforts by a remarkable young Paraguayan anthropologist, herself deeply committed to other Ayoreo communities. Despite this aid, each attempt caused new conflicts, and each was ultimately blocked. What can explain this masochistic persistence? Was he duped by the political sentiments that attracted him to anthropology in the first place? How might his failures illuminate the conundrums of public ethnography in the Gran Chaco?

In his inability to reconcile a self-legitimating drive for solidarity with the existing contexts of effective action, the Chronicler was unwittingly attuned to a significant point: public ethnography should be approached not as a finished program but as a project of becoming and an ethnographic question. It is a particularly unstable question when its topic is public policy that defines Indigeneity due to oscillations between two constitutive poles: ethnography's position within the disjunctive political fields of contemporary Indigeneity and anthropology's status as a unique genre inseparable from histories of internal colonialism, genocide, and dispossession. Among other things this means that affective claims to public ethnography are always inseparable from the ideal subject position of the anthropologist, whether fictional or real.

Recent efforts to consolidate such a project in lowland South America have been roughly grouped into four modalities: (1) those who apply anthropology as a tool for solving the questions posed by corporations, movements, governments, and transnational NGOs; (2) those who attempt to translate and package the basic insights of anthropological theory for consumption by diverse audiences; (3) those who authorize the strategic essentialisms of identity, tradition, custom, or history as a way to gain traction within contestatory fields of activism; and (4) those who use ethnography to bear witness abroad to the sociopolitical stakes around various sites and structures of intervention. However, each of these modalities alone has proven to be of limited use for those searching for ways to implement decolonizing methods or articulate with vital projects among those Indigenous populations who do not fit within those categories of difference that stabilize contemporary hierarchies of legitimate life.[4] One reason for this is that Indigeneity is widely considered a public problem whose terms and stakes have long been fixed. This leads to a central and definitive paradox: the appeal of public ethnography among aspiring anthropologists like the Chronicler no less than well-meaning audiences in North America and Europe often depends on overlooking or obscuring the conditions of its possibility.

The dilemmas of public ethnography are amplified to an extreme degree in the Paraguayan Gran Chaco, a perennial frontier region of dense thorn forests where state rule has always been sporadic and expeditionary. Imagined as a "Green Hell" where "the hand of civilization has never penetrated," it long offered refuge for utopian visionaries, fugitives, and displaced populations of one kind or another, such as Plautdietsch-speaking Mennonite agricultural colonists of Frisian origins and most recently from Canada and Russia, Argentine *criollo* jaguar hunters and subsistence ranchers, Angaite and Sanapaná Indians migrating west from the Rio Paraguay, Guarani Ñandeva uprooted from the Andean foothills, and Enxet-Enlhet and Nivacle moving north from the banks of the Rio Pilcomayo. Religious sects and missionaries from a dozen global denominations soon followed, as did entrepreneurs and corporations seeking to capitalize on commodities such as the tannin-rich wood of the *quebracho colorado*, the hides of large cats or caiman, oil, gas, hardwoods, marijuana, and cocaine. The quasi-communal Mennonite agricultural colonies prospered and drew transient wage laborers from eastern Paraguay and southern Brazil.[5] Today the Chaco is in the midst of an economic boom associated with cattle ranching: Paraguayan beef exports were worth $1.6 billion in 2014. Ranching, of course, requires a massive transformation of the thick forests to grass pastures; thus the Chaco has one of the highest deforestation rates in the world.[6]

As documented by the Chronicler and many others before him, these changes deeply affected the nomadic Ayoreo-speaking groups of the northern Chaco. Historically Ayoreo never existed as a unified ethnic group. Rather they belonged to local bands grouped into several politically autonomous and mutually suspicious federations, crosscut by ties of language and seven patrilineal clans. Increasingly pressured by introduced diseases and territorial loss, by the 1920s Ayoreo federations had turned against one another in wars of extermination. Northern groups withered before the assaults of the newly allied southern groups. Defeated and demoralized they established contacts with evangelical missionaries beginning in 1947. Armed with shotguns and machetes obtained on the missions, they launched devastating raids on their enemies, who in turn sought refuge with other Catholic and evangelical missionaries throughout the 1960s. Only the southernmost federation—the ABG—refused to make contact. Armed groups of Christian Ayoreo continued to hunt down these forest bands throughout the 1960s, 1970s, and 1980s. Entire bands were massacred, others captured and taken back to the missions as slave-like subordinates.

They joined approximately six thousand Ayoreo in Bolivia and Paraguay, who now inhabit three dozen settlements, mission stations, temporary work sites, and urban camps around the periphery of their ancestral territories. The new arrivals learned that one generation of their more settled relatives (in intense dialogue with evangelical missionaries) made a self-conscious decision to abandon nearly all of the practices that count as authorized "traditional culture" in Latin America, such as shamanic rituals, myth narratives, and ceremonial aesthetics. They were taught that contact caused a radical transformation of moral human life. This transformation of humanity was seen as a necessary condition for survival in the postcontact world. In contrast, enacting or remembering past selves put one at risk of illness and death, sent by a vengeful Christian God. The promise of this new life, however, was rarely fulfilled. Ayoreo are among the most severely marginalized of all Indigenous peoples in the region and are forced to create new forms of subjective positioning in dialogue with these conditions of marginality. As anthropologist Paola Canova insightfully explains, this is an especially fraught process for Ayoreo who inhabit the outskirts of the Mennonite towns in the central Chaco.[7] Meanwhile two or three bands of Ayoreo holdouts still pursue a life of nomadic concealment in the shrinking forest of the Bolivia-Paraguay borderlands.[8]

As the Chronicler discovered, such complex histories played out against the backdrop of a highly stratified, deeply divided, and multiethnic social milieu. Profound fissures of race, ethnicity, and class define life in the Chaco. An extreme income gap exists between wealthy investors, Mennonite colonists and ranchers, Paraguayan and "Brasiguayan" laborers, and a dispossessed Indigenous majority living mostly in poverty. Indians are discriminated against and confined to segregated and stigmatized spaces, where they must compete against members of their own and other Native ethnic groups for health care, education, food, and access to scarce jobs in towns or on ranches. Such local dynamics, in turn, are embedded in a wider system of Paraguayan governance that is characterized by extreme corruption, lack of transparency and accountability, weak institutions, contradictory legal codes, and hierarchical impunity. As Kregg Hetherington has convincingly argued, Paraguayan governance emerges as a complex dialectic between vertically ranked knowledge practices and contradictory interventions across distinct economies of scale.[9] In this context rights and resources are distributed through routine conflicts between an array of ideologically and structurally opposed institutions, each invested in its own forms of translation and intervention. Most of these institutions have markedly caudillistic tendencies. These include Mennonite development agencies, missionary groups from a dozen denominations, feuding NGOs in the Chaco and in the capital city, competing local and national government offices staffed by constantly rotating personnel, nascent Indigenous organizations, powerful landowner associations, and international development aid agencies. The end result is a system geared toward irrational economic production and structurally predicated on the dispossession of Indians. Contradiction, conflict, and corruption are the crucial operations through which it functions.[10]

In such a system there is no public sphere with its corresponding counters. No ideology of democratic or inclusive publicity exists as a local practice. Rather there are several competing microspheres in which shared identifications, moral codes of conduct, and participation are imagined to be exclusively restricted to fellow members and constantly at risk. Opposing worldviews are commonly viewed with suspicion, cynicism, and distrust. To a striking degree this attitude is shared by most local actors: Mennonites, missionaries, government officials, NGO staff, ranchers, and Indigenous peoples alike. Thus politics in the Paraguayan Chaco often flows through an unbalanced field of force composed of various local *antipublics*: vertically ranked collectives organized by explicit opposition to horizontal or ideological solidarities with other, competing constituencies.[11] Constant attacks, denouncements, and threats are mobilized through and against the figures of impending emergencies of opposed kinds. This cycle of hostility and urgency is the key generative dynamic, rendering all borders insecure and thus giving rise to another round of conflict. This friction, of course, is material, spatial, and economic. It is also cosmological and epistemological: each antipublic creates, evokes, and mobilizes a distinct set of truth-claims.

The social traction of ethnography derives from how it is deployed as a truth-claim within and against these competing regimes. As an ostensive science of difference, it provides a crucial function. In addition to its pragmatic utility for local governance, ethnography is a mode of translation that validates and imbues a perspective of difference with exchangeable forms of value. It is a critical technique for institutional claims to possess an exclusive knowledge of or proximity to Indigenous difference. At the same time it often seeks to instantiate the realities it ostensibly describes. It is no surprise, then, that "the ethnographic" is highly contested. There is no consensus about what kind of knowledge should count as ethnography or vice versa. Instead competing authorities endorse certain perspectives as ethnographic.

What is striking—and perhaps unique—about the Chaco is how, within its structural conditions, ethnography becomes a floating signifier. This is historic as well as political. Because academic anthropology has never been institutionalized in Paraguay, anthropology itself can and often does appear to feuding local groups as simply an additional antipublic: a foreign schema based on asserting and defending a particular cultural notion of difference against other models. Indeed the anthropological concept of Indigenous culture was an international imposition in the Chaco. It was uneasily translated, on one hand, from Mennonite theories of ethnicity and, on the other, from the North American context imported by missionaries and by government technocrats in the 1930s and 1940s as a kind of expert rubric for solving the "Indian problem" in the region.[12] In each case ethnography was never intelligible in the Chaco as a Boasian or grassroots research practice premised on fieldwork, participant observation, historical particularism, cultural relativism, or fluency in Native languages. Instead ethnography was a domain of technical expertise and a problem-solving technique. Today it primarily figures in the Chaco as a recognizable gesture, marshaled by competing interests, oriented toward objectifying actualities for local governance or an international audience, and aimed at validating one of the contradictory economies premised on preserving, developing, or eradicating Indian difference.[13]

Policing Surface and Depth

The strategic duality of the ethnographic in the Chaco is largely a product of NGO labor. It emerged during the "NGO-ization" of Paraguayan civil society after the 1989 fall of the military dictatorship and the de facto privatization of defending cultural difference this implied throughout the 1990s.[14] In Paraguay such advocacy NGOs occupied the role filled by Indigenous movements elsewhere in Latin America. Besides consultancies in multisector development projects, such institutions were the sole source of local employment for anthropologists. In the Chaco many of these NGOs emerged as the primary gatekeepers, censors, and arbiters of the normative exercise and circulation of what counts as ethnographic knowledge. Keenly aware that their platforms gain traction only if they are perceived to represent empirical realities and "the voice of the voiceless," most of these institutions are fiercely territorial about the products and processes of knowledge production. They actively promote sympathetic representations as ethically valid and empirically ethnographic, while bitterly denouncing others in the press and in private as ethically compromised, politically influenced, or anti-Indigenous. Managing the ethnographic, in other words, is a technique by which such institutions produce and manage the imagery of the suffering they claim to alleviate.

This dynamic is based on two premises: managing the practice of ethnography as research method and ensuring actual Indigenous voices are in agreement, co-opted, contradicted, or silenced. This was particularly clear in the political environment negotiated by the Chronicler. He describes constant NGO efforts to diminish or dismiss the validity of his ethnographic findings by public ridicule in meetings with government officials and by elementary attempts to discredit his presence in the communities. He also details how NGO leadership routinely manipulated the information available to ABG leaders; fabricated and published institutional positions as letters representing the "voice of the people"; operated as if the everyday exercise of Indigenous rights and participating in an endless cycle of meetings was a form of wage labor assigned only to select individuals; threatened to withhold the provision of food, medicine, and transport if the tribal organization disagreed with certain NGO positions; attempted to manage divisions among families and groups to their advantage; and created forms of dependence that meant the tribal organization was not able to function independently at the time. In this context, the NGO leadership accused the Chronicler of sowing mistrust.[15]

Such tales—which of course are already archival—are too sordid and too uncomfortable to recount at any greater length here. Details aside, what emerges from the Chronicler's accounts is a remarkably charged anthropological field, in which ethnographic images of Native difference were actively standardized, policed, and politicized in a way that was profoundly antithetical to the critically reflexive understandings that characterize public ethnography as a research strategy elsewhere. That is, it may be useful to distinguish the conditions associated with critical public ethnography in general from those conditions under which the ethnography of Indigeneity was politicized and popularized in the Paraguayan Gran Chaco. There insights derived from fieldwork methodologies were always interrupted by contradictory truth-claims that appealed to the ethnographic not as research method but as a way to contest and claim the status of fact in transnational domains of project evaluation, assessment, and financing or, conversely, juridical domains of veri-diction. What counted as ethnographic, then, was less the result of empirical research or academic review and more the outcome of intense political nego-tiations in which some understandings became intelligible as ethnographic within local and global political economies of Indigenous difference while countervailing truth-claims were discredited as insufficiently so.

This fractured regime of truth can be considered a kind of *tactical public ethnography*, which refuses—in its tactics and terms of publicity—the kind of hermeneutics that define a critical, *reflexive public ethnography*. This first, tac-tical approach is less a theoretical program than an indexical schema aimed at specific, predetermined, and exclusive audiences: local power brokers and the always distant managers of an international political economy, with all the paternalism and hierarchy it implies, focused on preserving, developing, or managing artificially culturalized Others in "underdeveloped" areas. What typifies the tactical approach is the use of ethnography as a brokerage tech-nique. In complex fields of contradictory local antipublics, each feuding insti-tution requires, funds, authorizes, defends, and purifies its own version of ethnographic truth in explicit opposition to others. It is this move away from critical ethnography and toward tactically effective images—from critique to versioning—that distinguishes such ethnographic regimes. They are predi-cated on complicity with already existing structures of intervention. In this complicity tactical ethnographic knowledge sustains a wider system in which increasingly sharp forms of inequality are masked, sustained, and enabled by fictions of democratic horizontality and the local efficacy of witnessing.

As our pitiable Chronicler soon discovered, to write field-based accounts of Indians in the Chaco was to write in opposition to these speculative re-gimes of truth. And the problem was not that ethnography lacked political traction; the opposite was true. Rather it was how slippages in the category of ethnography allowed it to frequently serve as an essential metanarrative for reinscribing the inequalities it purportedly described. Among other things this meant that tactical ethnography was often misaligned with the actual concerns of its ostensive subjects, which it actively labored to render invisible, illegitimate, and concealed.

Ethnographers and Their Secrets

It is striking how much of ethnography's tactical efficacy derives from its Janus-faced relationship to secrecy. The paradox is that this occurs in two opposite ways at the same time. What must remain secret on the local level is the kind of empirical insight that promises to rudely interrupt the very kind of known secrecy that makes the ethnographic an effective political gesture for international audiences.

The Chronicler reported numerous and darkly humorous interactions with tactical ethnographers, in which recognized experts expressed their conviction that the people the Chronicler had been living among for months were actually conducting traditional rituals and ceremonies in secret. In each case they said that Ayoreo were only acting Christian in order to deceive missionaries and other outsiders. They implied that the Chronicler himself had also been duped by the Indians, who were inveterate liars and secretly resistant to any Western norms, social forms, or beliefs. The fact that these experts could not understand the Ayoreo language and had not spent any substantial time living in an Ayoreo village—that is, their complete lack of evidence for such claims—was precisely the point. The alluring power of the Primitive, the Savage, is so great that we can perceive it even when it is imperceptible. The promise to reveal and operationalize these hidden repositories of tradition—secreted away in bodies, memories, whispers, myths, chants, and undiscovered clearings in the thick brush, where they await intrepid and imminent rediscovery—is what unifies those ethnographic images that have been most effectively politicized as they traverse transnational scales.

This promise, in turn, is predicated on a simple equation: the legitimacy of Ayoreo life is coterminous with authorized forms of traditional culture. There is a broad consensus on this point among tactical public ethnographers. This includes the work of the "ergon and myth" school, based at the Centro Argentino de Etnología Americana at the Universidad de Buenos Aires. Associated with Marcelo Bórmida, his students, and the contemporary accounts his work inspires, this body of scholarship is exhaustively cited by development consultants and missionaries alike. It is based on the notion that Ayoreo are guided by a timeless, mythic consciousness that is antithetical to modern rationality. This mythic consciousness explains Ayoreo culture as an ethos of terror and death. The resonance with missionary ideologies—which demonized traditional Ayoreo religion—is no coincidence. Bórmida's theories were based on lengthy interviews he conducted during visits to the highly surveilled space of New Tribes Missions. New Tribes missionaries were his translators and thus his primary informants.[16]

Other tactical ethnographers were associated almost exclusively with advocacy or development NGOs. The great German ethnologist Bernd Fischermann authored his painstaking magnum opus over two decades while employed by several of the most prominent institutions involved with Ayoreo. His work argues that the cosmological order of the world established by myth narratives is eternal and unchanging for Ayoreo; myths explain "the conformation of the structure of human society and nature in the form in which it is currently encountered." Because a core of traditional cosmology endures beneath the appearance of change, he concludes that contemporary Ayoreo people have an "intact cultural identity."[17]

Likewise, while working as a consultant, the German anthropologist Volker von Bremen authored a report that remains one of the most influential accounts of Indigenous relations to aid projects. It was based on the classic colonial tropes of Indians as essentialized others, ruled by deterministic cosmologies. He argues that Ayoreo and other Chaco Indians act upon the world based on a radically different system of "reproduction, values and social order," corresponding to a hunter-gatherer mode of production. According to von Bremen, this means that Indians perceive of development aid projects in traditional terms, as a modern source of sustenance to be gathered and hunted. If they do not play their proper roles it is because they imagine modern goods are "the gods of civilization" and relate to white men as "traditional spirits" they hope will "communicate to them the wisdom that encompasses the new [material] phenomenon."[18] The astounding popularity of von Bremen's work led to its adoption in policy guidelines by several development organizations, and the author became a consultant and a key broker for European aid money in the region. Accounts by such tactical ethnographers inform the frameworks for a variety of projects, from social impact statements for gas pipelines to legal arguments for land titles or health and education programs.[19]

Such images become tactically effective because they are also interventions that amplify the fetish power of an artificially constrained category of Indigenous tradition and imbue its taxidermic qualities with the status of empirical reality. The subsequent failure of these same interventions is beside the point. Tactical public ethnography in the Chaco is a regime of truth that depends on the ways knowledge of an imaginary tradition operates globally as both governmental matrix and public secret, or that which is known by how it is actively not known but hidden and concealed. As Michael Taussig insightfully argues, the standardization of knowability and mystery is what ties the doubled operations of revelation and concealment so closely to the exercise of colonizing power.[20] The crucial point is that what matters is not the ever-retreating contents of the secret but the shared recognition of something that is forcefully significant because it is elusive. Routine and always doomed efforts to transgress such boundaries and unmask these secrets do not threaten the system at all; in fact they are necessary for its renewal. Tactical ethnographies of Indigenous difference in the Chaco traffic in precisely this kind of dynamic. Ultimately their power flows from the fetish image of tradition as an authorized public secret.

The power of an artificially fixed and exclusionary tradition is predicated on a darker labor of obscurantism. What is new about contemporary politics is the constant slippage in the culture concept, deployed as both a space of critique and an enforceable governmental matrix at the same time. One result is the standardization of authorized Indigenous difference, and the restriction of palatable critique to its terms, known in advance. This threatens to amplify and mask the dispossessing violence against those Indigenous populations who resemble "ex-primitives": those whose ties to legitimating origins are tenuous, suspect, impossible, or refused. In such ways tactical ethnography plays a key role in sustaining a wider system of Indigenous hypermarginality, in which the invigorated political agency of those networked Indigenous populations able to claim authorized culture is predicated upon the largely invisible sociospatial relegation of multitudes of supposedly deculturated ex-primitives to devastated hinterlands, the bottom of class hierarchies, and the margins of civic space, where the stigma of culture loss or death is added to the stigmas of race, place, and class.[21]

This leads to an uncomfortable conclusion: the conditions of possibility for tactical ethnography in the Chaco depend on repressing ethnographic insights that might interrupt this play of secrecy and the political economies it mobilizes. This means that tactically effective ethnography is predicated on intensifying the fetish power of the very secrecy that animates the political system that such ethnography claims to be against. It also reveals a crucial inability of tactical ethnography to encompass actually existing Indigenous life. Lest we forget, Indigenous humanity always exceeds any ethnographic image of it.[22] This raises the question: What kind of public ethnography could prioritize this excess instead of the predictable kinds of exteriority it supposedly conceals?

Conclusion

In the entry that marks the abrupt end of his notes, the Chronicler finally admits his failures and succumbs to the negativity that has surrounded him. In a rambling message he renounces his faith in anthropology, expresses a profound regret at beginning his journey to the Chaco, and claims that his entire project has been based on self-deception. After carefully perusing his record I wish I could send him a message about concealment and revelation. Although I doubt he would listen, I would tell him that his failures were field notes and ethnographic questions.

How can one write against the system sustained by tactical public ethnographies in the Chaco while not undermining the few sources of Ayoreo political agency?[23] Such a project may well be impossible within the existing terms of tactical analysis in the Chaco. The most basic idioms of anthropological advocacy—public, tradition, culture, interculturality, community, cosmology, and so on—are revealed to be complicit in sustaining the systemic relations of power and secrecy they ostensibly protest. The political efficacy of such terms often flows from an instrumentally impoverished theory of the Indigenous subject, in which Indigenous life is presumed to be publicly relevant only in relation to the degree it contains the kind of alterity that is valuable for the moral redemption of non-Native society at large.

What is required, then, is an ethnographic praxis aimed at creating a revised political lexicon, one attuned not to the existing frames of intervention but to the dynamic and creative capacities of Ayoreo themselves. This kind of praxis—which ironically finds one footing for advocacy in a repurposing of ethnographic objectivity and the anticipated futures of anthropological texts—may entail the Indigenization of public ethnography. This Indigenization emerges from an ethnographic prioritization of those vital excesses that always escape the categorical typologies of neocolonialism and that tactical ethnography labors to conceal but which actually existing Indigenous people all inhabit. Bringing Indigenous life projects into dialogue with the aims of critically reflexive ethnography is one place such a project can begin.[24] As Didier Fassin has argued, this may mean embracing the strange social duality of ethnography as simultaneously a descriptive form and a reflexive reifying technology, one that self-consciously objectifies and resignifies the sociopolitical contexts of meaning-making itself.

Where tactical public ethnography holds people to the normative categories of governance, an Indigenized public ethnography protests, appropriates, or ignores these categories and reveals the artifices they contain. Where tactical public ethnography takes nonconformity as evidence of insufficiency or illegitimacy, an Indigenized public ethnography is predicated on nonconformity. It presumes open-ended subjects—always fluid, transforming, becoming, unfinished. Where tactical public ethnography purifies and sanctifies tradition as a foreclosed exteriority, an Indigenized public ethnography presumes that tradition is never stable but always incomplete and deployed in a variety of oppositional ways.[25] Where tactical ethnography serves existing structures of intervention, an Indigenized public ethnography embraces Indigenous concept work as the crucial prompt for theoretical revision and political critique. Such an Indigenized public ethnography promises to act back upon the basic analytic frames of ethnography more generally. Through its Indigenization public ethnography should be able to take seriously what Georges Bataille refers to as "subversive sovereignty," the strange power that surges from inhabiting contradiction and living beyond authorized utility: loss, abjection, insufficiency, and the breakdown of memory itself.

It is, of course, not likely that my efforts will be any more successful than those of the Chronicler. Like him I fear my conceptual fantasies will appear before others only in a bastardized, corrupt way or will be invoked to make the very arguments they mean to unsettle, oppose, and trip up. Even less predictable are how these arguments will appear to later generations of Ayoreo and anthropologists, including to my future self. Yet, as the Chronicler reminds us, it is precisely the rotational temporality and unfinished nature of ethnography that allows it to operate as a potent and collaborative world-making project of its own, one that may reveal unexpected spaces for future inhabitation by ourselves no less than our subjects.

Notes

1   By "public ethnography" I refer to Fassin's (2013: 628) definition of it as "the principle of bringing to multiple publics . . . the findings of an ethnography analyzed in light of critical thinking, so that these findings can be apprehended, appropriated, debated, contested and used . . . to contribute to a transformation of the way the world is represented and experienced." Fassin shows that public ethnography involves two linked operations: popularization and politicization. Where the first refers to questions of genre, market, and medium, the second dimension refers "to debate and change, to the opening of the public sphere to certain questions. . . . It

deals with forums and arenas as well as activism and reform" (626). On the "ethno-graphic taxidermy" of Native peoples, see Rony 1996.

2   Michael Taussig (1999) develops this definition of public secrecy at length.

3   As the Mohawk anthropologist Audra Simpson (2007) reminds us, writing about the public ethnography of Indigeneity inevitably means writing about techniques of colonial governance and ongoing dispossession, as well as social movements and resistance.

4   See Bessire 2012, 2014a, 2014b.

5   For a detailed historical overview of the Mennonite movements, social organ-ization, and economic conditions, see Klassen 2003.

6   For more on the scale of environmental devastation in the Gran Chaco, see Guyra Paraguay 2014. The politico-theological relation between ecological destruction, extractive economies, and the hidden fetish power of Indigenous tradition merits further exploration elsewhere.

7   See Canova (2011) for a pioneering analysis of these dynamics and processes.

8   For more on the social history of the Chaco, see Kidd 1995. For accounts of institu-tional politics within wider contexts of agrarian reform, Indigenous organizing, de-velopment, and social conflict, see Cerna Villagra 2014; Gordillo 2004, 2006, 2014; Hetherington 2013; Horst 2007, 2010. Braticevic (2010) draws a productive com-parison between missionary models and those of developmentalist NGOs in the Ar-gentine Chaco.

9   See Hetherington 2008, 2013, 2014.

10 See Bessire (2014a) and Fischermann (2001) for overviews of Ayoreo ethnohistory.

11 "Antipublics" are distinguished from "counterpublics" in that the second insist on a basic publicist orientation and a shared social space wherein agitation, directed out-ward, is fundamentally concerned with the dissemination of particular values throughout society as a whole. The first is a more radical form, in which such publicity is fractured or negated on a local level and restricted to international, displaced audiences. See Calhoun 2010; Fraser 1990; Warner 2005.

12 See International Labor Organization 1954; Rodriguez-Piñero 2005. The anthro-pological (i.e., multilinear, pluralistic, historically particular) category of Indige-nous culture was cocreated in the first decades of the twentieth century by states and international technocrats, including a large number of academic anthropolo-gists, before being imported and imposed as a way to denominate, integrate, and govern those populations believed to constitute the "Indian problem" in Latin America. Labor, in other words, was one crucial concern responsible for the vertical ranking and uneven distribution of the culture concept at a hemispheric scale. The (pluralistic, multilinear) culture concept—which, as originally developed in the North American context, was often used to validate a position of radical critique—was first active in Latin America as a self-styled technique for solving the political and economic dilemmas posed by recalcitrant, undeveloped, and nonintegrated Indians.

13 It is important to note that there are several significant exceptions to this general description, including more collaborative advocacy institutions such as Tierraviva and several of the independent anthropologists doing important, challenging work in the Chaco, most notably the Ayoreo expert and longtime advocate Paola Canova.

14 Stoll (2011, 2013) makes a similar point about governance in his analyses of NGOs and Indigenous relationships in Guatemala: "The disproportionate purchasing power of international donors not only provides leverage but breeds patron-client relationships rife with favoritism and opportunism, factionalizing the population they wish to pull together" (2011: 139). For more on NGO-Indigenous relationships in Latin America, see, among others, Albro 2005; Fisher 1997; Mato 2000; Offen 2003; Postero 2007; Ramos 1998; Tilley 2002.

15 This passage refers only to the description of a particular time and place. I am not claiming that such tactics are typical of all institutions working in the region and am unable to comment here on current politics or dynamics of the ABG case.

16 For example, see Bórmida 1984; Bórmida and Califano 1978; Dasso 2004; Mashnshnek 2012.

17 See Fischermann 2001: 104, 246–47.

18 Von Bremen 1987: 7, 13–15, 16, 18. See also von Bremen 2000; Renshaw 2002.

19 For an important counterpoint to this general overview of tactical ethnography in Paraguay, see Heijdra's (1996) important insights on Ayoreo co-optation and factionalism in a megaproject on the Bolivian side of the border. Stahl's (2007) reflections on decades of work as the leader of ASCIM, the Mennonite Indigenous development association, offer another comparative framework.

20 For more on public secrecy, see Taussig 1999.

21 The point is that contemporary Indigeneity is a disjunctive political field comprising several causally linked elements: a government of life realized through a malleable legal-theological category of culture that is increasingly robust but applied with ever-narrowing and exclusionary precision; the invigorated political agency of those globally networked Indigenous populations or individuals able to successfully claim authorized culture by conforming in part to externally imposed definitions thereof; the transnational hypervisibility of "isolated" or "uncontacted" primitive life, cosmology, or supposed ontological alterity; and the largely invisible sociospatial relegation of multitudes of supposedly "deculturated" ex-primitives to devastated hinterlands, the bottom of social class hierarchies, and the margins of civic space, where the stigma of culture loss or death is added to the already trebled stigmas of race, place, and class.

22 For instance, Indigenous media and analyses of it offer productive counterpoints to the narrow categories of such representational politics. See, especially, Ginsburg 1995, 2011, 2012; Salazar and Córdova 2008; Turner 1992.

23 Scholars, of course, have long recognized the governmental and neocolonial stakes of legalizing a narrow notion of "traditional culture" as the primary basis for Indigenous rights to territory and resources. For nuanced accounts of such dynamics, see

especially Abercrombie 1998; Clifford 2001; Conklin and Graham 1995; Graham 1993, 2002; Hale 2006; Jackson 1995; Niezen 2003; Ramos 1998; Sieder 2002. Moreover action-oriented scholars have long grappled with the dilemmas this poses for ethnographic research, as in Hale 2006; Prins 2006; Speed 2006; Tax 1975. See Turner (1993, 2009) for one of the most interesting attempts to reclaim an Indigenous notion of culture and turn it back against the narrow frameworks of political action, an attempt that inspires my own.

24 See Smith (1999) on Indigenizing research, and Fassin (2013) on reflexive public ethnography.

25 Many scholars in anthropology and critical Native studies have made this or a similar point (e.g., Browner 2005). See, especially, Barker (2011) and Coulthard (2014) on the politics of refusal.

References

Abercrombie, Tom. 1998. *Pathways of Memory and Power: Ethnography and History among an Andean People*. Madison: University of Wisconsin Press.

Albro, Robert. 2005. "The Indigenous in the Plural in Bolivian Oppositional Politics." *Bulletin of Latin American Research* 24.4: 433–54.

Barker, Joanne. 2011. *Native Acts: Law, Recognition and Cultural Authenticity*. Durham: Duke University Press.

Bessire, Lucas. 2012. "The Politics of Isolation: Refused Relation as an Emerging Regime of Indigenous Biolegitimacy." *Comparative Studies in Society and History* 54.3: 1–32.

———. 2014a. *Behold the Black Caiman: A Chronicle of Ayoreo Life*. Chicago: University of Chicago Press.

———. 2014b. "The Rise of Indigenous Hypermarginality: Culture as a Neoliberal Politics of Life." *Current Anthropology* 55.3: 276–95.

Bórmida, Marcelo. 1984. "Como una cultura arcaica conoce la realidad de su mundo." *Scripta Ethnologica* 8: 13–183.

Bórmida, Marcelo, and Mario Califano. 1978. *Los indios Ayoreo del Chaco Boreal*. Buenos Aires: Fundación para la Educación de la Ciencia y la Cultura.

Borofsky, Robert. 2011. "Defining Public Anthropology: A Personal Perspective." Center for a Public Anthropology. http://www.publicanthropology.org/public-anthropology.

Braticevic, Sergio. 2010. "Reconversion territorial del modelo evangelizador en el chaco central: Desde el modelo misional hacia la ayuda al desarrollo y las ONGs." *Estudios Sociales del NOA* 11: 5–21.

Browner, Tara. 2005. "Indigenizing the Academy: Transforming Scholarship and Empowering Communities." *American Anthropologist* 107: 536–37.

Calhoun, Craig. 2010. "The Public Sphere in the Field of Power." *Social Science History* 34.3: 301–35.

Canova, Paola. 2011. "Del Monte a la ciudad: La producción cultural de los Ayoreode en los espacios urbanos del Chaco Central." *Suplemento antropológico* 46.2: 275–316.

Cerna Villagra, Sarah. 2014. "Los censos indígenas en Paraguay: Entre el auto-reconocimiento y la discriminación." *Journal of Iberian and Latin American Research* 20.3: 423–35.

Clifford, James. 2001. "Indigenous Articulations." *Contemporary Pacific* 13.2: 467–90.

Conklin, Beth, and Laura Graham. 1995. "The Shifting Middle Ground: Amazonian Indians and Eco-politics." *American Anthropologist* 97.4: 695–710.

Coulthard, Glen. 2014. *Red Skin, White Masks: Rejecting the Colonial Politics of Recognition*. Minneapolis: University of Minnesota Press.

Cowan, Jane. 2006. "Culture and Rights after Culture and Rights." *American Anthropologist* 108.1: 9–24.

Dasso, María Cristina. 2004. "Alegría y coraje en la alabanza guerrera de los Ayoreo del Chaco Boreal." *Anthropos* 99: 57–71.

Fassin, Didier. 2013. "Why Ethnography Matters." *Cultural Anthropology* 28.4: 621–46.

Fischermann, Bernd. 2001. "La Cosmovision de los Ayoreode del Chaco Boreal." Translated by Benno Glauser. PhD dissertation, University of Bonn.

Fisher, William. 1997. "Doing Good? The Politics and Antipolitics of NGO Practices." *Annual Review of Anthropology* 26: 439–64.

Fraser, Nancy. 1990. "Rethinking the Public Sphere: A Contribution to the Critique of Actually Existing Democracy." *Social Text* 25/26: 56–80.

Ginsburg, Faye. 1995. "The Parallax Effect: The Impact of Aboriginal Media on Ethnographic Film." *Visual Anthropology Review* 11.2: 64–76.

———. 2011. "Native Intelligence: A Short History of Debates on Indigenous Media and Ethnographic Film." In *Made to Be Seen: Perspectives on the History of Visual Anthropology*, edited by Marcus Banks and Jay Ruby, 234–55. Chicago: University of Chicago Press.

———. 2012. "Indigenous Counter-Publics: A Foreshortened History." In *Sensible Politics: The Visual Culture of Nongovernmental Activism*, edited by Meg Lagan and Yates McKee, 563–87. New York: Zone Books.

Gordillo, Gaston. 2004. *Landscapes of Devils: Tensions of Place and Memory in the Argentinean Chaco*. Durham: Duke University Press.

———. 2006. *En el Gran Chaco: Antropologias e historias*. Buenos Aires: Prometeo.

———. 2014. *Rubble*. Durham: Duke University Press.

Graham, Laura. 1993. "A Public Sphere in Amazonia? The Depersonalized Collaborative Construction of Discourse in Xavante." *American Ethnologist* 20.4: 717–41.

———. 2002. "How Should an Indian Speak? Amazonian Indians and the Symbolic Politics of Language in the Global Public Sphere." In *Indigenous Movements, Self-Representation, and the State in Latin America*, edited by Kay B. Warren and Jean E. Jackson, 181–228. Austin: University of Texas Press.

Guyra Paraguay. 2014. *Informe de Deforestacion en el Chaco Paraguayo*. Asuncion: Guyra.

Hale, Charles. 2006. "Activist Research vs. Cultural Critique: Indigenous Land Rights and the Contradictions of Politically Engaged Anthropology." *Cultural Anthropology* 21.1: 96–120.

Heijdra, Hans. 1996. *Participación y exclusión indígena en el desarrollo: Banco Mundial, CIDOB y el pueblo Ayoréo en el proyecto tierras bajas del Este de Bolivia*. Vol. 6. Santa Cruz de la Sierra: APCOB.

Hetherington, Kregg. 2008. "Populist Transparency: The Documentation of Reality in Rural Paraguay." *Journal of Legal Anthropology* 1.1: 45–69.

———. 2013. *Guerilla Auditors*. Durham: Duke University Press.

———. 2014. "Regular Soybeans: Translation and Framing in the Ontological Politics of a Coup." *Indiana Journal of Global Legal Studies* 21.1: 55–78.

Horst, René Harder. 2007. *The Stroessner Regime and Indigenous Resistance in Paraguay*. Gainesville: University Press of Florida.

———. 2010. "The Peaceful Revolution: Indigenous Rights and Intellectual Resistance in Paraguay 1975–1988." *Latin American and Caribbean Ethnic Studies* 5.2: 189–205.

International Labor Organization. 1954. "The Second Session of the ILO Committee of Experts on Indigenous Labour." *International Labor Review* 70: 418–42.

Jackson, Jean. 1995. "Culture, Genuine and Spurious: The Politics of Indianness in the Vaupés, Colombia." *American Ethnologist* 22.1: 3–27.

Kidd, Stephen. 1995. "Land, Politics and Benevolent Shamanism: The Enxet Indians in a Democratic Paraguay." *Journal of Latin American Studies* 27.1: 43–75.

Klassen, Peter. 2003. *The Mennonites in Paraguay: Kingdom of God and Kingdom of This World*. Vol. 1. Translated by Gunther Schmitt. Hillsboro, KS: Print Source Direct.

Marcus, George. 2005. "The Anthropologist as Witness in Contemporary Regimes of Intervention." *Cultural Politics* 1.1: 31–50.

Mashnshnek, Celia. 2012. "Las categorías de discurso narrativo y su significado en la cultura de los Ayoreo del Chaco boreal." *Anthropologica* 9.9: 19–38.

Mato, Daniel. 2000. "Transnational Networking and the Social Production of Representations of Identities by Indigenous Peoples' Organizations of Latin America." *International Sociology* 15.2: 343–60.

Niezen, Ronald. 2003. *The Origins of Indigenism: Human Rights and the Politics of Identity*. Berkeley: University of California Press.

Offen, Karl. 2003. "The Territorial Turn: Making Black Territories in Pacific Colombia." *Journal of Latin American Geography* 2.1: 43–73.

Postero, Nancy. 2007. *Now We Are Citizens: Indigenous Politics in Postmulticultural Bolivia*. Palo Alto: Stanford University Press.

Prins, Harald. 2006. "Pragmatic Idealism in Challenging Structural Power: Reflections on the Situational Ethics of Advocacy Anthropology." In *Ethik, Ethos, Ethnos*, edited by Annette Hornbacher, 183–200. Bielefeld: Verlag.

Ramos, Alcida. 1998. *Indigenism: Ethnic Politics in Brazil*. Madison: University of
Wisconsin Press.

Renshaw, Jonathan. 2002. *The Indians of the Paraguayan Gran Chaco: Identity and
Economy*. Lincoln: University of Nebraska Press.

Rodriguez-Pinero, Luis. 2005. *Indigenous Peoples, Postcolonialism, and International
Law: The ILO Regime (1919–1989)*. Oxford: Oxford University Press.

Rony, Fatimah. 1996. *The Third Eye: Race, Cinema, and Ethnographic Spectacle*.
Durham: Duke University Press.

Salazar, Juan Francisco, and Amalia Córdova. 2008. "Imperfect Media and the Poetics
of Indigenous Video in Latin America." In *Global Indigenous Media: Cultures,
Poetics, and Politics*, edited by Pamela Wilson and Michelle Stewart, 39–50.
Durham: Duke University Press.

Sieder, Rachel, ed. 2002. *Multiculturalism in Latin America: Indigenous Rights,
Diversity and Democracy*. New York: Palgrave Macmillan.

Simpson, Audra. 2007. "On Ethnographic Refusal: Indigeneity, Voice and Colonial
Citizenship." *Junctures*, no. 9: 67–80.

Smith, Linda Tuhiwai. 1999. *Decolonizing Methodologies: Research and Indigenous
Peoples*. London: Zed.

Speed, Shannon. 2006. "At the Crossroads of Human Rights and Anthropology:
Toward a Critically Engaged Activist Research." *American Anthropologist* 108.1:
66–76.

Stahl, Wilmar. 2007. *Culturas en interacción: Una antropología vivida en el Chaco
paraguayo*. Asuncion: El Lector.

Stoll, David. 2011. "The Obligatory Indian." *Dialectical Anthropology* 35: 135–46.

———. 2013. "Strategic Essentialism, Scholarly Inflation and Political Litmus Tests:
The Moral Economy of Hyping the Contemporary Mayas." In *Anthropology and
the Politics of Representation*, edited by Gabriel Vargas-Centinela, 33–48. Tusca-
loosa: University of Alabama Press.

Taussig, Michael. 1999. *Defacement: Public Secrecy and the Labor of the Negative*. Palo
Alto: Stanford University Press.

Tax, Sol. 1975. "Action Anthropology." *Current Anthropology* 16.4: 514–17.

Tilley, Virginia. 2002. "New Help or New Hegemony? The Transnational Indigenous
Peoples' Movement and 'Being Indian' in El Salvador." *Journal of Latin American
Studies* 34.3: 525–54.

Turner, Terence. 1992. "Defiant Images: The Kayapo Appropriation of Video."
Anthropology Today 8.6: 5–16.

———. 1993. "Anthropology and Multiculturalism: What Is Anthropology That
Multiculturalists Should Be Mindful of It?" *Cultural Anthropology* 8.4: 411–29.

———. 1999. "Indigenous and Culturalist Movements in the Contemporary Global
Conjuncture." In *Las identidades y las tensiones culturales de la modernidad*, edited
by Francisco Fernández del Riego, Marcial Gondar Portasany, Terence Turner,
Josep R. Llobera, Isidoro Moreno, and James W. Fernández, 53–72. Santiago de
Compostela: Federacion de Asociaciones de Antropología del Estado Espanol.

————. 2009. "The Crisis of Late Structuralism: Perspectivism and Animism. Rethinking Culture, Nature, Spirit and Bodiliness." *Tipiti* 7.1: 3–42.

von Bremen, Volker. 1987. *Fuentes de caza y recolección modernas: Proyectos de ayuda al desarrollo destinados a los indígenas del Gran Chaco.* Stuttgart: Servicios de Desarrollo de las Iglesias.

————. 2000. "Dynamics of Adaptation to Market Economy among the Ayoreode of Northwest Paraguay." In *Hunters and Gatherers in the Modern World*, edited by Peter Schweitzer, Megan Bisele, and Bob Hitchcock, 275–86. London: Berghahn.

Warner, Michael. 2005. *Publics and Counterpublics.* New York: Zone Books.

7

Experto Crede?

A Legal and Political Conundrum

JONATHAN BENTHALL

An eerie calm reigns in the attorneys' offices, high above the seething streets of a U.S. megalopolis and at odds with the gritty world of checkpoints, detentions, bombings, demolished houses, and subsistence handouts that are the background to this upcoming trial. There have been many days of preparation for your deposition, that is to say, seven hours' cross-examination recorded by Min-U-Script stenography and video camera. They will seek to impeach (discredit) your expert testimony, particularly by trying to find inconsistencies between it and publications dating back a decade, which have been photocopied and neatly bound into ad hoc volumes. A pity about that interview some years ago with a lazy journalist whose misquotations on an obscure European website did not seem worth your taking the trouble to correct. But one thing has been made clear to you: "They aren't in the least bit interested in you or your work. They just want to trip you up."

Q. Do you understand today that you are under oath and that that requires you to tell the truth to the best of your ability?

A. I do.

Q. Is there any medication that you are currently on that might affect your ability to provide accurate or truthful testimony today?

A. No.

Q. Is there any other reason, medical condition or otherwise that might impair your ability to give accurate and complete testimony today?

A. Not as far as I know.

Stop. Confidentiality precludes any further quotation, even any reference to this case. Social researchers are accustomed to respecting confidentiality in order to protect the interests of their interlocutors, but this is usually left to the exercise of discretion. Entering a formal commitment to confidentiality as an expert witness is another matter and highlights the role conflict that ensues when one has agreed to take part in a legal proceeding whose forms and goals, in the words of Lawrence Rosen, "often appear foreign, if not overtly antithetical, to scholarly capacities and purposes."[1] Hamstrung as I am by an inability to discuss some important cases, I take an oblique approach here, replacing them with other material where similar issues and tensions have arisen: two other cases where confidentiality does not apply.

The outcome of trials, both civil and criminal, often depends on submissions by expert witnesses. A number of published studies explore the tensions that arise when ethnographers provide services of this kind. The subject matter at issue has included racial theory and indigenous rights claims, asylum cases, female genital mutilation, and war crimes.[2] My subject matter in this essay is social welfare with an Islamic coloring in the Palestinian West Bank, especially during the Oslo period, 1993 to 2007. This is an instance of an antinomy between humanitarian or charitable values and security concerns, which has probably always existed at times of political and military conflict—there was never a humanitarian golden age[3]—but which has become more salient since September 11, 2001, and, before that, the designation of Hamas as a foreign terrorist organization by the United States in 1997. In particular the doctrine of "asset substitution," based on the fact that money is "fungible," has become entrenched in U.S. counterterrorist law; this doctrine holds that a donation of a thousand dollars to a hospital deemed to be controlled by Hamas relieves Hamas of some costs of running the hospital and hence frees up a thousand dollars to be spent on bombs. The donor is held to be guilty of "material support" for terrorism, incurring the same punishment as terrorism itself.

The basis for my expertise dates back to a period of field research in early 1996 in Jordan and the West Bank, where I visited some *zakat* committees and interviewed officials responsible for administering zakat, the Islamic tithe.[4] I was staying in Amman in the guesthouse of Centre d'Études et de Recherche sur le Moyen-Orient, the French research center, and soon after my arrival the first general election took place in the Palestinian territories. The international media coverage was optimistic, but most of the French researchers who dropped in at the center, having crossed from the West Bank via the Allenby Bridge (King Hussein Bridge), took the more negative view that the new administration under Yasser Arafat was as corrupt as any African kleptocracy, and they doubted whether Israel really wanted the new proto-state to succeed. Some non-Arab commentators, severely critical of Arafat and his Fatah faction, tended to romanticize the Muslim Brotherhood and Hamas, though Hamas took responsibility for some lethal bombings of civilians in Jerusalem when I was in Amman; others, more trusting of Arafat, dismissed them as more indebted to their Leninist influences than to Muslim tradition. In investigating the Islamist charities in Jordan, and in particular a Jordanian committee that sent funds and other charitable resources to the Palestinian territories, I was already aware of the Jordanian authorities' suspicious view of them. The Hashemite leadership's policy of normalization with regard to Israel following the 1993 Oslo Accords was at that time opposed by a majority of Jordanians, especially those inclined toward Islamism.

I tried to keep an open mind on these matters, but when I visited Nablus, a medium-size town in the Palestinian West Bank, and saw the work of its zakat committee, I was impressed by the initiative of its members in having expanded its work from modest beginnings centered on a mosque. This work included cow and sheep farms, a modern dairy (planned in 1996 but not opened till a few years after my visit), beehives, a medical and dental clinic, training for typists, income payments for destitute orphans and families, and bursaries for students—drawing substantial support from Jordan, other Arab countries, and international donors. I satisfied myself as far as I could that the committee's policy was to help the most vulnerable, without political or other discrimination, while keeping expenses to a minimum. The committee members gave their services pro bono, though the staff were paid salaries. I learned that Nablus had set a lead for other towns throughout the West Bank to expand their zakat committees. In Jordan I interviewed Sheikh Abdul-Aziz Al-Khayyat, then a professor at Jerash University but formerly the minister of religious affairs in the Jordanian government, author of an authoritative monograph on zakat,[5] and a cofounder of the Nablus committee in 1978. He insisted that the primary beneficiaries of zakat should be "the poor"—all the poor, for the definite article in the Arabic *al-fuqara'* has the same inclusive weight as in English. This meant no discrimination in favor of Muslims—contrary to much standard practice in traditional Islam. He spoke emphatically against the politicization of zakat, which some of the Islamist factions in Jordan were engaged in.

Later I referred in passing to the Palestinian zakat committees in a general book on Islamic charities published in 2003,[6] but I did not pay them close attention until my participation as an advisor to the Montreux Initiative (later renamed the Islamic Charities Project), sponsored by the Swiss government. This was a mediation or conflict-resolution exercise, launched in 2005, with the practical aim of removing unjustified obstacles from Islamic charities since they had been generally under a cloud following allegations that some were involved in financing terrorism—especially the September 11 attacks on the United States. A major potential source of relief and development aid in troubled regions was being seriously inhibited. The Montreux Initiative chose the Palestinian territories as one of the Muslim-majority areas to be given special attention.

The character of these Palestinian zakat committees and some related Islamic charities during the Oslo period—more precisely, 1993 until 2007, the year of the momentous Fatah-Hamas split—has been the core issue underlying much litigation in the United States and Europe. Were they façades for Hamas, exclusively aimed at gaining political advantage and even facilitating "martyrdom operations" directly? Or were they authentic community-based, decentralized, voluntary organizations, working with minimal overhead expenses and widely respected and trusted—unlike many of the local NGOs associated with the dominant faction in the West Bank, Fatah?

How one approaches this question must depend on the investigative tools that one brings to bear. The analysis of flows of finance and webs of association has a vital place in uncovering criminality and protecting the public. But was charity, and in particular Islamic charity, being selected because it was an easy target rather than because it was really a major vehicle for terrorist finance? An approach giving due weight to the charitable imperative—widely acknowledged as common to people of all religions as well as to nonreligious humanists—and to humanitarian law seemed to me to be equally compelling. This was the approach adopted by the Montreux Initiative. The tradition of Swiss neutrality enabled the government to bring together people from different humanitarian traditions to explore common ground. Though the Swiss project failed to meet its institutional objectives,[7] it provided me incidentally with an opportunity for some transnational ethnography.

It is frequently argued today in the academic study of humanitarian programs that they are extensively instrumentalized.[8] This is not to decry efforts to restore to charity and humanitarianism the high-principled purity of aspiration that historically has underlain their practical manifestations.

The subtitle of the book I coauthored with Jérôme Bellion-Jourdan, *The Charitable Crescent: Politics of Aid in the Muslim World* (2003), has sometimes been misunderstood to suggest that politicization of aid is peculiar to the Muslim world. But we wrote in our conclusion, "The abuse of charitable activities to fulfil personal, political or military aims can . . . be considered a practice shared in various traditions. We mentioned in our introduction that it has become received wisdom to expose the political aspects of humanitarianism. This is overdue but should be applied consistently, and not arbitrarily by Westerners to discredit the activities of Muslim charities or vice versa. . . . The borrowing of the humanitarian figleaf by governments either to excuse themselves for taking no action against war crimes, or to make their own wars more palatable, has become highly sophisticated."[9]

The revival of my special interest in Palestine resulted in large measure from contact with the representatives of Interpal, the British Muslim charity, in the Montreux Initiative "core group." The Montreux Initiative was essentially devoted to encouraging complete transparency, accountability, and nondiscrimination in charities, easing the way for them to demonstrate their bona fides and eventually get themselves removed from blacklists. I knew that the United States had designated Interpal a terrorist entity—in a process that allowed for no defense or appeal—though it had already in 2005 been cleared twice by the U.K. Charity Commission.[10] The U.S. authorities' allegation that Interpal was a prime organizer for Hamas seemed at odds with the conduct of its representatives in Geneva and other places where the Montreux Initiative core group met. For the Interpal members were at the forefront within the core group in arguing the need for regulation, monitoring, and the rule of law, while their own charity since its launch in 1984 had kept meticulous records available for inspection. This contrasted sharply with the guarded attitude toward information that on the whole I have found to be characteristic of institutions in the Arab world. The representatives of Interpal were certainly devout Muslims, and they were passionate in responding to the hardships experienced by Palestinians, both in the territories and in refugee camps in Syria, Lebanon, and Jordan. But were they "Hamas operatives," as the Israeli and U.S. counterterrorists alleged?

Hamas elicits strong feelings. As part of a nationalist movement opposed to military occupation it is widely recognized as exercising the right to self-determination, while allegations that it supports global jihadism are unsustainable. Its reputation is compromised by its anti-Jewish charter, published in 1988 and never renounced (though its defenders claim that the charter is no longer a guide to its practical policies), and by its cult of death and its glorification of attacks on Israeli noncombatants, including children. But if one tries to enter the *Lebenswelt* of Palestinians, the picture becomes more blurry. As the successor to the Muslim Brothers of Palestine since its foundation in 1988, Hamas inherited the Muslim Brothers' institutional ambivalence, combining religious, political, and welfarist goals. Whereas the official ideology of the Muslim Brothers sets store by the principle of the "seamlessness" of Islam (*shumūliyyah*), this can manifest in practice as a strategic many-sidedness. How else can we explain that many Christians voted for the Hamas-backed coalition Change and Reform, which succeeded in the 2007 parliamentary elections? This was in part a protest vote against the corruption of the dominant political party, Fatah, and the Palestinian Authority (PA). Even Hamas's sharpest critics acknowledge its reputation during the Oslo period for financial honesty.[11]

The latest interpretation of the organization of Hamas by its leading counterterrorist opponent outside Israel concedes that a strict interpretation of the concept of membership does not apply to it.[12] My own conclusion is that, whereas no doubt there was a hard core of Hamas "members" during the Oslo period, they did not all necessarily toe the party line. Moreover Israeli and PA intelligence services tended to categorize as Hamas anyone who had a beard and prayed, whereas in fact there was a penumbra that also included private Islamists (not affiliated with any party), Muslim Brothers owing primary allegiance to the Brotherhood's Jordanian branch (which is less committed to violence than Hamas and in Jordan in 2016 still formed a kind of loyal opposition to the Hashemite leadership), and unaffiliated individuals who were repelled by the PA's maladministration and corruption. Even in the case of committed Hamas supporters it should not be presumed that their endorsement of paramilitary resistance was incompatible with a commitment to implementing the Islamic teachings on zakat. Let us reverse the argument: many people in the Arab and Muslim world, and indeed elsewhere, find Euro-American foreign policy immoral, criticizing its double standards in support of dictatorships, its authorization (under the George W. Bush administration) of torture, and its exercise of lethal military power from remote locations. In October 2001 Secretary of State Colin Powell commended nongovernmental organizations as a "force multiplier" for the U.S. military.[13] Yet most U.S. NGOs saw themselves as committed to a humanitarian ideal.

My own research on Palestinian Islamic charities is limited to the West Bank. In Gaza, by contrast, the connections between Islamic charities and

Hamas have been indirect but rather stronger.[14] In the West Bank they had fallen under Jordanian influence, as offshoots of the Ministry of Religious Affairs (Awqaf). Emanuel Schaeublin, who has carried out extensive field-work in the territories, concludes that until the reorganization in 2007 the West Bank zakat committees were established by "social coalitions" between the pious bourgeoisie (mainly prosperous businessmen), imams, persons known for their Islamic literacy, and activists belonging to Hamas, the Muslim Brotherhood, and other groups such as the pan-Islamic Hizb Al Tahrir.[15] Three opinion surveys, conducted under the auspices of the UN Development Programme and published between 1998 and 2003, indicated wide popular confidence in the zakat committees, whereas political parties of all complexions earned little popular trust.[16] Another important strand of evidence, albeit negative, results from two independent investigations of coverage of West Bank zakat committees in the Palestinian press before 2007, the year they became a topic of public controversy in the territories. The Palestinian newspapers during the period 1998 to 2007—even the two leading newspapers in the Occupied Territories, which were closer to Fatah than to Hamas—seem to have contained no reports of illegal or inappropriate conduct by these committees.[17] A published study by a Palestinian researcher, based on a sample of diverse newspaper coverage before 2007, finds that the only coverage of zakat committees was respectful.[18]

In 2007, as part of an exercise in amassing documentary evidence for a trial in the United States, I was able to engage a Palestinian research assistant in London to procure as much information as he could about the Nablus zakat committee by telephone, email, and fax. This was just before Hamas took power in Gaza. Shortly afterward the Israeli Defense Force raided the Nablus zakat committee, removing or destroying most of their files since it regarded the committee as a front for Hamas. The documents we were able to assemble prove that since its formal registration in 1978 the committee had been acting in accordance with Israeli and Palestinian law and had been receiving financial support from major organizations, including USAID, the World Food Program, and CARE.[19] Yet Islamic charities in Europe and the United States that supported the Nablus zakat committee, and other, similar Palestinian charities, during the same period were charged with "material support for terrorism." Later in 2007 the Palestinian Authority dissolved the ninety-two zakat committees in the West Bank, dismissing all their members, and replacing them with a centralized structure under direct ministry control. The Hamas administration in Gaza acted in a similar way, so that after that date, in both Palestinian territories, the fabric of Islamic charities became indisputably politicized. (In 2015 some steps were taken by the PA in Ramallah to strengthen the work of the West Bank zakat committees with some degree of decentralization.)

Security concerns evidently motivated the decision to restructure the West Bank zakat committees. Three public opinion surveys, published between 1999 and 2004, might have given them pause, as well as a finding in 2003 published by Nathan J. Brown, a professor of political science and international affairs at George Washington University and an authority on Middle East politics, that the committees enjoyed "a tremendous amount of legitimacy. Even secular leftists admire their authenticity and ability to operate without reliance on Western funding."[20] The International Crisis Group had published a carefully sourced report in 2003 that scrutinized the concept of charities' "affiliation" with political entities, arguing that it was problematic and a matter of degree.[21] Yet even if the results of more extensive field research had been available to the PA, it would almost certainly have paid no attention, according to the record of a secret meeting held in Tel Aviv in 2008 between Israeli intelligence and the U.S. Treasury Department.[22] At that meeting the Israeli and U.S. governments applied heavy pressure on the PA prime minister to remove any remaining influence of Hamas on the zakat committees.

The Tariq Ramadan Visa Case

One of the legal cases that hinged on the character of these zakat committees, and where there is no continuing obligation to confidentiality, was that which ensued from the application by Tariq Ramadan, the celebrated Swiss academic and writer on Islamic matters, for a U.S. visa. In February 2004 he accepted a tenured professorship in peace studies at the University of Notre Dame. He was granted a nonimmigrant visa, but in July it was revoked by the State Department. The government cited the "ideological exclusion provision" of the USA PATRIOT Act as justification. Ramadan resigned his position from the university. In September 2005 he filed an application for a visa to allow him to participate at speaking engagements with various organizations and universities. The government did not issue a decision on Ramadan's visa application. The American Civil Liberties Union (ACLU), supported by representatives of Ramadan's prospective hosts, filed a lawsuit against the government in January 2006. In September 2006 the government formally denied Ramadan's visa application, citing the decision of a U.S. consular officer in Bern: between December 1998 and July 2002 Ramadan had given donations totaling the equivalent of $940 to a charity organization registered in

Switzerland, the Association de Secours Palestinien (ASP). In August 2003 the U.S. Treasury had designated the ASP a terrorist fundraising organization for its alleged links to Hamas-linked charities—that is to say, over a year after Ramadan's donations ceased. The ACLU continued its litigation, adducing the First and Fifth Amendments. District Judge Paul A. Crotty ruled that the government's justification for denying Ramadan's visa was "facially legitimate and bona fide" and that the court had no authority to override the government's consular decision. In July 2009 a U.S. federal appeals court ruled that a lower court should review whether the consular officer had properly confronted Ramadan with the allegations that he had knowingly rendered material support to terrorism. In January 2010, after more than five years, the State Department decided to lift the ban that prohibited Ramadan from entering the United States; the document was signed by Secretary Hillary Clinton.[23] Since then Ramadan has made numerous visits without apparent incident.[24]

It was fairly clear that the real grounds for the exclusion of Ramadan were that he had been a critic of U.S. foreign policy or that he is the grandson of Hassan Al-Banna, founder of the Muslim Brotherhood, and that some Americans believed Ramadan to be spearheading a campaign to introduce a caliphate in the United States. The allegations of "material support"—under one thousand dollars over four years—were no doubt a smokescreen. I have never met or had any personal contact with Professor Ramadan. My role was to write an expert affidavit pro bono for the ACLU in February 2007, pointing out that when he made his donations ASP was regulated under Swiss charity law and had not been designated by the U.S. government and stating my opinion that, though the designation of ASP apparently rested on the fact that it had remitted funds to Palestinian zakat committees, there was no persuasive evidence that these committees were fronts for Hamas. I was rewarded by an observation in Judge Crotty's judgment (puzzling to make sense of) that my evidence, "while objectively illuminating, provides little comfort to the Court that Ramadan, subjectively, lacked the requisite knowledge." More satisfying was the eventual decision by Secretary Clinton in January 2010, to whom on behalf of the ACLU I had written in October 2009 a letter reaffirming my opinion, which had been reinforced by the results of field research carried out by Emanuel Schaeublin. Nathan J. Brown also wrote to Clinton, in October 2010, in full support of the content of the affidavit.

In retrospect Clinton's exercise of her discretionary authority on account of "national security and foreign policy interests" may have resulted more from a wish to break from the policies of the Bush administration—widely criticized as seeming to be unsympathetic to Muslims—than from any submissions on behalf of the ACLU. However, the government did choose not to contest the affidavit. It was based on firsthand research and on publications available at the time and reached cautious conclusions that called in question the government's position.[25]

I was untroubled by any thought that my affidavit and the resulting letter could amount to a distortion of academic inquiry. The fact that I was giving up my time pro bono was doubly reassuring.[26] But in retrospect the adversarial system cannot but distort—at least when the subject matter is ethnographic. In my own country, the United Kingdom, the system of expert testimony has led to controversy in many different fields of specialist knowledge, and I must hesitate to claim superiority for it over the U.S. system. Indeed two Hong Kong–based consultants in the construction industry recently compared U.S. and U.K. jurisdictions and concluded, "We experienced little difference between the professional conduct of the expert witnesses, lawyers and judges who participate in the legal proceedings."[27]

A British court, however, can order discussions between experts in order to identify and discuss the expert issues in the proceedings and, where possible, reach an agreed opinion on those issues; it may specify the issues the experts must discuss; and it may direct that following a discussion between the experts they must prepare a statement for the court setting out those issues on which they agree and disagree, with a summary of their reasons for disagreeing. The British system also emphasizes experts' "overriding duty to help the court on matters within their expertise."[28] I have not heard of such discussions taking place in the course of U.S. trials—certainly not in the context of counterterrorist allegations—and no such statements are to be found in the official U.S. guidance on the use of expert witnesses. In the United States it is left to trial judges to be the gatekeepers and exclude expert testimony whose reasoning or methodology they deem invalid or inappropriate.[29] In the United Kingdom a new procedure seems to be gaining ground, developed in the Australian courts and known colloquially as "hot-tubbing," whereby experts are sworn in concurrently before the judge.[30] Such a procedure would change the whole character of expert testimony if introduced in the United States.

While maintaining a cautious tone, neither the affidavit nor the ensuing letter about the West Bank zakat committees refrained from going so far as my conclusions a little later, in 2008, which admitted that I could not actually demonstrate the committee's independence from Hamas: "It is logically impossible to completely disprove any conspiratorial theory, because its adherents are able to argue that all evidence against it is mendacious or otherwise flawed. One can only set out to advance an alternative theory, accepting that if new, clinching evidence in favour of the conspiratorial theory were to come to light, one would change one's mind."[31]

The 2008 Occasional Paper

Matthew Levitt's *Hamas: Politics, Charity, and Terrorism in the Service of Jihad*, published in 2006 by Yale University Press in cooperation with the Washington Institute for Near East Policy, received a mixed reception from reviewers.[32] I would endorse criticisms by some of them of the bias of his analysis and his lack of scholarly and ethical scruple. Brown, giving expert evidence in the Holy Land Foundation criminal trial in Dallas in 2007, said, "It's not a real scholarly book. A real scholarly book would weigh research more, and he relies on the information of others and doesn't include evidence that would undermine his conclusions."[33] Most social science ethics committees would look askance at Levitt's practice of interviewing Palestinian prisoners in Israeli jails.[34] But the aspect that especially interested me was that of charity and welfare. He allowed the principal subjects of his research no voice: no statements or publications by charity organizers were cited. In fact, relying on inadequate evidence Levitt smeared the reputation of a charity that operates in the United States without legal impediment to this day (KinderUSA).[35] The puzzle of how the book passed normal standards of peer review is partly solved by a letter from Yale University to an attorney in 2006, which stated, "Yale University Press is not involved in the fact-checking of material submitted by the authors of manuscripts it publishes."[36]

Rather than indulging in name-calling I decided to pay Levitt the compliment that he was advancing a strong hypothesis that deserved to be tested in the spirit of Popperian falsificationism.[37] My paper published in 2008 scrutinized his claim that the West Bank zakat committees were fronts for Hamas, drawing on material that was not available to me when writing the affidavit for the ACLU in early 2007.[38] Levitt likened the organization of Hamas to a pyramid, with a political section at the top, which rests on a military section, which in turn rests on a broad social welfare section. I called this the "pyramid model," though this is not a term used by Levitt himself—and indeed it was articulated more clearly in his expert evidence in the 2007 Holy Land Foundation criminal trial than in his book *Hamas*.[39] There is no dispute that Hamas operated some relief and welfare services of its own directly; what was in contention was the status of the zakat committees, all of which were legally separate entities inspected and regulated by the PA Ministry of Awqaf, accountable to various specialist ministries (social welfare, education, health, agriculture) and subjected to annual audit.

I argued that the pyramid model was an etic (analytical) construct. As such it overlooked two foundation stones that underpinned Hamas's popularity: opposition to the Israeli occupation and religious conviction as a social determinant in itself. An alternative etic interpretation, that of the French researcher Jean-François Legrain,[40] contended that the military and political functions of Hamas were subordinate to an overriding priority to promote a moral and spiritual reawakening, seen as a resource to enable Palestinians to stand up to oppression and humiliation. (This seemed at the time a persuasive interpretation, though since 2007 and Hamas's assumption of power in Gaza it might be seen as losing relevance, for Hamas greatly extended its control of the Gazan voluntary sector, just as Fatah did after 2007 in the West Bank.)[41] I then attempted to interpret the organization of the pre-2007 zakat committees in emic terms—those recognized by all participants—and to test Levitt's various allegations against the zakat committees, which I concluded were exaggerated. Finally I proposed an alternative etic model: the Palestinian zakat committee as an instance of a deeply embedded "civil society institution" that had been operating unobtrusively for centuries across the Muslim world: "It would . . . appear that the zakat committees provided a meeting-point between the new-style Islamism and the old-style Muslim piety. Hence it was not necessary, to achieve its objective of stimulating a vigorous Islamic welfare sector, for Hamas to establish control over the zakat committees." I concluded, "The 'pyramid' model strips Palestinian Islamic institutions both of their geopolitical context—a military occupation widely considered to be illegal—and of their religio-political context, the resurgence of Islamist movements in many parts of the world that gathered force over the past thirty years. Our alternative etic model allows the Palestinian zakat committees to be seen in a different light, as local instances of a worldwide trend, the growth of Islamic NGOs, which are themselves a special case of Faith Based Organizations—but within the unique historical context of the Israel–Palestine conflict."[42]

Since the publication of this paper in 2008, Schaeublin—working with my assistance but independently—has pursued in-depth fieldwork in the Palestinian territories and has subjected the Levitt pyramid model to further testing.[43] He declines to see the pre-2007 zakat committees as subsidiaries of Hamas. Other scholars have broadly concurred in criticizing Levitt's rigid interpretations.[44] Rather than being vehicles of terrorism, autogenous voluntary institutions of this kind may be seen as a protection against terrorism in that they counteract the despair and sense of victimhood which are among the drivers of terrorism.

Local Contextualization

As indicated in the title of his paper, Schaeublin focuses on the "local context." His study and my own emphasize the fluidity of a social movement. This kind of local contextualization is a hallmark of the kind of evidence that ethnography can typically bring to bear. Gerhard Anders has analyzed a loosely comparable example, the testimony given in Freetown in 2006 by a U.S. anthropologist, Danny Hoffman, at the Special Court for Sierra Leone rebutting the expert evidence of a British Army colonel.[45] Hoffman testified for the defense in the trial of a leader of the Civil Defence Force, a pro-government militia, also known as *kamajors*, which fought the rebels who had toppled the democratically elected government in 1997. The issue was whether the kamajors were, as alleged by the prosecution, a military organization such that its leaders could be held responsible for their subordinates' criminal acts. Hoffman denied that the kamajors had a "command and control" structure, arguing that it was a polycentric, dynamic web of social relations based on the clientelism that is prevalent in African societies. The judges made no reference to Hoffman's testimony, implicitly accepted the military expert's model of command responsibility, found the defendant guilty, and sentenced him to fifty-five years in prison, which sentence was later confirmed by the appeal chamber.

This trial might seem to have little in common with a controversy over the integrity of charitable giving in Palestine, apart from the element of huge penalties being imposed. But in both cases ethnography leads to a questioning of the allegation of hierarchic responsibility. Schaeublin has given careful attention to various possible meanings of the term *affiliation* in the Palestinian context.[46] In an academic exchange one would underline the salience of patron-client relations in the Arab world, which undoubtedly affects all aspects of life in Palestine, even though the religious underpinning of zakat as a mechanism to redistribute wealth is supposed to act as a counterbalance.

For an academic or public policy readership I would also pursue the concept of "purism" as an analytical tool. For devout Muslim donors zakat is a means to purify their lives and their wealth (analogous, though not identical, to the Christian concept of charity). Hard-line Zionists and hard-line Islamists have both sought to purify their land, thus "religionizing" the Arab-Israeli conflict. The U.S. government developed a new commitment in 2001 to peer into the motivations of charitable donors to descry the taint of terrorism even when the end product is a maternity hospital or a bakery.[47] But such nuances would be lost in the context of adversarial trials, especially before juries, when arguments tend to be whittled down to black and white, yes and no.[48]

Selective Inattention as an Expert Strategy

Disagreement over the zakat committees might have receded into history if it were not for some major court cases that were still ongoing in 2017. Levitt's testimony in the second Holy Land Foundation criminal trial in Dallas in 2008 was partly responsible for the directors of that organization, which was the largest U.S. Islamic charity in the 1990s, being given life sentences in prison for "material support" to terrorism—and at the time of this writing a postsentencing appeal is still pending.[49] Certain international financial institutions have been sued for huge sums in U.S. courts because of their provision of financial services to disputed charities, also to a great extent on the basis of Levitt's expert reports and publications. Levitt's methodology was hailed in the U.S. Sixth Circuit Court of Appeals and by some of his counterterrorist colleagues as setting a "gold standard."[50]

But Levitt has not joined in the academic debate. If he wished to take part in a cooperative search for truth, he would surely have replied to criticism of his work that has been circulating since the publication of his *Hamas* in 2006. The nearest I have found to a reply to academic critics is in a passage in a recent transcript from a case focusing on the period 2001 to 2004:

Q. Your view is that visiting one of these Zakat charities would tell you what they were doing openly, but it would not give you a clue as to what they were doing behind closed doors?

A. That's one issue. There [is] also an issue as a former U.S. government official, that when—very frequently when former U.S. government officials meet with a group like Hamas, Hamas then makes it public that there was a meeting and make it as [if this is] some type of U.S. government back channel. I have not wanted to be a part of that. If I were an anthropologist or someone who is studying the movement of funds, how charities work, then there is utility going to meet people across a broad array of charities, some affiliated to Hamas, some not, to get a sense of how things work. The part of this that I have [been] investigating is, how Hamas uses these public institutions as cover for their secret work. That they are not going to tell you about.[51]

Levitt's assumption here is that a whole category of informants, including charity organizers, is discredited by obfuscation and lying, whereas another category, including Israeli intelligence officials, can be trusted completely. He has set out to investigate *how* rather than *whether* Hamas uses public institutions. Opportunistic abuse of the privileges of charities occurs in every jurisdiction because they rely on trust; the question is whether or not such abuse is systemic in a given case. Possibly some kind of smoking gun exists that could prove that a given zakat committee had received direct instructions from Hamas, or had systematically disbursed funds in a discriminatory manner, or had financed suicide bombings. Yet no such smoking gun has so far come to light after many years of judicial proceedings.

Meanwhile, if the more benign view of the character of the Islamic charities before 2007 is justified, they can be seen in retrospect as practical expressions of the Palestinian virtue of *ṣumūd*, best translated as "steadfastness," with Qur'anic connotations.[52] Less well known than the Palestinian capacity for active resistance (*muqāwama*), which extends to the cult of the "martyrdom operation," ṣumūd motivates the assertion of national cultural values, the determination not to give up land or emigrate, and the building up of local institutions of mutual aid, including the zakat committees.

One might hope that the process of cross-examination would expose the weaknesses in Levitt's position, but as a former FBI investigator and U.S. Treasury official, now an accredited academic, experienced expert witness, and media commentator, he has considerable power to sway a judge and jury.[53] I have been assured by U.S. attorneys that the personal impression made on a jury by an expert witness's demeanor is often likely to outweigh its assessment of the detailed opinions and evidence presented. Moreover legal hearings, especially in the United States, are like fast-moving games of professional tennis, in the course of which even veteran attorneys are apt to make unforced errors. To understand how such an expert has had so much influence in the U.S. courts we need to consider how the media and the justice system interpenetrate.

The Finance-Security-Media Nexus

Can judges be their own expert witness? An article I published in a law journal, "An Unholy Tangle: *Boim versus the Holy Land Foundation*," was adapted from a presentation given at a UCLA seminar in 2010 on the "criminalization of Islamic philanthropy." It respectfully calls attention to the haste with which a noted American judge, Richard Posner, jumped to conclusions in 2008 without examining the evidence about the tortious liability of this American

Islamic charity, which had remitted funds to the Palestinian zakat commit-tees. I also showed that it is evidently acceptable in the United States for a blogging judge to express a pronounced political opinion on matters relevant to cases on which he adjudicates, for Posner published a controversial blog in 2006 calling for "massive military force" against the Hamas leadership.[54]

President Bush had denounced the defendant in this case in December 2001. This amounted to prejudgment of its guilt in the media during the intense disquiet after 9/11, though no one has ever claimed that the Holy Land Foundation had any connection with Al Qaeda. More recently a senior British barrister, Francis FitzGibbon QC, has criticized the Holy Land Foundation criminal hearings as a "show trial," "a tale of legal chica-nery by the government, of moral panic and of complicity on the part of the judiciary."[55]

Marieke de Goede has outlined what she calls the "finance-security assem-blage," "the transnational landscape of laws, institutions, treaties, and private initiatives that play a role in fighting terrorism financing."[56] She describes "in-termediality" as crucial to "fostering a broad cultural space in which terrorism financing became perceived as an urgent security problem as well as to recy-cling persistent myths and narratives about terrorist financing for which sometimes there has been little concrete evidence."[57] Judge Posner blurred the distinction between the judiciary and political journalism in publishing his blog. In his judgment in the *Boim* case he appeared to accept media represen-tations of the operations of Islamic charities and "Arab terrorism" while ig-noring the extensive literature on the law and ethics of humanitarianism that his colleague on the bench, Judge Ilana Rovner, recording her minority opin-ion, was attentive to. His judgment has been relied on as an authority in other courts.

Conclusion

The very notion of expertise invites quizzical treatment. On the one hand, ethnographers typically set out to inquire into everyday knowledge and the experiences of ordinary people as a counterbalance to the manipulative power of elites who profess to know better.[58] On the other hand, ethnographers should not be ashamed of drawing on the cumulative understanding gained by social science. If one submits to the constraints of giving expert testimony, one implicitly accepts that social research needs to maintain the links to its anchor-age in science—however distinct in its methods it has to be from natural sci-ence. To those who would cast off this anchorage Georges Guille-Escuret has put a pertinent question: "In what branch of anthropology has field research not made advances on the standards that were accepted half a century ago?"[59]

More than other social scientists, anthropologists are routinely trained to examine their own prejudices, and many ethnographers now find it useful to dwell explicitly on their own cultural and personal backgrounds as elements in their research data. There is some common ground with what is supposed to happen in an adversarial legal system, when advocates for each party have the chance to try to convince the judge or jury to lay aside their prejudices. Anthropologists could do more to draw attention to the difficulty we all have in correcting for our stereotypic thinking and stigmatization of others, especially when these tendencies are reinforced by the media; these principles could be applied to the training of lawyers—even in a country like the United States where, despite the separation of powers, the most senior judges often have known party-political sympathies.

Australian-style "hot-tubbing" of expert witnesses would no doubt reduce some of these problems. So would the responsibility of independent publishers to remember, when checking submissions on patently contentious topics, that academic accreditation can have unforeseen consequences for human lives and well-being. Levitt's book on Hamas, hallowed as it is with the imprimatur of Yale University Press, would have carried less weight if it had been published as a report by the Washington Institute for Near East Policy, a think tank considered to be friendly toward Israel. Given the continuing polarization of Israeli-Palestinian geopolitics and extreme turmoil in the region as a whole, the ethnographic initiatives outlined in this chapter can probably do no more than lay down a documentary record that may provide some stimulus toward rebuilding the Palestinian social fabric if the Fatah-Hamas split is eventually mended.

Notes

I am most grateful to Nadia Abu El-Hadj, Didier Fassin, and Emanuel Schaeublin for constructive criticism of earlier drafts of this chapter. The usual disclaimers apply.

1   Rosen 1977: 555.
2   See Anders 2014; Campisi 1991; Good 2007; Piot n.d.; Rosen 1977. Anders provides an excellent list of references.
3   Donini 2012: 1–4.
4   I also visited Israel and Palestine in 1999, 2009, 2011, and 2012.
5   Al-Khayyat 1993.

6   Benthall and Bellion-Jourdan 2003.

7   Benthall 2014.

8   See Fassin 2011; Donini 2012.

9   Benthall and Bellion-Jourdan 2003: 154, 155.

10 Interpal was essentially cleared by the Charity Commission for a third time in 2009, though with some specific directions for changes. Since 2010 and up to the time of writing, it has been fully compliant with the Charity Commission's rulings.

11 Levitt 2006: 1, 238.

12 *Linde et al. vs. Arab Bank*, U.S. District Court, Eastern District of New York, Matthew Levitt, questioned by Shand Stephens for the defense, August 19, 2014, p. 736:

> Q. And you prefer not to use the word members when referring to people associated with Hamas, isn't that right?
>
> A. It's difficult to use the term member when referring to an organization like Hamas or any other organization that includes covert—I don't like to use the term membership or affiliation. Because they don't necessarily keep a list. They don't necessarily carry membership cards in their wallet. So you try and be as specific as possible when you can. So when citing to a government report you try and use the words they use. Presumably, they have reason to use the word they use. Or to try and be specific, if someone was engaging in an operation, Hamas operative, you might call them an operative. If someone was providing support, supporter. They were providing funding, fundraiser, to the extent possible.

On another occasion, Levitt drew an analogy between an affiliation to Hamas and the affiliation of U.S. alumni to their university (*Linde et al. vs. Arab Bank*, deposition by Matthew Levitt, New York City, September 20, 2011, questioned by Kevin Walsh for the defense, p. 536).

> A. I went to the Fletcher School of Law and Diplomacy. I get people who come to me all the time, straight out of school or mid career. They're looking for advice, they want an informational interview, whatever. And what's their connection to me? They saw I went to Fletcher. There's a network. It doesn't have an address. It's not done through the Fletcher School. It's not done through anybody, right? It's just—but there's a sense of connection, and they're probably right, that if I can, I will take the time and sure.

13 Powell 2001.

14 See Schaeublin 2012. The Jordanian model for modern zakat committees, following the example of Nablus as described above, did not extend to Gaza, which until 1967 was under Egyptian administration and had inherited a different legal culture. Zakat committees were indeed formed in Gaza, but they were overshadowed by three large Islamic nonprofit organizations founded in the 1970s operating under an old Ottoman law of association, all of them playing a major role in mitigating the most oppressive rigors of military occupation and having some success in raising funds internationally. In all of them there was considerable overlap between their founders and the founders of Hamas, though to different degrees. Each of them

seems to have been operated with considerable autonomy, competing with one another in raising external funds, including grants from USAID.

15 Schaeublin 2009: 5.
16 For an analysis of the surveys conducted in 2000 and 2004, see Benthall 2008: 20–21. An earlier survey conducted in 1998–99 gives figures roughly in line with the later surveys (Birzeit University 2000: 112–13).
17 Schaeublin 2009: 57.
18 Abu Saif 2012: 24.
19 The Nablus committee was declared an "unlawful association" by the Israeli Ministry of Defense in June 2006 but was allowed in practice to continue functioning.
20 Brown 2003: 14.
21 International Crisis Group 2003: 10.
22 U.S. Embassy, Tel Aviv, "Terrorism Finance: GOI Says Now Is the Time to Act against the Central Bank of Iran and Increases Its Financial Isolation of Gaza," WikiLeaks, cited in Schaeublin 2012: 80.
23 Lall 2010.
24 Most of the documents relating to the case have been archived on the ACLU website: https://www.aclu.org/national-security/american-academy-religion-v-napolitano -case-profile.
25 See Brown 2003; Hroub 2006a; International Crisis Group 2003.
26 An hourly fee of $150 to $200 for experts is very much on the low side in U.S. courts and can become a major source of their income. Sheila Jasonoff (1995: 45–48) has argued that the expert witness system has become commodified; it tempts science professionals to exaggerate, be overdefinitive, and express opinions beyond their competence.
27 Huyghe and Chan 2013: 18.
28 U.K. Ministry of Justice Civil Procedure Rules 2016, part 35, "Experts and Assessors," September 2014, paras. 35.12, 35.3. Similar directions apply to criminal trials (U.K. Ministry of Justice Criminal Procedure Rules 2016, part 33, "Expert Evidence," October 2014).
29 See Cromwell 2011.
30 Huyghe and Chan 2013: 17; U.K. Ministry of Justice Civil Procedure Rules: Practice Direction 2016: 35, "Experts and Assessors," January 2015, paras. 11.1–11.4.
31 See Benthall 2008: 14n22.
32 Favorable reviews: Kershner 2006; M. Rubin 2007; L. Rubin 2006. Qualified review: Erlanger 2006. Negative reviews: Hroub 2006b; Roy 2007.
33 *United States of America vs. Holy Land Foundation et al.*, U.S. District Court for the Northern District of Texas, Dallas Division, September 10, 2007, 11.08. Questioned by Joshua Dratel for the defense.
34 See Roberts and Indermaur 2007–8.
35 Levitt 2006: 151–52.

36 Dorothy K. Robinson, vice president and general counsel, Yale University, letter to John P. Kilroy, attorney-at-law, Lorain, Ohio, November 9, 2006. Consulted by the author, September 18 2016.

37 Anthony Good (2007: 141–42) points out that the rules of expert testimony applied in U.S. federal legal proceedings since 1993, the "*Daubert* standard," include a reference to Popper's principle of falsifiability. Good argues that in 1993 "Popper's views were already seen as old-fashioned by science studies students."

38 Benthall 2008; Lundblad 2008; Malka 2007.

39 *United States of America vs. Holy Land Foundation et al.*, U.S. District Court for the Northern District of Texas, Dallas Division, July 25, 2007, 09.47. Questioned by Barry Jonas for the Government.

    Q. Dr. Levitt, do you see it on your screen now?
    A. I do.
    Q. And Dr. Levitt, can you explain the triangle?
    A. What you have here is a graphic depiction of the three wings or branches of HAMAS that we discussed, the political at the top of the pyramid, the military which is called the Izz Al-Din Al-Qassam Brigades, and the base at the bottom is the social wing sometimes referred to as the Dawa.

40 Legrain 2006.

41 See Schaeublin 2012.

42 Benthall 2008: 24, 26.

43 See Schaeublin 2009, 2012.

44 See Gunning 2007, 2008; Høigilt 2010, 2013; Lundblad 2011; Roy 2011. Schaeublin conducted renewed fieldwork in Nablus in 2013–14 and confirms that his view of that particular committee as having been run by a "social coalition" before 2007 has not changed. His recent fieldwork is comprehensively documented in Schaeublin 2016.

45 See Anders 2014; Hoffman 2007. Hoffman emphasizes that he has offered no opinion on the question of culpability; his role was to assist the court in understanding the dynamics of the movement.

46 Schaeublin 2012: 50–62.

47 This is discussed further in Benthall 2016: chapter 9, "Puripetal Force in the Charitable Field."

48 As closely argued by Good 2007.

49 The first trial, in 2007, resulted in a hung jury.

50 Washington Institute 2012. See Silverstein 2012 for the offending article.

51 *Linde et al. vs. Arab Bank*, U.S. District Court, Eastern District of New York, questioned by Shand Stephens for the defense, August 19, 2014, 740–41.

52 The term has Islamic resonance, for Al-Ṣamad ("The Self-subsisting") is one of the names of God (Qur'an 112.2). Leonardo Schiocchet (2011) argues that ṣumūd also has a secular history but has recently become "re-Islamized."

53 My criticisms of Levitt are confined to his interventions on the question of Palestinian charities, and I do not question his sincerity or good intentions. More recently he has given practical attention to confronting the threat of international jihadism (Levitt 2015).

54 See Benthall 2010–11.

55 FitzGibbon 2015: 13.

56 I prefer the term *nexus* to *assemblage*. Cf. Ingold 2014.

57 De Goede 2012:5.

58 Sillitoe 2007: 154–55. In her biography of Claude Lévi-Strauss, Emmanuelle Loyer (2015: 732–35) notes that, though he made personal interventions in various public debates throughout his long career, he was wary of all "applied" social science and its appropriation in political controversy, and he rejected the notion that dilemmas of public policy could be resolved by means of deference to expertise (including his own scholarship): "Les choix de société n'appartiennent pas au savant en tant que tel, mais—et lui-même en est un—aux citoyens" (Lévi-Strauss, letter to Éric Fassin, in Borillo et al. 1999: 110, cited in Loyer).

59 Guille-Escuret 1999: 1. The tradition of Middle East ethnography had earlier roots, but ethnographic studies of NGOs did not exist before, for example, Barbara Harrell-Bond (1986) and Alex de Waal (1989).

References

Abu Saif, Atef. 2012. "Reforming or Instrumentalizing Zakat? A Study of Palestinian Media Coverage." Geneva: CCDP Issue Brief, Graduate Institute.

Al-Khayyat, Abdul-Aziz. 1993. *Al-zakāh wa taṭbīqāt-ha wa istithmārāt-ha* (Zakat and Its Applications and Profitable Uses). Amman: Ministry of Awqaf and Islamic Affairs.

Anders, Gerhard. 2014. "Contesting Expertise: Anthropologists at the Special Court for Sierra Leone." *Journal of the Royal Anthropological Institute* 20.3: 426–44.

Benthall, Jonathan. 2008. "The Palestinian Zakat Committees 1993–2007 and Their Contested Interpretations." Occasional Paper. Geneva: Graduate School of International and Development Studies, Program for the Study of International Organization(s). Reprinted in Benthall 2016, 57–80.

———. 2010–11. "An Unholy Tangle: Boim versus the Holy Land Foundation." *UCLA Journal of Islamic and Near Eastern Law* 10.1: 1–10. Reprinted in Benthall 2016, 99–107.

———. 2014. "The Islamic Charities Project (Formerly Montreux Initiative)." In *Gulf Charities and Islamic Philanthropy in the "Age of Terror" and Beyond*, edited by Robert Lacey and Jonathan Benthall, 285–305. Berlin: Gerlach Press. Reprinted in Benthall 2016, 81–98.

———. 2016. *Islamic Charities and Islamic Humanism in Troubled Times*. Manchester, UK: Manchester University Press.

Benthall, Jonathan, and Jérôme Bellion-Jourdan. 2003. *The Charitable Crescent: Politics of Aid in the Muslim World*. London: I. B. Tauris.

Birzeit University. 2000. "Palestine Human Development Report 1998–99."

Borillo, Daniel, Éric Fassin, and Marcella Iacub, eds. 1999. *Au-delà du Pacs: L'Expertise familiale à l'épreuve de l'homosexualité*. Paris: PUF.

Brown, Nathan J. 2003. "Palestinian Civil Society in Theory and Practice." Paper presented at the annual meeting of Structure of Government Section, International Political Science Association, Washington, DC.

Campisi, Jack. 1991. *The Mashpee Indians: Tribe on Trial*. Syracuse: Syracuse University Press.

Cromwell, Thomas A. 2011. "The Challenges of Scientific Evidence." Macfadyen Lecture. Scottish Council of Law Reporting. http://www.scottishlawreports.org .uk/publications/macfadyen-2011.html.

De Goede, Marieke. 2012. *Speculative Security: The Politics of Pursuing Terrorist Monies*. Minneapolis: University of Minnesota Press.

de Waal, Alex. 1989. *Famine That Kills: Darfur, Sudan*. Oxford: Clarendon Press.

Donini, Antonio, ed. 2012. *The Golden Fleece: Manipulation and Independence in Humanitarian Action*. West Hartford, CT: Kumarian Press.

Erlanger, Steven. 2006. "Militant Zeal." *New York Times*, June 25.

Fassin, Didier. 2011. *Humanitarian Reason: A Moral History of the Present*. Berkeley: University of California Press.

FitzGibbon, Francis. 2015. "Low-Hanging Fruit." *London Review of Books*, January 22: 13–14.

Good, Anthony. 2007. *Anthropology and Expertise in the Asylum Courts*. London: Routledge-Cavendish.

Guille-Escuret, Georges. 1999. "Need Anthropology Resign?" *Anthropology Today* 15.5: 1–3.

Gunning, Jeroen. 2007. *Hamas in Politics*. London: Hurst.

———. 2008. "Terrorism, Charities, and Diasporas." In *Countering the Financing of Terrorism*, edited by Thomas Biersteker and Sue Eckert, 93–125. London: Routledge.

Harrell-Bond, Barbara E. 1986. *Imposing Aid: Emergency Assistance to Refugees*. Oxford: Oxford University Press.

Hoffman, Danny. 2007. "The Meaning of a Militia: Understanding the Civil Defence Forces of Sierra Leone." *African Affairs* 106: 639–62.

Høigilt, Jacob. 2010. *Raising Extremists? Islamism and Education in the Palestinian Territories*. Oslo: Fafo.

———. 2013. *Islamism and Education: The Nature and Aims of Islamic Schools in the Occupied Palestinian Territories*. Oslo: Fafo.

Hroub, Khaled. 2006a. *Hamas: A Beginner's Guide*. London: Pluto Press.

———. 2006b. Review of Matthew Levitt's *Hamas: Politics, Charity, and Terrorism in the Service of Jihad. Journal of Palestine Studies* 35.4: 73–75.

Huyghe, Steve, Sr., and Adrian Chan. 2013. "The Evolution of Expert Witness Law under UK and US Jurisdictions." *Construction Law International* 8.4: 14–18. http://www.fticonsulting.com/~/media/Files/us-files/insights/articles/the -evolution-of-expert-witness-law-under-uk-and-us-jurisdictions.pdf.

Ingold, Tim. 2014. "On Human Correspondence." Huxley Memorial Lecture, Royal Anthropological Institute, November 13. Awaiting printed publication; podcast on https://www.youtube.com/watch?v=1vIq5s04wBU.

International Crisis Group. 2003. *Islamic Social Activism in the Palestinian Territories.* Brussels: International Crisis Group.

Jasonoff, Sheila. 1995. *Science at the Bar: Law, Science, and Technology in America.* Cambridge: Harvard University Press.

Kershner, Isabel. 2006. "Rise of the Zealots." *Washington Post*, May 7.

Lall, Sarah. 2010. "In Shift, U.S. Lifts Visa Curbs on Professor." *New York Times*, January 20.

Legrain, Jean-François. 2006. "Le Hamas et le Fatah: Doivent-ils dissoudre l'autorité palestinienne?" http://www.lefigaro.fr/debats/2006/11/23/01005-20061123 ARTFIG90059-le_hamas_et_le_fatah_doivent_ils_dissoudre_1 _autorite _palestinienne.php.

Levitt, Matthew. 2006. *Hamas: Politics, Charity, and Terrorism in the Service of Jihad.* New Haven: Yale University Press.

———, ed. 2015. *From the Boston Marathon to the Islamic State: Countering Violent Extremism.* Washington, DC: Washington Institute for Near East Policy.

Loyer, Emmanuelle. 2015. *Lévi-Strauss.* Paris: Flammarion.

Lundblad, Lars Gunnar. 2008. "Islamic Welfare, Discourse and Practise: The Institutionalization of *Zakat* in Palestine." In *Interpreting Welfare and Relief in the Middle East*, edited by N. Naguib and I. M. Okkenhaug, 195–216. Leiden: Brill.

———. 2011. *Islamic Welfare in Palestine: Meanings and Practices. Processes of Institutionalization and Politicization of Zakat, the Third Pillar of Islam.* Saarbrücken: Lambert Academic.

Malka, Haim. 2007. "Hamas: Resistance and Transformation of Palestinian Society." In *Understanding Islamic Charities*, edited by Jon Alterman and Karin von Hippel, 98–126. Washington, DC: Center for Strategic and International Studies Press.

Piot, Charles. N.d. "Representing Africa in the Kasinga Asylum Case, and Beyond." Unpublished paper.

Powell, Colin. 2001. "Remarks to the National Foreign Policy Conference for Leaders of Nongovernmental Organizations." U.S. Department of State. October 26. http://avalon.law.yale.edu/sept11/powell_brief31.asp.

Roberts, Lynne, and David Indermaur. 2007–8. "The Ethics of Research with Prisoners." *Current Issues in Criminal Justice* 19.3: 309–26.

Rosen, Lawrence. 1977. "The Anthropologist as Expert Witness." *American Anthropologist* 79: 555–78.

Roy, Sara. 2007. Review of Matthew Levitt's *Hamas: Politics, Charity, and Terrorism in the Service of Jihad. Middle East Policy* 14.2: 162–66.

―――. 2011. *Hamas and Civil Society in Gaza*. Princeton: Princeton University Press.

Rubin, Lawrence. 2007. Review of Matthew Levitt's *Hamas: Politics, Charity, and Terrorism in the Service of Jihad*. *Terrorism and Political Violence* 19.1: 152–54.

Rubin, Michael. 2006. "Popular Notions Laid Bare." *New York Sun*, May 23.

Schaeublin, Emanuel. 2009. "Role and Governance of Islamic Charitable Institutions: The West Bank Zakat Committees (1977–2009) in the Local Context." CCDP Working Paper 5. Geneva: Graduate Institute.

―――. 2012. "Role and Governance of Islamic Charitable Institutions: Gaza Zakat Organizations (1973–2011) in the Local Context." CCDP Working Paper 9. Geneva: Graduate Institute.

―――. 2016. "Zakat in Nablus (Palestine): Change and Continuity in Islamic Almsgiving." Doctoral thesis in anthropology, University of Oxford.

Schiocchet, Leonardo. 2011. "Palestinian Sumud: Steadfastness, Ritual and Time among Palestinian Refugees." Working Paper 51. Ramallah: Birzeit University.

Sillitoe, Paul. 2007. "Anthropologists Only Need Apply: Challenges of Applied Anthropology." *Journal of the Royal Anthropological Institute* 13: 147–65.

Silverstein, Ken. 2012. "The Government's Man: How to Read the Résumé of a Terrorism Expert." *Harper's Magazine*. June: 58–59.

U.K. Criminal Procedure Rules. 2016.

U.K. Ministry of Justice Civil Procedure Rules. 2016.

U.K. Ministry of Justice Civil Procedure Rules Practice Direction. 2016.

Washington Institute. 2012. "Counterterrorism Experts Defend Levitt from Unfair Attack in 'Harper's.'" September 10. http://www.washingtoninstitute.org/press-room/view/levitt-colleagues-object-to-harpers-article.

8

Policy Ethnography as a Combat Sport

Analyzing the Welfare State against the Grain

VINCENT DUBOIS

"It's our bible." That was how the deputy director of research at an important French national welfare agency described a book I had published on the encounters between welfare offices and their clients. Such an enthusiastic sentence came as a surprise. The research from which my book was issued had been commissioned by this organization, but the report had sat on a shelf for a long time before gaining the attention of my institutional partners. My ethnography of face-to-face interactions between the low-level bureaucrats who sit behind desks and the impoverished welfare recipients who stand before them underlined relationships of domination from a critical perspective and was never intended to provide advice on how to improve "client relationship management." Such an orientation was inauspicious for my book to become an official reference, which, if not always read, seemed widely acknowledged by policy managers ("a bible"). Its long and circuitous road to canonization was helped along the way by academic recognition and, to a lesser extent, media attention. Yet thanks to this postponed institutional acknowledgment, I was able to access even more information, enjoyed a fair amount of leeway in choosing research topics (even controversial ones) and defining my framework, and secured support for further research I conducted in collaboration with the welfare organization in question.

This personal experience provides an occasion to reflect on ethnography and policy and, more precisely, on how to ensure favorable conditions for autonomous critical ethnographic research when it comes to public policy. In light of this opportunity I address the questions of how this body of knowledge is received and by whom, bearing in mind that the public of policy ethnography is not limited to policymakers. By drawing a link between the conditions of production and the conditions of reception of my work by various audiences, I explore how policy ethnography can become public with the aim of contributing to the ongoing debates on public ethnography beyond the specific domain of policy.

The relationship between policymaking and ethnographic research indeed raises numerous questions at the core of the debates on public ethnography.[1] To list but a few: Who is ethnographic research intended for? What can its outcomes in the real world be? What, in turn, are the possible effects of external expectations on the research design? How do the ethnographers define their role and combine academic rationales with other potential agendas? These various issues are not specific to the field of policy, but since the ethnographer is directly, concomitantly, and profoundly confronted by them, probably more so in this domain than in others,[2] it provides a good opportunity to address them.

What Type of Knowledge Is Policy Ethnography?

Following Burawoy, policy is one of four types of sociological knowledge, the others being professional, critical, and public sociology.[3] According to him, policy sociology (or ethnography) is "in the service of a goal defined by a client," and its "*raison d'être* is to provide solutions to problems that are presented to us, or to legitimate solutions that have already been reached."[4] In this perspective policy research is an "instrumental knowledge" (as opposed to reflexive knowledge) intended for an extra-academic audience.

This analytic definition clearly establishes the boundary between policy-driven knowledge and its audiences and other types of knowledge with their respective audiences. However, such a distinction is not as self-evident as it may seem, insofar as it runs the risk of taking for granted that policy sociology equals research *for* policy, that is, an expert knowledge supposedly useful to policymakers and, conversely, of lesser value according to academic standards. There is no doubt that this equation is relevant to account for much of policy sociology when it is defined as applied research providing information and advice to policymakers. There is, however, another way of defining policy sociology, this time as sociology or ethnography *of* policy processes. According to this alternative and far less common definition, social scientists do not provide answers to questions posed by their policymaking clients. Instead they formulate their own problems and questions, construct policy as a research object, and use frameworks and methods employed by their scientific counterparts to study other objects. This redefinition has been advocated for and illustrated in several branches of the social sciences, in anthropology, and under the banner of critical policy studies.[5] According to this new definition, policy ethnography is therefore "professional" (academic) and possibly also "critical," as I show later. But strictly sticking to this conception and never crossing the line that distinguishes it from policy-oriented research is no easy task. These difficulties are at the core of the reflection I develop in this chapter.

These introductory remarks lead me to my main point: it is possible to reconsider some common oppositions such as applied versus critical or policy-driven versus academic or political as well as distinctions between the categories of recipients of public research (policymakers, the general public, or academia). These oppositions are fully relevant at an analytical and general level, but they are not permanently established and mutually exclusive categories. They designate tensions and polarities rather than strict oppositions, for blurred lines are much more common than clear-cut distinctions in the concrete practices of social scientists. Moreover it is possible to reinterpret Burawoy's typology in a dynamic way and to view his four types as describing successive steps in a career or a research process rather than final options.[6]

This is how I gradually came to define an unplanned but nevertheless conscious strategy in my research in general and in policy ethnography in particular. This strategy relies on two basic principles: first, the adoption of an uncompromising attitude toward the autonomy of research (e.g., refusing to address questions in the way they are defined by policymakers or to write policy recommendations); second, the use of ethnographic methods, among others, both in opposition to mainstream approaches to policy analysis and as a tool to challenge official views on policy problems.[7] This fits Burawoy's models of "professional" and "critical" sociology.

Yet the achievement of these models may paradoxically require making compromises, if not partially and temporarily adopting some contradictory features of "policy knowledge." The problem of access to the field, which is of course crucial for ethnography in particular, poses a challenge to a straightforward and rigid application of such principles. Unlike in other domains it is usually very difficult, if not impossible, to conduct proper ethnographic fieldwork on policy processes without accreditation granted by policy officials, who have their own agenda, their own (often vague) notion of social science, and their own understanding of how research could be useful to them or, on the contrary, damage the public image of their institution. As a result standard practices of ethnographic fieldwork—opening the closed doors of bureaucracy, accessing files, collecting internal documents, talking to people at various levels in the hierarchy—require a negotiated agreement with policy authorities and therefore a compromise between what the researchers intend to do and what policy officials would like them to do or avoid doing.

This is all the more the case as commissioned research is one of the main possibilities for such an agreement. Since it includes a financial aspect, possibly turning policymakers into clients, to use Burawoy's term, commissioned research may impact the selection of problems to investigate, impose an official view on them, or define the purpose of the study in managerial rather than scientific terms. In other words, a loss of scientific autonomy may be the price of access to the field necessary to conduct empirical research. In the conception of policy ethnography I defend, this is too high a price to pay: there is no point in conducting empirical research if it does not follow strict academic criteria or if it does not pursue scientific and critical goals. The challenge is therefore to overcome the contradictions that exist between the goals of critical policy ethnography and the scientific, political, and practical conditions of its implementation.

I will account for the way I have coped with these difficulties in my research on social welfare in France, which makes extensive (but not exclusive) use of ethnographic methods. The narrative of this personal experience, with its successes and failures, is intended to contribute to a collective discussion on how to make autonomous policy ethnography possible and how to make policy ethnography public. Before getting to that, however, it is necessary to outline the academic, institutional, and general context in which my experience takes place.

Public Ethnography in the French Context

The division between academic disciplines in the French social sciences is not quite the same as in other countries. Disciplines and subdisciplines are not as strictly separated as they are in North America. My discipline, for instance, is political science, which in France is virtually a synonym of political sociology and shares theoretical frameworks and methods with sociology. There is a long-standing tradition of qualitative sociology based on in-depth interviews and long-term observation, which could be regarded as anthropology or ethnography from a U.S. point of view. References to ethnographic fieldwork and methods have become popular among the other disciplines of social science over the past two decades. One of the handbooks most commonly used to train social science students in the conduct of fieldwork, written by two sociologists, is actually a guide for ethnographic research,[8] and nowadays many doctoral theses in sociology and political science include ethnography in their methodology. Yet despite its strength as a research practice, anthropology is quite weak as an academic discipline. Many bachelor's and master's programs have closed in recent years, and ethnologists are far less numerous than their colleagues from other disciplines in university faculties.[9] Therefore in the French context it is certainly more relevant to speak of public social scientists (some of whom use ethnographic methods) than of public ethnographers per se.

Public social science does exist, insofar as we refer to the presence of social scientists outside of academia. On a daily basis national newspapers such as *Le Monde* and *Libération* publish op-eds (*tribunes*) on social and political issues by sociologists, historians, or (less frequently) anthropologists. The increasing media demand for expertise has multiplied the number of interviews with social scientists in the past decades, which has itself become a topic of debate within the profession.[10] As Laurent Jeanpierre and Sébastien Mosbah-Natanson have shown in their study of social scientists published in *Le Monde*, their dominant model of intervention in the public space remains influenced by the historical French definition of intellectuals as "universal specialists" (i.e., speaking out in the name of universal values), far from the competing definition of "the expert," in the narrow sense of the term.[11] Over the past twenty years several independent publishers have opened a new space for political books, mostly written by academics who use their knowledge of social science to engage in public debates.[12] Short books intended for a wide audience have become a model set by publishers issuing book series promoting critical if not radical orientations.[13] Well-established publishing companies have followed this model, working with more moderate reformist authors.[14]

Lastly, and this is more specifically related to the topic of this chapter, there is in France a strong tradition of collaboration between social scientists and public bodies such as ministries and national agencies.[15] In this rich and complex tradition applied research and the model of "useful" expert knowledge unsurprisingly prevail. There has nevertheless always been room for autonomous research, even under radically critical forms. For instance, in the 1970s neo-Marxist and Foucauldian analyses of urban planning and welfare that denounced capitalist state power or punitive social control over underprivileged populations were state funded and influential in the training of civil servants in these domains. More recently, and more in tune with my own approach, the fieldwork later published in *The Weight of the World* under Bourdieu's supervision was initially funded by a state financial organization, the Caisse des Dépôts et Consignations (Deposits and Consignments Fund).[16] Despite its unusual format (almost one thousand pages, mainly consisting of interviews), the book garnered considerable attention far beyond academic circles.

There are examples of ethnographic research funded by ministries and public policy agencies, mainly in order to collect information on the lifestyles of specific social groups. For instance Pierre Bonte and Anne-Marie Brisebarre's study of the sacrifice of 'Id al-kabir in the French suburbs was funded by the Ministry for Social Affairs as part of its policy program dedicated to immigrants.[17] Yet in contrast to what has long been the case in the United States, ethnographers are rarely asked to turn their attention to policy organizations and processes.[18] The neoliberal trend in public administration resulted in cuts in research budgets and a preference for what C. Wright Mills calls—in a totally different context—"bureaucratic empiricism," namely standardized methods intended for direct use by bureaucrats, such as applied management, economics, or positivist quantitative sociology.[19] The least I can say is that there have been more favorable contexts for autonomous critical research to collaborate with policy agencies and therefore for what I call "critical policy ethnography."[20] There are still, however, opportunities to do so.

I will relate three of my own experiences (the third still ongoing) with the same institution, which is one of the main public agencies in France for social welfare, housing, and family benefits, the Caisse Nationale des Allocations Familiales (National Family Allowances Fund). Since these experiences extend over almost twenty years now, this narrative will account for several changes in my own position, in the dissemination of my research, and in my relationship with the institution. In the process I illustrate how Burawoy's types of sociology contradict each other but also combine one with another, and ultimately designate steps in a research process rather than once and for all mutually exclusive options.

Translating Managerial Concerns into Critical Policy Ethnography

My first research in policy ethnography started in 1995, when I analyzed the relationships between clients and clerks in welfare offices. This was an institutional commission in response to various organizational concerns, such as improving the image of the agency among its clients, finding the reasons for the increasingly long waiting lines, explaining the attitudes of impoverished clients, and developing the agents' relational skills. The initial idea was to find ways to improve client satisfaction and to overhaul the institution's internal organization from a perspective at least indirectly inspired by new public management. The watchword of the time was the "modernization" of public services, which in this case meant both the questioning of the supposedly "archaic" attitude of bureaucrats toward their clients and the hope that the latter would themselves contribute to modernizing the bureaucratic organization by expressing their wishes, adopting a more active attitude instead of being targets of bureaucratic power, and becoming coproducers of public services.

Initially this agenda appeared to be of no interest to me as a researcher. At the time I had just defended my PhD thesis on an entirely different topic, but I was looking for a job and did not find myself in a position to turn down an employment opportunity. As it quickly turned out, I was nevertheless able to translate these managerial concerns into a totally different project. First, the research program was under the supervision of two colleagues known for their unflagging support for the independence of social scientists and their refusal to compromise with narrowly applied or managerial research. Second, the research managers I was dealing with at the welfare agency soon became precious allies. They were willing to convince their superiors of the value of independent research rather than impose a practice-driven agenda on the researchers. Having kept abreast of the new trends in social science research, they originally designed the research project in reference to the sociological framework freshly constructed by Luc Boltanski and Laurent Thévenot.[21] Contrary to Bourdieu's critical sociology, these authors advocated for "a sociology of critique," adopting the point of view of persons acting in the social world to understand critical operations undertaken by these persons (e.g., evaluating people and situations, finding agreements). Using that framework was a scientifically exciting theoretical and methodological challenge—again a far cry from a narrowly defined applied and managerial form of research. Eventually, for reasons that would take too long to explain here, I did not rely on Boltanski and Thévenot's model and was able to make my own theoretical and methodological choices. My contact in the research department of the welfare organization gave me free rein to pursue my own lines of inquiry, provided that I give detailed information on what was happening and on what was at stake during bureaucratic interactions. (These apparently mundane encounters remained quite enigmatic for the managerial staff.) In the end the vagueness of this commission allowed me to interpret it and redefine it in my own way. Quite unexpectedly what could have been a public management-driven case study of little interest from an academic social science point of view became a research project I was free to frame as I saw fit and which offered me the opportunity to make my first attempt as a policy ethnographer and raise theoretical questions that had nothing to do with improving client satisfaction or implementing a managerial modernization of public services.

This enabled me to conduct proper ethnographic research. I spent six months in two welfare offices, observing clients in the waiting room and talking to them, sitting at the desk alongside the caseworkers during their encounters with impoverished people, and conducting extensive interviews regarding their work, personal histories, and attitudes. Based on an empirical descriptive approach, this fieldwork resulted in findings that contradicted the most common predefined notions of bureaucratic encounters conveyed by the official managerial discourse. I showed, for instance, that the actual functions of these daily encounters were far more complex and diversified than their official implicit definition suggested. What the management saw as useless visits resulting in long lines to the detriment of the efficient processing of people and files appeared to be motivated by social anxiety, the need of isolated individuals to talk to someone and be advised on many aspects of life, far from mere paperwork requirements. Similarly, whereas the dominant discourse blamed the degradation of these relationships on the growing "incivility" of clients, I showed that the problem lay less in their "aggressiveness" than in the social violence they were subjected to (poverty, unemployment, despair); street-level welfare bureaucracies became the place where they could express their anger toward "the social system," which these institutions embodied. While the work of reception agents was mostly seen as unimportant and routine, I unveiled its unexpected difficulties and the complexity of their social roles, from compassionate assistance to police-like control, from cold anonymous bureaucratic attitudes to individual involvement, from technical efficiency to personalized advice and support. Lastly, whereas "communication skills" and "individual character" were regarded as the two variables of reception work, I identified both the structural causes in the problems and the variety of factors coming into play, including social backgrounds, previous work experience and socialization, race, gender, generation, local organizational features, and the characteristics of clients.

Having no special reason to please policy officials by writing a report fulfilling their (vague) expectations, I was able to present these results quite bluntly and to conceptualize them in my own scientific language without fear of possible negative reactions from those who had commissioned the study; unlike them I was able to claim, as ethnographers do, that "I was there."[22] Most important, I endeavored to present a systematic demonstration that could not be reduced to the personal feelings or preferences of a young scholar.

An Ethnographic Research and Its Publics

The question I would like to address now is precisely one that deals with the reception of this research. This will allow me to show how policy ethnography can become public, what its various publics can be, and how in turn the reception of research can impact the autonomy of a scholar in his or her subsequent work.

I initially presented my research in a 150-page report to the welfare agency I worked on (and, to some extent, for). During this first official reception nothing really happened. My partners in the research department of the welfare organization were very satisfied with my work. The managers of this agency showed polite interest but were hardly enthusiastic—to say the least—about research insisting on domination and micropower relationships, when the problems were officially framed in terms of coproduction, negotiation, good communication, and service relationships. In the local offices where I had conducted my fieldwork, my research was not greeted with unanimous approval either, especially in one case I had described as following a "bureaucratic" model of client reception, contrasting it with a "social work" model. Our meeting mostly revolved around explaining my use of the term *bureaucratic* in reference to Max Weber, without the negative connotation it carries in ordinary language. I did not succeed in convincing my interlocutors, and this unfortunate adjective prevented them from hearing what my research could possibly bring to their reflection. I had better feedback from the street-level bureaucrats I had observed, who, even though my study occasionally shed light on negative aspects of their attitudes and behaviors, were happy to see their work acknowledged as difficult and worthwhile for academic research. Some of them thanked me and expressed the wish that my findings would draw the attention of their superiors to their working conditions. If this was at all the case it was in a delayed and indirect way. The contact I had with the reception agents after I finished my fieldwork was unfortunately only indirect. They were not invited to the meetings at which I presented my research and could only react by sending me a letter after they had read my report.

Unfortunately, and this says a lot about how welfare agencies envisioned their relationships with the public at the time, no meeting with clients was organized, and as a result I could not have any conversation with them about my research.

Three years later this study was published as a book in a new political science series by a second-rank academic publishing company with mostly law and economics handbooks in its catalogue.[23] I was invited to present it at a few conferences organized by charities, such as ATD Quart Monde, influential in the field of French philanthropy. The book received unexpected media coverage, with a dozen reviews or interviews in the press and some TV and radio appearances. This was far more than I could have anticipated as an unknown young scholar living far from Paris with no connections to journalists and working in a university department that, at the time, had no regular contact with the national press. This media attention was mainly due to a few aggressions of officials by clients in public services that had occurred around that same period and had stirred public discussions of bureaucratic encounters. After debunking the official problematic of "the modernization of public services," I was given the opportunity to explain why the media's framing of the "violent events at the frontline of public services" in terms of "incivilities" and "antisocial behavior" should at least be examined from the broader perspective of the various forms of violence involved, including the social and symbolic violence welfare recipients were subjected to.[24]

The book gained even more attention in academic circles than I could have hoped for. It was awarded a prize by the Académie des Sciences Morales et Politiques, received numerous positive reviews in many French social science journals (again far beyond my expectations), and appeared to be of interest to a wide array of scholars with varying interests. Those interested in social work and welfare found in it useful insights on the bureaucratic aspects of these domains. Political scientists and policy analysts welcomed the book's contribution to the political sociology of institutions and to the street-level bureaucracy approach of public policy,[25] which was then burgeoning in France. The reception of my research also benefited from the growing interest in ethnographic methods, which were often used in methodology courses as an example of how to conduct fieldwork. And the book's theoretical framework, combining a structural approach inspired by Bourdieu with close attention to strategic face-to-face interactions from a Goffmanian perspective, attracted the attention of scholars from various fields.

My writing strategy certainly helped in gaining this attention, both inside and outside of academic circles. This strategy was inspired by Goffman's focus on details and concrete situations in the service of theoretical assertions. Instead of abstract considerations and long literature discussions followed by empirical vignettes, I organized the book as a step-by-step demonstration simultaneously based on sociological assertions and fieldwork descriptions. The care I took in the writing style was aimed at illustrating the point I wanted to make: bureaucratic encounters cannot be reduced to an instrumental, functional, and routine exchange but are situations involving various important aspects of the clients' lives, and therefore imply strategic issues, tactics, values, and emotions. I considered these encounters an example of individual relationships with institutions, which resonated with the interests and personal experiences of readers in other settings.

The book sold quite well by French standards (around 4,000 copies, whereas most social science books typically sell 450 copies), especially for a volume based on fieldwork and published by a second-rank publisher. Three successive editions were issued by the original publisher (in 1999, 2003, and 2010); then came an English translation;[26] last a major publishing company (Points-Seuil) issued a new paperback edition in 2015.

It was only after the book received media coverage and academic attention that public administrations, including the one that originally commissioned the research, showed real interest in it. In short the research was initially a policy commission, which I was able to turn into critical academic research; it was well received by academics and to a lesser extent by the public; as a result of these favorable reviews rather than its contents (or perhaps I should say despite its contents), the work eventually attracted some interest from the agency that had commissioned me to do the study but had remained unconvinced by my findings. The book is now read or at least known by welfare managers. It is used as a reference for the training of bureaucrats in contact with clients to draw their attention to the social complexities of apparently mundane interactions at welfare offices. Yet its contents and style barely differ from the original report, which was largely ignored. This rather erratic circulation serves as a primary example of how the same policy ethnography research can cross the boundaries between professional, critical policy, and public knowledge, to borrow once again from Burawoy's typology. What could have been policy-driven research with a critical and academic orientation became public, and then, but only then, was it eventually used for policy purposes.

When Acknowledgment Allows Risky Strategies

The acknowledgment of my work by various types of interacting publics enabled me to propose a new research project to policymakers in 2000, a year after the book was published. This was the start of the second experience I will now discuss. This time the topic was of my own choosing, and it was a more controversial one. My intention was to study welfare fraud, not in order to analyze deviant behaviors but to investigate institutional practices of surveillance over the poor. At the time these control practices were seen as the dark side of welfare administration, and nobody wanted to talk about them. Welfare fraud was not yet the controversial topic that it already was in the U.S. and British media and in the political debates of those countries or that it would later become in France, especially under Sarkozy (2007–12). Far from informing the general public on how they weeded out the undeserving poor, as they would later do, welfare agencies kept quiet on these aspects, which were far less present than they currently are.

It would have been inconceivable for me to make such a proposal without the benefit of my previous experience. The research was nevertheless far more difficult. It took a year and a half of long and complex negotiations, with legal and bureaucratic obstacles piling up mainly because of internal conflict within the national welfare agency (Caisse Nationale des Allocations Familiales) between advocates and opponents of my project. For obscure reasons the new director, seemingly opposed to the project, canceled the research contract we had just signed. The story could have ended there, but I refused to give up and received internal support. After another year of negotiations I was finally able to conduct the research according to my own agenda. The fieldwork, however, was no cakewalk. At the local level some of the managers were reluctant to let me and my coworkers access their staff for interviews or observation. In one case the obstacles were so discouraging that I decided to move to another site. I was quite surprised to watch a television documentary on fraud investigations in this same welfare office a few weeks later. Evidently they viewed journalists, but not social scientists, as allies. I also encountered some rather unenthusiastic welfare investigators who did not want to be bothered in their personal routine by an external observer, often suspected of being assigned by their superiors to assess their work. At the time these investigators had recently created a union and were (unsuccessfully) organizing to improve their status and salary. Despite these difficulties I was able to conduct my fieldwork, which resulted in a report submitted to the commissioner in 2003.

I knew it was a touchy subject, but, as before, I decided not to water down the presentation of my findings in anticipation of the reactions from my institutional partners, even though I did not expect that they would find my conclusions very pleasant. These conclusions completely undermined the official discourse on legal rigor and pointed to the fuzziness of the rules to be enforced, the incoherence of bureaucratic practices, and the arbitrariness of decisions.[27] I showed how the emerging welfare surveillance and sanction policy, which some promoted as a way to enforce the rules more strictly, actually relied on what I called a "legal bricolage" by welfare investigators, who themselves did not strictly stick to the rules: in the making of their decisions, personal social stereotypes were just as involved as official norms.

I was aware that it could well be my last collaboration with the agency. However, I made these statements acceptable by giving a very detailed account in a report that was longer and more thorough than the ones they were used to. Even though they were not very happy with my conclusions, they could not say I was wrong or underinformed, even on technical aspects. In other words, I had to display expert knowledge on institutional rules, practices, and mechanisms to legitimize my critical approach.

I decided not to publish my results immediately in order to ease possible tensions and to complement this research with further work. My plan was, first, to publish a few serious academic papers (which I have done), then to put out a book, which could draw the attention of a wider public (which I have yet to do), and finally to disseminate my results as a way to intervene in the public debate (which I have not really done either). Because of other ongoing projects and various academic duties, I was unable to achieve this program in the time frame I had initially scheduled. As a result it was necessary to update my data, especially as dramatic changes concerning surveillance and sanctions in welfare have occurred since I conducted my first researches.

Therefore, and this will be my third and last example, I contacted my institutional partners again, in 2012, and offered to update my previous research. This time they expressed immediate and enthusiastic interest. They gave me valuable information on how to proceed, asking me to send my proposal just in time to benefit from the remaining funds available in their budget. While I did have to go through the formal review process, I already knew that my project would be accepted before I sent it (provided, of course, it was a serious one!). Over the previous five years welfare fraud had become a major topic, and welfare agencies were more willing to show their results in that domain than they were when I conducted my previous fieldwork. But I think the main reason my contacts were unexpectedly supportive lies in the reception of that first book, almost fifteen years after its initial publication. During our first meeting, and to my surprise, they told me of the book, "It's our bible." Given the reception of my original research, I was completely unsuspecting and unaware of the book's prominence, but it served me greatly.

It conferred on me both academic and institutional legitimacy, which helped me get my proposal accepted, gain access to people and confidential documents, get assistance in collecting data, and so on. Despite the very sensitive nature of the topic of welfare fraud and surveillance, which was and is often debated in the media and political arena, I had never before been granted support as keen as what I enjoyed in this still ongoing research. Naturally certain precautions had to be considered. On a few occasions I have received requests for interviews from the media and once from one of the main trade unions in France for a piece in its newsletter. Before accepting I made sure to inform my institutional partners and to secure their formal agreement since our contractual relationship is still ongoing. I have also made sure to avoid openly controversial answers and to prevent negative reactions that could have an impact on the continuation of my research.

In such situations one is never too cautious. For instance, I was invited to talk about surveillance of the poor and the unemployed at a social forum organized in a small town by alternative and activist organizations. There were around twenty people in the audience, the atmosphere was lively and warm, and I felt I could speak freely, which I did. I did not know there was a journalist among the twenty people there. She did not talk to me, but she later published an account of my presentation in the local newspaper, claiming that I had "shocked" the audience when I explained how intrusive welfare investigations could be. This journalistic account of my modest experience as a public ethnographer unveiling some hidden aspects of current policies to political activists could have been the end of my access to the local welfare organization in which I was conducting the fieldwork. Apparently I was lucky enough that nobody from the agency "read what the paper wrote I said."[28]

This misadventure shows that there is a time for policy ethnography to become public, here in the sense of the dissemination of research results in activist networks. Addressing an audience of policymakers, radical political activists, or the general public is a matter of timing more than a permanent option. The necessary collaboration with policy agencies requires that some encounters be postponed to avoid conflicts liable to endanger one's ability to carry out fieldwork. This caution does not amount to self-censorship; it is above all pragmatic—and temporary.

Conclusion

Having started this chapter with Burawoy's plea for public sociology, I wish to come back to him in this conclusion. In his introduction to a special issue on "precarious engagements in the realm of public sociology" published in *Current Sociology*, Burawoy uses Bourdieu's phrase and his concept of *field* to describe sociology as a "combat sport" and to consider the difficulties for sociology to become "public" by situating them at the intersection of the academic and the political fields.[29] Burawoy usefully elaborates on the notion of "combat sport" applied to sociology by distinguishing three forms of struggle in which sociologists have to engage: the fight against common sense, the combat with "doxosophers" (such as journalists, experts, and politicians) who wish to impose their view of the social world as the only relevant and legitimate one, and the internal competition in the academic field with other disciplines (such as philosophy or economics) and within the discipline of sociology. However, he misses an important point in the fact that Bourdieu's analogy does not refer to just any combat sport but specifically to martial arts. This is worth mentioning because the reference to martial arts invites us to think of a form of combat in which one manipulates the opponent's force against him or her rather than to confront it with one's own force (*jitsu*). The "opponents" here are those in power who exert social, political, economic, and symbolic domination: governments, political leaders, dominant media, financial institutions, and others. Sociologists and, by extension, social scientists are never in a position to engage in a direct confrontation with them. Instead they may use the resources accumulated by the powerful (information, finances, opportunities for dissemination) to conduct critical research challenging dominant views and to intervene in the public debate on this basis.

In this sense policy ethnography can be defined as a combat sport and, more precisely, as a martial art. It requires using the informational, financial, or symbolic resources provided by policy institutions to construct critical knowledge of these institutions and of the policies they implement. There is indeed no other choice than to simultaneously or successively play at different levels (policy organizations, academia, the media) and to address different publics (policymakers, academics, journalists, activists, the general public) in order to combine a study of bureaucracy from the inside with a critical approach and, on this basis, to propose analyses aimed at achieving both academic and public relevance.

In my view this combination is necessary for policy ethnography to claim political relevance. Providing an insider's view without a critical horizon would be akin to reducing policy ethnography to instrumental expert knowledge. Conversely, making critical statements without detailed internal knowledge would pose the risk of oversimplifying and of doing nothing but preaching to the choir. In my case criticizing the coercion and surveillance of the poor on moral and political grounds can convince only those who share these moral and political preferences. Unveiling how coercion and surveillance actually work, their rationales, their impact on people, which is in my view what policy ethnography is about, is probably more effective in forcing policymakers to examine the contradictions in their policies and in challenging the popular views disseminated among the general public on these questions.

Notes

I want to thank Jonathan Benthall and Didier Fassin for their comments and Jean-Yves Bart, Patrick Brown, and Marion Lieutaud for their linguistic revisions on a first version of this chapter. Jean-Yves is supported by the Excellence Initiative of the University of Strasbourg, funded by the French government's Future Investments program.

1   Discussed in Tedlock 2005; Fassin 2013.
2   See, for instance, Manuela Ivone Cunha's chapter in this volume on policy-oriented audiences of ethnography.
3   See Burawoy's (2005) call for a public sociology. To avoid burdening the text, from now on I use the terms *ethnography* and *sociology* indifferently when I refer to problems they have in common. I return to a more specific distinction between the two disciplines when necessary.
4   Burawoy 2005: 9.
5   For anthropology, see Shore and Wright 1997; Shore et al. 2011; Wedel et al. 2005. For critical policy studies, see Orsini and Smith 2011.
6   See, for example, my paper on Bourdieu as a policy advisor (Dubois 2011).
7   See my paper on the topic (Dubois 2014a).
8   Beaud and Weber 2010.
9   In 2009 there were 192 assistant professors and full professors in anthropology, ethnology, and prehistory, in comparison with 344 in political science and 835 in sociology and population studies (Ministère de l'Enseignement Supérieur 2008–9).

10   Castel 2000; Lemieux et al. 2010.

11   Jeanpierre and Mosbah-Natanson 2008.

12   See Noël 2012.

13   The first series of this kind was "Liber–Raisons d'agir" (Liber–Reasons for Action), launched by Bourdieu (1998) in 1996 with his pamphlet on television.

14   See, for instance, the series "La République des idées" launched by the historian and sociologist Pierre Rosanvallon in 2002 and published by Le Seuil.

15   Bezès et al. 2005.

16   Bourdieu 2000.

17   Brisebarre 1993.

18   See my chapter (Dubois 2015).

19   Mills 2000.

20   Dubois 2009, 2015.

21   Boltanski and Thévenot 2006.

22   To use Clifford Geertz's (1988) phrase.

23   Dubois 1999.

24   For instance, in an interview on violence in public services published in *Libération*, October 18, 1999, or during a TV debate on the same question channel *La Cinquième*, January 31, 2000.

25   Inspired by Lipsky 1980.

26   Dubois 2010.

27   Dubois 2014b.

28   To paraphrase Greenberg 1993.

29   Burawoy 2014.

References

Beaud, Stéphane, and Florence Weber. 2010. *Guide de l'enquête de terrain*. 4th ed. Paris: La Découverte.

Bezès, Philippe, Michel Chauvière, Jacques Chevallier, Nicole Montricher, and Frédéric Ocqueteau, eds. 2005. *L'État à l'épreuve des sciences sociales: La fonction recherche dans les administrations sous la Ve république*. Paris: La Découverte.

Boltanski, Luc, and Laurent Thévenot. 2006. *On Justification: Economies of Worth*. Princeton: Princeton University Press.

Bourdieu, Pierre. 1998. *On Television*. Translated by Priscilla Parkhurst Ferguson. New York: New Press.

———, ed. 2000. *The Weight of the World: Social Suffering in Contemporary Society*. Translated by Priscilla Parkhurst Ferguson. Stanford: Stanford University Press.

Brisebarre, Anne-Marie. 1993. "The Sacrifice of 'Id Al-Kabir: Islam in the French Suburbs." *Anthropology Today* 9.1: 9–12.

Burawoy, Michael. 2005. "For Public Sociology." *American Sociological Review* 70.1: 4–28.

———. 2014. "Introduction: Sociology as a Combat Sport." *Current Sociology* 62.2: 140–55.

Castel, Robert. 2000. "La sociologie et la réponse à la 'demande sociale.'" *Sociologie du Travail* 42.2: 281–87.

Dubois, Vincent. 1999. *La vie au guichet: Relation administrative et traitement de la misère*. Paris: Economica.

———. 2009. "Towards a Critical Policy Ethnography: Lessons from Fieldwork on Welfare Control in France." *Critical Policy Studies* 3.2: 221–39.

———. 2010. *The Bureaucrat and the Poor: Encounters in French Welfare Offices*. Aldershot, UK: Ashgate.

———. 2011. "Cultural Capital Theory vs. Cultural Policy Beliefs: How Pierre Bourdieu Could Have Become a Cultural Policy Advisor and Why He Did Not." *Poetics* 39.6: 491–506.

———. 2014a. "The Economic Vulgate of Welfare Reform: Elements for a Socioanthropological Critique." *Current Anthropology* 55.S9: 138–46.

———. 2014b. "The State, Legal Rigor and the Poor: The Daily Practice of Welfare Control." *Social Analysis* 58.2: 38–55.

———. 2015. "Critical Policy Ethnography." In *Handbook of Critical Policy Studies*, edited by Frank Fischer, Douglas Torgerson, Michael Orsini, and Anna Durnova, 462–80. Cheltenham-Northampton, UK: Edward Elgar.

Fassin, Didier. 2013. "Why Ethnography Matters. On Anthropology and Its Publics." *Cultural Anthropology* 28.4: 621–46.

Geertz, Clifford. 1988. "Being There: Anthropology and the Scene of Writing." In *Works and Lives: The Anthropologist as Author*, 1–24. Stanford: Stanford University Press.

Greenberg, Ofra. 1993. "When They Read What the Papers Say We Wrote." In *When They Read What We Write*, edited by Carol B. Brettell, 107–18. Westport, CT: Bergin and Garvey.

Jeanpierre, Laurent, and Sébastien Mosbah-Natanson. 2008. "French Sociologists and the Public Space of the Press: Thoughts Based on a Case Study (Le Monde, 1995–2002)." In *Intellectuals and Their Publics: Perspectives from the Social Sciences*, edited by Christian Fleck, Andreas Hess, and E. Stina Lyon, 173–91. Farnham, UK: Ashgate.

Lemieux, Cyril, Laurent Mucchielli, Erik Neveu, and Cécile Van de Velde. 2010. "Le sociologue dans le champ médiatique: Diffuser et déformer?" *Sociologie* 2.1. http://sociologie.revues.org/351.

Lipsky, Michael. 1980. *Street-Level Bureaucracy: Dilemmas of the Individual in Public Services*. New York: Russell Sage Foundation.

Mills, C. Wright. 2000. *The Sociological Imagination*. Oxford: Oxford University Press.

Ministère de l'Enseignement Supérieur. 2008–9. "Quelques éléments démographiques détaillés relatifs aux personnels enseignants de l'enseignement supérieur." http://cache.media.enseignementsup-recherche.gouv.fr/file/statistiques/08/3/demo g09fniv2_172083.pdf.

Noël, Sophie. 2012. *L'édition indépendante critique: Engagements politiques et intellectuels*. Lyon: Presses de l'ENSSIB. http://www.decitre.fr/livres/1-edition -independante-critique-engagements-politiques-et-intellectuels-9791091281041 .html.

Orsini, Michael, and Miriam Smith. 2011. *Critical Policy Studies*. Vancouver: UBC Press.

Shore, Cris, and Susan Wright. 1997. "Policy: A New Field of Anthropology." In *Anthropology of Policy: Critical Perspectives on Governance and Power*, edited by Cris Shore and Susan Wright, 3–39. London: Routledge.

Shore, Cris, Susan Wright, and Davide Però, eds. 2011. *Policy Worlds: Anthropology and the Analysis of Contemporary Power*. New York: Berghahn Books.

Tedlock, Barbara. 2005. "The Observation and Participation of and the Emergence of Public Ethnography." In *The Sage Handbook of Qualitative Research*, edited by Norman Denzin and Yvonna Lincoln, 151–71. Thousand Oaks, CA: Sage.

Wedel, J. R., Cris Shore, Gregory Feldman, and Stacy Lathrop. 2005. "Toward an Anthropology of Public Policy." *Annals of the American Academy of Political and Social Science* 600.1: 30–51.

Part III

—Tensions

9

Academic Freedom at Risk

The Occasional Worldliness of Scholarly Texts

NADIA ABU EL-HAJ

It was August 2007, following two institutional votes in favor of my tenure, when a petition turned up online: "Deny Nadia Abu El-Haj Tenure." The petition was posted on petitiononline.com, and by the end of the month approximately 1,900 people had signed it. Presumably initiated by a Barnard College graduate and West Bank settler, the petition placed my tenure case in the public domain. Over the next several months the *Jewish Weekly*, the *Boston Globe*, the Jewish *Forward*, the *Nation,* and the *New York Times,* among other publications, printed articles or op-eds about the so-called controversy. There was one vote left—that of Columbia University's Ad-Hoc Committee on Tenure. As I elaborate in what follows, this public brouhaha was but one instance of a broad political attack aimed at the U.S. academy (and its teaching of Palestine and the Middle East) at the time: Was I yet another instance of rampant anti-Semitism masking itself as anti-Israel critique in U.S. universities? Had the U.S. academy become such a bastion of liberalism that it was out of touch with the country as a whole? Should the public have any say in adjudicating tenure cases inside the academy? Was the petition legitimate?

In this essay I think about how and why my first book became an object of public controversy. An academic book that had its origins in a PhD dissertation, it was not written for the public at large. Based on archival and ethnographic research, *Facts on the Ground* (2001) is an anthropological study of the practices of biblical and Israeli archaeology in Palestine and Israel from the late nineteenth century through the post-1967 period. It traces the emergence of a specific historical imaginary, embodied in archaeological remains and architectural designs, through which Israel's founding was produced as the accomplishment of a nation "returning home." The book analyzes one domain of practice—scientific, cultural, political—through which a project of *settler* nationhood effaced the very colonial foundations on which it was built: that is, the expulsion of Palestine's already existing population and the erasure of alternative histories of the land.

This essay unfolds in five parts. First, I sketch the book's argument. Second, I give an account of the campaign against my tenure by placing criticisms of my work within the larger context of the culture wars that have rocked the U.S. academy at different times and in different ways since the 1980s. Third, I consider the broader conditions of possibility within which attacks on academics writing on the Middle East in general and on Palestine in particular emerged as particularly powerful within U.S. society in the post-9/11 period. And fourth, I take my discussion into the present and discuss current campaigns to silence critical speech about the Israeli state on U.S. college campuses. In so doing I trace the emergence of specific tactics as they have shifted over the past decade or more, and I consider their wider resonance and effects. In my conclusion I return to the question of authorship, the public domain, and the worldliness of a scholarly text.

More generally this essay considers the public life of a specific anthropological text in order to address a broader set of questions about scholarship, academic freedom, and free speech in the context of American society over the past decade or more. Specific to the topic of public ethnography, I ask: What difference might it make that the book is an *anthropology* of Israel? On what forms of evidence and authority are anthropological texts understood to rest, and what kinds of problems might those foundations pose for our credibility in the public domain? Even more generally, in this essay I think anthropologically—albeit not ethnographically—about the conditions of possibility within which such public campaigns operate. Moving into the present, I trace the ways in which a campaign against professors, their scholarship, and the question of academic freedom has morphed into a much broader attack on free speech itself: today student groups face sustained campaigns to silence their activism on the question of Palestine. I explore the terms—the facts, the affects—through which particular persons or groups of persons are interpellated as subjects to whom such Zionist-activist campaigns speak. And I ask: Who are the publics brought into being through this work of interpellation? And how and why might these campaigns resonate?

The Book

Facts on the Ground examines the significance of archaeology to the Israeli
state and society, the role the discipline played in the formation and enactment of the state's settler-national historical imaginary and in the substantiation of its territorial claims. It focuses on select archaeological projects that
formed the foundations and cultural contours of settler nationhood (1880s
through 1950s) and that facilitated its territorial extension, appropriation,
and gradual reconfiguration following the 1967 war. These same archaeological research projects, I argue, were simultaneously fundamental to the work of
building the discipline of Israeli archaeology, to demarcating its central research
agendas, and to crystallizing the discipline's paradigms of argumentation and
practice. Looking at Israeli state formation through the lens of archaeology—
as scholarly discipline, as cultural and political practice—I demonstrate the
particular form that Jewish settler nationhood took and specific struggles it
faced as it emerged ever more powerfully in Palestine and Israel.

Palestine and Israel, the colony and the metropole, were and are the same
place, the former rapidly and repeatedly transformed into a cultural and historical space to which Jewish settlers would lay *national* claim and over which they
would assert sovereign ownership. Archaeology's centrality to Jewish settler-
nationhood can be understood best in relation to its continual assertion and
repeated enactment of that national claim through its very work. Positioned
squarely within a literature in the history and philosophy of science, *Facts on the
Ground* analyzes the epistemological practices, historical arguments, and material artifacts and landscapes through which the truth of the historic Jewish
claim to Palestine was made visible and demonstrable. (For example, I do close
readings of the evidentiary terrain of the Israelite settlement debate in the 1950s
and I examine the work of excavating and rebuilding the Old City of Jerusalem
in the post-1967 period.) Rather than reading Israeli archaeology as simply a
handmaiden of Zionist ideology, I elaborate the ways in which settler-national
ideology and archaeological and historical practice met and informed one
another on shared epistemological ground—that is, on the ground of a shared
commitment to a culture of fact (geographic, historic, biblical, material).

The Controversy

The petition was not the start of the campaign against my tenure. The campaign had begun well over a year before. In May 2006, not long after my
department's decision to put me up for tenure was sent to the Barnard College

provost's office, an article appeared on the *History News Network* website. A mother-daughter team, both Barnard alumnae and neither of whom I had ever met or taught, wrote a review of my book. They began by equating me to a magician's assistant: "You know, the girl who stands on the stage looking so good that you watch her and miss the sleight of hand that lets the magician make a rabbit vanish into thin air." The rabbit that I make disappear is the very facts of Zionist claims to Palestine, "archaeological evidence of an ancient Jewish presence in the land [that] constitutes a compelling claim to Jewish indigeneity."[1] According to Diana Muir and Avigail Applebaum, the book's sleight of hand operates through its theoretical-qua-epistemological commitments: taking a quotation entirely out of context, they argue that the book is written "within a scholarly tradition that 'reject(s) a positivist commitment to scientific methods . . .' and is 'rooted in . . . post structuralism, philosophical critiques of foundationalism, Marxism and critical theory . . . developed in response to specific postcolonial political movements.'"[2] Grounded in the repeated charge of the book's being mired in "post-modern theory" (and for the two authors, it really is a charge) and the argument that I reduce Zionist claims to the land to the status of "mere myth" (meaning unabashed fabrication), the mother-daughter team refute what they understand to be the book's major historical claims and reveal its purported political intent. Rather than rehearse their polemic here, I want to consider more generally the contexts within which Muir and Applebaum's reading had traction and the polemics into which the book was cast.

Criticisms of *Facts on the Ground* and the broader opposition to my tenure rotated around a series of accusations: about competence (Did I know Hebrew? Had I spent any time in Israel? Did I know anything about archaeology?) and about bias (Was the book nothing more than an ideological assault? Can a Palestinian really write about Israel?). But those criticisms were also the tip of a much larger iceberg. Critical reviews and the Zionist campaign more broadly spoke a language of critique and accusation characteristic of much longer-term battles within and over the academy; twenty-plus years after the culture wars of the 1980s and a decade after the science wars of the 1990s acrimonious arguments over the canon versus postpositivist epistemological commitments, about postcolonial theory, identity politics, and scholarly authority had deep roots in the United States, inside the academy and beyond it. As Jonathan Cole argues, "The attack on free inquiry has been a feature of the culture wars for decades. The advocacy groups surrounding these efforts have long had the resources to lobby government figures, and to organize alumni and students, with the goal of generating public outrage and eventual pressure on the university to abandon some of its basic commitments." Cole notes, however, that there was something distinct about attacks on the academy during the George W. Bush administration: those groups now had "a powerful voice in the White House." Moreover, following the 9/11 attacks "the ranks of their followers swelled."[3] As external pressure rose on the right of the public—and politicians[4]—to adjudicate hiring and tenure cases, academic freedom came under increasing assault. The post-9/11 campaigns against specific faculty members notwithstanding, this was not a political project aimed at individuals per se, Cole insists. It was an assault on the whole structure of the university and on its very commitment that the authority to "establish what is or is not valued or labeled as 'high quality work'" resides with the professoriate, not with the administration or outside groups.[5]

In the post-9/11 period the question of Palestine was at the vortex of the culture wars, now reconfigured around the threat of (Islamic) terror and the U.S. war on it. *Facts on the Ground* is a book about Palestine and Israel, a conflict understood to harbor its own (Muslim) terrorists.[6] But in terms of what it signaled in the latest culture wars, it was about much more than that: it is a book squarely situated within the legacy of postcolonial studies and, to boot, one that takes its inspiration from a critical literature on the history and philosophy of science.[7] As such *Facts on the Ground* was the perfect object to be pulled into that post-9/11 storm. In Edward Said's terms it emerged as an "event," "part of the social world" in that time and place because it brought together a series of issues—political, epistemological, cultural—that spoke to culture wars, old and new.[8] To quote James R. Russell, a professor of Armenian Studies at Harvard University, "*Facts on the Ground* fits firmly into the postmodern academic genre, in which facts and evidence are subordinate to, and mediated by, a 'discourse.' There is no right or wrong answer, just competitive discourses." With Said as its father figure, not just Middle East Studies but "other branches of the humanities" as well have "fallen prey to ideology," Russell continues.[9] Aren Maeir likewise argues, "This book is a highly ideologically driven political manifesto, with a glaring lack of attention to details and to the broader context. In part, this perspective can be explained as the product of a postmodern/postcolonial deconstructionist approach to the social sciences." (The other part is my hostility to the Israeli state.)[10]

As an *anthropological* text, however, there were also more specific problems that *Facts on the Ground* posed. According to Alexander Joffe, a biblical archaeologist and neoconservative Zionist activist, "The lack of comparison is the final, and fatal flaw, since it means *the reader must rely on the total immersion experience of the author, and her observer-dependent conclusions*, including her political agenda."[11] More bluntly Maeir writes, "Throughout the book she repeatedly quotes anonymous archaeologists to support her contentions. Although it might be claimed that she does this to 'protect' her sources, one wonders whether the real purpose is to protect the verifiability of these statements."[12] With a "counterpolitics [that] is explicitly Palestinian," writes Joffe, and "without that even quavering aspiration to self regulation, objectivity, and truth, however vague and elusive these may be," *Facts on the Ground* is written from within a "Marcuse-Said-Foucault tradition," a tradition of "celebrity provocateurs," and that leaves us with "results [that] may be dark indeed."[13] The unreliability of the postcolonial intellectual—the *Palestinian*[14]—converges here with a distrust of ethnographic methods to produce a profound state of suspicion: Was I just making things up? How could we possibly know? If as Steven Shapin and Simon Shaffer have argued in *Leviathan and the Air-Pump*, only "gentlemen" were considered "reliable witnesses" to the experimental method in early modern science, for my critics a Palestinian scholar doing ethnographic research on Israeli society is an unreliable witness prima facie.[15]

The Conditions of Possibility

Following the attacks on the Twin Towers and the Pentagon in September 2001, U.S. society experienced a radical shift to the right—a shift in which the specter of the threatening Arab or Muslim terrorist loomed large in the national imaginary. But in providing a genealogy of the Zionist activist campaigns that targeted scholars of the Middle East in the early 2000s one needs to begin before that fateful day. Of course there is a long history in the United States of organized efforts to silence critical speech on Israel and Palestine. As documented by Zachary Lockman, beginning in the 1980s both the American Israel Public Affairs Committee and the Anti-Defamation League of B'nai B'rith "compiled and circulated material accusing various scholars of being anti-Israel propagandists and pro-Arab apologists." They produced "blacklists" of scholars, and "there is evidence that efforts were also made to try to prevent otherwise qualified scholars (some of them Jews) from securing academic positions because they were deemed critical of Israeli policies."[16] The attacks on Said, including the death threats that he faced for decades, are but the most prominent examples of such attempts at public defamation and intimidation.

Nevertheless the Second Intifada that began in the fall of 2000 marked an important turning point. It produced the possibility for a reinvigorated Zionist activist campaign that targeted intellectuals critical of the Israeli state. From my experience working and writing in the American academy, I would argue that there was a significant shift between the time of the Oslo Accords (signed in 1993) and the beginning of the Second Intifada. Following Oslo, with a two-state solution presumably on the table, it became more possible to speak critically of Israel (especially if one did not touch the question of 1948). Why? Perhaps because there was a well-articulated discourse (a fantasy, one might suggest) that a solution was now in the cards. Political critique emerged as seemingly inconsequential; we could now "all" agree that the occupation was bad and a two-state solution was in the offing; what one thought about 1948, well, perhaps it no longer mattered very much at all. In the context of a relatively liberal discipline such as anthropology, the post-Oslo period was a moment in which it became markedly easier to engage in critical speech about the Israeli state. There was still significant push-back, especially if one spoke or wrote about the foundations of Zionism and about 1948, but that push-back was no longer characterized by the near total silencing that had once dominated the field.

The Second Intifada shattered that "liberal opening." Almost immediately I faced strong and angry reactions to my work—and to my politics more generally. How could I not unequivocally condemn Hamas? How could one even try to explain suicide bombings? The stakes had shifted. The barriers to critical speech were going back up. Suicide bombers targeting Tel Aviv, Haifa, and other cities and towns brought Israeli society and even many of its most anemic and ambivalent supporters in the United States to the point of near hysteria. The peace movement in Israel and its counterparts in the U.S. Jewish community fell apart; (many) liberals in the United States saw the Palestinian resistance as monstrous. The space for speaking and writing critically about Israel in the United States narrowed, including within liberal and left-wing intellectual circles. Quite crucially the problem of trying to explain suicide bombings in Tel Aviv prefigured the way discussions about Al Qaeda and its attack were going to unfold in the United States after 9/11.[17] To explain was to condone. To condone was to align oneself with a politics considered beyond the pale.

If the Second Intifada marked one crucial turning point in critical speech about the Israeli state in the academy and among the public at large, September 11 sealed the deal. It blew open a space for neoconservative Jewish pundits and activists who had long been struggling to realign U.S. policy in the Middle East to enter the political mainstream.[18] The Israeli state and its supporters in the United States had the perfect framework for equating the U.S. fight against "Muslim terrorists" with their struggle against Palestinians: *This is the same fight. Israel has long been on the front line. You now (finally) know what we have to deal with all the time.* Douglas Feith, Richard Perle, and Paul Wolfowitz, neoconservative Jewish thinkers and policymakers, worked hard to align U.S. interests ever more tightly to the defense of Israel; they were powerful figures in framing U.S. policy on the Middle East within the Bush administration.[19] More generally, new neoconservative Zionist groups were founded, and they launched well-funded and vociferous public campaigns to monitor and censor public debate on the question of Israel and Palestine in particular, and on U.S. policy in the Middle East more generally—focusing on the academy, where they believed anti-U.S. and anti-Israel speech and sentiment had taken hold, especially in the field of Middle East Studies. To focus on two groups most central to campaigns against professors of Palestine and Israel and of the Middle East more broadly at the turn of the millennium, 2002 marked the founding of both Campus Watch and the David Project. Campus Watch is an arm of the Middle East Forum—a neoconservative Zionist think tank founded by Daniel Pipes in 1990—and it generated dossiers on professors it deemed anti-American and anti-Semitic. It called upon students to report on the content of class lectures, promoting a culture of surveillance among Zionist activists on campus. The David Project was a major player in the fight that unfolded at Columbia about its "teaching of" Palestine and the Middle East in the years immediately prior to my tenure battle; it produced a film on what they claimed to be evidence of anti-Semitism among Columbia's Middle East faculty. And that film, *Columbia Unbecoming*, was used to make public the presumably secret crisis of anti-Semitism on campus and to force Columbia's administration to respond—both internally and for the public at large.[20] Monitoring and intervening in campus speech on Israel and Palestine was the mandate of all such groups. Smear campaigns, accusations of anti-Semitism, and efforts to intervene in hiring, promotion, and tenure decisions on specific faculty were their tactics.[21]

Tactics have shifted since those early post-9/11 years. No longer running just smear campaigns, activists have also turned to the legal domain, and they increasingly target not just professors and their writings but student groups as well.[22] These tactical shifts speak to a changing political landscape. With the country having pulled back from the mass hysteria of the immediate post-

9/11 period, the "swift-boating" tactics of the U.S. right don't play quite as well in the public domain. Moreover, with Palestine activism on the rise on college campuses, and with the Boycott, Divestment and Sanctions movement gaining momentum and support, Zionist groups are working hard to counter what they fear might be a tipping point in public support for the State of Israel—at least among the young and well educated. What, then, does this more recent work of Zionist political organizing look like? Through what forms of address is it extending from a challenge to academic freedom to a challenge to free speech? With what effects?

On the Existence of an Injured Public

March 2014. As part of Israel Apartheid Week, members of the Columbia Students for Justice in Palestine (SJP) applied for permission to hang their banner on Barnard Hall. This is a place where for as long as anyone can remember student groups have hung banners advertising student events. SJP hung their banner late on a Monday afternoon. Almost immediately the head of Columbia Hillel put out a call on Hillel's Facebook page to contact the Barnard administration. By allowing SJP to put their banner next to the Barnard logo, he wrote, the college was endorsing their politics. And that politics was anti-Semitic: the SJP logo was superimposed over a silhouette of the map of all of Palestine.[23] Within a few hours the president's office was inundated with hundreds of calls and emails from students and their parents, demanding the sign be taken down. By eight o'clock the next morning the sign was gone. The president apologized to the Hillel students, and the SJP was left out in the cold. The administration was worried about having "offended" Jewish students on an issue that "we all know," I was told, is "very difficult and sensitive" on college campuses. (After much negotiation Barnard's president hosted an event with SJP in the fall of 2014 as a way to make them feel more supported by the college and the community.)

September 2014. President Roderick J. McDavis of Ohio University challenged the newly elected Student Senate president, Megan Marzec, to take the "ice bucket challenge," that is, to dump a bucket of ice water over her head in order to raise awareness about ALS. Instead she chose to perform her own rendition of the Palestinian activist version of the ice bucket challenge. Rather than taking the "rubble bucket challenge," she poured fake blood over her head. As part of this politics as theater she recorded her own performance, during which she said, "I'm urging you and Ohio University to divest and cut all ties with academic and other Israeli institutions and businesses. . . . This bucket of blood symbolizes the thousands of displaced and murdered Palestinians, atrocities which OU is directly complicit in through cultural and economic support of the Israeli state."[24] The Student Senate's Twitter account condemned her almost immediately, and the campus group Bobcats of Israel and the Jewish Fraternity Alpha Epsilon Pi called for her resignation. The president of OU delivered a speech on civility: "I take great pride in the fact that Ohio University is a community that tackles hard issues head-on. The conflict in Israel and Gaza is no exception. But *the manner in which we conduct ourselves* as we exercise our right to free speech is of utmost importance.... When we engage in difficult dialogue on issues such as this, *we must do so with civility* and a deep appreciation for the diverse and resilient international community in which we live."[25]

August 2014. During the Gaza War in July 2014 Stephen Salaita, a scholar of Indigenous Studies who had recently accepted a position as associate professor in the American Indian Studies Program at the University of Illinois–Urbana Champaign, tweeted a series of critical remarks about the Israeli assault and about Israel's prime minister. In response to those tweets, and in the name of "civility," the provost of UIUC rescinded the job offer to Salaita, who had already resigned his job at Virginia Tech and moved his family halfway across the country.

What drives these kinds of administrative interventions into critical scholarship, speech, and political activism on the question of Palestine on university and college campuses today? The most obvious answer, and not an inaccurate one for being obvious, is donor money. Donors had threatened to discontinue contributing to the University of Illinois.[26] During the height of attacks on my colleagues and me at Barnard and Columbia donors threatened to never again give money to either institution. Did the defense of academic freedom trump the risk of losing donor money? That was the question the presidents of Barnard College and Columbia University faced.

Nevertheless far more is going on here than a simple financial calculus. *What is the language in and through which donor money speaks?* If instances of senior university administrators silencing critical scholarship and speech on the Israeli state are not merely cynical gestures of caving to donor pressure, what is the political imaginary in which it *might make sense* to shut down certain kinds of speech acts? Here enters a particular liberal sensibility, the appeal to which characterizes many a university response of late: civility.

The president of Ohio University is not alone in invoking the importance of civility in discussions of Israel and Palestine on college campuses. But what is civility? And what constitutes evidence of incivility? Let me turn the clock back a few years and discuss an interview that Nicholas Dirks, then incoming chancellor of the University of California at Berkeley, gave to the Berkeley News Center in 2012. An anthropologist and former vice president and dean of the faculty at Columbia University, Dirks produced a retrospective account of the so-called controversy involving Middle East Studies faculty that had rocked Columbia's campus nearly a decade before. The interviewer stated, "Floating around the Internet is a claim that at some point in your past . . . you signed a petition for Columbia to divest in all things Israel." He then asked the chancellor-designate to clarify his role. And let us be clear: this was not a question; it was a demand. If you want to be a powerful public figure, the interviewer effectively said to Dirks, distance yourself from that petition. And Dirks did just that. He never signed the petition, he told the interviewer. He somehow "found" his name on it and asked that it be removed.[27]

But Dirks said a lot more than that. He offered a description of Columbia in 2002, a time in which faculty members such as Joseph Massad, Rashid Khalidi, and Hamid Dabashi were under attack by Campus Watch and the David Project and, a few years later in the case of Khalidi, also by the chancellor of the New York public schools.[28] And in his account he made a specific claim. Flying in the face of the final report of an internal committee that Dirks himself had convened to investigate claims of anti-Semitism and the intimidation of Jewish students by faculty at Columbia's Department of Middle Eastern Languages and Cultures, Dirks said, "It seemed very difficult for some [Jewish] students *to find safe spaces* in which to talk about Israel where *they didn't feel* that the basic context in which they found themselves wasn't hugely not just anti-Israel, but by implication, anti-Jewish and anti-Semitic."[29]

The "safety," the "feelings" of Jewish students in an allegedly anti-Semitic atmosphere—those were the terms the David Project and Campus Watch had used to campaign against professors of Middle East Studies at Columbia in the early 2000s. While their campaigns ultimately failed at Columbia,[30] by the latter part of the decade that tactic was being taken to state legislatures and to the courts. Instead of (just) trying faculty in the public court of appeal, activists turned to antidiscrimination statutes that were designed to protect racial minorities and women in the U.S. educational system. Anti-Semitism constituted discrimination against Jewish students and thus could be adjudicated through the law. In fact, on moving to Berkeley in the summer of 2013, Dirks was walking into a situation in which the California State Assembly had passed a bill that equated the defense of Palestinian rights and criticism of the state of Israel with anti-Semitism. Moreover he was taking over a campus under investigation for violations of the antidiscrimination statutes of Title VI.[31] Complaints filed by Israel advocacy organizations in 2012 alleged that Palestine activism and scholarly lectures critical of Israeli policy created an anti-Semitic, hostile climate for Jewish students. Legal cases filed in the name of "defending Jewish students" have all since failed, dismissed as groundless.[32] But the story does not end there.

Enter *civility*. As Ali Abunimah has argued, while "the strategy . . . so far failed at the legal level, it is succeeding with university administrations, who are rushing to issue 'civility' statements explicitly or implicitly targeting utterers of speech critical of Israel."[33] In September 2014, on the occasion of UC Berkeley's celebration of the free speech movement and the return of students to campus for the new academic year, Dirks issued a public call for civility. "We can only exercise our right to free speech," he wrote, "insofar *as we feel safe* and respected in doing so, and this in turn requires that people treat each other *with civility*."[34] And Dirks is not alone: charges of incivility, together with calls for civility, are aimed at Students for Justice in Palestine organizations countrywide, and the UIUC is not giving Salaita his job back—even though, as a group of civil rights organizations declared in a letter to university administrations, there is no "civility" exception to free speech.[35]

But I want to shift this conversation away from the question of free speech and onto the meaning—or signs—of in/civility in such contexts. In his defense of the U.S. university Cole insists on the importance of civility, writing that a "basic commitment to civility and professional responsibility is part of the code of conduct at Columbia and at every other major American research university." But civility has nothing to do with comfort, Cole says. It has nothing to do with avoiding difficult topics, with making sure everyone feels emotionally safe. "Great universities," Cole writes, "are designed to be unsettling. They challenge orthodoxies and dogmas as well as social values and public policies." "In this process," he continues, "students and professors may sometimes feel intimidated, overwhelmed, and confused. But it is by working through this process that they learn to think better and more clearly for *themselves*."[36]

In the public domain today—and more specifically in relation to critical scholarship and speech on Israel and Palestine—the call for civility is being harnessed for very different ends. What does it mean to say that one (or certain people) can speak critically only if one makes sure that *others feel safe*? That one can *learn*—these are universities we are speaking about, after all—only if one feels comfortable, if one is not challenged in any way that might be disturbing to one's core values, commitments, beliefs? We are not talking about physical violence; no bodily threats have been documented or punished. We are talking about *speech* that apparently leaves one *feeling* upset, ill at ease, "unsafe."

What kinds of publics and subjects are being interpellated by such calls for civility—through accusations of anti-Semitism, of making Jewish students feel unsafe? The call for needing to make sure "Jewish students" feel safe and its implications for education as a critical and challenging project resonates with other demands being made on (some) college campuses. Take the call for trigger warnings on class syllabi. In March 2015 the student union at UC Santa Barbara passed a nonbinding resolution calling for warnings to be added to any assignments that might "elicit feelings of emotional or physical distress." Oberlin College issued the following guidelines to its faculty: "Triggers are not only relevant to sexual misconduct but also to anything that might cause trauma. Be aware of racism, classism, sexism, heterosexism, cissexism, ableism and other issues of privilege and oppression. Realize that all forms of violence are traumatic." According to the *Los Angeles Times*, Oberlin's instructions to faculty listed Chinua Achebe's novel *Things Fall Apart* "as one possible 'trigger' book because of its themes of colonialism, racism, religious prejudice and more."[37]

We can dismiss this as the effect of an overly coddled generation, as have some. Or of political correctness gone awry, as other critics have said. But perhaps the problem runs much deeper: trigger warnings, calls for civility, administration policies driven by the claim that *students feel unsafe*—rather than that they might actually *be unsafe*—is symptomatic of a political imaginary that resonates among many publics in the United States today.

In his book *The Shape of the Signifier*, Walter Benn Michaels writes critically about a politics rooted in a conception of (and commitment to) *difference* rather than *disagreement*. This is a form of politics, he argues, that emerged in the United States after the fall of the Soviet Union. Michaels maps what he sees as a shift in understandings of history and politics in the post–cold war era: the posthistoricists (whether of the left or right, Michaels insists) see a world divided not by ideology but by cultures. Moving from the question of culture to that of subject positions, Michaels argues that we have come to speak from the position of *who we are* rather than *what we might think*.[38]

The question of speaking from subject positions that are always already constituted is key to the political imaginary within which all this talk of feelings, safety, and civility appears and operates. Such speech is addressed to and works through publics imagined as structured around identities that can be injured and (only some of) which we must protect through "respect"—by limiting certain kinds of presumably inherently injurious speech.

But there is also a more specific story here. These subject positions, more accurately, *some of these* subject positions are saturated with what Joseph Masco has identified as a contemporary U.S. sensibility of ongoing, proliferating, and anticipatory danger and threat. In *Theater of Operations,* Masco elaborates the "national security affect" that structures anticipation politics and citizenship in the contemporary United States. Ours is a society organized around the anticipation of risk and by the infrastructures (including affective infrastructures) that ground and enable the War on Terror. This war operates in a world of endlessly proliferating and shifting "anticipatory dangers." Take the domain of biosecurity: even though the number of casualties that have resulted from bioterrorism is statistically insignificant (seven hundred injured by a salmonella attack in Oregon in 1984 and five by anthrax in 2001), it is a threat that preoccupies the political imaginary of the national security state. "The U.S. biosecurity project," Masco argues, relies on "a post-statistical mode of thinking . . . that makes strategic calculations about potential catastrophic threats and then mobilizes state resources against them *as if* they were confirmed events." Biosecurity posits hypothetical dangers (viruses, weapons of mass destruction) through which fear—an ongoing and proliferating *affective emergency*—is brought into being. And not only is that affective emergency essential to—not only is it *constitutive of*—the U.S. nation-state and its contemporary operations of power; so too does it have to be made. "The counterterror state, like the counter-communist state before it, attempts to install through domestic affective recruitments a new perception of everyday life that is unassailable."[39]

Masco's insights are helpful for making sense of all this talk of civility as it is elicited by and aimed at critical speech on Israel in the U.S. academy. Contrary to what many university administrations have assumed in responding to attacks on professors and students critical of the Israeli state, it is not simply that there is a public out there composed of the offended, the uncomfortable, or even the afraid Jewish student to which the administration must be sensitive, whom it must protect. That public was and is interpellated by well-funded organizations and centralized campaigns. That "Jewish public" is brought into being (to the extent that it is) by calls to respond *urgently* to the "existential threat" to Israel, to the rise of anti-Semitism on college campuses and elsewhere—to "post-statistical risks" that, through their constant iteration, through training fellowships by Hasbara, through Birthright trips to Israel are *produced as if they were real*.[40] And that is generating an affective politics—of unease, of being out of place, of fear—to which university administrations must now urgently respond. Zionist organizations proliferate risks. They testify to and circulate signs of anti-Semitism that seem to be everywhere, on the rise, all the time. And they name the *forms* anti-Semitism takes, just in case we don't already know. The Amcha Initiative's website lists the following three forms of anti-Semitism on U.S. campuses, among others: delegitimizing Israel, holding Israel to a higher standard, and promoting Boycott, Divestment, and Sanctions against Israel. Amcha, Campus Watch, the Louis D. Brandeis Center for Human Rights under Law—theirs is an urgent call to action, an affective emergency in the making.[41] And that affective emergency has been and is being made in and through the law.

On September 13, 2004, Kenneth L. Marcus, Deputy Assistant Secretary for Enforcement, delegated the authority of the Assistant Secretary for Civil Rights, issued a public memo on the problem of discrimination in education: "On the seventeenth day of September, we will observe Constitution Day. . . . It is appropriate, as we approach this day of education and remembrance, to address the protections that we receive through the Constitution and laws of the United States. On this occasion, I would like to address the right of all students, including students of faith, to be free from discrimination in our schools and colleges under Title VI of the Civil Rights Act of 1964 (Title VI) and Title IX of the Education Amendments Act of 1972 (Title IX)."[42]

The memo clarified, "The Office for Civil Rights (OCR) of the U.S. Department of Education (the Department) ensures compliance by recipients of the Department's financial assistance with federal laws prohibiting discrimination on the basis of race, national origin, sex, disability, or age." Protecting against discrimination on the grounds of religion, however, falls to other agencies, including the Department of Justice. Nevertheless the "OCR does aggressively enforce Title VI, which prohibits discrimination on the basis of race or national origin, and Title IX, which prohibits discrimination on the basis of sex. In OCR's experience, *some cases of religious discrimination may also involve racial, ethnic or sex discrimination*" (emphasis added).[43] What comes next is striking. In the wake of the September 11 attacks, Marcus reports, "OCR has received complaints of race or national origin harassment commingled with aspects of religious discrimination against Arab Muslim, Sikh, and Jewish students." Arab Muslim and Sikh students—we all know of the racist acts against Muslims and Sikhs that emerged after the September 11 attacks. That makes sense. Against Jewish students? It is not clear to me whether or how that would have come to pass, what the connection to September 11 could possibly have been. It is not clear to me whether or not his claim is even true, whether or not such reports could possibly have risen to a level in any way comparable to what Muslims and Sikhs (by way of "mistaken identification") suffered in the aftermath of 9/11. But perhaps in our post-statistical political imaginary in which risk and terror and the war on it operate, numbers matter not at all. What I do understand is what the effects of Marcus's work at the Office of Civil Rights have been.

As staff director at the U.S. Commission on Civil Rights, Marcus was appointed Assistant Secretary of Education for Civil Rights. He used that power to have Jews designated as a race who would thereby be entitled to protection under both Title VI of the Civil Rights Act of 1964 and Title IX of the Educational Amendments Act of 1972. And in his subsequent role as founder, president, and general counsel of the Brandeis Center for Human Rights under Law, he has been one of the prime movers of legal and legislative fights against critical speech on Israel in the academy. Marcus has helped to spearhead attacks on Title VI (of the Higher Education Act) funding for Middle East Centers deemed "biased" against Israel and legal suits brought under the provisions of Title VI (of the Civil Rights Act of 1964) and Title IX to protect Jewish students from a seemingly spiraling epidemic of anti-Semitism on U.S. college campuses.[44] The affective, legal, and rhetorical infrastructure of the ever expanding counterattack on Palestinian and other critics of the Israeli state are firmly in place even as they incite—and require—continuous reiteration.

Conclusion

Let me close by returning to the campaign against my tenure and, more generally, to the question of how one might want to think about scholarship— and not just free speech—in relation to political campaigns of this sort. The antitenure campaign was never really about me. At the most obvious level it wasn't about me because I was but one in a series of targets of Zionist political activism around the country. Moreover it wasn't about me because I didn't recognize myself in the representations that emerged in the public domain. Being a public figure of any sort must involve some kind of dissimulation of one's "real" self, but in this case it was a whole other person and certainly not my own voice or speech circulating in the public domain. As a specter of the

Palestinian, Arab, Muslim (and sometimes "inauthentic" because Christian Palestinian) scholar and her increasing presence and power in the United States and its academy,[45] or more generally as a specter of the postcolonial intellectual taking over "our" universities, "I" was circulating as but a sign in a renewed culture war in which, during the post-9/11 period, the question of Palestine stood center stage.

What about my scholarship? How do we think public ethnography vis-à-vis forms of misunderstanding, denial, ignorance, and criticism that seem to be deliberate misrepresentations of scholarly work? There were those who gladly proclaimed they had never read my book. (For example, the Barnard graduate-cum-settler admitted never having read the book when interviewed by Jane Kramer of the *New Yorker*.)[46] And there were those who, had they actually read the book, could not possibly have concluded what they did: (former) colleagues of mine, writers of scholarly reviews and journalistic renditions of the argument(s) that were either deliberate misreadings or signs of stunning intellectual incompetence. Let me be clear: these were individuals who would have disagreed with my arguments even if they had engaged and understood them. But they had not read *the book*. And in a context in which one's work is overpoliticized in the crudest of terms—that is, in which one's work is dragged into a polemic as a sign of political bias or intellectual fashion or as evidence of a tainted and unreliable witness (the wrong kind of Subject), how does one respond? Can one respond? *Should* one respond? For that matter, how does one write the *next* book?

I chose not to respond publicly. But it was not because I was worried about going public during a tenure decision. It was because I recognized that this wasn't a fight that was going to be won by me. More specifically this wasn't a fight that was going to be adjudicated on the basis of facts: Did I know Hebrew? Did I do more than two weeks of fieldwork? What was my position on the existence or nonexistence of ancient Israelites? What did I actually say about Palestinian demonstrators who destroyed Joseph's tomb?[47] This was a public argument about more fundamental ethical and political positions and divisions in the United States: it was about the value of free speech and intellectual debate; about academic freedom and the autonomy of universities; about who would be recognized as having the authority or right to speak and *about what or whom* in U.S. universities and beyond; about U.S. policy in the Middle East, quite centrally during the raging war in Iraq; and about the ethical and political responsibility of U.S. citizens vis-à-vis their state's increasingly voracious imperial reach. Had I chosen to intervene I would not have been heard. And perhaps that is as it must be.

Ian Hacking has felicitously described scientific objects that emerge from experimental work as (sometimes) acquiring a life of their own.[48] That is what happened to *Facts on the Ground*. My authorship mattered only to the extent that it was seen to speak to the kind of Subject I was, and thus the kind of politics that from some perspectives seamlessly emerged from that essential Self. If it came to circulate as "public ethnography," it was not because of a choice I made. And maybe that is more common than one might suspect. Public ethnography—in the sense of scholarship that enters into public debate, that helps to frame political arguments in the public domain—may emerge and perhaps sometimes most powerfully from writings taken up for various reasons, at various moments, and in various ways by particular publics and counterpublics for reasons of their own. In other words, our public interventions may well be born of the seemingly surreptitious "worldliness" of the texts we write—at a particular time and in a particular place.[49]

Notes

1   Muir and Applebaum 2007. This review first appeared in the summer of 2006. The only online version I can find now was one reprinted by the *History News Network* in 2007.

2   This quotation is taken from the introductory chapter. It is a description of the work of reflexive archaeologists approaching their own discipline critically, from within specific frameworks that they name as such. In other words, those are their epistemological and theoretical commitments, not mine (Abu El-Haj 2001: 8–9).

3   Cole 2009: 368–69.

4   During a teach-in on Columbia University's campus in the spring of 2003, for example, Nicholas de Genova, an assistant professor of anthropology, stated that he wanted to see "a million Mogadishus." His comment hit the airwaves, and both he and Columbia came under serious scrutiny. According to Cole (2009: 370), Lee Bollinger, the university's president, "received a letter from 104 Republican members of the House of Representatives asking that Professor de Genova be fired." See also Chatterjee and Maira 2014.

5   Cole 2009: 383. As Cole explains, the notion of academic freedom defines the very "employment relationship between professors and universities," putting in professors' hands the power and authority to evaluate scholarship and thus to "determine standards for hiring and promotion" (383). Cole argues that in the post-9/11 period many an academic has failed to understand the extent of the assault on the "American university." By focusing on the "effects of the repression on individuals rather

than its effects on the institution" we may be missing the larger and more dangerous picture. For an extended discussion, see Cole 2009: chapter 12.

6 On the decades-long history of reframing the Palestinian resistance as a terrorist movement, which converges with the question of radical Islam in the wake of the Iranian Revolution and the bombing of the U.S. marine barracks and embassy in Lebanon in 1982, see Lockman 2010. It is worth noting, as Lockman shows, that Benjamin Netanyahu played a key role in that transformation, as a think tank pundit, long before he was prime minister of Israel.

7 For an extensive discussion of my postcolonial, postmodern (they tend to be read as the same thing) *and* science studies commitments, see especially Joffe 2005.

8 Said 1983: 4.

9 Russell 2007.

10 Maeir 2004: 523–24. For similar arguments, see Joffe 2005; Muir and Applebaum 2007. For a somewhat different twist, see Lassner 2003.

11 Joffe 2005: 302, emphasis added. At the time his review was published in the *Journal of Near Eastern Studies*, Joffe was the director of Campus Watch, an arm of a right-wing Zionist think tank that I discuss below. He later became research director of the David Project, a key organization in the attack on Columbia University and its teaching of the Middle East, which I also discuss below.

12 Maeir 2004: 523.

13 Joffe 2005: 302–3.

14 It is worth emphasizing that I never wrote or spoke *as a Palestinian*. During the campaign critics both produced my identity as "a Palestinian" scholar and then argued over it: Was it a genuine claim? Was I *really* a Christian (and by implication, inauthentic)? Who is a Palestinian anyway?

15 Shapin and Shaffer 1985.

16 Lockman 2010: 254.

17 In making that parallel here I want to be clear that I am not equating the two movements. Al Qaeda and the various Palestinian factions that engaged in suicide bombing are radically different kinds of political movements, rooted in very different political visions, desires, and demands.

18 See Lockman 2010: 247–73.

19 For a discussion of Perle and Wolfowitz, see Lockman 2010: chapter 7. See also Beinin 2003. As discussed by Lockman and by Beinin, Perle and Wolfowitz, together with Douglas Feith, laid the groundwork for a rightward shift in U.S. policy toward Israel and the Middle East decades earlier through their work in the world of think tanks as well as in government posts. From 2001 to 2005 Wolfowitz served as deputy secretary of defense. Perle served on the Defense Policy Board Advisory Committee from 1987 to 2004, including as chairman in 2001. He is widely considered to have been a key architect of the 2003 invasion of Iraq. Feith was undersecretary of defense for policy from 2001 to 2005.

20 For a discussion of the David Project, the film, and what transpired at Columbia, see Kramer 2008; Cole 2009.

21   David Horowitz's Freedom Center was the third most powerful wheel in this work. For a discussion of Horowitz and his campaign, see Harter 2008. For an insightful discussion of accusations of anti-Semitism as a political tactic, see Butler 2003.

22   One of the most recent efforts to blacklist activists on the question of Palestine emerged in May 2015. See Nathan-Kazis 2015.

23   It is worth noting that when Columbia Hillel uses maps of Israel, they don't exclude East Jerusalem, the West Bank, or Gaza, or the Golan Heights.

24   https://www.youtube.com/watch?v=AJSmrgSOc40.

25   https://www.insidehighered.com/news/2014/09/16/ohio-u-debate-intensifies -over-anti-israel-twist-ice-bucket-challenge-and-4-arrests.

26   See de Garennes 2014. The University of Illinois released the email exchanges between administrators and donors in response to a request for the information filed under the Illinois Freedom of Information Act.

27   *Berkeley News* 2012.

28   See Lockman 2010: 269.

29   *Berkeley News* 2012, emphasis added. The committee that Dirks appointed to investigate the allegations raised by the David Project and its film found no evidence to support accusations of either anti-Semitism or the intimidation of Jewish students.

30   Joseph Massad and I were granted tenure by Columbia, although Massad's battle, in contrast to mine, went on for years.

31   Title VI came into force as part of the Civil Rights Act of 1964. "It prohibits discrimination on the basis of race, color, and national origin in programs and activities receiving federal financial assistance," and insofar as educational institutions receive federal assistance, they are subject to the statute and can be sued on its basis. See U.S. Department of Justice 1964; U.S. Department of Education, Office for Civil Rights n.d. There is a second Title VI of the Higher Education Act that funds area studies programs, including Middle East Studies programs, first established during the Cold War.

32   Berkeley was not the only institution to face such charges. A complaint against Santa Cruz was filed in 2011, and UC Irvine in 2007. For extensive documentation of the cases, see the website of Palestine Legal, palestinelegalsupport.org/.

33   Abunimah 2014.

34   *Reclaim UC* 2014.

35   Palestine Legal 2014.

36   Cole 2009: 377.

37   *Los Angeles Times* 2014. For a discussion of the call for "safe spaces" on campuses more generally, see Shulevitz 2015.

38   I do not sign onto his wholesale dismissal of poststructuralist theory and politics. Nevertheless I think Michaels's critique here captures one powerful strand of politics that has emerged from within that turn. For a trenchant albeit far more sympathetic critique of the limits of identity politics, see Brown 1995.

39   Masco 2014: 163, 7.

40 Hasbara refers to the public relations (propaganda) work of the Israeli government; one of the things they do is train Jewish American college students to counter criticisms of Israel on university campuses. Birthright is an organization that offers free trips to Israel for young American Jews with a view toward deepening their connection to and support for the Jewish state.

41 See the Amcha website, http://www.amchainitiative.org/; the Brandeis Center website, http://brandeiscenter.com/; the Campus Watch website, http://www.campus -watch.org/. For recent articles on the presumed problem of anti-Semitism on college campuses, see also the following articles published in the *New York Times*: Nagourney 2015; Medina and Lewin 2015.

42 Department of Education, Office for Civil Rights 2004.

43 He is referring to Title IX of the Education Amendments of 1972 that prohibited discrimination on the basis of sex in any educational program or activity funded by the federal government. See U.S. Department of Labor 1972.

44 For attacks on Title VI (of the Higher Education Act) funding for Middle East Studies in the post 9/11 period, see Lockman 2010: chapter 7. For legal cases against student activists on university campuses, see note 32. See also Abu El-Haj 2005: 549–50; Wolf 2014.

45 See, for example, the BBC radio documentary on David Horowitz's work on soft jihad (Harter 2008). For an extensive discussion of my tenure case, see Kramer 2008.

46 Kramer 2008. There was also an extensive email exchange between a member of Columbia's History Department and a reporter for *Jewish Week* about my book, which the reporter forwarded to me as a more "reasonable" discussion of the matter. The exchange begins with the professor, who the reporter did not identify, saying, "I have never actually read the book, but what I hear from a colleague . . ." This purported scholar then proceeded to engage in a long explication of the argument, my credentials, and why neither of them stood up.

47 These questions cover four of the most commonly asserted claims of what I wrote: that I had spent only two weeks doing fieldwork in Israel; that I did not know Hebrew; that I denied the existence of ancient Israelites (a presumably anti-Semitic position, by definition); and that I justified the destruction of Joseph's Tomb by Palestinian demonstrators in Nablus in 2000.

48 Hacking 1983.

49 Said 1983: 549.

References

Abu El-Haj, Nadia. 2001. *Facts on the Ground: Archaeological Practice and Territorial Self-Fashioning in Israeli Society*. Chicago: University of Chicago Press.

———. 2005. "Edward Said and the Political Present." *American Ethnologist* 32.4: 538–55.

Abunimah, Ali. 2014. "'Civility' Is the Israel Lobby's New Weapon against Free Speech on U.S. Campuses." *Electronic Intifada*, September 7. http://electron icintifada.net/blogs/ali-abunimah/civility-israel-lobbys-new-weapon-against -free-speech-us-campuses.

Beinin, Joel. 2003. "Pro-Israel Hawks and the Second Gulf War." MERIP, April 6. http://www.merip.org/mero/mero040603.

Berkeley News. 2012. "Transcript Extra: Divestment." November 27. http://newscenter .berkeley.edu/2012/11/27/transcript-extra-divestment/.

Brown, Wendy. 1995. *States of Injury: Power and Freedom in Late Modernity*. Princeton: Princeton University Press.

Butler, Judith. 2003. "No, It's Not Anti-Semitic." *London Review of Books* 25.16: 19–21.

Chatterjee, Piya, and Sunaina Maira, eds. 2014. *The Imperial University: Academic Repression and Scholarly Dissent*. Minneapolis: University of Minnesota Press.

Cole, Jonathan. 2009. *The Great American University*. New York: Public Affairs.

de Garennes, Christine. 2014. "Salaita Prompted Donors' Fury." *News Gazette* (Champaign, IL), September 2.

Hacking, Ian. 1983. *Representing and Intervening: Introductory Topics in the Philosophy of Natural Science*. Cambridge: Cambridge University Press.

Harter, Pascale. 2008. "Soft Jihad." *Assignment*. BBC World Service.

Joffe, Alexander. 2005. "Review: Facts on the Ground. Archaeological Practice and Territorial Self-Fashioning in Israeli Society. *Journal of Near Eastern Studies* 64 (October) (4): 297–304.

Kramer, Jane. 2008. "The Petition. Israel, Palestine and a Tenure Battle at Barnard." *The New Yorker*, April 14.

Lassner, Jacob. 2003. "Review. *Facts on the Ground: Archaeological Practice and Territorial Self-Fashioning in Israeli Society.*" *Middle East Quarterly* 10.3: 79–82.

Lockman, Zachary. 2010. *Contending Visions of the Middle East: The History and Politics of Orientalism*. Cambridge: Cambridge University Press.

Los Angeles Times. 2014. "Warning: College Students, This Editorial May Upset You." March 31. http://www.latimes.com/opinion/editorials/la-ed-trigger-warnings -20140331-story.html.

Maeir, Aren. 2004. *Facts on the Ground. Archaeological Practice and Territorial Self-Fashioning in Israeli Society,* Book Review. *Isis: A Journal of the History of Science* 95.3: 523–24.

Masco, Joseph. 2014. *The Theater of Operations: National Security Affect from the Cold War to the War on Terror*. Durham: Duke University Press.

Medina, Jennifer, and Tamar Lewin. 2015. "Campus Debates on Israel Drive a Wedge between Jews and Minorities." *New York Times*, May 9. http://www.nytimes.com /2015/05/10/us/campus-debates-on-israel-drive-a-wedge-between-jews-and -minorities.html.

Michaels, Walter Benn. 2004. *The Shape of the Signifier: 1967 to the End of History*. Princeton: Princeton University Press.

Muir, Diana, and Avigail Applebaum. 2007. "Review of Nadia Abu El-Haj's *Facts on the Ground: Archaeological Practice and Territorial Self-Fashioning in Israeli Society*." http://historynewsnetwork.org/blog/25976.

Nagourney, Adam. 2015. "In UCLA Debate over Jewish Student, Echoes on Campus of Old Biases." *New York Times*, March 5. http://www.nytimes.com/2015/03/06/us /debate-on-a-jewish-student-at-ucla.html.

Nathan-Kazis, Josh. 2015. "Shadowy Web Site Creates Blacklist of Pro-Palestinian Activists." *Forward*, May 27. http://forward.com/news/308902/shadowy-web-site -creates-black-list-of-pro-palestinian-activists/.

Palestine Legal. 2014. "Warning to Universities: No 'Civility' Exception to First Amendment." December 2. http://palestinelegalsupport.org/2014/12/02/psls -and-partners-submit-letter-to-universities-warning-there-is-no-civility-exception -to-first-amendment/.

Reclaim UC. 2014. "From the Free Speech Movement to the Reign of Civility." September 5. http://reclaimuc.blogspot.com/2014/09/from-free-speech-movement-to-reign -of.html.

Russell, James R. 2007. "Ideology over Integrity." *Current* (Columbia University), Fall.

Said, Edward. 1983. *The World, the Text, and the Critic*. Cambridge, MA: Harvard University Press.

Shapin, Steven, and Simon Shaffer. 1985. *Leviathan and the Air-Pump: Hobbes, Boyle, and the Experimental Life*. Princeton: Princeton University Press.

Shulevitz, Judith. 2015. "In College and Hiding from Scary Ideas." *New York Times*, March 21. http://www.nytimes.com/2015/03/22/opinion/sunday/judith -shulevitz-hiding-from-scary-ideas.html.

U.S. Department of Education, Office for Civil Rights. 2004. "Title VI and Title IX Religious Discrimination in Schools and Colleges." http://www2.ed.gov/about /offices/list/ocr/religious-rights2004.html?exp=0.

———. N.d. "Education and Title VI." http://www2.ed.gov/about/offices/list/ocr /docs/hq43e4.html.

U.S. Department of Justice. 1964. "Title VI of the Civil Rights Act of 1964, 42 U.S.C. §2000D et seq." http://www.justice.gov/crt/about/cor/coord/titlevi.php.

U.S. Department of Labor, Office of the Assistant Secretary for Administration and Management. 1972. "Title IX, Education Amendments of 1972." http://www.dol .gov/oasam/regs/statutes/titleix.htm.

Wolf, Bekah. 2014. "Title VI and Middle East Studies: What You Should Know." MERIP, November 14. http://www.merip.org/title-vi-middle-east-studies-what -you-should-know.

10

Perils and Prospects of Going Public

Between Academia and Real Life

UNNI WIKAN

On November 11, 2003, I receive a phone call from a friend warning me not to read a review of my book *Generous Betrayal: Politics of Culture in the New Europe* that has just appeared in *Norsk Tidsskrift for Migrasjonsforskning* (Norwegian Journal for Migration Research). I am surprised at the intensity in her tone. Something is clearly at stake, and I am soon to find out.

The next day I am copied in on an email from two members of the journal's editorial board (none of whom I know personally) to the other two. They are resigning from their positions in protest against the publication of the review and are admonishing the others to do the same. The review, they write, is an ad hominem attack, the like of which should never have been published in a scholarly journal.

The matter might have ended there, but such was not the case. Instead it came to feature for over a month in the media, engaging different kinds of publics and *silencing* others. The issue was the principles and precepts of a scholarly debate, but my name was at the heart of it, for reasons beyond my control. I did not participate in person save for a single interview early on.[1] Nor did I have any contact during the process with those who did. Others, scholars and journalists, outlined my position and contribution to the "immigration debate" better than I could have at the time. That they could do so told me I had succeeded through the years of being in the public in conveying anthropological knowledge in clear language. Indeed that had been my aim throughout: to speak clearly.

A personal experience, such as I shall relate, might be dismissed as subjective and self-indulgent. Were it just that, I would know better than to tell it here. It is not without hesitation that I bring it to light, but there are lessons to be gained, I believe, in its telling. My aim is to shed light on processes of *silencing* within the liberal left that are little talked about and contestations over "the truth" that fly in the face of a quest for rational knowledge. As the two scholars who resigned from the editorial board wrote in the liberal daily *Dagbladet*, a poisoning of the very debate on critical social issues would ensue if it were left to degenerate to the level of the review.[2] This is crucial.

The media debate I relate has a specific anchoring in time and place. But the *issues* it raised are timeless and of particular consequence in today's world of hate mail, harassment, and the use of violence to suppress opponents, bringing them to silence. It is becoming tougher in academia, in my view, to speak out on sensitive issues, but the issues do not go away because of that. An open critical debate, with argument meeting argument, is needed more than ever. What the story told here provides is also a glimmer of hope as it shows how the public—committed citizens—can intervene to turn a bad case into a learning experience about the priority of argumentation over moral degradation, the categorization of persons as evil or good.

As human beings we are in need of support when the going gets rough. The kindness of strangers is needed in several fields of life. Mine is one such experience of strangers, persons I did not know, acting on my behalf as scholars and moral beings. That in itself is food for thought and well worth sharing. After all, the case was not about me or my book or a particular review. The stakes were higher, hence its relevance here.

Paradoxically the book that occasioned the debate had not been written for the general public. It was a scholarly book meant for a more limited audience and written in English. Yet it made its way into the Norwegian media. This is an example of how hard it can be to anticipate the way in the world of works we write.

Every society has persons who regard themselves as keepers of the truth. Stark conservatives or liberal leftists—that is not the issue. The one can be as bad as the other. Nadia Abu El-Haj (in this volume) relates an experience of political activists using her book on Palestinians, which they had not read, to launch a campaign against her and her prospects of tenure at a U.S. university. Using faulty citations and other tools, they were able to give a *factual* representation, as they saw it, of the truth of her work. My experience is similar but different. My detractors *had* read the book—or so they claimed by virtue of doing the review. They were researchers at an academic institution. They wrote for an academic journal published by a scholarly press and financed by the Norwegian Research Council. The enemy, if I may use the word, was within, not without. So I tell the story here to highlight the variety of publics that may align to prohibit, or encourage, research on critical social issues and its mediation into the public domain.

My story comes from a place on the margins, Norway, my home country. I myself come from way up north, an island in the Arctic Ocean. We were considered backward from the perspective of people down south. At the time of my coming south, in 1965, it was not unusual for advertisements for flats for rent to be marked "Not for North Norwegians." We tried to disguise our dialects back then, so as not to be taken to speak uncouthly. This experience remains with me, though in the present speaking your dialect has become an insignia of identity. I mention my background because it has something to do with the position I was to take within academia and the public realm. Speaking out, speaking up was important. If there was anything we *nordlendinger* learned to distrust, it was people who *smykket seg selv*—adorned themselves—with pretty words.

I found a similar attitude among the poor people in Cairo, where I did my first fieldwork, in 1969, and forever after through the years.[3] "Empty talk" they cannot stand. Perhaps marginality is a condition that *does* something to people, across the board, breeding skepticism toward authority and an emphasis on deeds rather than words. It would be all too easy to overgeneralize, but my work in Cairo prepared me for a life in anthropology that made me decide from the start to go *public*. What was the use of knowledge if it was not to be shared with the public? How to justify peeping into people's lives (as ethnographers do) if I did not try to bring something in return, even something as little as an understanding of and for their lifeworlds?[4] *Fattigfolk i Cairo* (*Life among the Poor in Cairo*) was published as a trade book in 1976 and reviewed in the *Guardian* and the *Times Literary Supplement* when the English edition came out in 1980, which was encouraging for an aspiring anthropologist. It was also translated into Japanese and made for invitations to Japan to talk to both public and academic audiences. Other public ethnographies based on fieldwork in the Middle East followed and helped to establish me in the Norwegian public realm as someone who knew Arabic and life among Muslims.[5] In a small country like mine, not many academics did.

Generous Betrayal: Politics of Culture in the New Europe

Labor migration to Norway had started in the late 1960s with men coming from Pakistan, Morocco, and Turkey. Soon it became clear that they had come to stay, and by 1975, when Norway, like other European countries, introduced an "immigration stop," a sizable number had already settled with their families, and more were to come via family reunification and political asylum. Vietnamese and Tamil refugees had also arrived, along with other categories of both immigrants (e.g., Indians, Chinese) and refugees (Somalis, Eritreans, and more).

In August 1992 the Ministry of Family and Child Affairs contacted me with an urgent request to chair a committee to do a situation analysis on children and youth of immigrant background. I was reluctant as I was bound up in research in Bhutan and had no particular interest in immigration in Norway. But I felt a civic obligation to take on the task once I realized its urgency: the materials my committee gained insight into, unofficial at the time, made it clear that youngsters of *Muslim* background were at a disadvantage compared with others. Why should that be? And what to do about it?

In spite of the urgency of the committee's report, it was shelved. I suspected the reason to be political: as long as the facts did not become public, it could be made to appear that integration *worked*, though at the time *integration* was practically a nonword. The focus was on the *fargerike felleskap* (colorful commonality) that would emerge if the majority was kind and generous to the minority. Social welfare and antiracism were to do the work of creating a well-functioning colorful commonality. This was an ideology shared by politicians and intellectuals on the liberal left, in Norway as in much of Europe.

Meanwhile teachers, social workers, government officials, and others began contacting me for advice regarding families of immigrant background, especially Muslims. It was clear that *knowledge* was required and desired regarding how to deal with a situation where "respect for their culture" was the slogan, but what did it mean? My colleague Thomas Hylland Eriksen argued for a multiculturalist approach with wide acceptance for cultural diversity, as did the late Marianne Gullestad. Others such as Ottar Brox and Inger-Lise Lien positioned themselves in a more pragmatic arena, asking how integration could actually proceed without entitlements being linked with duties and with seeing culture as a field for argument rather than downright acceptance.

Of course there were many others engaged in public debates on immigration, not just anthropologists, but for my purposes here I limit myself to naming some anthropologists.[6]

I entered the public debate in February 1995, with an op-ed in the daily *Aftenposten*, "Er 'kultur' blitt vårt nye rasebegrep?" (Has "Culture" Become a New Concept of Race?).[7] It was grounded in the ongoing international debate in anthropology about culture and warned against seeing people as *products* of their culture rather than as persons in their own right. I also took a stance against the majority/minority dichotomization that glossed over great diversity in real life. Most important, I argued for the equal right of youngsters, irrespective of background, to shape their own identity; this should not be the prerogative of just "our kids," as if the identity of "their kids" was given in the blood. Moreover I discussed how power and culture went hand in hand: somebody's treasured culture might be another's entrapment or oppression.

The op-ed got public attention and led to media interviews, which encouraged me to write other op-eds on the situation of children and youth of immigrant background, drawing on ethnographic materials I had started to collect as well as secondary sources. Then, in spring 1995, I was invited to address all the teachers in the Oslo elementary schools—four thousand—in the largest concert hall in town. The lights were blinding so that I could not see a single face, but I *sensed* the quest for knowledge about culture, about Islam, about identity. Perhaps it was then that I became motivated to write the book that came to be called *Mot en ny norsk underklasse: Innvandrere, kultur og integrasjon* (Toward/Against a New Norwegian Underclass: Immigrants, Culture, and Integration), published in October 1995.[8] It caused an uproar among the liberal left.[9] "Underclass" was an unspeakable category at the time in a country priding itself on social equality and justice. Racism might ensue if it became known that Muslims (though the book did not deal solely with Muslims) fared less well than others and depended more on social welfare. And did I not represent Muslim men as oppressors when I argued for Muslim women's right to equality and freedom on a par with "Norwegian" women? I was castigated in some quarters, portrayed as a "Norwegian fundamentalist in scientific garb" in a leftist daily, *Klassekampen*,[10] and brandished as a supporter of the rightist Progress Party. This is part of the history preceding *Generous Betrayal* and hence the *context* in which the debate about it (and me) took place.

What was *Generous Betrayal* about? Let me cite an informed foreign reader, Hugh Eakin, in the *New York Review of Books*: "In a controversial book published shortly after September 11, 2001, the social anthropologist Unni Wikan described the problem of Norway's treatment of its minorities as a 'generous betrayal': social benefits and well-intended rhetoric about multiculturalism were serving as stand-ins for more meaningful integration, with the result that an 'underclass' of immigrants was created."[11]

Published seven years after *Mot en ny norsk underklasse*, *Generous Betrayal* was a very different kind of book. The former was based on limited ethnographic and quantitative materials, using "informed guessing," in Geertz's sense,[12] and addressed entirely to a public audience of concerned citizens, politicians, government officials, and others. Its purpose was to raise an alarm: Beware, integration is *not* working; Norway is heading toward greater social inequality, with Muslims in particular as losers. *Generous Betrayal*, on the other hand, was an ethnographically based, longitudinal study that drew on comparative materials from other countries, hence the subtitle *Politics of Culture in the New Europe*. The analysis had benefited from critical discussions following presentations at several universities in Europe and the United States, and the book had been written entirely while I was a visiting professor at Harvard, which gave me the required distance from the local field. I never experienced any form of harassment on any occasion abroad. It was different at home.

Norway, the land of the midnight sun and a fine welfare state, also has a gloomy aspect. There is a *Jante* law, as it is called: "Don't you ever think you *are* something!"[13] Moreover political correctness has pertained in the realm related to immigrants, especially Muslims: the fear of being called a racist prevails to this day. It is not as severe as in Sweden—far from it (see below). But keepers of the truth are concerned to protect minorities, Muslims in particular, from what they perceive as racism and to render the image of Norway as a place where a "colorful plurality" works out much better than elsewhere, which may be true, depending on your reference point. But is it good enough? What is the measure? What should it be? Are we Norwegians truly offering people of immigrant background dignity and respect or just welfare colonialism?

Positioning itself right into the debate about multiculturalism, identity politics, and individual human rights, *Generous Betrayal* was inspired by the works of scholars and writers like Amartya Sen, Fatima Mernissi, Amin Maalouf, Susan Okin, Liah Greenfeld, Alain Finkielkraut, Michael Ignatieff, Eric Hobsbawm, and Slavenka Drakulic. But above all it was founded on *empirical* ethnographic research and extended case studies. It made no claim to be an analysis that had a solution to the harrowingly difficult question of how to balance group rights, or rights based on ethnicity or religion, with individual human rights—one of the most unsettling questions of our time. But it did dig deep into the matter, and *it took a stand*.

Full of notes and references, the obverse of what a trade book should be, *Generous Betrayal* might not have gained any attention in the Norwegian *public* realm had not one particular review ensued.[14] Going overboard in one's aspiration to blacken another's name is rarely a good idea; the effort may well backfire. The afterlife[15] of the book leads me to ask certain questions: For whom is the truth so frightening that one will resort to violence to keep it from surfacing?[16] What are the prospects of doing public ethnography on sensitive issues if "your own"—scholars like you—attack you rather than your argument? And how can the discussion get back on track, if at all?

Now to what came to be called "the Wikan debate": How did the particular review of *Generous Betrayal* enter the public? And to what effect?

I had followed my friend's warning not to read the review, but a few days later, on a Sunday morning while relaxing over my coffee and the daily *Dagbladet*, my eyes hit upon an article titled "Når forskere blir til fiender" (When Researchers Are Made into Enemies). The author was a prominent public intellectual, professor, and former cultural editor of *Dagbladet*. He had read the review and wrote that it was so full of swear words as to make one gasp for breath: "Unni Wikan, we are told, is an ideological propagandist for 'the new cancer epidemic of racist politics that is now spreading across the European landscape.' She is akin to the Third Reich's worst anti-Semites, besides [being] on a par with that century's most brutal colonialists . . . say the reviewers. . . . What is it that is actually going on in a scholarly milieu, when people think they can go at each others' throats this way? This is happening in the arena of the anthropologists and migration researchers."[17]

Dagbladet at the time was read by everyone; it was *the* liberal daily. Bringing the matter out there put it squarely in the public eye. Now other media too turned to the case. "Stemplet som nazist" (Branded a Nazi) was the headline staring at me in big bold letters in major media. But it was always in my defense, followed by quite nuanced presentations of what was known to be my viewpoints. The accusation against me was so absurd as to cause moral wreckage not of me but of its agents. Now morality and scholarship are not wholly distinct. The media too wanted to know what was actually going on among academics engaged in migration research. In a small country like mine, public accountability matters. Academics cannot seek refuge in their ivory towers. Norway is an anti-elitist country, likely to back the one who is done in by persons with academic credentials abusing their position. The Nazi damnation of me was a step too far. It was bound to bounce back if it reached the public. The authors may have thought that it never would or that it was a true characterization of me or that they were doing a public service. I have no clue. I had never even heard their names. But they were researchers at Oslo University College, *scholars*, in other words. And while the journal might not be the best on migration research, it was the best that Norway had. It should be a flagship. The Norwegian Research Council, the publisher, and the editorial board all had stakes in that.

Ten days after the matter reached the media, the two authors explained their position in an article in *Dagbladet*.[18] They expressed their surprise at the criticism launched against them when their text had been circulating for nearly two years and received much acclaim from scholars, nationally and internationally, some of whom they named. Two (unnamed) professors at the University of Oslo had even called it "brilliant" and "fantastic." So what was wrong?

Writing in the present, twelve years after the fact, I see their point. They are saying they were part of a larger international network and that their text had passed muster from a group of *likesinnete* (likeminded people). It takes the onus away from them and turns it into an achievement. I also wonder if the authors' role might not have been more that of messenger than originator. Trained people would not have committed the kind of mistake they did: to let the swear words rain in a scholarly journal. It shows how unprofessional they were. Indeed, as far as I know, they vanished from the scene after their debut in *Dagbladet*.

"The worst *ad hominem* attack I have ever seen!" is how one of the scholars resigning from the editorial board characterized the review in an interview in Norway's best-selling daily, *VG*. In an article in *Dagbladet* titled "Kunsten å få folk til å holde kjeft" (The Art of Getting People to Shut Up) the two who resigned wrote that the reviewers "did not just offend Wikan as a person and a professional, they poison the very debate. When her viewpoints qualify for the label cancer epidemic, with linkages to the interwar time's race research, the German Nazi regime and Holocaust, it shuts the mouth of anyone by inflicting on them the worst imaginable shame after World War Two."[19] They then set out what they saw as my contribution to the immigration debate, with special emphasis on the rights of the individual to dignity and respect, over and above culture or religion. The issue was not whether one agreed with me. The issue was the critical social scholarly debate and the need to observe certain ethical standards to enable it to proceed.

The editor of the journal agreed that moral standards had to be upheld. In an article in *Dagbladet* titled "Upresis Wikan-debatt" (Imprecise Wikan Debate) he wrote that countering racism was necessary. Minorities had to be protected. He did not accuse me of being a racist in this, an article he wrote at the very end of the debate, where he would have to watch his words as editor of the now infamous journal. But in an earlier interview in *VG* his language was harsh, calling me an anti-Muslim and a nurturer of racism that had to be subdued.[20]

Each and every one of us, scholar or nonscholar, speaks from a particular position. In repeating these different views, as well as my own, I lift the protagonists out of their social spaces. I do not adequately contextualize the position from which they (or we) speak. There is no flesh and blood to the protagonists (except perhaps me). I want to point this out so as not to be unfair and also to make the following analytic claim: Debates are never just about issues; they are also about you and me. The editor who debunked me, who was he? What was at stake? Had I not taken on the Fadime case, the case of an honor killing in a Kurdish community in Sweden, and written a much publicized book about it earlier in the year? I could not help wondering if my engagement over the past year on the issue of honor killings, well publicized, had added fuel to the fire as far as the editor was concerned. I did not know him nor his work, but he would have known my work well. Within the Kurdish community in Scandinavia I was no hero.

On the home front, in my department, what were the reactions? Silence. Two colleagues on the technical staff expressed their empathy and their surprise at the overall silence. Nobody else mentioned the matter, though at most everyone could be counted on to know of the debate.

To the public this did not look good. Some grew concerned about the image of anthropology mediated by the silence. One senior anthropologist, himself a public anthropologist, approached the chair of the department to suggest they make a public statement. Nothing came of it. And I knew nothing of it at the time. But I will not forget the day an op-ed titled "Sosialantropologi og innvandringsdebatt" (Social Anthropology and Immigration Debate) appeared in *Dagbladet*. The author was Arne Martin Klausen, a former chair of the Anthropology Department at the University of Oslo and a highly respected public intellectual. The subtitle stated, "Wikan had challenged to a more open and fearless debate about one of the most difficult and most important phenomena in modern society." The text was about the role anthropology *could* play. Klausen wrote, "This is my moral support for Wikan in this connection."[21] I did not know him personally, yet he spoke up for anthropology and for me at this critical point in time.

I have tried to relate the factual events of this debate in plain language, though the whole experience was laden with emotion for me and my family. The Nazi branding was a serious thing, not so much for what it said but for where it pointed to: the discrediting of my name and work to an international audience. On my home ground it couldn't really do much harm. People knew me. I was a public figure with a certain standing. Perhaps the essence of it all was to try to take ownership of what the truth about Norway's immigration and integration policies should be.

If so, *whose* ownership was at stake? The reviewers were not lone figures but aligned with others; this might help explain the silence within my own department.[22] Silence is typical when you don't know what to say or when you want things just to go away. That one of my colleagues was on the editorial board of the journal did not help matters. He later said that he regretted not speaking out publicly in my defense when I was personally morally attacked.[23]

Didier Fassin has noted that publics vary even within the academy.[24] My experience testifies to that. Just five months after these events the rector of the University of Oslo said in a public speech, "The University of Oslo is proud of you." It happened when I was awarded the Fritt Ord (Freedom of Expression) prize for 2004. After that nothing was the same.

It was on a rickety telephone line in Cairo, where I had just come from Yemen, that my husband told me, "Francis Sejersted has called. You have been awarded the Fritt Ord prize."[25] It was unbelievable and I went out to buy myself a chocolate bar to convince myself I deserved something. In its official statement the Fritt Ord committee said the prize had been awarded on account of my "insightful, openhearted, and challenging contribution to the debate about value conflicts in the plural society." Did the events at the end of 2003 play a role? I imagine so, but when I asked, the director of Fritt Ord said it was my *long-term* contribution to public debate that had earned me the prize.

With the Fritt Ord prize the silence broke within my department. I felt as if I had come in from the cold. This had consequences for how I could function in the teaching and supervision of students. I have pondered how the very public recognition of the value of one's work could engender such a change for an academic within academia. Perhaps the answer is that we are not compartmentalized as persons. Perhaps especially in a small society the whole person counts. Though the status of Fritt Ord[26] in my country clearly made a difference.

Next-Door Neighbor, Sweden: Another Place, Another Controversy

To a non-Scandinavian the Nordic countries Norway, Sweden, and Denmark might appear to be close cousins, which they are in many respects. But not as regards immigration and the role of the public anthropologist. Here the differences are more conspicuous than the similarities, especially between Sweden and the other two. The story I told above is local to Norway as well as international. It is deeply embedded in a particular local mold within an egalitarian society wedded to transparency and civic courage and with a public press taking its role of watchdog seriously. Sweden has another history, with an aristocracy, larger differences of wealth and class, a broader international outlook, and a consensus-based polity. *Presis* (precisely): that's how Swedes conduct their dialogues, punctuating sentences to underscore agreement. In an insightful article on engaged anthropology, Signe Howell makes much of the fact that public anthropology has exceptionally good standing in Norway.[27] I know Swedes who could write a different story based on their experiences in Sweden, and some have.[28] Howell discusses why the Norwegian public is so receptive to anthropology. The Swedish anthropologist Ulf Hannerz too has a view on that which is interesting, given his comparative perspective.[29] I shall get back to that. It should be noted, however, that the difference between the countries is especially great as regards immigration, with its load of sensitive issues. But then this needs to be placed in context. Alone among the Nordic countries Sweden has celebrated an ideology and politics of multiculturalism.[30] And Sweden has opened its borders completely to immigrants and refugees for decades. Only as of late November 2015 was the government compelled to call for a halt: the country could not cope any longer with the masses of refugees entering from Syria and elsewhere, Sweden and Germany being their preferred destinations in Europe.

A country that seeks to take in all immigrants and refugees that come to their door will naturally meet with challenges that ought to be aired in public debates. Should not anthropologists contribute to that? "Unless we describe reality, we will awaken one day to a reality that is indescribable," said the Israeli author and human rights advocate David Grossman. Sweden has felt the full force of this point. Most anthropologists and intellectuals chose, for reasons of their own, either to stay away from public engagement on immigration or to describe reality in line with the multicultural ideology. Hence, while in Norway public intellectuals engaged in debate that had them sharpen their arguments and battle for the truth, in Sweden the debate hardly existed. Not until some destroyed the illusion of harmony, some who were not born Swedes and were not academics. Several were women with an immigrant background. A key figure was Fadime Sahindal, to whose story I now turn.

Silencing has been a running thread through this essay. Let me now relate a case of silencing in its most brutal form: putting an opponent to death on account of her speaking out for individual freedom and for integration. It was a wake-up call for Sweden and had the effect of changing policies on child marriage and forced marriage; it also made Sweden a forerunner internationally in work against honor-related violence.

The case highlights the perils of going public, in word and deed, for persons compelled by an honor code; it also lays bare the prospects of doing so against all odds, and the possible rewards. I discuss risks involved for the ethnographer wanting to research such a case and ways to handle obstacles without violating ethical standards. Further, on genre and presentation to publics: how to proceed? I share some of my experiences in various countries calling for different kinds of argumentation and discuss issues of translation. By way of summing up I revert to the comparison between doing public anthropology in Norway and Sweden, especially on sensitive social issues.

My engagement with the Fadime case began on the morning of January 22, 2002, when the news of her murder was broadcast throughout the world: Muslim father kills his daughter in Sweden. It was not the first honor killing in Sweden, but Fadime's death rocked the nation and had international effects. In Norway too the media searched for an explanation: How could a father kill his own child for honor's sake? That's how I came to be involved as an ethnographer: through the media. It began with requests for interviews, then an op-ed in the daily *Aftenposten* (also published in Poland), then a research project that eventuated into a book that was published in several languages and also led to public engagements in Sweden.

The book opens with two questions: What makes a father murder his child for honor's sake? What makes a mother testify *for* a man who has murdered their child for honor's sake? It was published in Norwegian on the first anniversary of Fadime's death, on January 21, 2003. The Swedish translation followed exactly a year later. It was written with the aim of enlightening the general reader, policymakers, and professionals, hoping to contribute to policy changes. I also wanted to pay my respects to Fadime and help carry her mission forward.

Fassin has coined the phrase "the black holes of ethnography" to alert us to areas, fields, and spaces where ethnographers are reluctant to tread.[31] The reasons may be various, from physical discomfort to social or cultural disquiet and outright fear. With my research on the Fadime case I ventured into such a black hole. What were the challenges? How to proceed methodologically? How to reach out to a public? And to what effect?

Public ethnographies are *motivated*, not just made. I had never intended to research honor killings; the mere thought would have been abhorrent to me. What drove me now was the urge to understand something that was beyond my comprehension. Again the media played a role. When, after Fadime's murder, journalists asked me, "Please, can you explain? Please, can you help us understand?," I felt a deep disquiet. It was certainly not the first time I had been approached by the media in similar cases, but it was the first time that I *could not put the matter out of my mind.* How could it be that with my knowledge and experience I still could not understand what honor killing was all about at a human, existential level? It seemed a failure on my part and a failure on the part of anthropology.

What I did understand was that Islam was not the culprit. I had specific ethnographic knowledge from specific places in Oman, Indonesia, and Egypt that killing one's daughter would be seen as abhorrent, a violation of Islam.[32] In the international climate after September 11, 2001—Fadime died just five months later—it was important to convey this information to the public. I felt a civic duty to use my knowledge to undertake wider ethnographic research that might help illuminate "the problem of evil" in the particular form of a child being killed by her own family for honor's sake.

Shortly after Fadime's death I wrote an op-ed in *Aftenposten* trying to explain the rationale of honor killings without exonerating the act.[33] An honor killing has its own logic; that much some anthropologists working in the Middle East had made clear. It is deliberate, premeditated, done on behalf of a larger collective to retrieve honor lost, usually by a brother or father or other paternal kinsman who reaps "honor" by killing a young woman believed to have disgraced the family. But with few exceptions, cases were missing that could offer insight into the human dilemmas of what it means to practice what the honor code preaches.

Reaping honor for murdering one's child presupposes a certain social environment where the act is perceived as congratulatory, an admirable deed. How was such a society constituted? This murder did not happen far away, among "others" in some remote place. Fadime's family was one of "us." They had lived in Sweden for twenty years; their home was in Uppsala, a beautiful old university town, and they were not poor. Yet in a speech given shortly before she died Fadime had described her parents as living in *utanförskap*, an evocative Swedish noun that means "outside of society." For this she blamed society (*samhället*), not her parents. So who had the power of life and death in Fadime's family's community? It would be all too easy to think people like her father are "monsters," though some said, "He had no choice, no alternative." Persons do have alternatives, in the usual run of things.

In my op-ed in *Aftenposten* I attempted to explain what at that point I could understand, in the hope of helping to prevent the stigmatization of Muslims. I had not yet realized that I would run into the problem of how to deal with the fact that certain ethnic communities had an especially bad record regarding honor-based violence, and that among them were Kurds. Again a black hole. Kurds were freedom fighters. Were they also especially violent to their women? And if so, why?

My engagement in public debate in Norway had made me take a critical stance against the concept of culture in line with several anthropologists internationally. The Fadime case was to make me revise my position in recognizing a larger role for culture and its hold on some people's lives. What to call it? Custom, culture, tradition? I landed on all three, taking my cue from Kurdish human rights activists, which is not to say that our *conceptions* necessarily were the same, but you need some concepts, and culture or custom may do.[34]

Here is Fadime's story, briefly told:

On February 4, 1998, twenty-two-year-old Fadime Sahindal made use of her freedom of speech to tell her story to the Swedish daily *Aftonbladet*. Her decision to go public was made after the police would not grant her protection. "Perhaps if I become known to the public," she said, "they will not dare to kill me." She was referring to her extended family (*släkten*). Their homeland was Kurdistan in eastern Turkey. The Sahindals comprised about a thousand family members, of whom over three hundred lived in

Sweden. Fadime's parents had settled in Uppsala sixteen years before. She had four sisters and a brother. Now she had committed the disgrace of falling in love with a boy.

He was Patrick Lindesjö. They had met at a computer course two years earlier. For a year they kept their relationship secret. But in September 1997 her father spotted them walking on the street. He was enraged and threatened to kill her. She was terrified and never went home again. The police fetched her passport and belongings. At the end of the year, in an attempt at reconciliation, Patrick's father and grandmother went to Fadime's parents to ask for her hand. They spoke Turkish together, for Patrick's father was from Iran. Fadime's parents reluctantly agreed. But the decision was not theirs. It belonged with relatives higher up in the hierarchy, and they said no: "If Fadime gets to marry a Swede, then all the girls in the family might come to marry Swedes!"

Fadime was cast out by her family and ordered into exile. The message was conveyed through her mother on January 11, 1998. If she ever came back to Uppsala, that would be the end. Fadime contacted the police for help, but they didn't believe her story. It was then that she went public through the media. She saw it as her last resort. But there is no freedom of speech in societies ruled by an honor code, where loyalty to and respect for the family are all-important, and to expose family matters is a disgrace, a betrayal. The threats against Fadime increased.

She then made use of another freedom Swedish law gave her: she took her father and brother to court, and they were fined for threats on her life. She also participated in a TV documentary on her case, first broadcast on May 7, 1998. The intent was to draw public attention to the challenges faced by persons like her; Patrick too told their story. Asked by a journalist if she was not afraid to speak out, she said, "If what I do can save the life of just one person, it will be worth it."

Less than a month later, on June 3, 1998, Patrick died in an accident[35] as he was driving from Stockholm to Uppsala to move in with Fadime. A week later her brother tried to kill her on the streets of Uppsala. She suffered injuries, but no serious harm. A new court case followed in August, and her brother was sentenced to jail. Then Fadime withdrew from the public. She enrolled as a student of social work and made a new life for herself. Only on two occasions did she speak publicly after August 1998, once at a Red Cross event and then, on November 30, 2001, to a conference on integration. She was fearful and her name was not listed in the program.

The conference was held in the old Parliament building in Stockholm, and the minister of integration herself was due to appear. Fadime presented what would become known as "*Talet i Riksdagen*" (The Speech in Parliament). Less than two months later she was dead.

She was shot by her father while meeting secretly with her mother and two younger sisters in Uppsala. Sweden honored her with a state-like funeral attended by the crown princess, the head of Parliament, cabinet ministers, and other prominent people. It took place in the old cathedral in Uppsala, as she had wanted. She lies buried next to Patrick.

Stories can be told differently depending on audience and occasion. This rendering of Fadime's case is how I presented it to an international audience at a public event called "Challenges to Multiculturalism: A Conference on Migration, Citizenship, and Free Speech," arranged by the New York Review of Books Foundation and Fritt Ord in Oslo in June 2012. I participated with Kwame Anthony Appiah, who had written a major book on cosmopolitanism,[36] in a session called "Concepts of Multiculturalism and Cosmopolitanism," chaired by Robert Silvers, editor of the *New York Review of Books*. I used the case as my entry into the analytic discussion, the whole of which is available on YouTube.

I needed a strong beginning, something that would engage the audience and keep their attention. Fadime's case could provide that. But it had to be pared down to a minimum and framed so as to open up for a discussion of analytical points. Twenty-five minutes was the time frame for each presentation, quite considerable in fact, but the longer part would be needed for the argumentation. This is the public ethnographer's constant dilemma: how much time to devote to narrative and how much to analysis, and how to integrate the two. Especially in a case like Fadime's, where you have drama upon drama, it is easy to be caught: the audience wants more, you sense it and want to give it, but you need to hold back. Ethnography is about keeping one's distance, about embodying that sense of disengaged empathy that Gananath Obeyesekere writes so well about in his *Work of Culture*.[37]

How did the audience respond? I cannot really tell, but it seemed to go well. I was no enthusiast for the concept of cosmopolitanism, but having read Appiah's book closely in preparation for the session, I found much to agree with, especially his critique of anthropology's bent toward moral relativism. "Toleration requires a concept of the *intolerable*" was one statement I took note of.[38] Otherwise, once you have a powerful ethnographic case to tell, you can console yourself, I think, that the audience might forget everything you said except perhaps a fragment of the case. Is that good enough? No, but it may be the best one can hope for in today's world, with its overload of information (and paradoxically an overload of stories).

Methodological and Ethical Issues

How had I produced my ethnographic materials on the Fadime case? By playing it by ear and relying on my long experience of doing fieldwork. It also mattered that we were a team at home: my husband, Fredrik Barth, had done his first fieldwork among Kurds in Iraq and also worked in other Middle Eastern societies with a strong honor code.[39] Being able to discuss the fieldwork and analysis with him was of inestimable value; it was more of a collaboration than I recognized until now.

I had no definite plan or schedule to begin with because it was impossible to know when key events would take place. The trial against Fadime's father would be crucial to follow. I expected it to be about a year later; that is how long it would have taken in Norway. So I almost missed it. By sheer luck I discovered one afternoon in early March, just six weeks after her death, that the trial would start the next morning! I threw myself on the plane to Stockholm and lined up in the biting cold outside Uppsala District Court at 6 the next morning. The doors would open at 8. By luck I got a seat amid the family members, enabling me to speak with some of them and to listen in to parts of their conversations.

Prior experience of doing ethnography at the court helped me to navigate the case.[40] The trial took just four days. Only two family members testified: a cousin and friend of the father and Fadime's sister, Songül. She had been warned not to testify and appeared in court with a police escort. "My father fired the pistol, but others stood behind," she said, telling of family meetings. Rahmi Sahindal was sentenced to life in jail.

After the trial I realized that I must not interview any of Fadime's family or friends. It was too risky, for them and for me. I decided to use only materials that were public, that in each and every instance had a documented source. By "materials" I mean conversations, statements, utterances. Ethnography must draw on the unutterable, the silences, the gestures and innuendos, and I did, as well as on observation of behavior. But the decision I made not to quote anything that could not be documented in a public source is memorable and unique in my experience as an anthropologist. But then I had never before or afterward faced a situation like this.

The appeals case followed six weeks later, in Stockholm in early May. This time Fadime's mother testified in support of her husband, confirming a story full of holes aimed to make him seem innocent. It was heartbreaking to see and hear her. The eyes of her son and her brother stared at her from the audience. I was grateful for all I had learned about attending to nonverbal communication and taking in the wider social situation. Observation was key here, not just listening.

This was a living tragedy played out before my eyes. After the experience I was unwell for over a week. Then I realized that Fadime would probably have said, "Poor Mama." When a close friend of Fadime confirmed this, I had the running thread of the book I was to write: the conflicting feelings and loyalties experienced by persons caught in circumstances not of their making but that they could alter in sometimes minute, sometimes dramatic ways through their choices of how to act.

The context, the social structure would need to be spelled out: how a family like Fadime's was situated both within Sweden and transnationally. Kurds I knew in Norway with linkages to Sweden and Turkey could fill me in on this. But "the problem" was not Kurdish. Researching multiculturalism in Sweden would be necessary, and here anthropology had little to offer me. I could only scratch the surface in the time I had.

An unexpected and invaluable source of material was the police report, the recording of oral testimony during the police investigation. It enabled me to hear how persons differently positioned had responded, reacted, reflected— if with the police—when the tragedy was still raw. That such records were publicly available in Sweden (after the verdict) came as a surprise. Further rich materials were the TV documentary on Fadime, her "Speech in Parliament," interviews she had given, media interviews with members of the Kurdish community, and more. It is rare for the victim of an honor killing to leave behind such a record that can be used as a resource for a researcher. That Fadime had an analytic, empathetic view of family members and their traditions made the testimonies she left behind even more valuable.

On Genre, Timing, and Critique

Thinking through cases is an ethnographer's best friend. Nothing can outclass a story that resonates at the human level for being remembered for what it says of larger social realities. This is one point of Fassin's "True Life, Real Lives."[41] The story I came to write of the Fadime case is an example of what in Norway would be called *sakprosa*, a documentary genre; *sak* means "case" or "matter." Opinions vary as to what leniency an author can take with the empirical materials, or lack thereof, for the sake of a good read. I kept to the facts as closely as possible, refrained from attributing thoughts and feelings to people, and used a narrative style that had drive and hopefully impelled the reader to hold on to the end. The story itself was so full of drama as to ease the job of the author. But four concerns arose: multiple viewpoints; theory; representativeness; policy and debate. Some words about the first three.

First, multiple viewpoints is the basis of good ethnography. I was limited in that I could not talk with key persons, such as Fadime's father, mother, brother, and mother's brother. But I could use materials from the police report, public interviews, court cases, TV documentaries, and more to explore different vantage points and ensure that different voices would be heard. It was a balancing act, and not all readers approved; some of them felt I betrayed Fadime.

Second, on theory: What *is* honor when it can rank above the life of your own child? What is *the stuff of social relations* if society rewards child murder with honor?[42] I was no novice to the scholarship on honor and shame,[42] but it was only thanks to Frank Henderson Stewart's *Honor* that things finally started to make sense.[43] It is a book that is hard to read, is underrated in anthropology, contains a wealth of insights, and may finally be gaining the importance it deserves.[44] This is not the place to go into Stewart's theories, save to say that he makes clear why disgrace is so much worse than shame, and how a particular kind of lost honor confers disgrace on a patrilineal group, reducing them to nothing in the eyes of others until honor is restored. But, and this is a key point, murdering a girl who is perceived to have caused the lost honor is not unavoidable; there are alternatives. Fadime's being sent into exile was a lesser vengeance. She was killed when she broke out of exile, just as she had been warned.

Third, representativeness: questions were bound to arise of how special Fadime's case was. At the time of her death, in 2002, honor killings in Europe were just starting to become publicly known. Presently we have name upon name, faces, personal stories, biographies, films, documentaries. Sweden has been especially afflicted. Could we Norwegians think of ourselves as better than the Swedes in tackling integration? Perhaps. At least integration was on the agenda in Norway, with some effect. But I included in the book three clear cases of honor-based violence in Norway, in two cases with deadly effect. When revising the book in English, I came to think of these cases as intrusive in drawing attention away from the main narrative. Yet I did not exclude them.

I have tried to share my thoughts on the composition of a book I wrote thirteen years ago and some of the hard decisions I faced. At the time they did not seem so hard for I had little time at my disposal, so I could not rewrite. Timing can be of the essence if you want to reach out. I wanted the book to be published on the first year anniversary of Fadime's death, as did my publisher. Without my editor's expert nudging, we should never have made it. But we did.

The book was launched at a press conference and widely covered in reviews and interviews in the media. Overall the reception was positive, giving me credit for having made honor killing intelligible from a social and a human vantage point. But I want to consider here one of the harsh criticisms I received. It was written by Shabana Rehman, a prominent public figure, a journalist, standup comedian, author, human rights activist, and Fritt Ord prizewinner. In a full-page review in *Dagbladet* titled "Du skulle holdt kjeft, Fadime" (You Should Have Shut Up, Fadime) she took me to task for betraying Fadime.[45] Arguing that Fadime was killed because she went public and warning other girls like her to think twice before going public with their stories was treason, Rehman wrote. The criticism was not entirely fair, in my view, as my analysis concluded that it was the combined circumstances of Fadime's "Speech in Parliament" and her breach of the exile, so close in time, that spelled her end. But Rehman has a point. One need not go public to risk being killed for honor's sake in certain communities. Indeed the first Norwegian who brought the matter to public attention, in 1993, was a girl who was forced to marry in Pakistan under threat of being killed by her family. She later escaped back to Norway and contacted a journalist who wrote her story anonymously; she had not gone public beforehand. She later wrote a fictional account of her experiences.[46]

Rehman's critique is like a fist in the face, more now than when I first read it. Then I just dismissed it, thinking she had not got the point of the book. Now I realize there was more to her critique than I had been ready to consider. At the time of my writing the book I knew that the Romeo-and-Juliet story was what the public wanted to hear. It was the running story. But Fadime was not just killed; she was *allowed to live* long after the death threats against her had subsided. This was a conundrum I, as an ethnographer, faced and had to try to explain. Did I go overboard in doing so? Did I make too much of it? Would she have been killed in any case? Did I misunderstand? Was I too much taken up in my "humanizing" endeavor?

I still stand by my analysis. But I also see the point of Rehman's critique more clearly now; in her eyes—she and her family have been subject to severe violence for her going public—here was another anthropologist with a moral relativist view, and this though I was not even a leftist. Marianne Gullestad and Thomas Hylland Eriksen had been the ones to truly feel her ire. Rehman would have expected better of me.

Another well-recognized reviewer in the financial daily *Dagens Næringsliv* also criticized me for my empathetic view of the father. At the time I felt that this critique too was unjust; with hindsight it is easier to understand. "I love all my characters, also the bad," says the Egyptian author Alaa Al-Aswany.[47] As an ethnographer I cannot say the same of all the persons who populate my narratives, but his words are food for thought. I certainly felt a tinge of unease, bordering on deep disquiet at times, while writing the Fadime book. I had to try to enter the hearts and minds of people I despised but whose thoughts mattered immensely to me if I were to understand, as much as I could, their motives and actions. It meant, for instance, sympathizing if not empathizing with Fadime's murderer.

At stake here, from an outside point of view, is anthropology and cultural relativism. I felt I had been clear enough in the book on distancing myself from cultural relativism as a moral code. But was it good enough?

Douglas Hollan has written that one requires feedback to know whether one has achieved empathy.[48] Fadime's father, Rahmi Sahindal, indicates I did not. In an interview with two Kurdish journalists he said he had my book by his side in prison and that I had written many lies, I should have spoken with him.[49] He may well be right, but it was impossible. The risk was too high.

I have written as if empathizing with the murderer and his supporters came easily to me. It did not. In fact there were to be several cases after the Fadime case where I was completely unable to take an empathetic view toward some of the perpetrators. One that I covered extensively in the media in several op-eds and also later in books was the case of Ghazala Khan, an eighteen-year-old Danish-born girl. A Punjabi, she had fallen in love with a Pashtun. Nine persons were convicted of her murder in Copenhagen in 2006.[50] A grotesque Norwegian case involved a brother who axed his three sisters to death in 2006; they too were of Punjabi origin. Again I wrote articles for the media on the case and a critical analysis of the court proceedings in a book. In both cases my public engagement was to use anthropological knowledge to help shed light on the crimes and the court proceedings. I published a strong critique of the Norwegian trial that I have also voiced publicly on numerous occasions, hopefully to some effect.[51] Through these other experiences I came to understand that there were particular facets of the Fadime case that enabled the anthropologist to take an empathetic view. Fadime's own consistent view that her family should be understood, not condemned, helped. So did the fact that the perpetrator displayed strong emotions, coming across as someone of heart and mind. In some other cases I have researched, the perpetrators acted as if they were made of stone, and they used such excessive force or brutality as to put me off. I could not empathize, I would not empathize.[52]

Language and Translation

The English version of my book on Fadime could be freer in its use of sources than the Norwegian version. I wrote the Norwegian text confident that it would be translated into Swedish and Danish. Sweden was what mattered. The book was sure to gain much publicity there, as it did. Knowing this held me back. My family feared for me, and I was not too confident myself.

Indicative of the sensitivity of the case in Sweden was the fact that my Norwegian publisher, Universitetsforlaget, did not get its collaborator in Sweden, Natur- og kulturfôrlaget, to bring it out. This was surprising to my publisher and to me. A friend, Arne Ruth, former cultural editor of *Dagens Nyheter*, took it to another press, Ordfront, who published several editions of the book. Since its publication in Sweden I was invited annually to Sweden for many years on Fadime's memorial day. I addressed publics at the same place in the old Parliament Building where she had stood giving her *"Talet i Riksdagen."* Throughout the years I have had numerous public engagements in media, lectures, talks to police lawyers and social workers, and more. Not once have I experienced any unpleasantness. It is as if a Norwegian anthropologist can say things in Sweden that would be unacceptable from one of their own. A Swedish anthropologist who did speak publicly through his writings on the Fadime case was Michael Kurkiala, and very reflectively so.[53] His was a brave venture, and in a forthcoming article he provides insight into the challenges of doing public anthropology in Sweden that is unique and worthy of wide attention.[54]

When the English edition of my book appeared, six years had passed since Fadime's death. In the meantime I had met with Fadime's younger sisters and her best friend, who helped her write "The Speech in Parliament." I believed it was safe to draw on what they told me, having gotten their approval. And I was sure the book published in the United States would be something so foreign no one except possibly some academics in my part of the world would even notice it.

Language is at the core of writing. Hard choices have to be made if you come from a small language community. Norway comprises just five million people. Our PhD students write their thesis in English, as do many MA students. This means that for the most part their work won't be read by Norwegians. This has consequences for public ethnography. Anthropologists writing for the broader public have written in Norwegian, sometimes with critical political intent; most of these works have not been translated into English. While translators working from English into Norwegian are easy to find, the opposite is far from the case. Moreover translation means *rewriting*. Especially if you have written a piece of public anthropology in Norwegian you will have taken so many common referents for granted it will be difficult to make the work available to an international audience. You will ask yourself, *Do I really want to spend time on that?*[55]

Other considerations impinge. What about your academic career? When doing the Norwegian Fadime book I had the luxury of choice. Had I needed to have a book, like anthropologists establishing themselves, I should have gone for English. I think public ethnography, and surely political public ethnography, will come to suffer from the dominance of English as an academic language. For me working in Norwegian was also crucial from a timing perspective: things could move quickly, efficiently; the book was released just four months after I handed in the manuscript.

From English the book was translated into Portuguese (Brazil), Arabic, and Turkish, whereas the Kurdish (Sorani) edition was based on the Swedish text, which again was based on the Norwegian, as was the Danish. What happens to an ethnographic text in these processes of rewriting, as translation is bound to be, would be well worth an article but beyond my scope here. I have experienced delights and nightmares. With both the Swedish and the Danish translations I worked closely with the translators, who were superb, and it was thrilling and challenging to note the differences between even such close languages as Norwegian, Swedish, and Danish. With the English edition, based on the Norwegian, such problems arose that I felt in retrospect I would have done better writing the whole book anew myself in English; the translator was good but well versed in Swedish rather than Norwegian, and, crucially, she had not worked on nonfiction before. For the Arabic and Kurdish translations I could trust that the translators, whom I knew, really knew what they were doing and had a much better understanding of their readership than I. But there is always the risk with translations that one has no way of knowing what actually is transposed. Translation *should be* rewriting, and as authors we simply have to let go if we want our works translated into languages we do not know.[56]

Fadime's story brought me to places I had not expected to go: Taiwan, Iraqi Kurdistan, Lithuania, and elsewhere. Some of the publics were academic; in Taiwan students had read my book thoroughly and were eager to discuss it. Fadime's story resonated with them, except for the crucial fact that she was murdered; in Taiwan, they said, those who disgrace their family are expected to commit suicide. In Iraqi Kurdistan, by contrast, killing is precisely what a family might have done. In December 2010, thanks to an invitation from the Women's Rights Center in Suleimani, two Swedish Kurds, Ahmed Eskandari and Rasool Awla, and I traveled about Kurdistan with a gunman in the front seat and gave talks to public audiences on honor-based violence, followed by discussions. In one place we sensed a deep disquiet among the schoolgirls in the audience, and then learned that one of their classmates had been killed by her family the night before. Did it matter that we spoke? The Women's Rights Association in Suleimani thought that it could matter, that the fact of our coming all the way from Scandinavia to engage in discussions on problems we had in common would matter.

A memorable experience from the discussions was my failure at times to phrase the argument against honor killing adequately. Whereas I believed it was important to emphasize the role of custom or tradition—in line with the position taken by Kurdish human rights organizations in Europe—this was contrary to the perception of some Kurds, who were secular Marxists and held Arabs—that is, Muslims—responsible for honor killings, thereby exonerating their own traditions. In their view Islam was the culprit. It was a valuable lesson about ethnographic misperceptions.

In the United States Carol Breckenridge and Arjun Appadurai responded to the Fadime book by organizing a public event in New York bringing together journalists and scholars working on issues of honor-based violence; among them was the Canadian journalist Fabian Dawson, who had researched and made an NBC documentary on a Canadian Indian Sikh case that I have used in teaching a course on honor for years. Thanks to his and his team's work, the uncle and mother who ordered the murder of Jaswinder (Jassi) Kaur Sidhu in India were finally brought to justice in Canada. Thanks to the

English edition of the Fadime book I was invited to be one of the commentators in a documentary film on honor killing drawing on a German case, that of Hatun Sürücü. With Desmond Tutu and His Holiness the Dalai Lama also taking part, it was an honor to be asked.[57] I found it touching that the Dalai Lama, who spoke with the producer, David Gould, for more than an hour, did not (or would not) get the gist of what honor killing was about. The idea seemed beyond him.

Listing all the places to which I was invited thanks to the Fadime book is not testimony to my work as much as to her legacy. Moreover the black hole I had entered by virtue of researching honor killing in modern Europe created interest. Ethnographically the field was underexplored. Time was on my side, as one case after another caught public attention. The question now is this: Why do honor killings continue? And how is honor linked with extremist movements that also think it necessary and heroic to kill?

Conclusion

In the last course I gave on honor to a class of sixty students at the University of Oslo in spring 2014 (it was the eighth in a row), five top investigators from Kripos (Norway's Scotland Yard) attended. They took it not for credit but for learning. To the students their attendance was special: it meant that honor counts; it is a form of practical knowledge that even police investigators have need for. Through the years this ethnographer's knowledge of honor has been applied in numerous court cases as an expert witness; in Norway as in Great Britain, the role of the cultural expert is to serve the court, not the defense or the prosecutor, and she is obliged to bring up any information or knowledge she deems relevant to the case at hand.[58] My knowledge has also been applied by the police in crime investigations, by child welfare authorities in child custody cases, and by other agencies and organizations. This kind of work is time-consuming and can be taxing, and my regret is that there are so few of us in my country who have developed the relevant ethnographic expertise. Clearly people are reluctant to go into such fields; that is the black hole syndrome Fassin notes.

Doing this kind of work has been anthropologically lonesome. Honor-based violence continues to be a theme shunned by anthropologists, not just in Sweden. I understand this impulse well for in its grossest form research on honor killing does deal with the problem of evil. Anthropologists have been prepared to deal with that in the form of genocide—which puts it far away, Bosnia at the closest in recent times. Ethnographers can help shed light on why ordinary people, who by all accounts are caring parents and responsible community members, may feel obliged to pass a death sentence on their child, or why others, subject to similar social pressure, will not. It is in the particulars of ethnographic cases that humans come alive and expose themselves, with their dignity and their demons.

In her article "Norwegian Academic Anthropologists in Public Spaces" Signe Howell provides very valuable insights into how and why public anthropology on a variety of issues has been so strong in Norway over the past fifty to sixty years.[59] However, she omits significant contributions of some persons who are not part of the Oslo scene or not well connected with the anthropology department in Oslo, among them Ottar Brox, a prominent public intellectual for over thirty years who was critical in raising immigration issues and who continues to contribute to the public debate.[60]

This takes me back to Sweden. In an interview he gave in 2012 Hannerz makes an interesting comparison of doing public anthropology in Sweden and Norway.[61] He says, "Our Norwegian colleagues have been particularly successful here." As to why that should be, Hannerz explains, "In part I think they have simply tried harder. One of them had a regular newspaper column for quite some time, in the 1970s or 1980s or so,[62] and then in the next generation there were several who took an interest in reaching a wider public, and who may also have stimulated each other. This has been true not only of anthropologists; I think a number of other Norwegian social scientists have been noticeable as public commentators as well."[63] Hannerz goes on to observe that in a small language community an academic wanting to reach the public will need to use her national language and that works in English mostly go unrecognized at home, similar to what I have noticed. But it is his point about Norwegian anthropologists "simply trying harder" than Swedes to reach a general public that I want to focus on here. *Why* did we try harder? What was at stake?

Hugh Eakin writes in the *New York Review of Books* that Norway has a stronger tradition of freedom of expression than Sweden. That might be true and might help explain the much less strongly developed public anthropology in Sweden. Surely Sweden is a much more consensus-based society, with stronger censure for those who break out. What might be celebrated in Norway as courage may in Sweden come across as foolhardiness. This is not to put Norway in a better light but to point to some differences between the two countries that have consequences for the prospects of doing public political anthropology in either place. I escaped censure in Sweden because I was a Norwegian and we are known to be more outspoken—or less cultured. Had I been a part of the Swedish academic scene I am not sure that I would have managed. The cost might simply have been too high.

The narrative I have presented here and the heated debates generated by my publications speak to the combative nature of intellectual exchanges in Norway. However, rather than making it a personal affair, I have tried to show that conflicts between scholars reveal conflicts among ideas, values, and perspectives. Such disputes become particularly tense when they involve sensitive issues, such as honor killings, and occur in difficult times, such as after 9/11. These topics and contexts illuminate the fact that the sort of description of reality and quest for truth that social scientists produce are never beyond debate—which is precisely what public ethnography is about.

Notes

I am deeply indebted to Didier Fassin for convening the workshop and inviting me to participate in it. My gratefulness to all the participants for stimulating discussions. A very special thanks to Didier Fassin for his rich, challenging, and invaluable feedback.

My husband, Fredrik Barth, did not live long enough to see the publication of this essay. For the first time in forty-four years he won't be there to share with me the pleasure of a work done. All I ever did as an anthropologist, not least the public political part of it, would have been impossible without him. For my gratitude, and loss, there are no words.

1 The interview was in Norway's best-selling liberal daily, *VG*.

2 Djuve and Borchgrevink 2003.

3 I have conducted fieldwork in Cairo's poor quarters almost yearly since 1969. One of my monographs (Wikan 1996) was translated into Arabic and published in Egypt in 2013.

4 See Fassin (2013: 640): "Carrying on an ethnography is cumulating debts. Making it into an intellectual production is repaying them—at least in part."

5 Wikan (1982) 1991, 1983.

6 Ottar Brox, a prominent social scientist, does not actually have a degree in anthropology but he was trained in anthropology.

7 Wikan 1995a. Thanks to the invitation of Jean-Claude Galey, editor of *Social Anthropology*, an expanded scholarly version was later published in the journal (Wikan 1999).

8 The Norwegian *mot* means both "toward" and "against," which made it well suited for my title.

9   In connection with the fiftieth anniversary of the Faculty of Social Sciences at the University of Oslo, *Morgenbladet*, a liberal weekly, featured the ten most important debates during the history of the faculty; Ingrid Kvittingen (2013) interviewed Thomas Hylland Eriksen and me as the key debaters on immigration and integration.

10 "Norsk fundamentalist i vitenskapsklær" (*Klassekampen*, October 26, 1995).

11 Eakin 2015.

12 Geertz 1973.

13 The term *janteloven* (Jante law) was coined by the author Axel Sandemose. All the rules are versions of the idea that you should not stand out or think of yourself as better than others. The Jante law is commonly perceived as summing up an ethos of Norwegian culture.

14 There had been several reviews earlier in scholarly journals incurring no public attention, for example, Borchgrevink and Brochmann 2003; Fuglerud 2003.

15 On "afterlife," see Fassin 2015.

16 Here I follow Fassin (2013: 635), who has argued that the category of violence "could not be restricted to brutality but had to include other forms [he] designated as moral, such as humiliation, vexation, debasing comment and racist insult, and the conditions making violence possible."

17 Dahl 2003.

18 Seltzer and Ylvisaker 2003.

19 Djuve and Borchgrevink 2003.

20 Kayed 2003.

21 Klausen 2003.

22 The reviewers named Peter Hervik, a Danish anthropologist, as supporting their view. My department had hired him for a temporary vacancy. The senior reviewer, Seltzer, features in the acknowledgment to an article published not long after by Marianne Gullestad (Gullestad 2004) that deals with my work and that of Inger Lise Lien.

23 In an interview in *Morgenbladet* in 2013, Thomas Hylland Eriksen said he regretted his silence: "I could have reminded them of [*minnet om*] the difference between case matter and person [*sak og person*]. There were pure personal attacks. People claimed she was immoral." I much appreciated him saying so. See Kvittingen 2013.

24 Fassin 2013.

25 The late Francis Sejersted was the chair of the Nobel Peace Prize committee for a number of years and an outstanding academic and public intellectual.

26 Fritt Ord, founded in 1974, is a private, non-profit foundation that works to protect and promote freedom of expression and the environment for freedom of expression in Norway, particularly by encouraging lively debate and the dauntless use of the free word. Fritt Ord also supports projects in several other countries, and it cooperates closely with the New York Review of Books Foundation, arranging conferences and seminars. A Fritt Ord prize winner is selected yearly.

27 Howell 2010.

28 See especially Kurkiala (forthcoming) for a succinct presentation and discussion.

29 Boyer 2012.

30 See Carlbom 2003.

31 See Fassin 2013.

32 See Barth (1993) for a discussion of honor and elopement among Muslims in northern Bali.

33 Wikan 2002b.

34 See Begikhani 2003.

35 The accident was investigated by the police, but no evidence was found that Fadime's family had been involved, as some (including Patrick's family) suspected. It was raining heavily that day, the road was slippery, and as Fadime's best friend later told me, Patrick liked to drive fast. Fadime herself never believed her own family to have been involved.

36 Appiah 2007.

37 Obeyesekere 1990.

38 Appiah 2007: 144.

39 Barth 1953, 1959, (1980) 2004.

40 Wikan 2000a.

41 Fassin 2014.

42 Wikan 1984.

43 Stewart 1994.

44 Appiah (2011) makes good use of Stewart's (1994) *Honor*, which may help draw attention to it.

45 Rehman 2003.

46 Karim 1996.

47 Al-Aswany 2015.

48 See Hollan 2008.

49 Güngör and Dervish 2009.

50 Wikan 2008b: 71–114, on Ghazala and Emal.

51 Wikan 2008b: 157–92, on "Sobia, Sadia, Nafisa."

52 In my book *Resonance* (2012) I discuss the Ghazala case and the problem of evil and empathy.

53 Kurkiala 2003, 2005.

54 Kurkiala forthcoming.

55 Fredrik Barth wrote several books for the public in Norwegian, both popular ethnography (Barth [1980] 2004, [2004] 2008) and political public ethnography (2008), yet did not have them translated into English because it truly meant, as he saw it, *rewriting*, and though he was entirely bilingual, he didn't want to spend his time on that. See also Eriksen 2015a.

56 On the problem of translation, see Hymes 2002; Shreve 2002. See also the extremely interesting discussion in the *New York Review of Books* (September 29, 2016, page 93) following an essay by Janet Malcolm on translation of Tolstoy's *Anna Kare-*

nina (Malcolm 2016). Though the discussion deals with the translation of fiction, I think the issues are very relevant for the translation of anthropological works too.

57 Gould 2011.

58 On British courts, see Jonathan Benthall's chapter in this volume.

59 Howell 2010.

60 See Brox 1966, 1991. Howell may have omitted Brox because he does not have a degree in anthropology, but see note 6.

61 Boyer 2012.

62 Hannerz may have had Arne Martin Klausen in mind. I don't know of any other Norwegian anthropologist who has had a regular column for so long; Brox has one to this day.

63 This is also noted by Howell (2010).

References

Al-Aswany. Alaa. 2015. Untitled talk at the House of Literature (Litteraturhuset). Oslo. February 11.

Appiah, Kwame Anthony. 2007. *Cosmopolitanism: Ethics in a World of Strangers*. New York: Norton.

———. 2011. *The Honor Code: How Moral Revolutions Happen*. New York: Norton.

Barth, Fredrik. 1953. *Principles of Social Organization in Southern Kurdistan*. Oslo: Ethnographic Museum.

———. 1959. *Political Leadership among Swat Pathans*. London: Athlone Press.

———. 1993. *Balinese Worlds*. Chicago: University of Chicago Press.

———. (1980) 2004. *Andres liv—og vårt eget*. Oslo: Universitetsforlaget.

———. (2004) 2008. *Vi mennesker: Fra en antropologs reiser*. Oslo: Pax.

———. 2008. *Afganistan og Taliban*. Oslo: Pax.

Begikhani, Nazand. 2003. *Open Letter to His Honour Neil Denison*. October 10.

Borchgrevink, Tordis, and Grete Brochmann. 2003. "Det generøse forræderi. Individer og kollektiver under velferdsstatens vinger: Bokanmeldelse av Unni Wikan, *Generous Betrayal*." *Tidsskrift for samfunnsforskning*, no. 1: 87–97.

Boyer, Dominique. 2012. "An Anthropologist of the World: Interview with Ulf Hannerz, September 2." In *Anthropology Now and Next: Essays in Honor of Ulf Hannerz*, edited by Thomas Hylland Eriksen and Janet Carsten. Oxford: Berghahn.

Brox, Ottar. 1966. *Hva skjer i Nord-Norge? En studie i norsk utkantpolitikk*. Oslo: Pax.

———. 1991. *Jeg er ikke rasist, men . . . Hvordan får vi våre meninger om innvandrere og innvandring*. Oslo: Gyldendal.

Carlbom, Aje. 2003. *The Imagined versus the Real Other: Multiculturalism and the Representation of Muslims in Sweden*. Lund: Lund Monographs in Social Anthropology.

Dahl, Hans Fredrik. 2003. "Når forskere blir til fiender." *Dagbladet*, November 16.

Djuve, Anne Britt, and Tordis Borchgrevink. 2003. "Kunsten å få folk til å holde kjeft." *Dagbladet*, December 1.

Drakulic, Slavenka. (1991) 1996. *Café Europa: Life after Communism*. London: Penguin Books.

Eakin, Hugh. 2015. "Norway: The Two Faces of Extremism." *New York Review of Books*, March 5.

Eriksen, Thomas Hylland. 1995. *Det nye fiendebildet*. Oslo: Cappelen Damm.

———. 2006. *Engaging Anthropology: The Case for a Public Presence*. London: Bloomsbury Academic.

———. 2015. *Fredrik Barth: An Intellectual Biography*. London: Pluto Press.

Fassin, Didier. 2013. "Why Ethnography Matters: On Anthropology and Its Publics." *Cultural Anthropology* 28.4: 621–46.

———. 2014. "True Life, Real Lives: Revisiting the Boundary between Ethnography and Fiction." *American Ethnologist* 41: 40–55.

———. 2015. "The Public Afterlife of Ethnography." *American Ethnologist* 42.4: 5592–609.

Finkielkraut, Alan. 1995. *The Defeat of the Mind*. New York: Columbia University Press.

Fuglerud, Øyvind. 2003. "Generøst forræderi eller antropologisk vådeskudd: Bokanmeldelse av Unni Wikan, *Generous Betrayal*." *Tidsskrift for samfunnsforskning*, no. 1, 98–108.

Geertz, Clifford. 1973. *The Interpretation of Cultures*. New York: Basic Books.

Gould, David. 2011. *Two Sides of the Moon: The Honor Killing of Ayun Hatun Surucu*. Documentary film. My Sweet Lord Entertainment. www.twosidesofthemoon .com.

Gullestad, Marianne. 2004. "Blind Slaves of Our Prejudices: Debating 'Culture' and 'Race' in Norway." *Ethnos* 69.2: 177–203.

Güngör, Emre, and Nima Dervish. 2009. *Varför mördar man sin dotter?* Stockholm: Norstedts.

Hollan, Douglas. 2008. "Being There: On the Imaginative Aspects of Understanding Others and Being Understood." *Ethos* 36.4: 475–89.

Howell, Signe. 2010. "Norwegian Academic Anthropologists in Public Spaces." *Current Anthropology* 51, suppl. 2: 269–78.

Hymes, Dell. 2002. "Translation of Oral Narratives." *Anthropology News*, May 2002, 23.

Ignatieff, Michael. 1999. *Whose Universal Values? The Crisis in Human Rights*. The Hague: Foundation Horizon.

Karim, Nasim. 1996. *Izzat—For ærens skyld*. Oslo: Cappelen.

Kayed, Mehmed S. 2003. "Upresis Wikan-debatt." *Dagbladet*, December 12.

Klausen, Arne Martin. 2003. "Sosialantropologi og innvandringsdebatt." *Dagbladet*, December 2.

Kurkiala, Michael. 2003. "Interpreting Honour Killings: The Story of Fadime Sahindal (1975–2002) in the Swedish Press." *Anthropology Today* 19.1: 6–7.

———. 2005. *I varje trumslag jordens puls: Om vår tids rädsla för skillnader*. Stockholm: Ordfront.

———. forthcoming. "Treading a Minefield: Anthropology and the Debate about Honor Killings in Sweden." In *Engaged Anthropology: Views from Scandinavia*, edited by Tone Bringa and Synnøve Bendixen. Basingstoke: Palgrave Macmillan.

Kvittingen, Ingrid. 2013. "Multi-kultidebatten." *Morgenbladet*, August 30.

Lien, Inger Lise. 1993. "Når gjestene kritiserer vertskapet." *Aftenposten*.

———. 1997. *Ordet som stempler djevlene: Holdninger blant pakistanere og nordmenn*. Oslo: Aventura.

Maalouf, Amin. 2012. *In the Name of Identity: Violence and the Need to Belong*. London: Arcade.

Malcolm, Janet. 2016. "Socks." *New York Review of Books,* June 23.

Obeyesekere, Gananath. 1990. *The Work of Culture*. Chicago: University of Chicago Press.

Rehman, Shabana. 2003. "Du burde holdt kjeft, Fadime!" *Dagbladet*, January 25.

Seltzer, Michael, and Signe Ylvisaker. 2003. "Kritikken av Wikan." *Dagbladet*, November 27.

Sen, Amartya. 1990. "Individual Freedom as a Social Commitment." *New York Review of Books,* June 14: 49–52.

———. 2006. *Identity and Violence: The Illusion of Destiny*. New York: Norton.

Shreve, Gregory. 2002. "Translation, Fidelity, and Other Mythical Beasts I Have Sighted." *Anthropology News*, October: 7.

Stewart, Frank Henderson. 1994. *Honor*. Chicago: University of Chicago Press.

Wikan, Unni. 1976. *Fattigfolk i Cairo*. Oslo: Gyldendal.

———. 1980. *Life among the Poor in Cairo*. Translated by Ann Henning. London: Tavistock/Methuen.

———. 1983. *I morgen, hvis Gud vil: Kvinneliv i Cairos bakgater*. Oslo: Universitetsforlaget.

———. 1984. "Shame and Honor: A Contestable Pair." *Man* 19: 635–52.

———. (1982) 1991. *Behind the Veil in Arabia: Women in Oman*. Chicago: University of Chicago Press.

———. 1995a. "Er 'kultur' blitt vårt nye rasebegrep?" *Aftenposten*, February 27.

———. 1995b. *Mot en ny norsk underklasse: Innvandrere, kultur og integrasjon*. Oslo: Gyldendal.

———. 1996. *Tomorrow, God Willing: Self-Made Destinies in Cairo*. Chicago: University of Chicago Press.

———. 1999. " 'Culture'—A New Concept of Race?" *Social Anthropology* 7.1: 57–64.

———. 2002a. "Citizenship on Trial: Nadia's Case." In *Engaging Cultural Differences: The Multicultural Challenge in Liberal Democracies*, edited by Richard Shweder, Martha Minow, and Hazel Rose Markus, 128–44. New York: Russell Sage.

———. 2002b. "For ærens skyld." *Aftenposten,* January 26.

———. 2002c. *Generous Betrayal: Politics of Culture in the New Europe.* Chicago: University of Chicago Press.

———. 2003. *For ærens skyld: Fadime til ettertanke.* Oslo: Universitetsforlaget.

———. 2004. *Medmennesker: 35 år i Kairos bakgater.* Oslo: Pax.

———. 2008a. *In Honor of Fadime: Murder and Shame.* Translated by Anna Paterson. Chicago: University of Chicago Press.

———. 2008b. *Om ære.* Oslo: Pax.

———. 2012. *Resonance: Beyond the Words.* Chicago: University of Chicago Press.

11

Ethnography Prosecuted

Facing the Fabulation of Power

JOÃO BIEHL

"Absolutely not." I would not meet Dr. X at the Solicitor General's Office. The medical researcher and I were in the midst of a tense disagreement over the interpretation and publication of data we had collected, as collaborators, on right-to-health lawsuits against the southern Brazilian state of Rio Grande do Sul. This was nothing short of intimidation, I told Dr. A, a head researcher who knew Dr. X and was a kind of informal mediator in our unfolding feud. After all, Dr. X was an evidence-based medicine consultant for the state and worked closely with the attorneys reviewing the lawsuits. The Solicitor General's Office was hardly a neutral setting for our meeting.

What a hellish situation. It was mid-August 2010, and I had plans to fly out of Porto Alegre the next day. After multiple failed attempts to contact him, Dr. X had finally approached me, requesting that I remove all criticisms of the health system's malfunctioning from the article I had drafted over the summer, together with three other collaborators in the United States. He also insisted that our ethnographic references to patient plaintiffs were irrelevant and nonrepresentative, and should therefore be removed from the text. Beyond this Dr. X was oscillating between unwarranted claims for first authorship and the need to list the state attorneys as coauthors of the article, neither of which we had previously agreed upon. The results of our research were becoming an affair of the state, I thought, and my anxiety was reaching new heights, as I couldn't imagine a clear way forward.

In this chapter I draw on my own uneasy experience of collaborative research in order to engage polemics surrounding the widespread Brazilian phenomenon of right-to-health litigation, commonly referred to as the *judicialization of health*.[1] As I reflect on the results of our research alongside the fraught collapse of the collaboration, I critically assess the antilitigation arguments and truth claims jointly articulated by officials, evidence-based public health scholars, and the media. Taken together, our work sought to elucidate the field of the judicialization and ultimately revealed something about *the fabulation of power* and the potential of critical public ethnography to produce counterknowledge.

The project in question was a statistical and multisited ethnographic analysis of right-to-health lawsuits in the state of Rio Grande do Sul, which has the highest number of health-related lawsuits in the country.[2] I worked with research collaborators in the United States and Brazil to develop a quantitative and qualitative portrait of the people who are turning to judicialization and to illuminate their travails. But frictions with Dr. X and state representatives started to surface when our initial statistical analysis of lawsuits found that judicialization was in fact a widespread practice, accessible even to the very poor, and that judicialization had, to a large extent, become an alternate path to health care when administrative mechanisms failed to uphold people's constitutional rights (thus confirming our ethnographic findings). Tensions over the interpretation and dissemination of data ultimately led to an explosive face-off between my university's legal counsel office, on the one hand, and a Brazilian research institute, and state prosecutors, on the other, and to the demise—and, in a sense, failure—of the collaboration.

This failed collaboration might be read as an experiment in public ethnography, whose meanings and stakes, as Didier Fassin has argued, are foregrounded in challenges to local knowledge production and circulation.[3] Such challenges highlight tensions over the reception of counterevidence by the guardians of orthodox knowledge and hint at the interests and political projects imbricated in the making and policing of local truths.

This ethnographic episode itself has a deeply public character: not only are the questions at stake of crucial relevance to public interest—health, rights, truth, policy, and the delivery of care—but the work itself is public, involving direct collaboration with public officials, themselves engaged in judicial, policy, and scholarly projects. Distinct from—although by no means antithetical to—engaged or activist anthropology that speaks truth to power or makes its findings public, this kind of public ethnography simultaneously emerges from and reflects upon work with social actors who themselves work, in theory, for the public good. And while ethnography does indeed have a public afterlife that raises new questions and debates,[4] this public life can further participate not only in enlarging the ethnographic record but also in providing new openings for conceptual work. Carving out a retrospective *public self-reflexivity* thus brings into view the broader paradigms of statecraft and the specific mechanisms of veridiction and falsification at play in contemporary Brazil, particularly in the field of public health, and opens up new avenues for theorizing power and the political field.

When Ethnography Is a Failed Collaboration

In recent years, there has been an emergent emphasis on the role of collaboration in anthropological work, particularly in relation to the studying-up of scientists and other experts. Noting the "profoundly altered conditions in which relations of fieldwork today must be negotiated," Douglas Holmes and George Marcus, for example, make a case for collaboration as a crucial feature of contemporary fieldwork, envisioning a new form of ethnographic inquiry that brings anthropologists together with other "para-ethnographers" to engage in collective projects as reflexive, active "epistemic partners."[5] If, however, anthropologists engaged in successful collaborative work might learn from the analysis and knowledge practices of their collaborator-subjects, what is revealed when such epistemic partnerships break down?

In a much publicized example, Paul Rabinow's work with Berkeley's Synthetic Biology Engineering Research Center as a kind of anthropological collaborator-consultant fell apart over disagreements about scientific ethics and public risk, highlighting the fraught sharing of terrain by different kinds of experts and the challenges of critique within collaboration.[6] In working on the judicialization project, I found myself, like Rabinow, caught up in the broader interests of my collaborators, who brought their own strategies, political projects, and rhetorical needs to our (then) shared endeavor. Where Holmes and Marcus argue that the point of collaboration is "to integrate fully our subjects' analytical acumen and insights to define the issues at stake in our projects as well as the means by which we explore them," the moments where our insights and analytics clash with those of our collaborators might also become openings to the deeper issues at play.[7] Trained on the points of tension within collaboration, these "second order observations" lend a kind of dual reflexivity to the work, repurposing them as subjects of ethnographic attention.[8]

In the social and natural sciences negative results are seldom published. Yet, as is increasingly acknowledged in scientific research communities, these often unpublishable nonresults might be differently understood as important contributors to knowledge production. Reconsidering them positively, not as absence but as content, opens up new opportunities for learning from failure, directing attention to the sometimes invisible dynamics of experimental mechanisms and machineries, their assumptions and entanglements, and their contradictions, uncertainties, and political stakes.

In her work on the offshoring of clinical trials, for example, Adriana Petryna notes that models of drug development and testing frequently underestimate adverse effects, operating within what she calls a "paradigm of expected failure": real risks are known and harms are anticipated, but such failures are normalized under a rubric of experimentality.[9] If, for Petryna, paying attention to failure sheds light on deeper questions about ethical variability, risk, and accountability, how might attending to the failure of the research collaboration in Brazil similarly illuminate core issues of statecraft, evidence-making machines, and political rationality at work?

Returning to the debacle of my collaborative work in Brazil, I am interested in what can be learned from the wreckage. In the first section I trace the origins and context of our project on judicialization in Brazil, arguing that particular government and market dynamics are tied to processes of veridiction *and* falsification that shore up postneoliberal political discourses. In the second section I discuss moments of tension with my collaborators, reading these face-offs as openings to the underlying evidentiary regimes and conflicting interests that shape *state data*. The third section draws on close analysis of one material artifact of our failed collaboration to attend to the ways official narratives are produced and mobilized to particular ends, illuminating what I have called a *de-pooring of people*. Ultimately, I reflect on the kinds of politics and publics at stake, problematizing the criteria for inclusion in contemporary political communities (real or imagined).

Fabulation of Power

In his lectures on biopolitics and neoliberalism Michel Foucault argues that we can adequately analyze biopolitics only when we understand the economic reason within government. In his words, "Inasmuch as it enables production, need, supply, demand, value, and price, etcetera, to be linked together through exchange, the market constitutes . . . a site of veridiction-falsification for governmental practice. Consequently, the market determines that good government is no longer simply government that functions according to justice." In an inversion of older relations between state and economy, the market and its liberal principles are no longer subject to state power but rather determine the "truth" of government, that is, its jurisdiction and self-limitation. Guided by the principle that it is already in itself too much, government "is now to be exercised over what we could call the phenomenal republic of interests."[10] Excluded from this reality is the possibility that the collective good might be an object of governance or an organizing principle in individual lives.

The late liberal Brazilian political economy complicates Foucault's analytics. Over the past two decades the country has moved through a period of intense neoliberal reform and decentralization of services under the Social Democratic Party to the growth of social programs aimed at reducing inequality during the rule of the Workers' Party, which took power in 2002. Without radically breaking with neoliberal policies, the Workers' Party's poverty-reduction programs and expanded social services led to a redefined self-conception of the government as "beyond the minimal state."[11]

Brazilian state policy and political discourse emphasize the government's active role in guaranteeing the rights of citizenship and in eliminating poverty via cash transfers, for example, while the promotion of a market-friendly environment remains a central priority: "A rich country is a country without poverty," as an early slogan of (recently impeached) President Dilma Rousseff proclaimed. Brazil's political rationality today thus does not neatly align with Foucault's account, instead suggesting a more complex arrangement between state and economy, where the market, while critical, is not the sole dimension shaping governmental reason. The state itself is also entangled with personal interests and the demands of electoral politics, with the recent popular outcry over entrenched corruption highlighting the uses to which government is put even as it operates under the veneer of transparency and social equity.[12]

As I showed in my study of Brazil's model universal AIDS treatment policy, the consolidation of state activism has been coupled with extraordinary market expansion and the vanishing of civil society as a viable transactional reality.[13] In this mounting sphere of "state activism without statism,"[14] public institutions, in their frugality or futility, act in the name of equity while remaining largely unresponsive to the people they serve. While the verification of one thing normally serves as the mechanism for disqualifying another, in Brazil today there is *a decoupling of veridiction and falsification*. The state not only produces and authorizes particular kinds of policy truths but also actively falsifies renderings of its people and their needs. A different kind of unmoored falsification is at work, which coexists with but is also distinct from the joint machine of veridiction-falsification. These dual processes together constitute what I call *the fabulation of power*. They are the mechanisms that make possible the coexistence of supposed social protection—or "a politics of distribution"—and market expansion, thereby shoring up particular political projects and interests.[15] As Brazil's current crisis shows, state resources are used and depleted to such ends, while the public continues to insist on the importance of social services; as a recent survey showed, an overwhelming 45 percent of Brazilians list health as the country's principal concern.[16]

Thus in the Brazilian judicialization of health we see not a top-down biopolitical model of governance in which population well-being is the object of knowledge and control, but rather a struggle over the utility and purpose of government by multiple private and public stakeholders. Here both market and government are leveraged by people seeking access to services amid crumbling public infrastructures, as well as by regional public officials in the spheres of improvised evidence-based policy and electorally motivated politics, and by a federal government invested in a reclassification of the poor as middle class. By attending not only to how evidence-based policy is fabricated and deployed but also to how claims to need and accountability are falsified, we begin to see a more complex phenomenon of fabulation that coexists with political ideologies and market mechanisms within government. As real people become a part of these strategies, aggregates, and data, public ethnography and the counterknowledge it makes possible open up core questions about paradigms of statecraft and political mobilization.

In her recent work on precarity and political assembly, Judith Butler highlights the ways infrastructures are simultaneously the grounds from which and the demand for which bodies enter into collectives. "Everyone," she writes, "is dependent on social relations and enduring infrastructure in order to maintain a livable life." The demand for infrastructure is thus "a demand for a certain kind of inhabitable ground, and its meaning and force derive precisely from that lack."[17] How, then, might the struggle for workable infrastructures in Brazil shed light on state accountability and politics in-the-making in emerging democratic economies?

Critical Numbers

Allow me to contextualize. Just two years before the 2010 confrontation with which I began this chapter, I had embarked on a multidimensional and collaborative study of an intriguing new medico-socio-legal phenomenon in Brazil: individuals I came to understand as "patient-citizen-consumers" suing the government for access to treatment in the name of their constitutionally guaranteed right to health.[18] The rights-based demand for treatment access championed by AIDS activists throughout the 1990s had quickly migrated not only to other patient advocacy groups but also to the general population. People were not waiting for new medical technologies to trickle down, and they were using all available legal levers to access them. This judicialization of the right to health opened a new chapter in the pioneering history of patient-citizenship and pharmaceutical access in the country.

States were now seeing the number of lawsuits brought in their courts—particularly for access to pharmaceuticals—reaching the tens of thousands. With a population of about eleven million people, the state of Rio Grande do Sul was an epicenter of this phenomenon: right-to-health lawsuits rose from 1,126 new cases in 2002 to 17,025 in 2009; 70 percent of these lawsuits were for access to medicines.[19] Right-to-health litigation had become a subject of contentious debate in political arenas and in the media throughout Brazil. According to government officials and some public health scholars, this practice was dramatically altering administrative practices, encroaching upon state budgets, and ultimately producing new inequalities.[20]

Despite the circulation of numerous opinions, there was no reliable and comprehensive information concerning this avalanche of health-related judicial cases, their medical and anthropological character, and their impact on lives and on health systems. Official data-collecting systems were tenuous at best, and what little scholarly evidence on right-to-health litigation existed was constrained by small samples, limited geographic coverage, and the examination of few variables. I was intrigued by this lacuna and, detective-like, I wanted to identify real-time accessible data in order to get a clearer sense of who was judicializing and what was being judicialized: What sort of citizenship rights were these patient-litigants exerting on what sort of state, and what kind of politics was being enacted here?

I was familiar with Dr. X's health care research, and he was familiar with my work on the pharmaceuticalization of health care, which has tracked how, in both delivery and demand, public health has shifted from prevention and primary care to access to medicines, making Brazil a profitable platform of global medicine.[21] We agreed that a more comprehensive understanding of judicialization was in order and assembled an interdisciplinary "dream team" (as we called it *then*) of Brazilian and North American scholars in anthropology, medicine, epidemiology, and health policy.

Our initial work together was off to a positive start, and Dr. X introduced us to public officers at the Health Secretariat and Solicitor General's Office of Rio Grande do Sul. Dr. X and his colleagues welcomed the resources and prestige that came with such an international collaboration and, given the dearth of available information, they were interested in participating in the production of new scientific knowledge. The narrative of judicialization as a tool of wealthy patients seeking access to high-cost medicines was already deeply entrenched, and state officials saw the research as a way of showing how the role of market forces shapes physician prescriptions and patient demands. The officers, ever eager to demonstrate state transparency, authorized the state prosecutors to make the right-to-health legal cases they were reviewing available to our team.

With funding from my university and an external foundation, we gathered information from over one thousand active lawsuits, collecting data on demographic and medical characteristics of patient-plaintiffs as well as on their legal claims and judicial outcomes. In addition to this quantitative work I teamed up with local social scientists and started full-scale ethnographic research. I wanted to study this phenomenon from multiple perspectives and to produce a comprehensive view of judicialization on the ground. The broader idea, as I articulated it in an initial proposal, was "to create a critically informed public space in which social actors can move beyond polarized positions and, hopefully, identify a common good."

The findings from our initial analysis of the database were startling, and I was enthralled by the power of numbers to corroborate our ethnographic evidence. In contrast to official state and media accounts, which presented judicialization as a practice of the wealthy, our results revealed that patients who procured medicines through the courts were mostly low-income individuals who were not working (because they were either retired or unemployed) and who depended on the public system for obtaining both health care and legal representation.

The numbers plainly confirmed what we had been chronicling at public defenders' offices, where the poor get free legal assistance and where more than half of the lawsuits requesting medicines from the state originated. Roughly two-thirds of requested medicines were already on governmental drug formularies, suggesting that government pharmaceutical programs were failing to fulfill their role of expanding access. The medicines most frequently requested were for common problems such as hypertension, high cholesterol, asthma, and mental illness. The vast majority of lawsuits indicated that treatment was requested for a continuous duration, reflecting the chronic character of the diseases that afflict these patient-citizens. Moreover judges at the district and higher court levels almost universally granted access to all medicines requested, recognizing that their provision was consistent with Brazil's constitutional right to health.

While it is now common in anthropology to think about the power of numbers through Foucauldian analytics or in relation to biopolitical modes of governance,[22] what is particularly striking in this case is how the obscuring or unavailability of certain kinds of numbers mobilizes nonknowledge in the service of state agendas and interests. As Jacques Rancière has pointed out, being uncounted—or unaccounted for—is crucial to how political exclusion takes place, where the "part of no part" is invisibilized within a given social field.[23] Before our study, data on right-to-health litigation was unsystematized and not publicly available, leaving open a space easily filled with assumptions, self-serving narratives, and large claims based on small-scale studies with limited representativeness.

Numbers are indeed powerful tools in the game of veridiction-falsification that is at the heart of policymaking. They can, however, also buttress critique—especially when found within the state machine, like the lawsuits that composed our database. Taken together these 1,080 lawsuits refuted mainstream (government, academic, and popular media) antijudicialization arguments—that is, that judicialization was driven by urban elites and private interests and was used to access high-cost drugs that were not part of government formularies. Coupled with ethnography *our* numbers told a different story, exposing such arguments as part of what I came to think of as a broader *mythology of judicialization* that, in fact, undercut the complexity of the phenomenon and ultimately misinformed public opinion and health policy.

Entranced by the power of the numbers we were uncovering, I wanted to build upon our initial quantitative findings and secured funding for a second, more rigorously representative database, drawing from all medical lawsuits filed against the state of Rio Grande do Sul in 2008, when relevant information was first digitized. Work on this more comprehensive database was close to complete when tensions heightened with Dr. X over the meaning and destiny of our data, and our cooperation reached a breaking point.

State Data

How could I have not seen this coming? The fact is that I needed Dr. X's contacts within the state apparatus to access the much coveted information for our databases. At the time I truly did not think much of the rituals of power in which I partook, performing a kind of courtship ultimately aimed at data access. As is perhaps inevitable in collaborative research, and especially striking in the contact zones engendered through this kind of public ethnography, all parties came to the project with distinct views on its import, value, and potential, with certain sacrifices and compromises undertaken, especially at first, to appease one another and keep the project afloat.

In retrospect such moments of compromise and participation in uncomfortable rituals of state and academic politics serve as openings to the underlying tensions and maneuvering at work in both the collaborative encounter and public health policy. On one occasion I spoke to a conference of two hundred state attorneys about my work on the pharmaceuticalization of health care,[24] a talk preceded by the singing of anthems and pledging of allegiance to state and country flags, interspersed with interminable populist political discourses and an interview with the region's largest newspaper about my research in partnership with the Health Secretariat. In other fora both Dr. X and state officials had referred to my research as proof of how business interests were corrupting the meaning of the right to health. These sound bites were inevitably linked with pronouncements about "public money" and "equity," explicitly giving voice to the logics of state actors. There has also been growing global interest on the part of public health specialists and policymakers in engaging with anthropologists, and in corridor talks officials also voiced pride in the "scientificity" and "transparency" I supposedly bestowed upon state institutions simply by researching in their precincts.

On another occasion, at a public lecture, an officer from the Health Secretariat adamantly denounced judicialization as "a scandal," driven by well-off patients seeking high-cost and largely ineffective medicines new to the market and by overprescribing doctors in cahoots with profit-driven laboratories. He repeatedly emphasized the role of public disinformation, the draining of public health funds, and the inequity inaugurated by this demand for new medical technologies: "We try to guarantee the availability of medicines. But it is extraordinarily perverse that we have to guarantee the most expensive medicines, which have no effect whatsoever. The laboratories use patients to increase profits."

For this and other state actors such criticisms were, at least in part, a means of insisting upon a certain vision of public health and of the public itself, one that emphasizes population well-being and rejects the injustice of unevenly shared collective funds and services. There are limits, after all, to what the state can actually provide for its citizens, given that there are other pressing infrastructural needs and that medical technologies are developing and circulating ever more quickly.

The same officer proudly proclaimed that the state's Solicitor General's Office had created its own taskforce of medical consultants to verify or disqualify claims for treatment access and efficacy. Indeed Dr. X and this group of evidence-based medicine (EBM) consultants were now crucial assets in the state's efforts to contest judicialization cases and contain costs. Premised on the positive relationship between the use of experimental evidence and improved health outcomes, EBM has become, in the past two decades, a dominant force in health care research, policymaking, and delivery.[25]

If EBM emerged as a "rigorous" scientific means of improving medical decision making, evidence-based policy followed as a rational foundation for standardization, efficiency, and cost-effective rationing in health policy.[26] For example, a paragon of such approaches, the Cochrane Collaboration, was founded in 1993 under the motto "Trusted Evidence, Informed Decisions, Better Health," and now represents an international network of over twenty-eight thousand people in over a hundred countries, including Brazil, preparing and disseminating health care information and research.

The retrofit of EBM to public health has been neither easy nor uncontroversial. Criticism has focused on the narrow conceptions of evidence EBM creates and the incommensurability of population evidence and individual patient needs.[27] Many see EBM's experimental metric as a scientific legitimation of neoliberal political and economic models of health governance. As Vincanne Adams argues, this new landscape of evaluation is displacing the previous goals of interventions, making the purveyance of actual health services secondary to the development of reliable methodologies and the generation of comparable data.[28] In this context statistics are presented as objective, value-free, and abstracted from social and political contexts. Yet in reality, as Susan Erikson notes, "they operate as administrative apparatus that shape health futures by reducing contextualizing 'noise' and enabling business management rationalizations and decision making."[29]

Unlike certain health systems in the Global North that have been practically reorganized around the principles of evidence-based medicine,[30] in southern Brazil the pretense of evidence-based approaches is not borne out in solid institutional structures. While little has changed in the allocation of resources or the organization of health care services, state officials invoke the language of EBM as a stand-in for a certain kind of scientific modernity that works in the service of political interests that are both electorally motivated and publicly marketable. Deployed in the name of equity and the public good, these evidentiary regimes stand in for social concerns while effectively absolving the state of responsibility for actually attending to people's needs and demands or working to remedy administrative and infrastructural failures.

As our research continued I started to see the cracks where social fields and the fabulation of power were coming into view: moments where deception and discomfort were made visible and state agents revealed contradictions, ambivalence, posturing, and manipulation. In one such moment a representative of the state's Solicitor General's Office proudly announced to the media that the office was no longer contesting lawsuits for medicines that were part of government drug formularies, while behind the scenes attorneys told me about devising other ways of disqualifying claims (allegations that the prescribing doctor was not part of the public health system, for example, or—in the name of EBM—that dosages were incorrect or a prescription did not follow protocols). "It is no secret," said a state pharmacist who asked for anonymity, fearing for her job, that pharmaceutical programs were "a mess," with no efforts to upgrade drug formularies or to address problems with distribution and access.

On another occasion, when Ms. Z, an attorney working on health-related lawsuits, had started to feel at ease with us, she let slip her discomfort: "This is tough work we do: to deny treatment. When it is a lawsuit concerning a child, the lawyers generally enclose a photo of the plaintiff. I have a child. This is too much. I hide the picture in order to go through with it." While she was perhaps articulating an attempt to remain objective rather than be swayed by emotion, I could not help but hear in her words inklings of a broader process through which people were invisibilized from the state's handling of judicialization. Despite my unease, I kept quiet. Throughout this research enterprise I had trained myself to read the warning signs popping up from Dr. X and other members of the research team as idiosyncratic markers of stress, narcissism, ambition, academic theater—you name it. Nothing insurmountable, or so I reasoned with myself in order to keep the research going. But no longer.

I agreed to meet my collaborator-turned-adversary in the neutral grounds (or so I supposed) of the research institute managing the project's finances. As planned, the meeting would be an opportunity to address growing points of tension, moderated by the institute's executive director and Dr. A, the head researcher I had reached out to for some clarity on how to navigate the treacherous terrain of this international interdisciplinary research collaboration gone awry. To my total surprise Dr. X came into the conference room escorted by three state prosecutors, including Ms. Z.

Instead of easing frictions the meeting exacerbated them. I was shocked and furious to hear Dr. X tell blatant lies—that "the American team" (I was born and raised in southern Brazil!) had, for example, simply translated what he himself had written and then added an irrelevant anthropological veneer (so much for the work of critique!)—not to mention his unwarranted personal attacks coupled with self-praise of his role as the pioneer scholar of judicialization in Brazil. I was equally incredulous that the prosecutors seemed to condone the alternate reality so shamelessly being woven. I could not help myself and did not hold back in expressing the wrongs inflicted throughout our collaboration. Among other things I exposed Dr. X's earlier attempt to publish some of the database results without consulting me—a move I was made aware of only because he had listed me as coauthor and the journal had contacted me to verify.

In this back and forth of accusation the tone of the meeting had become unbearable. With no resolution on the horizon we all agreed to the head researcher's suggestion: Dr. X and the state attorneys would have two weeks to provide substantial comments on the draft article that three collaborators and I had crafted, which had been the catalyst for this painful confrontation. As I had heard a rumor that Dr. X had prohibited the project's IT assistant from giving us a copy of the second database, which was now complete, I made sure, before fleeing the meeting, to have him agree to share it with us in the next few weeks, although he added the caveat "after it is ready for analysis."

To make a long and tortuous story short: the face-off continued for almost two years, and ironically we almost had to judicialize ourselves. After several months and numerous reminders Dr. X's team finally sent comments on the article. Their request for the removal of all critical assessments from the text amounted to intellectual censorship and spoke volumes to the political and evidentiary stakes of our findings, as well as to our incommensurable takes on truth and the place of the human subject in the production of state knowledge and the political sphere. Moreover Dr. X was now denying us access to the second database.

We had no other recourse but to reach out to my university's legal counsel, who assessed the situation. Ultimately, in accordance with the agreements between the research institutions involved, we made the data from the first database publicly available on our website (with due reference to all researchers and sponsors). Later we finalized the article and published it on our own terms, without Dr. X, including all authors who met criteria for authorship consistent with best practices for scholarly publications.[31]

As for the second database, the counsel reached out to the research institute with which the university had contracted and, in an effort to ensure access, proposed to make the results publicly available on the Internet so that everyone (collaborators and ex-collaborators alike) could access and analyze them and write freely. But as the institute now claimed that the database whose production it had been paid to facilitate was "state data," the counsel began suggesting that legal action might be necessary. Two years after the start of the collaboration it seemed that we would be denied access to the data because our initial results did not support the biased narrative of the state.

How, then, did we finally gain access to the second database?

In a welcome, if unexpected, turn of events a federal judge in Porto Alegre learned of our travails and found our results too crucial for health policy to remain locked up. The Workers' Party had recently come into power in the state, and transparency was a key political buzzword of the moment. The progressive judge made some calls and put me in contact with the human rights attorney of the state's revamped Solicitor General's Office. A few weeks later Ms. Z released the second database, which closely corroborated our initial findings.

Epistemic Machine

The saga of our collapsed research collaboration adds more texture to the critique that emerged from the data itself. Particularly telling were the state prosecutors' comments on our original article draft, read in light of a broader sense of prevalent (and ultimately misconstrued) accounts of judicialization and who it is for.

Backing up to when we finally received the comments from the state prosecutors, before anything had been published, the comments on our draft came with the warning that "any publication based on the database must be submitted to the review of the Solicitor General's Office and the Health Secretariat." While there were no comments on or requests for changes to the actual numbers drawn from the database, there were plenty of highlighted notes throughout the text signaling "things with which we disagree" and orders such as "This must be removed," together with a few minor editorial suggestions. The objective (so to speak) labor of the social scientists was acceptable; the problem was with contextualizing, making connections across scales, and moments of interpretation and critique.

The officer of special affairs who signed off on the document did so in the name of the Solicitor General's Office and the Health Secretariat, lending the views expressed an official, public character. Considered as a document, the draft made visible certain assumptions and positions, laying bare the core tensions underlying our faltering collaboration. As Anneliese Riles has shown, documents are "paradigmatic artifacts of modern knowledge practices": they instantiate and render legible ways of knowing, doing, and studying. She calls for attention to documents as artifacts that enable us to "take other people's knowledge practices as an ethnographic subject" seriously, shedding light on the commitments of their and our own knowledge.[32] In this sense the document in question—our article draft with commentary—becomes a window into conflicting epistemic practices as they play out over time.

This particular document gains analytic currency not only as an embodiment of our failed collaborative project but also as a critical artifact of political rationality.[33] In this capacity it embodies how evidence is constructed and deployed in the service of political schemes and an improvised statecraft ultimately removed from the people it supposedly represents and governs. As I have shown elsewhere, judicialization has become a "para-infrastructure" that allows the state to disqualify claims and delay action;[34] in the logic of state actors, if the poverty of claimants can be denied, so too can the pressing need to change policy and improve the delivery of services.

Our draft of the article began with a case study: that of Mrs. Y, a patient-litigant I knew from my ethnographic research who was suing the state for medication to treat her pulmonary hypertension. Forty-eight years old and HIV-positive, married to a taxi driver, and living in a shantytown of Porto Alegre, Mrs. Y lost her job as a custodian when shortness of breath made it impossible for her to perform her duties. Unlike her HIV treatment, which is provided free of charge, Sildenafil, the drug her doctor prescribed, is not offered through the public health care system and costs US$1,300 a month. With free legal representation from the Public Defender's Office, Mrs. Y sued the state for the medication, losing her initial lawsuit but winning on appeal. As we noted later in our article draft, Mrs. Y was in many respects (middle age, female gender, low income, ill health) a "typical" patient-litigant, although in other ways (HIV status, losing her initial lawsuit) somewhat anomalous.

The state prosecutors' response to this story in the introduction and throughout the article was unequivocal: *It must be excised from the text.* There was no place for particular stories, and ethnographic knowledge was refused as unscientific. Taking issue not only with the chosen vignette—which, they claimed, was not representative of the larger sample and was therefore misleading to readers—but with the broader possibility of acknowledging or learning from life stories, they dismissed such personal narratives as working against objectivity. They wrote, "There is no one specific case that could represent the issue of judicialization." From this perspective no singular life story has value against the supposedly generalizable aggregate of data. An appeal to accuracy becomes a means of erasing human stories, and the fetishization of data performs a kind of scientific legitimacy. Staying with the numbers lends the guise of objectivity while leaving space for tinkering with interpretations, unbound by the precarious realities of bodies and voices. Visible in this interpretive machinery are efforts to erase the singularity of circumstances and to reduce dissensus. These efforts enact political work as they circumscribe state accountability.

The commentators also objected to much of the interpretive and analytic work of the article. They denounced contextual information on the health system and public bureaucracy as irrelevant and decried commentary on the failings of current drug formularies and systems of provision as "speculative" and "opinion," even though it was backed up by interviews with local patient-plaintiffs, families, pharmacists, caregivers, and public defenders, all of whom alluded to local and regional administrative failures. They cast aside arguments about the limitations of the public health system in adequately meeting the needs of the public as "not based on the data." Data come to stand in for infrastructure here, and, in a strategic inversion, where there are no data there can be no problems with existing services. This reasoning buys time, as it were, postponing the need to address gaps and lacks in the system and slowing the immediacy of judicialization's temporality. The political thus becomes a means of controlling time.

As a demonstration of an incipient, grassroots form of counterpower, judicialization is subject to a war over interpretations. As Rancière reminds us in *Moments Politiques*, "All transformation interprets, and all interpretation transforms."[35] Dismissing our analysis as "differing opinions" and "value judgments" and relying on a narrow view of evidence, the state officials suggested edits and commentary managed to reduce our findings—which in fact *countered* dominant accounts of judicialization—to the self-same stories we sought to challenge, all in the name of science. Rehashing arguments that place blame on individual patient-litigants claiming unnecessary and unjust use of the system while denouncing our analysis as irrational and value-laden, their policing of relevance becomes a means of controlling the judicialization narrative. These explanations both erase critique and its power to enlarge public conversation, and foreclose broader political questions. In this way an epistemic machine comes into being through which evidentiary claims are mobilized and perpetuated, performing a work that folds all data (even counterknowledge) into its own logics.

De-Pooring People

The story is still being written. The judicialization of the right to health remains a contentious subject in Brazil, extending its reach into the national sphere of media and political discourse, where the narratives I encountered in the field continue to circulate and gain strength.[36] "Judicialization Increases Health Inequity" was a recent headline in *Folha de São Paulo*, one of Brazil's most influential newspapers. The article framed judicialization as a scandal of the "haves" triumphing over the "have-nots," a view echoed by government officials. Brazil's health minister has said that lawsuits seeking medicines "take resources away from the poorest to benefit those who have more." "It's a kind of Robin Hood in reverse," added the health secretary of the State of São Paulo, "to take from the poor to give to those who can afford to pay for a good lawyer." The director of Brazil's Cochrane Center for evidence-based medicine has speculated that the pharmaceutical industry is behind the phenomenon of judicialization: "Why does no one file a lawsuit for the government to give calcium to pregnant women and prevent hypertension? Because calcium does not cost anything, there is no lobby behind it."[37]

I searched online and found the study most likely mentioned in the *Folha* article: "The Right to Health in the Courts of Brazil: Worsening Health Inequities?" by the legal scholar Octavio Luiz Motta Ferraz.[38] As in his other publications the author unsurprisingly responded yes to the leading question in his title, resting his judgment on studies that "confirm that a majority of right-to-health litigants come from social groups that are already considerably advantaged in terms of all socioeconomic indicators, including health conditions."[39] Repeated and self-reinforcing, these portrayals congeal into a dominant myth that casts patients as malingerers and the state as a just defender of equity, depoliticizing the actions of patient-plaintiffs while buttressing state actors' political projects.

What comes into view in the prosecutors' comments on our article draft is precisely the production and perpetuation of such state stories. "In all legends," writes Foucault, "there is a certain ambiguity between the fictional and the real—but it occurs for opposite reasons. Whatever its kernel of reality, the legendary is nothing else, finally, but the sum of what is said about it. It is indifferent to the existence or nonexistence of the persons whose glory it transforms."[40] For Foucault legends walk the line between the fictional and the real, between what is known and how it is talked about, thereby gaining a kind of story-life of their own and crystallizing into truth. The stakes of such circulating stories are both real and unfettered by human concerns, "indifferent" to the "persons whose glory it transforms." These stories thus come to serve as a kind of machine of fabulation, managing how evidence is absorbed, reconfigured, or put to work.

A recent review article on lawsuits for access to medicines, published in a Brazilian public health journal, sought to aggregate available research (our own study included) in order to offer a more general, comprehensive account of the phenomenon of judicialization. Read critically the article speaks to the extent to which the mythology of judicialization operates largely unchecked; the authors misread and inaccurately report on our research, restating conclusions that, while unsubstantiated by available evidence, have already made their way into the dominant narrative.[41] For example, on drug costs, the authors state, "In most cases, the prescribed drugs can be classified as medium to high cost"—an assertion that is at odds with the strong evidence in our results. Moreover only one study under their review actually contained specific drug costs.[42] Self-reinforcing and recounted as fact, such arguments insidiously stand in for the truth of judicialization, where the fictional is recast as the real. Attending to falsehood thus opens up space for asking what stories are told and how they gain currency, offering entry points into both the conditions of their making and their force in the world.

An ethnographic approach to our numerical data produced an entirely different empirical portrait than the one relied on by officials and public health scholars.[43] This highlights the potential of publicly engaged ethnography to produce counterknowledges that might render pressing infrastructural challenges visible and support the mobilization of counterpublics. Indeed as cost-cutting public officers kidnap the discourse on equity, one wonders how the inequalities produced by government policies (or lack thereof) can be alternatively politicized.

While a reduction in inequality under the federal rule of the Workers' Party and the associated rise of the so-called new middle class, which supposedly now occupies 50.5 percent of the population,[44] have been heralded as the end of endemic poverty, mainstream narratives about judicialization frame the phenomenon as a practice of the wealthy. In a sense these stories dovetail with the knowledge and policy systems through which this new middle class is being fashioned, as new forms of statecraft and ideas of citizenship and legitimate politics accompany a massive social recasting of Brazil's poor in terms of market inclusion and the potential to consume. While in the United States poverty has been stigmatized and rewritten as illness,[45] in the populist, "postneoliberal" state of Brazil the erasure of poverty takes a different form, whereby those who were once poor now find themselves categorized as middle class.

Ultimately, critical ethnography allows us to call into question the *fabulation of power* that not only makes poor patient-citizens publicly invisible, but also *proves* (through stylish modeling and bizarre quantitative maneuvers) that the subjects of judicialization are not poor at all—an epistemic mechanism I think of as *de-pooring people*. This supposed proof is generally offered in the name of the country's neediest, who, the argument goes, suffer from the impact of judicialization on health care budgets and policies. The mythology of judicialization which de-poors actual people seeking access, care, and justice in a faltering public health system thus sits in awkward tension with a state caught up in projects of championing and speaking for "the new middle class." These shifting categorizations and ways of imagining citizenship, justice, and politics actually render the poor less visible—all in the name of the public good. As ethnographers we must attend to these forms of statecraft and to the kinds of evidence and political subjectivities built into the para-infrastructure of rights and interests that the judicialization of health has occasioned.

Entering Justice

This experiment in public ethnography asks what happens when the ethnographer approaches the black box of power and grapples with what might be learned from it. In this attempted entry, failure itself opens space for considering how and to what ends truths about both citizens' needs and rights and state accountability are mobilized. Opening the failed collaboration to self-reflexive scrutiny I assembled elements for a critique of contemporary political rationality, showing how public ethnography might simultaneously contribute to an enlargement of the ethnographic record of statecraft and evidence-making machines and to theorizing on power and politics more broadly. It is only through second-order ethnographic reflexivity that it becomes possible to consider the explicit logics of what state actors say and do but also, through careful exegesis, to move beyond face value to the more entrenched political rationalities at play.

Arguments about the reality and impact of the rampant judicialization of the right to health in Brazil are often crafted around economic analyses and appeals to evidence-based medicine and policy. Critics fail to recognize that judicialization can itself help to create alternative sources of practice-based evidence, showing where existing administrative mechanisms fail people and offering clues on how to improve the system. A rhetorical machinery is at play that not only denies poverty but also erases people. Just as evidence-based medicine is mobilized to rationally allocate resources, fictions and falsehoods are marshaled in the name of equity and the public good, even though there are no existing mechanisms to actually assess or act on public needs. A fetishization of evidence lends an aura of authority to the aggregates of quantitative data while refusing the value or evidentiary force of the singular lives out of which all data are ultimately produced.

The individual patient-citizen here is at once blamed for abusing the system for personal gain and dismissed as a potential embodiment or representative of the collective. Such subjects do not meet the threshold of acceptance for political inclusion, even as the state supposedly guarantees universal health coverage for all. In the fallout of our collaborative research we glimpse the calculus of this exclusion, where fabulation and the machineries of veridiction and falsification are thrown, ever so briefly, into stark relief. Truth production is tied to forms of political rationality that depend on slippages of scale between individual and collective, the person and the public, where claims for the broader collective are defended at the expense of the individuals who actually compose it, obscuring unexpected grassroots politics around workable infrastructures while shoring up state politics-as-usual.

Countries have legitimate concerns about regulating new and high-cost medicines, and resource constraints mean that trade-offs will inevitably occur.[46] Brazil's experience highlights the importance of ensuring explicit and functional mechanisms for participation, transparency, and accountability in health systems. It also illustrates the significant role of counterpublics and the judiciary in monitoring the quality of health care and assessing the need for new medical technologies amid competing and contested considerations of value, cost-effectiveness, and efficiency.

Referring to their lawsuits, people often use the expression *entrar na justiça*, "to enter the judiciary" or, literally, "to enter justice." This suggests a more capacious reading of individual acts of suing the state in light of the broader forms of "entry" at stake—into politics, an emergent collective, and a different conception of truth, justice, and the public sphere. It is only through ethnographic work, and an undoing of the mythology surrounding judicialization, that such moments and mechanisms come into view, allowing a politics of entry to complicate prior understandings about the judicialization of health and its subjects.

Going against the grain of appearances and affirming dissensus, public ethnography thus illuminates the improvised quality of late liberal democratic institutions of government and challenges the remodeled logics of today's inequality. It also breaks open a distinct sense of politics in the making, in which people find means to hold the state locally accountable, creating an alternative political space from dire infrastructural conditions. Only by working against the fabulation of power and insisting on a space where precarity is actually a mobilizing force might we restore the place of the poor in political community.

Notes

This chapter draws from a research project developed with Adriana Petryna, Mariana P. Socal, and Joseph J. Amon, and I am deeply grateful for their amazing collaborative efforts and illuminating critical insights. I benefited greatly from the comments and suggestions of the participants of the Public Ethnography workshop, and I am thankful to them, and especially to Didier Fassin for his guidance at every step. I want to express my deepest gratitude to Naomi Zucker for her critical reading and wonderful editorial help. I am also grateful to Igor Rubinov, Heath Pearson, and Serena Stein for their insightful comments. To protect anonymity the names of all institutions and actors have been changed, along with their professional positions. This chapter is based on the article, "The Postneoliberal Fabulation of Power," *American Ethnologist* 43.3 (2016). Copyright © 2016 by the American Anthropological Association. Republished with permission of the publisher.

1   Biehl et al. 2012; Messeder et al. 2005.
2   Bassette 2011.
3   Fassin 2013.
4   Fassin 2015.
5   Holmes and Marcus 2008: 81.
6   Gollan 2011; Rabinow and Bennett 2012.
7   Holmes and Marcus 2008: 86; Marcus 2009.
8   Luhmann 1993.
9   Petryna 2009, 2010: 60.
10 Foucault 2008: 32, 46.
11 Maillet 2012.
12 Nobre 2013; Romero 2015.
13 Biehl 2007b.
14 Arbix and Martin 2010: 6.

15 Ferguson 2015.

16 Leite 2014.

17 Butler 2015: 21, 127.

18 Biehl 2013.

19 Biehl et al. 2012.

20 Azevedo 2007; Ferraz 2009; Vieira and Zucchi 2007.

21 Biehl 2007b.

22 Foucault 2008, 2009; Hacking 1982.

23 Rancière 2006: 12; Rancière 2001.

24 Biehl 2007a.

25 Daly 2005; Evidence-Based Medicine Working Group 1992; Lemieux-Charles and Champagne 2004.

26 Klein et al. 1996; Timmermans and Mauck 2005.

27 Behague 2007; Lambert 2006.

28 Adams 2013a, 2013b.

29 Erikson 2012: 369.

30 Such as the United Kingdom's National Health Service. See Harries et al. 1999.

31 Biehl et al. 2012. See International Committee of Medical Journal Editors 2016.

32 Riles 2006: 2, 17.

33 Hull 2012.

34 Biehl 2013.

35 Rancière 2014: xii.

36 Chieffi and Barata 2009; Da Silva and Terrazas 2008; *Economist* 2011.

37 Collucci 2014.

38 Ferraz 2009.

39 Ferraz 2009: 33; see also Ferraz 2011a, 2011b.

40 Foucault 2000: 162.

41 Biehl et al. 2016.

42 Gomes and Amador 2015: 9, 6.

43 Biehl 2013.

44 Neri 2011; Kopper 2016; Souza 2010.

45 Hansen et al. 2014.

46 Dittrich et al. 2016; Yamin 2014.

References

Adams, Vincanne. 2013a. "Evidence-Based Global Public Health: Subjects, Profits, Erasures." In *When People Come First: Critical Studies in Global Health*, edited by João Biehl and Adriana Petryna, 54–90. Princeton: Princeton University Press.

———. 2013b. *Markets of Sorrow, Labors of Faith: New Orleans in the Wake of Katrina*. Durham: Duke University Press.

Arbix, Glauco, and Scott B. Martin. 2010. *Beyond Developmentalism and Market Fundamentalism in Brazil: Inclusionary State Activism without Statism*. Paper presented at the Center for World Affairs and Global Economy, University of Wisconsin–Madison. March 12–13. http://law.wisc.edu/gls/documents/paper _arbix.pdf.

Azevedo, Solange. 2007. Remédios nos tribunais. Revista Época, December 12. Accessed April 21, 2016. http://revistaepoca.globo.com/Revista/Epoca/0,,EDG 80696-8055-501,00-REMEDIOS±NOS±TRIBUNAIS.html.

Bassette, Fernanda. "RS réune metade das ações judiciais de saúde." 2011. *O Estado de São Paulo*, April 29. Accessed September 20, 2015. http://www.estadao.com.br /noticias/geral,rsreune-metade-das-acoes-judiciais-de-saude-imp-,712418.

Behague, Dominique. 2007. *An Ethnography of Evidence-Based Policy-Making in International Maternal Health: Full Research Report*. ESRC End of Award Report, Res-000–1039. Swindon, UK: ESRC.

Biehl, João. 2007a. "Pharmaceuticalization: AIDS Treatment and Global Health Politics." *Anthropological Quarterly* 80.4: 1083–126.

———. 2007b. *Will to Live: AIDS Therapies and the Politics of Survival*. Princeton: Princeton University Press.

———. 2013. "The Judicialization of Biopolitics: Claiming the Right to Pharmaceuticals in Brazilian Courts." *American Ethnologist* 40.3: 419–36.

Biehl, João, Joseph J. Amon, Mariana P. Social, and Adriana Petryna. 2012. "Between the Court and the Clinic: Lawsuits for Medicines and the Right to Health in Brazil." *Health and Human Rights* 14.1: 1–17.

———. 2016. "The Challenging Nature of Gathering Evidence and Analyzing the Judicialization of Health in Brazil." Cad. Saúde Pública 32.6 [online]. Accessed September 23, 2016. http://www.scielo.br/scielo.php?script=sci_arttext&pid =S0102–311X2016000607001&lng=en&nrm=iso.

Biehl, João, and Adriana Petryna. 2013. *When People Come First: Critical Studies in Global Health*. Princeton: Princeton University Press.

Butler, Judith. 2015. *Notes toward a Performative Theory of Assembly*. Cambridge, MA: Harvard University Press.

Chieffi, Ana Luiza, and Rita Barradas Barata. 2009. "'Judicialization' of Public Health Policy for Distribution of Medicines." *Cadernos de Saúde Pública* 25.8: 1839–49.

Collucci, Claudia. 2014. "Judicialização Faz Desigualdade na Saúde Avançar." *Folha de São Paulo*, March 29. http://www1.folha.uol.com.br/fsp/especial/158639 -judicializacao-faz-desigualdade-na-saude-avancar.shtml.

Daly, Jeanne. 2005. *Evidence-Based Medicine and the Search for a Science of Clinical Care*. Berkeley: University of California Press.

Da Silva, Virgilio Afonso, and Fernando Vargas Terrazas. 2008. *Claiming the Right to Health in Brazilian Courts: The Exclusion of the Already Excluded*. Social Sciences Research Network.

Dittrich, Rebecca, Leonardo Cubillos, Lawrence Gostin, Kalipso Chalkidou, and Ryan Li. 2016. "The International Right to Health: What Does It Mean in Legal Practice and How Can It Affect Priority Setting for Universal Health Coverage?" *Health Systems & Reform* 2.1: 23–31.

Economist. 2011. "An Injection of Reality." Editorial. July 30.

Erikson, Susan. 2012. "Global Health Business: The Production and Performativity of Statistics in Sierra Leone and Germany." *Medical Anthropology* 31.4: 367–84.

Evidence-Based Medicine Working Group. 1992. Evidence-Based Medicine: A New Approach to Teaching the Practice of Medicine. *Journal of the American Medical Association* 268.17: 2420–25.

Fassin, Didier. 2013. "A Case for Critical Ethnography: Rethinking the Early Years of the AIDS Epidemic in South Africa." *Social Science and Medicine* 99: 119–26.

———. 2015. "The Public Afterlife of Ethnography." *American Ethnologist* 42.4: 592–609.

Ferguson, James. 2015. *Give a Man a Fish: Reflections on the New Politics of Distribution*. Durham: Duke University Press.

Ferraz, Octavio Luiz Mota. 2009. "The Right to Health in the Courts of Brazil: Worsening Health Inequities?" *Health and Human Rights Journal* 11.2: 33–45.

———. 2011a. "Brazil. Health Inequalities, Rights, and Courts: The Social Impact of the Judicialization of Health." In *Litigating Health Rights: Can Courts Bring More Justice to Health?*, edited by Alicia Ely Yamin and Siri Gloppen, 76–102. Cambridge, MA: Harvard University Press.

———. 2011b. "Harming the Poor through Social Rights Litigation: Lessons from Brazil." *South Texas Law Review* 89.7: 1643–68.

Foucault, Michel. 2000. "The Lives of Infamous Men." In *Power: Essential Works of Foucault 1954–1984*, edited by James D. Faubion, 157–75. New York: New Press.

———. 2008. *The Birth of Biopolitics: Lectures at the Collège de France 1978–1979*. Translated by Graham Burchell. New York: Picador.

———. 2009. *Territory, Security, Population: Lectures at the Collège de France 1977–1978*. Translated by Graham Burchell. New York: Picador.

Gollan, Jennifer. 2011. "Lab Fight Raises U.S. Security Issues." *New York Times*, October 22.

Gomes, V. S., and T. A. Amador. 2015. "Studies Published in Indexed Journals on Lawsuits for Medicines in Brazil: A Systematic Review." *Cad Saude Publica* 31.3: 451–62.

Hacking, Ian. 1982. "Biopower and the Avalanche of Printed Numbers." *Humanities in Society* 5: 279–95.

Hansen, Helena, Philippe Bourgois, and Ernest Drucker. 2014. "Pathologizing Poverty: New Forms of Diagnosis, Disability, and Structural Stigma under Welfare Reform." *Social Science and Medicine* 103: 76–83.

Harries, Ursula, Heather Elliott, and Alan Higgins. 1999. "Evidence-Based Policy-making in the NHS: Exploring the Interface between Research and the Commissioning Process." *Journal of Public Health* 21.1: 29–36.

Holmes, Douglas R., and George E. Marcus. 2008. "Collaboration Today and the Re-imagination of the Classic Scene of Fieldwork Encounter." *Collaborative Anthropologies* 1: 81–101.

Hull, Matthew S. 2012. "Documents and Bureaucracy." *Annual Review of Anthropology* 41: 251–67.

International Committee of Medical Journal Editors. 2016. "Defining the Role of Authors and Contributors." http://www.icmje.org/recommendations/browse/roles-and-responsibilities/defining-the-role-of-authors-and-contributors.html.

Klein R., P. Day, and S. Redmayne. 1996. *Managing Scarcity: Priority Setting and Rationing in the National Health Service*. London: Open University Press.

Kopper, Moisés. 2016. "Arquiteturas da esperança: Uma etnografia da mobilidade econômica no Brasil contemporâneo." PhD diss., Programa de Pós-Graduação em Antropologia Social, Universidade Federal do Rio Grande do Sul. Accessed May 15, 2016. http://hdl.handle.net/10183/141243.

Lambert, Helen. 2006. "Accounting for EBM: Notions of Evidence in Medicine." *Social Science and Medicine* 62.11: 2633–45.

Leite, Marcelo. 2014. "Datafolha aponta saúde como principal problema dos brasileiros." *Folha de São Paulo*, March 29.

Lemieux-Charles, Louise, and Francois Champagne, eds. 2004. *Using Knowledge and Evidence in Health Care: Multidisciplinary Perspectives*. Toronto: University of Toronto Press.

Luhmann, Niklas. 1993. "Deconstruction as Second-Order Observing." *New Literary History* 24.4: 763–82.

Maillet, Antoine. 2012. "Beyond the Minimal State: Sketching an Alternative Agenda." *Revista de Ciência Política* 32.3: 687–701.

Marcus, George. 2009. "Introduction: Notes toward an Ethnographic Memoir of Supervising Graduate Research through Anthropology's Decades of Transformation." In *Learning Anthropology's Method in a Time of Transition*, edited by James D. Faubion and George E. Marcus, 1–31. Ithaca: Cornell University Press.

Messeder, Ana Marcia, Claudia Garcia Serpa Osorio-de-Castro, and Vera Lucia Luiza. 2005. "Mandados judiciais como ferramenta para garantia do acesso a medicamentos no setor público: A experiência do Estado do Rio de Janeiro, Brasil." *Cadernos de Saúde Pública* 21.2: 525–34.

Neri, Marcelo Côrtes. 2011. *A nova classe média: O lado brilhante da base da pirâmide*. São Paulo: Saraiva.

Nobre, Marcos. 2013. *Imobilismo em movimento: Da abertura democrática ao governo Dilma*. São Paulo: Companhia das Letras.

Petryna, Adriana. 2009. *When Experiments Travel: Clinical Trials and the Global Search for Human Subjects*. Princeton: Princeton University Press.

———. 2010. "Paradigms of Expected Failure." *Dialectical Anthropology* 34.1: 57–65.

Rabinow, Paul, and Gaymon Bennett. 2012. *Designing Human Practices: An Experiment with Synthetic Biology*. Chicago: University of Chicago Press.

Rancière, Jacques. (1990) 2001. "Ten Thesis on Politics." *Theory and Event* 5.3.

————. 2006. *The Politics of Aesthetics*. Translated by Gabriel Rockhill. London: Continuum International.

————. 2014. *Moments Politiques: Interventions 1977–2009*. Translated by Mary Foster. New York: Seven Stories Press.

Riles, Annelise, ed. 2006. *Documents: Artifacts of Modern Knowledge*. Ann Arbor: University of Michigan Press.

Romero, Simon. 2015. "Scandals in Brazil Prompt Fears of a Return to Turmoil." *New York Times*, August 12.

Souza, Jessé. 2010. *Os batalhadores Brasileiros: Nova classe média ou nova classe trabalhadora?* Belo Horizonte: Editora UFMG.

Timmermans, Stefan, and Aaron Mauck. 2005. "The Promises and Pitfalls of Evidence-Based Medicine." *Health Affairs* 24.1: 18–28.

Vieira, Fabiola Sulpino, and Paola Zucchi. 2007. "Distorções causadas pelas ações judiciais à política de medicamentos no Brasil." *Revista de Saude Pública* 41.2: 1–8.

Yamin, Alicia Ely. 2014. "Promoting Equity in Health: What Role for Courts?" *Health and Human Rights Journal* 16.2: 1–9.

12

How Publics Shape Ethnographers

Translating across Divided Audiences

SHERINE HAMDY

Is "publicly engaged" ethnography always a laudable aim? With what public does an ethnographer engage in contexts of political repression? Or in contexts in which news networks grossly manipulate public opinion and perpetuate misinformation? In this essay I hope to make an intervention into current debates about the extent to which academics engage, should engage, or *can* engage with publics, and with what affective sensibilities. While much has been made of academics as distant, aloof, or unnecessarily obscure,[1] I point to the much less discussed political and structural obstacles that can stand in the way of academic public engagement. A major part of this problem, I contend, is the very different types of audiences with which one seeks to engage and the difficulties of translating social scientific research across different political and social contexts, and even across different affective norms and registers.

I reflect on barriers to public ethnography based on my own experiences conducting ethnographic fieldwork in Egypt and, later, my equally frustrated attempts to present my work to people with different political and social worldviews. Reflecting on these experiences I try to make sense of how a deep cynicism came to pervade my ideas of ethnography's potential to enact radical social change. The work of a younger colleague in my field, Sa'ed Atshan, encouraged me to critically interrogate my frustrations and ask what work my skepticism was doing. Thus I consider the work of Atshan as a counterpoint to what I had earlier come to know as the doom-and-gloom of public ethnography.[2] Following Atshan I reconstruct a form of critical hopefulness in scholarship and public engagement.

Preventing Ethnography

When I began my fieldwork on medicine, religion, and ethics in Egypt in 2002 I met with university hospital administrators around the Nile Delta, hoping to gain access to patients in their clinical encounters. This was inordinately difficult, as social science perspectives are not valued in general among clinicians in Egypt, who early in their academic lives (before high school) move to the sciences track and have little exposure to the perspectives of social sciences and the humanities. Thus they had difficulty imagining what benefit could possibly come from a social science analysis of medical ethics in Egypt.

The ability of the ethnographer to observe social and political dynamics is necessarily informed by factors such as her gender, race, background, linguistic abilities, and citizenship, all of which shape—but do not necessarily predetermine—her ability to access particular field sites. Social anthropologists also face the more specific problem of what I call *the ethnographer's illegitimacy*: a condition shaped by many factors, including a dominant celebration of hard science and technology that dismisses the softer fields of humanities and social sciences, as well as many ethnographers' focus on marginalized communities that challenge reigning structures of power.

The fact that I was born and educated in the United States and that I was now merely returning to "take" from Egyptian society in order to benefit my own career trajectory "over there" did not help matters. Many of the physicians on the clinical faculty had completed fellowships in their specialties in the United States, Canada, or Western Europe. Upon their return they had learned to feel ashamed of the state of the university hospitals they now served: their dilapidated walls, overflowing waiting rooms, and general lack of resources to adequately serve the high number of patients seeking heavily subsidized care. Suspiciously they asked what purpose I could possibly serve other than to "expose" the shame of poverty and "technological backwardness."

My response then was that I was interested in patients' perspectives on life-or-death decisions: how they and their families come to understand the possibility of a kidney transplant, for example, as an ethical or viable treatment amid contentious public debates over the ethics of organ transplantation. There were heated debates among religious scholars about whether doctors could ethically transpose body parts from one person to another, given that the body as a whole was the creation and property of God. The university hospital clinicians in one particular Nile Delta province subjected me to a constant barrage of questions about my "real intentions" in speaking with poor patients. I was told, "They are ignorant and cannot answer questions about medicine. As for religion, if you want to study religious perspectives, you can go to Al Azhar and ask the religious scholars for the correct views. No one else has the right to voice a religious opinion." Al Azhar is the beacon of traditional Islamic scholarship of the Sunni Muslim world, located in Cairo; it is one of the main sources of the Egyptian state's official position on Islam. At another university hospital, which specialized in eye diseases, the director told me that talking to cornea-opacity patients would only give them an outlet to voice anger and frustration at the government for not providing an eye bank. Giving the poor patients a platform to voice their grievances, he warned, would open a host of problems, leading to a potential clash with the government.[3]

During my long-term fieldwork in Egypt in 2002–4 political tensions were high; everyone seemed glued to Al Jazeera's coverage of the Second Intifada and violence in the Palestinian territories. Having little success in gaining access to Egyptian university hospitals, I subsequently received a call from the Fulbright office informing me that there was a bureaucratic problem and that I had no Egyptian government clearance to carry out my research project. Months later the United States invaded Iraq. At one university clinic where I had hoped to work, one of the faculty physicians asked me whether or not I believed that Saddam Hussein was *truly* a brutal dictator. I replied that it was obvious he was. The clinician and his colleagues then shook their heads dismissively and described me as "the daughter of George Bush." I protested that I could think that Hussein was a brutal dictator and at the same time that the United States should not invade Iraq. Again I was bidden farewell, yet another door seemingly closed in my face.

I wondered then: What is this endeavor we call "ethnography"? While many ethnographers have raised questions about which sites are available to field workers and why, there remain many ethnographies of the heroic trope that depict an unflappable researcher with the wherewithal to drop into any place on earth, pick a topic, and have a scene of human activity available to observation and analysis. Social settings are already more or less accessible to us. Unobservable spaces are like all those moments in history that are left undocumented and unarchived;[4] we end up commenting only on what is made available, all the while patting ourselves on the back for our ability to present "marginalized" and "alternative" viewpoints. Following Trouillot it seems we have more work to do in uncovering the conditions of visibility and accessibility as themselves phenomena of anthropological investigation and analysis.[5]

In Egypt the middle-class intelligentsia and professionals act as gatekeepers to recording the voices and views of the poor that are seen as both "dangerous" and a source of deep shame for the nation, views that are naturalized in the mainstream media.[6] This social gatekeeping is infused with elitism, intolerance of the poor, and the naturalization of inequality. It also coincides with brutal political repression, adding yet another layer to what can and cannot be said and who is allowed to speak and be heard. I also understand the offensive silencing on the part of a relatively empowered social class as a simultaneously defensive (and misguided) measure against Euro-American hegemony. In the doctors' own experiences training abroad there was a chance they could earn their European or U.S. colleagues' respect when they excelled alongside them in medical research. They learned that they could use their education, their cosmopolitanism, and their diligence to change those colleagues' preconceived views of Arabs and Muslims as backward and inferior.[7] Many of these physicians felt that their own personal work to combat these prejudices would be undone, the prejudices justified, if the outside world was exposed to those with less social capital in Egypt whom they themselves considered to be backward and irrational. Performing what is now referred to as "respectability politics," they sought to silence and render invisible Egyptian Others with less education, lower income, or offensive religiopolitical stances.

Delegitimizing the Ethnographer

My acute frustrations with these predetermined structures of access and intelligibility resurfaced a decade later, in June 2012, when I presented my work at the Islamic Bioethics conference in Qatar. At this public event, held at the Georgetown University campus in Doha, the audience included medical clinicians from different Arab countries who were practicing in Qatar and several Canadian and American nurses. The audience also included students from the surrounding university city. They had come to the conference on their own initiative, presumably because they found the topic—Muslim bioethics— to be of interest. I presented my research on the wide and intractable debate in Egypt over the ethics of organ transplantation.

My main argument, based on my ethnographic fieldwork in Egypt, was that religious objections to organ transplantation were part of a larger context in which a vibrant black market in Cairo in kidneys and liver lobes had generated antipathy to transplant medicine. Further, I argued that patients were largely disempowered in the face of rampant medical mismanagement and that wider concerns about the alarming increase in kidney and liver failure throughout the country could never be adequately addressed through transplantation. In the context of a widening gap in socioeconomic classes, organ transplantation surfaced as yet another bodily instantiation of the rich exploiting the poor.

Audience members were interested in my arguments about the entanglement of religious ethics, politics, medical efficacy, and larger questions about social justice. For this highly educated audience of mostly Muslims or people living in a Muslim country, attending a lecture from a U.S.-trained female Muslim professor may have been an infrequent occurrence, but it was not implausible to them that I could be a source of information or insight. Nor was it necessarily damning for this audience that I would approach the topic of Islam from a social science perspective, analyzing how and why people make claims to what is Islamic. And none of the audience members was invested in defending Egypt on nationalist grounds.

In contrast, on the presenters' panel, there were two faculty members from Al Azhar University for whom my presence presented an immediate problem. Because these are well-known figures in Egypt, I will name them: Saad El Din Al-Hilali and Mohamed Raafat Osman. The conference organizers were graduates of Al Azhar who went on to receive PhDs in Europe and the United States and were intent on bridging the gap between U.S.-based academics who work on Islam and Azhari scholars. In addition to Al Azhar's centrality in institutionalizing contemporary Sunni authority, it is also the site of strong political struggles between Salafi, Muslim Brotherhood, and traditional approaches to Islam that were *madhhab-based* (that is, according to classical Islamic schools of jurisprudence).[8]

It happened that this conference was held on the eve of the first presidential elections in Egypt in 2012, after the popular protests resulted in the forced resignation of Hosni Mubarak. It was clear that the Azhari professors, and in particular Dr. Al-Hilali, were uncomfortable with the minute-to-minute news updates we were getting from Egypt that resulted in the election of the Muslim Brotherhood candidate, Mohamed Morsi. Hilali's stance toward Tariq Ramadan, a leading public intellectual among European Muslims, who was the keynote speaker, showed that he had little tolerance for what he took to be Ramadan's divergence from canonical religious interpretations, not to mention his suspected sympathies with the Muslim Brothers.

As I described my research in Egypt among patients with kidney failure, I spoke of the poor management of public health, concerns about the unreliability of water and about food quality, and dangerous labor conditions that can predispose people to organ failure. I detailed people's well-founded mistrust of a corrupt medical system coupled with the government's inability and seeming unwillingness to curb the problem of organ selling. I also detailed the circumstances under which the much loved television personality and Muslim preacher Shaykh Sha'rawi had argued on Egyptian state television that Muslims could not donate organs for transplantation because they are not theirs to donate but rather the property of God Almighty. I explained that Sha'rawi's words resonated among patients and family members and even medical professionals in the context of larger misgivings about the transplant enterprise, not because of a scriptural or fatalistic opposition to medicine.

Hilali's outbursts during and immediately following my talk—beginning with "Is she *Egyptian*?!"—made clear that he did not think I had any authority to speak about Islam or to offer an opinion about Shaykh Sha'rawi. He asked how I could present such untruths about the contamination of Egypt's water supply and how I could ignore the scientific accomplishments of Egypt's leading transplant surgeon, Dr. Mohamed Ghoneim (about whom I had in fact spoken). His anger came from positions that I had heard many times before during the course of my research in Egypt in official institutions that are very much places where "ethnographers are not welcome."[9] Those objections were based on the following assumptions:

1. To speak to foreign audiences about problems in Egypt like pollution or corruption is a betrayal of Egyptian national interests and leaves Egypt open to attacks by its enemies.
2. To offer perspectives on the rural poor or uneducated (e.g., patients suffering from kidney failure) stains Egypt's image.
3. To speak of government mismanagement or corruption is to fuel the flames of opposition parties, such as the Muslim Brotherhood, whose aim is to destabilize Egypt.
4. Social science is not a valuable or justifiable form of research.
5. Islam cannot be subject to social scientific analysis.
6. A figure like Shaykh Sha'rawi is above scrutiny by social scientific methods.

Hilali's outbursts echoed the justification of Egyptian state power and repression against political dissidents. Thanks to the national media in Egypt, this perspective is shared by a larger and larger majority of the population. The defensiveness about Egypt's "national image" now carries a particularly dark tenor considering the erosion of outlets for public and social debate.

As for the Canadian and American female members of the audience, they were appalled by the treatment I received, convinced they had witnessed an ugly instantiation of Arab Muslim patriarchy. While complicating Muslim views of organ transplantation, a professor of Islamic studies at the prestigious Al Azhar University publicly shut me down in a way that seemed to confirm people's worst misgivings about Islam. One of these women told me sympathetically, "These types of men are not only used to having the *last* word, but they are used to having the *only* word." While I welcomed her sympathy and I agree it is probable that Hilali's interlocutors are mostly if not exclusively men, I still chafed at the words "these types," which I understood to point to an assumed Muslim patriarchy. It was abundantly clear to me that Hilali's motivation to silence me came from his pro-state nationalism, not his being Muslim or speaking in defense of the Islamic tradition. Although he carried the weight of the Islamic authority that comes with his institutional affiliation with Al Azhar, none of his objections to my work came from disagreements with my analysis of Islamic theological, ethical, or legal positions. Rather, by questioning my national allegiance, he questioned my right to speak at all.

Given his demeanor and disregard for the female participants at the conference, I have no doubt that Hilali also views men as superior to women intellectually, politically, and socially and that my very presence as a speaker on matters of Egypt and Islam was disconcerting to him. But there was something discomfiting about the way his response could *only* be read by these audience members in terms of Arab or Muslim patriarchy and not his ultranationalist fervor. Nationalism is often both animated by and further entrenches patriarchy, whether in the Middle East, Europe, or North America. I felt I had little space from which to argue that political and gendered repression are interrelated and that global political economic forces (not just cultural ones) support systems of exclusion.

In my attempts to engage with public Anglophone audiences I often sense that no matter what work I present, there are inevitably those who only hear me saying "Islam prohibits . . ." or "Islam condemns . . ." even if my argument is making the contrary claim: that people have made *claims* about religion preventing this thing or that, and that these claims are better understood in terms of particular political economic factors. Inasmuch as my ethnography is already predetermined by structures of power within Egypt that grant or deny my access, it is also the case that such structures of power within my potential Anglophone audiences set the terms of receptivity and intelligibility of my work. Thus before I can present my ethnography and describe how things *are*, I must first argue *what they are not*. My work argues *against* the received wisdom in the United States, Canada, Western Europe, and Australia that Islam is a religion that necessarily breeds authoritarianism, intolerance, misogyny, and violence and *against* the dominant view in Egypt that only the educated middle and upper classes can speak, lest the uneducated, illiterate, marginalized, peasant, or urban poor shame the nation, or all Arabs, or all Muslims. Insofar as I intend to engage with a public, I know I am not starting on neutral territory, where all people are given a fair hearing. As much as my audience members may meet my words with defensiveness, my anticipation of their assumptions breeds a defensive posture in me, the ethnographer, as well.

Translating across Divided Audiences

One of the many challenges of public engagement is to know how to address different audiences, a process that requires a translation from what is intelligible for one public to another. Yet in the case of certain publicly engaged scholars hoping to address—and even bridge gaps between—multiple audiences, the continual translation of messages from one setting to another can be met with grave suspicion. As someone whose very identity and presence blurs boundaries—Muslim, Arab, American—my necessary shift in discourse from Muslim-majority to Muslim-minority settings is readily interpreted by both publics as "hypocrisy" or "double-speak."[10] For many audience members my critique of Euro-American hegemony in the Middle East sits uncomfortably with my willingness to simultaneously expose problems within Middle Eastern societies. Indeed speaking against dominant misconceptions held by one public audience risks offending another.

In the Anglophone media the Egyptian state is often depicted as a "secular ally" to justify and bolster the Camp David Accords of 1978 signed under U.S. president Jimmy Carter, in which Egyptian president Anwar Sadat broke from the pan-Arab alliance against Israel. In these media accounts the Egyptian government's overt attempts to control interpretations of Islam are largely ignored. Meanwhile non-state-sanctioned versions of Islam—what the Egyptian state regards as "bad Islam" (e.g., that of the Muslim Brotherhood and

Salafi groups)—are often regarded in Anglophone media outlets as unproblematized representations of Islam writ large, whose putatively intolerant views and volatile potential are used as justification for the superiority of secular democracy. In fact these political actors are violently and brutally repressed by the (undemocratic) Egyptian state, and their (unpalatable, in my view) use of "Islamic" rhetoric cannot be properly understood outside of this context.

Thus global media accounts misconstrue the fact that politicized groups in Egypt that identify under the banner of Islam are not opposing a secular democracy but rather are opposing an authoritarian government that attempts to tightly control interpretations and practices of Islam. In eliding the Egyptian state's orchestration of an official Islam, U.S.-centered media accounts further conflate Islam-at-large with the Islam of oppositional politicized groups. By labeling the self-consciously modern, rational version of Islam promoted by the Egyptian state[11] with something like secularism itself, U.S.-centered narratives fail to recognize overlaps between secular liberalism and Islam and reserve the label *Islam* for that which is alien or antithetical to U.S. political interests and cultural dispositions.

I find it difficult in public settings to explain my position on Islam and the Egyptian state because the dominant Arabic-speaking and English-speaking mass media render such a position impossible. That is to say, I am critical of how the Egyptian state wields its power to define the "true" place and interpretation of Islam—in part via state surveillance of Al Azhar—and of the Egyptian state's right to rid the nation of all its opponents who are cast as dangerous terrorists who threaten national security. At the same time, I also refuse to defend or apologize for certain antistate actors in Egypt with whom I adamantly disagree who mobilize in the name of Islam. Many public audiences find it unintelligible that one would mobilize a critique against the Egyptian state's use of national security to quash dissent *and simultaneously* critique Egyptian antistate actors' use of religious identity politics. I abhor the religiopolitical movements that cause major social divisions and strife within Egyptian society. Yet I refute the notion that there is something problematic and violent-prone about Islam writ large—or its place in the modern world—that determines these problems. In these politicized depictions of Islam, which inevitably influence scholarly output, little attention is paid to everyday Muslim practices and beliefs that are neither oppositional to nor directly promoted by the Egyptian state.[12]

In the global Anglophone media the "good Muslim" assimilates and naturalizes Euro-American hegemony and its attendant dispositions and affective sensibilities, while the "bad Muslim" rejects both Euro-American hegemony and its accompanying enlightenment ideals.[13] Hilali, wearing a suit and tie, not the traditional robe of an Azhari sheikh, can be easily glossed as a "good Muslim" according to this calculus. He is a vociferous opponent of the politicization of Islam in the form the Muslim Brotherhood has taken. It is not until the massacre of nearly one thousand people during August 2013, following the overthrow of Egypt's short-lived President Morsi, that this form of nationalist, modernist, secular politicization of Islam begins to appear troublesome in the Anglophone media. Only recently might we begin to wonder how Islam in Egypt can be so overtly politicized for two opposing aims: those of the military-state that *uphold* Euro-American political dominance and those agitating *against* the current state and military regime.

One year after I met Hilali at the Qatar conference, in February 2014, he was a speaker at an official state commemoration for the two hundred fallen and wounded members of the police force during the conflicts that followed the removal of Morsi from power. (It should go without saying that there was no official state commemoration for the hundreds of protestors who were killed by the state security during this conflict.) Speaking to officials serving a military state, Hilali justified not only the past killing of state opponents but also any future killing for the sake of Egypt's stability. He then went as far as to lift the military general who led the massacre to the status of a religious prophet.[14]

Hilali was addressing members of the Ministry of the Interior in the presence of the minister himself, Muhammad Ibrahim. In this speech he stated that history, ordained by God, repeats itself. God commanded on more than one occasion that there would be (false) leaders who try to force a religion upon the people of Egypt and pretend that it is the religion of God. The first time God sent Prophet Aaron and Prophet Moses to help Egyptians confront these false leaders so they could practice the "true religion of God." Today God sent General Abdul Fattah Al-Sisi (then the minister of defense) and Muhammad Ibrahim (then minister of the interior).[15] Hilali's speech and attendance at the event highlights for me the role of the Egyptian state apparatus and media in fueling a stark polarization between Egypt's supporters and detractors, of Egypt's worthy and despised, of those who count and those who must be silenced and rendered invisible.

Rejecting Cynicism

In my book *Our Bodies Belong to God* I presented an unlikely success story of organ transplants in the Nile Delta provincial city of Mansoura. In this anomalous tertiary medical care center, founded by the illustrious Dr. Ghoneim, almost all organ donations happened within families, and pious Muslim patients readily saw the good in organ donation. Predictably colleagues in critical Middle East ethnography were skeptical of the Mansoura story; surely we are more sophisticated and cynical than to believe in such things as success stories! If those who represent the interests of the political ruling class in the Arab world, like Hilali, refuse to hear or acknowledge political and social failures of their society, critical scholars in the U.S. academy can represent the opposite: a refusal to believe in *positive* social developments that can occur within the context of Euro-American hegemony and state authoritarianism. Critics questioned the source of the money for the Mansoura Kidney Center, as there had to be a more sinister story behind such an anomalous case.

After Edward Said's (1978) explication of the ways Euro-American hegemony-as-telos has saturated the production of scholarship on the Middle East, the post-Orientalist counterdiscourse has asserted the centrality of Euro-American hegemony as a form of unjust neocolonialism with profound social implications at nearly every micro level of social practice. Western imperialism thus looms large as the meta-object of our critique, and as such impinges on our ability to present micro *successes* (particularly if they are part and parcel of larger systems sustaining Western imperialism—but then what isn't?). There can be other options and possibilities besides the oversimplified binary of resistance versus power, such as when forms of Western imperialism can be repurposed to open up new possibilities. If an analyst is looking only for that moment of grand dismantling, then surely everything will fail that test, leaving us with nothing but cynicism (and self-satisfaction, perhaps, at our predictive powers). This stance also impinges on our ability to critique internal forms of violence and strife *on their own terms*.

This tendency is perfectly exemplified by a controversial debate that appeared in the popular Middle East online magazine *Jadaliyya* between the Palestinian hip-hop artists DAM and two U.S. academic colleagues who work on the Middle East, Lila Abu-Lughod and Maya Mikdashi. The hip-hop artists produced an Arabic music video as a social critique against domestic violence and, more specifically, against so-called honor crimes. The video presented a story, in reverse, of a young woman killed by her father and brother after refusing an arranged marriage and attempting to elope with her beloved. In the world of Palestinian social activism the Arabic-language media and popular music are powerful tools to broach sensitive topics like domestic violence. The DAM video asks how killing women can be linked with honor and asks its fans to take a stand against violence against women.

In the United States, where Islamophobic discourse looms large, sensationalist ideas about an oppressive Islamic structure that supposedly glorifies the killing and disposal of women circulate to bolster a sense of Euro-American moral superiority as well as to justify political interventions in the region. In this context Abu-Lughod and Mikdashi wrote an open letter to DAM critiquing their video for presenting an ahistorical and overly cultural view of honor killings, and hence of serving Western imperialist interests by depicting the Arab world as a caricature of angry violent men. They called for situating honor killings within the context of a brutal Israeli colonial occupation, the ultimate culprit in violating women's and men's social freedoms. The Abu-Lughod and Mikdashi piece sparked outrage from *Jadaliyya*'s readers and a rejoinder from DAM, who felt the sting of condescension from two academics unnecessarily reminding them, as Palestinians living under occupation, of the social detriments of that occupation.

As this debate unfolded on *Jadaliyya*'s website, I was reminded of Hilali, both of his refusal to allow for my exposure of Egypt's social ills and of my own embarrassment and refusal to vilify him as a sexist Arab man. These are the tight spaces of critical ethnography: the ethnographer is silenced by Arab political elites who refuse the airing of dirty laundry, but are also wary of the eager consumption by Euro-American publics of every social ill as evidence of Arab and Muslim backwardness. In this crowded space Abu-Lughod and Mikdashi's critique is, to my mind, nevertheless misplaced; it would be better pointed at self-gratified Euro-American feminists who want to "save" Muslim women than at Palestinian social activists working in their local communities.[16] Further their critique exonerates hypernationalists of the Arab political ruling class who cause direct suffering to people's daily lives and even echoes its mechanisms of silencing the local idioms and practices that naturalize gender-based and other social inequalities. Their misfiring is a clear symptom of the structural obstacles that stand in the way of translation across divided audiences, particularly when audiences' differences can be flattened across time and space. When a single article, post, letter, or lecture is delivered to an audience divided into vastly different social and political worlds, it becomes all the more challenging to perform the necessary act of translation to *each different subdivision* of that audience.

Reconstructing a Form of Critical Hopefulness

These thoughts roughly reflect my presentation at the May 2014 workshop organized by Didier Fassin on the various challenges to public ethnography. Yet since that time I have come to have a more tempered and more hopeful view after working alongside a new colleague in my field, Sa'ed Atshan. An ethnographer of the occupied Palestinian territories who grew up in the West Bank, Atshan tirelessly engages with publics that include those predisposed to justify Israeli occupation and to brand all Palestinians as terrorists. I have seen him numerous times speak to large audiences in which extreme supporters and defenders of Israel stand up to accuse him of lies and of engaging in Palestinians' convenient invention of the term *Palestine* simply to thwart the establishment of a Jewish homeland. The Israel-Palestine topic, as Lara Deeb and Jessica Winegar (2015) have recently documented, casts a shadow on the entire field of Middle East anthropology. It is the minefield around which we are required to dance in order to survive in the U.S. academy. My own engagement on Palestinian justice waxes and wanes, as the untenable and unsustainable situation of people living in Gaza and the West Bank so infuriates me that I quickly burn out. Atshan not only continues to engage on the issue, but he is relentlessly cheerful. He laughs readily and heartily. At first I didn't know what to make of his bubbly affect as he spoke of gross injustices. The bumper sticker "If you are not outraged you are not paying attention" came to mind. Why wasn't he more outraged? Wasn't he paying attention?

My friend and colleague Soha Bayoumi taught me the Arabic word *muzayada*, which is commonly spoken in Egyptian leftist activist circles, for which there is no ready English equivalent.[17] People who engage in muzayada are constantly upping the ante, asserting that they are even more morally pure and politically committed than their comrades. In addition to describing a form of political and moral competition, the term also suggests a cynical skepticism, an anticipation that what is to come is further oppression that must be condemned. Those who engage in muzayada are judgmental and suspicious of others' levels of commitment; they are always *more* committed, *more* dedicated than everyone else. If one expresses joy or a sense of accomplishment over a battle won, those practicing muzayada are suspicious that one could ever feel victory and still be a morally and politically committed subject who has not naïvely capitulated to the ploys of the oppressor. Like all political positions in the U.S. academy, solidarity with the freedoms and basic rights of people living in the Middle East, including Palestinians' struggle against the Israeli occupation, is riddled with muzayada.[18]

Muzayada disciplines affect; cynicism and negativity become markers of one's critical capacities; cheerfulness (gendered feminine) reeks of naïveté and a lack of political or moral commitment.[19] There has been much talk about cynicism, hope, and the "promise of happiness" in the academy and among leftists in general.[20] Among critics of hope and happiness, I suggest that hope is now regarded with the same suspicion as religion, providing an opium for the masses, anaesthetizing marginalized people to the brutality of their own exploitation. Indeed there is a temporal dimension to the call for cynicism that reasserts the finality of the secular world, denying an eschatological or other futuristic time and place in which true justice, equality, and bliss will one day become manifest.

For Lauren Berlant hope, anxiety, or stress can be the manifestation of a "cruel optimism" in our neoliberal era that produces desires for objects that in reality are unattainable and hence become obstacles to human flourishing.[21] Hope can be a disempowering form of magical thinking, leading someone to place her own autonomy and agency in someone else's hands (or God's?) in the hopes that it will all work out in the end. Following Berlant, Lisa Duggan critically reflects on her own discomfort with hope: "As a queer feminist anti-imperialist and utterly contrary and cranky leftist, I have my doubts about the political valences of hope. I'm suspicious of it. I associate it with normative prescriptions about the future I *ought* to want, with coercive groupthink, with compulsory cheerfulness, with subtly coercive blandness. I find a lot of pleasure in bitterness, cynicism, depressiveness and bitchiness. I raise my defenses against earnest optimism and its normative compulsions. It is within this framework of temperament and politics that I defend myself as a specifically *queer* leftist." Duggan later asks, "But must hope be made of these materials?" and turns to her interlocutor, José Muñoz, who affirms the dangers of ungrounded, abstract hope. But Muñoz too asserts, "We need hope to counter a climate of hopelessness that immobilizes us both on the level of thought and transformative behaviors. None of this is to say that hope is easy to find or never misleading or potentially appropriated by reactionary agents and movements. Hope is a risk. But if the point is to change the world we must risk hope."[22]

Hope and happiness, as Duggan poignantly writes, can be posited as "the affective reward for conformity, the privatized emotional bonus for the right kind of investments in the family, private property and the state." Duggan writes, "When I think about *hope*, I set it alongside *happiness and optimism*, which I immediately associate with race and class privilege, with imperial hubris, with gender and sexual conventions, with maldistributed forms of security both national and personal."[23] For those working on the contemporary Middle East there is much to be outraged and upset about: the "imperial hubris" of hope and happiness resonate poorly with economic insecurity, brutal political repression, civil wars, sectarian violence, Israeli settler-colonialism, nationalist fascism, religious intolerance, and the double standards of the international community regarding the rights and freedoms of Arabs and Muslims.

Yet asserting our right to be angry and outraged need not establish this affective disposition as an index of political or moral commitment to the lives and freedoms of people living in the Middle East today. The more we do so, the more we are likely to turn off the publics we most strive to engage. The intolerance of affective diversity and real-life complexity leaves those who practice muzayada with no other choice than to simply talk among themselves, preaching to choirs. Engagement requires messiness in that meeting space between speaker and audience. Those who practice muzayada are intolerant of the contamination that both precedes and follows engagement with others who do not share the same moral high ground.

In contrast Atshan's continual public speaking engagements make those who practice muzayada uncomfortable on many levels. He asks people to sit with the complexities of U.S. humanitarian assistance to occupied Palestine that enables Palestinians to survive and resist the occupation, as well as sustaining and naturalizing that occupation. Atshan espouses nonviolence as a strategy for Palestinian self-determination, while some aligned with the cause of Palestine believe this stance denies Palestinians the right, recognized in international law, to counter military occupation with means that include violence.[24] He distances himself from the tactics of Hamas, which some in the movement feel justifies Islamophobic double standards that stigmatize the political mobilization of Islamist groups. Atshan travels often on solidarity trips to Palestinian lands and communities, introducing groups committed to struggling against racism, homophobia, postcolonial violence, or sexism in the areas that were captured in 1948 as well as the areas occupied since 1967; his critics say that bringing observers to the Occupied Palestinian Territories is not helpful to the movement, that it turns Palestinians into objects to be observed and pitied rather than allies whose struggle should be shared. (Having taken part in such a trip, I believe this critique is unfair.)[25]

Atshan also addresses problems within Palestinian and Arab society, such as violence that occurs in families against women and youth; his U.S.-based critics attack him for allowing further justification for Israeli occupation by exposing the "backwardness" and patriarchy of Arab culture. Local Arab activists working to confront social problems such as violence against women and homosexuals can increasingly find themselves the objects of U.S. academic critiques that they are reifying Orientalist tropes about the Middle East and naïvely participating in larger imperialist projects. Ironically this stance relies on an outdated and static (and hence Orientalist, in the Saidian sense) view of Middle Eastern societies that is unwilling to grapple with the complexity of contemporary social change.

Muzayada privileges the purity of an ideological position over recognizing a good. When we practice muzayada, we refuse to celebrate any small gain as long as larger structural inequality persists. I understand muzayada to both contribute to political impotence and to result from it. Shunted from effective significant change, participants turn on one another and attempt to claim the pleasure of being the most radical and ideologically pure. The ethnographer's attention to the consolidation of global power and inequality, I fear, can easily lead to cynicism, intellectual laziness, and self-righteous moralizing. Has this particular affective disposition about the increase in militarism and social inequality permeated our intellectual endeavor as public ethnographers? What work is it doing? How is cynicism in particular shaped by the audiences we hope to engage, and how does it in turn shape our ability to engage them?[26]

Working alongside Atshan I encountered in his critics surprising levels of vitriol, cynicism, and suspicion. These were leveled against someone who I came to know as deeply committed, knowledgeable, and insightful about his material. His perseverance cast a new light on my earlier frustrations and feeling that there was simply no space in which I could maneuver my own work. In my own case muzayada was a knee-jerk response to being crowded out by heavy-handed ideologues—nationalist reactionaries on the one hand and Orientalists on the other. What I learned from Atshan was that a politics of compassion, aside from being a more pleasant way to see and be in the world, can be a powerful way to level one's political mobilization for social justice as well as remaining true to the complexities and contradictions of one's ethnographic findings.

Atshan continues his engagement with publics no matter how hostile and is able to appreciate and celebrate small gains in movements toward greater tolerance, egalitarianism, and social justice, even when he is attuned to the fact that Western imperialism and Euro-American hegemony persist. I learned from him that these small celebrations are not the same as complacency; on the contrary they fuel one's persistence. His scholarly work demonstrates how sovereignty is contested in the lives of Palestinians living under occupation—from the sovereignty of the Israeli state to the Palestinian Authority, international humanitarian organizations, family structures, and individual psyches. His ability to connect with so many different kinds of people at so many different levels is a model for a multiscalar approach to egalitarian social justice, specifically in the micro levels of everyday social encounters. In this Atshan enacts the Palestinian discourse of *sumud*—the steadfastness and fortitude required to see that the everyday acts of surviving and existing can be the greatest form of resistance. With sumud, people living under occupation replant their uprooted olive trees; with sumud they rebuild their demolished homes.

I am not suggesting that activists and academics merge roles entirely; for many pursuits separating labor and the exigencies of working at different paces and toward different goals makes sense. I am simply reasserting the truism that we each have much to learn from one another, particularly how to translate one's work across divided audiences. It does not take great intellect or moral integrity to practice muzayada and to feel self-righteous; it is much harder to maintain scholarly rigor while building solidarity for social justice struggles that require building people up, particularly in the face of the many political, social, and economic forces intent on tearing them down.

Conclusion

In situations in which political polarization is stark and there is little social space for public debate, how can ethnographers avoid being interpellated into this or that political faction? How does an ethnographer render her work with marginalized communities meaningful to the very public that has denied those communities the right of being represented? How can anthropologists consider themselves part of a critical discipline, presenting perspectives that challenge or upset dominant narratives, while at the same time hoping to engage with publics that are beholden to those narratives? Anthropologists' own ethnographic portrayals of seemingly pro-egalitarian efforts, such as development programs, human rights organizations, and humanitarian interventions, have revealed that even institutions meant to address inequality and injustice have to a large extent sustained the power structures in place. Hence, to some extent, anthropologists are doomed to frustration if their goal is to work toward egalitarian social justice by engaging publics with their scholarship.

If the mid-1980s have been characterized by a crisis in anthropology's identity (How do we avoid our own ethnography reflecting and perpetuating the political-economic hierarchies through which it was produced?), the 2010s have provoked our questioning of anthropological practice and engagement.[27] Writing of people living near France's housing projects who had little knowledge of the life there, Fassin suggests, "Ethnography can perhaps partially fill this cognitive gap."[28] Yet he also points to the very real impediments to this potential benefit, for instance the general lack of appetite for social critique, the fact that academic scholarship invites few readers and that when its content is made publicly available via the news media, the content is often radically transformed.

These impediments are real enough when people acknowledge that a lack of understanding of the lives of others is a problem; what about when there is an explicit rejection of understanding the Other? In the academy and beyond, the field of Middle East studies is so polarized that Palestinian narratives and voices are denounced at the outset as "dangerous" and "one-sided." Similarly in Egypt the current moment of intense political paranoia and xenophobia is hostile to critique. Any form of questioning is readily interpreted as an attack on the state and the Egyptian nation writ large and as the potential cause of further economic and political instability. Not only are ethnographers unwelcome; their words are also dangerous, as there is no agreed upon neutral territory one might claim. In such a context one can hardly hope for a public ethnography. If ethnography is a way to make audible the claims of marginalized people whose voices are readily dismissed, to make appeals toward social justice, then it is doomed from the start as it hinges on being acknowledged by the very powers that seek to silence these groups.

In this essay I have called for greater recognition and discussion of how publics come in with their own ideas, ideological commitments, and affective stakes that shape the ability of the ethnographer to engage audiences, as well as audiences' own receptivity to the alternative visions ethnography can produce. The obstacles to public ethnography—mainly of access, receptivity, and intelligibility—are real; I am not suggesting they are merely the effect of an overly cynical affective regime in the academy. But working alongside Sa'ed Atshan helped me see a model of continual engagement despite these obstacles. Doing so requires tremendous humility as well as faith in the soundness of one's own scholarship and trust in one's own moral and political commitments.

When presenting perspectives on Palestinian self-determination, Atshan speaks with compassion to his audience, but he also knows when to hold his ground; he strictly sidelines those who are there only to derail and obstruct conversations. It is true that we can never appeal to all publics evenly, and in that sense there is no use in trying. But it is also true that if we approach our positions with the sensibility of muzayada, fearful of contaminating our moral high ground, or of cynicism—already knowing that we will fail—then we will never know who or what we may be able to reach. Atshan's methods of engagement echoed the words of Howard Zinn:[29]

> To be hopeful in bad times is not just foolishly romantic. It is based on the fact that human history is a history not only of cruelty, but also of compassion, sacrifice, courage, kindness. What we choose to emphasize in this complex history will determine our lives. If we see only the worst, it destroys our capacity to do something. If we remember those times and places—and there are so many—where people have behaved magnificently, this gives us the energy to act, and at least the possibility of sending this spinning top of a world in a different direction. And if we do act, in however small a way, we don't have to wait for some grand utopian future. The future is an infinite succession of presents, and to live now as we think human beings should live, in defiance of all that is bad around us, is itself a marvelous victory.

If our goal as ethnographers is to illuminate and analyze, reinterpret and reframe particular moments, then perhaps it is enough to settle for knowing that at certain moments and in certain contexts ethnography's greatest value lies in its potential rather than immediate realization of moving conversations forward.

Notes

I would like to thank Didier Fassin for organizing these important discussions on public ethnography and all the workshop participants. I would also like to thank my many friends and colleagues who provided feedback during the writing process: Soha Bayoumi, Adia Benton, Amahl Bishara, Rina Bliss, Keith Brown, Manuela Cruz-Cunha, Margaret Cruz, Didier Fassin, Toby Craig Jones, David Kertzer, Yasmin Mol, Coleman Nye, Eve Spangler, Justin Stearns, Ian Straughn, and Kabir Tambar.

1   For example, Nicholas Kristoff's (2014) piece in which he contends that "Ph.D. programs have fostered a culture that glorifies arcane unintelligibility while disdaining impact and audience."

2   I use Sa'ed Atshan's actual name in this piece with his permission.

3   I succeeded in gaining access only by avoiding Cairo, where such nationalist fervor was most pronounced, and situating myself in provincial cities along the Nile Delta. In many cases it took me months and months of repeated requests before wearing down clinicians into granting me access.

4   Trouillot 1995.

5   Narayan 1993.

6   For discussions of this phenomenon in Egypt, see Abu-Lughod 1998; Saad 1998; Sholkamy 1999. For a more general discussion on the problem of "native" positionality and concerns about "airing dirty laundry," see Jacobs-Huey 2002.

7   The anthropologist Michael Herzfeld has described this phenomenon as "cultural intimacy."

8   The conference organizers had been optimistic about the possibility of setting aside political differences in the name of academic dialogue, for they had also invited Shaykh Yusuf Al-Qaradawi to attend (a leading religious scholar who had been exiled from Egypt for decades), but he declined due to a death in the family. Qaradawi is a globally recognized Egyptian figure in Islamic jurisprudence who is based in Doha. He is also an ideological supporter of the Muslim Brotherhood in Egypt and appears on the Al Jazeera show *Sharia and Life*, which boasts an estimated sixty million viewers across the Arabic-speaking world.

9   Fassin 2013: 630.

10   See, for example, Ian Buruma's (2007) article, which begins, "Tariq Ramadan, Muslim, scholar, activist, Swiss citizen, resident of Britain, active on several continents, is a hard man to pin down. People call him 'slippery,' 'double-faced,' 'dangerous,' but also 'brilliant,' a 'bridge-builder,' a 'Muslim Martin Luther.'" Later in the article Buruma cites Scott Appleby from Notre Dame, who says, "He's doing something extraordinarily difficult if not impossible, but it needs to be done. He is accused of being Janus-faced. Well, of course he presents different faces to different audiences. He is trying to bridge a divide and bring together people of diverse backgrounds and worldviews. He considers the opening he finds in his audience. Ramadan is in that sense a politician. He cultivates various publics in the Muslim world on a variety of issues; he wants to provide leadership and inspiration."

11   Skovgaard-Petersen 1997.

12   An exception is Hussein Agrama (2012), who describes these spaces indifferent to the policing of the boundary between religious and secular domains as *asecular*.

13   Hirschkind 2006; Mahmood 2005; Mamdani 2002.

14   Hilali was later criticized by the rector of Al Azhar for taking this stance; see Ali 2014.

15   https://youtube/kAkYzmi6fBM. Hilali says, "No one would imagine how God's will replays itself, that there would be those who came to say there is no Islam besides that which we force upon you. And that there is no religion except for that which we make known to you. And that God would stipulate for Egyptians that there would be those who stand up and confront them, so that they could achieve the religion that God had ordered. God sent also two men. As he had sent before two men: Moses and Aaron. He sent again two men. There was no one among Egyptians who

would have imagined these messengers that God had sent [as stated in the Holy Qur'an 74:31] *'And no one knows who those fighting on God's behalf are except for Him.'* The ones who came forth were Al-Sisi [minister of defense] and Muhammad Ibrahim [minister of the interior]. In order to accomplish the command of God, exalted be He. [quotes from Qur'an 2:193] *'Fight them until there is no more fitnah and until worship is acknowledged to be for God alone."* At that point, at least on the YouTube video that documents this speech, a woman in the audience audibly protests, but Hilali continues to speak over her until she is removed from the building.

16 Abu-Lughod 2002.

17 Yasmin Mol reports that this term is also used in Islamist circles (personal communication, 2015).

18 Eve Spangler (personal communication, 2015) refers to muzayada among American leftists as being "more Mao than thou."

19 For how these gendered affective dispositions in the academy are policed, see the interesting piece by Kelsky (2011).

20 Ahmed 2009.

21 Berlant 2011.

22 Duggan and Muñoz 2009: 279.

23 Duggan and Muñoz 2009: 276.

24 Of course the burden on Palestinians to be only the *recipients* of violence is itself a cynical way to further delegitimize their liberation struggle. The various strategies of struggle against occupation, however, should not be indices of people's commitment to their liberation.

25 For example, Jennifer Lynn Kelley (2014) argues that solidarity tourism through the Occupied Palestinian Territories avoids positing more privileged tourists or observers as the "saviors" come to "fix" Palestine by explicitly positioning their role in the struggle *back in their own communities*: the tours are meant to inspire people to return to their country of origin and mobilize their activism from there.

26 I thank Eve Spangler for sharing these ideas and for helping me to think of muzayada as both a structural and personality-driven phenomenon.

27 Of course, as Behar and Gordon (1996) demonstrate, these questions were raised long before the 1980s, even though James Clifford and George Marcus's (1986) book *Writing Culture* is often associated with this turn in anthropology.

28 Fassin 2013: 631.

29 Zinn 2010: 208.

References

Abu-Lughod, Lila. 1998. "Television and the Virtues of Education: Upper Egyptian Encounters with State Culture." In *Directions of Change in Rural Egypt*, edited by Nicholas Hopkins and Kirsten Westergaard, 147–65. Cairo: American University Press.

———. 2002. "Do Muslim Women Really Need Saving? Anthropological Reflections on Cultural Relativism and Its Others." *American Anthropologist* 104.3: 783–90.

Agrama, Hussein, 2012. *Questioning Secularism: Islam, Sovereignty, and the Rule of Law in Egypt.* Chicago: University of Chicago Press.

Ahmed, Sara. 2009. *The Promise of Happiness.* Durham: Duke University Press.

Ali, Loai. 2014. "Al Azhar Criticizes Hilali for Comparing Sisi to a Prophet." *Cairo Post*, February 9. http://www.thecairopost.com/news/87575/news/al-azhar -criticizes-hilali-for-comparing-sisi-to-a-prophet.

Behar, Ruth, and Deborah Gordon. 1996. *Women Writing Culture.* Berkeley: University of California Press.

Berlant, Lauren. 2011. *Cruel Optimism.* Durham: Duke University Press.

Buruma, Ian. 2007. "Tariq Ramadan Has an Identity Issue." *New York Times Magazine,* February 4.

Clifford, James, and George Marcus. 1986. *Writing Culture: The Poetics and Politics of Ethnography.* Berkeley: University of California Press.

Deeb, Lara, and Jessica Winegar. 2015. *Anthropology's Politics: Disciplining the Middle East.* Stanford: Stanford University Press.

Duggan, Lisa, and José Esteban Muñoz. 2009. "Hope and Hopelessness: A Dialogue." *Women and Performance: A Journal of Feminist Theory* 19.2: 275–83.

Fassin, Didier. 2013. "Why Ethnography Matters: On Anthropology and Its Publics." *Cultural Anthropology* 28.4: 621–46.

Gaffney, Patrick. 1994. *The Prophet's Pulpit: Islamic Preaching in Contemporary Egypt.* Berkeley: University of California Press.

Goodson, Ivor. 2003. *Professional Knowledge, Professional Lives: Studies in Educational Change.* London: Open University Press.

Hamdy, Sherine. 2012. *Our Bodies Belong to God: Organ Transplants, Islam, and the Struggle for Human Dignity in Egypt.* Berkeley: University of California Press.

Hirschkind, Charles. 2006. *The Ethical Soundscape: Cassette Sermons and Islamic Counterpublics.* New York: Columbia University Press.

Jacobs-Huey, Lanita. 2002. "The Natives Are Gazing and Talking Back: Reviewing the Problematics of Positionality, Voice, and Accountability among 'Native' Anthropologists." *American Anthropologist* 104.3: 791–804.

Kelley, Jennifer Lynn. 2014. "Itineraries through Occupied Spaces: Routinized Violence, Solidarity Tourism, and the Fraught Politics of Witnessing." Paper presented at the Annual Meeting of the American Anthropological Association, Washington, DC.

Kelsky, Karen. 2011. "Stop Acting Like a Girl! A Response to Feminist Critics." *Professor Is In*, October 17. http://theprofessorisin.com/2011/10/17/1787/.

Kristoff, Nicholas. 2014. "Professors, We Need You!" *New York Times*, February 15.

Mahmood, Saba. 2005. *Politics of Piety: The Islamic Revival and the Feminist Subject.* Princeton: Princeton University Press.

Mamdani, Mahmood. 2002. "Good Muslim, Bad Muslim: A Political Perspective on Culture and Terrorism." *American Anthropologist* 104.3: 766–75.

Narayan, Kirin. 1993. "How Native Is a 'Native' Anthropologist?" *American Anthropologist* 95.3: 671–86.

Saad, Reem. 1998. "Shame, Reputation and Egypt's Lovers: A Controversy over the Nation's Image." *Visual Anthropology* 10.2–4: 401–12.

Said, Edward. 1978. *Orientalism*. New York: Vintage Books.

Sholkamy, Hania. 1999. "Why Is Anthropology So Hard in Egypt?" *Cairo Papers in Social Science* 22.2: 119–37.

Skovgaard-Petersen, Rudolph. 1997. *Defining Islam for the Egyptian State*. Leiden: Brill.

Starrett, Gregory. 1998. *Putting Islam to Work: Education, Politics, and Religious Transformation in Egypt*. Berkeley: University of California Press.

Trouillot, Michel-Rolf. 1995. *Silencing the Past*. Boston: Beacon Press.

Zinn, Howard. 2010. *You Can't Be Neutral on a Moving Train: A Personal History of Our Times*. Boston: Beacon Press.

Epilogue

The Public Afterlife of Ethnography

DIDIER FASSIN

The French newspaper *Libération* was founded in 1973 by Jean-Paul Sartre and four young far-left journalists in the aftermath of the 1968 movement with the motto "People, speak up, take the floor, and keep it." In its earlier years it experienced various financial and institutional crises that resulted in occasional interruptions of its publication. In the 1990s, under the Socialist presidency of François Mitterrand, the editorial stance shifted toward an improbable combination of social democracy and libertarian ideal. In the 2000s it drifted further to the center left following the purchase of a controlling stake in the daily by the banker Edouard de Rothschild. Although ideologically distant from its radical beginnings, *Libération* nevertheless remains today the main progressive national newspaper in France. As a sign of its unique position within the world of journalism, it devotes the entirety of its front page and the next three as well as its main editorial each day to the coverage of a single "event." The selection of this topic is intended to highlight some of the defining problems of contemporary society.

For its January 8, 2015, issue, the "event" chosen by the editorial board was the publication of *L'Ombre du monde*, a book based on the fieldwork I had carried out in a French prison over the course of four years. This showcase was a unique opportunity to discuss what constituted the matter of the research, namely the punitive turn of society, the inequality of citizens before the penal system, and the grim experience that inmates have of the "carceral condition." Prison hardly ever makes the headlines, and the decision by the editorial board to give the topic such visibility as well as the content of the articles written by the journalist in charge of the "justice section" along with the substantial interview she conducted with me clearly indicated the intention to have the questions that were raised by my ethnography widely debated. Actually, hoping that this would have been the case, I had paid particular attention to the writing of the book so as to make it accessible to a larger audience in spite of its unusual length and thus allow for a national discussion on the politics of punishment in France.

The day before the planned publication, however, the window of opportunity for this discussion was suddenly and unexpectedly closed: another "event" took the place that had been allotted to my book. On January 7 two men attacked the offices of the weekly satirical journal *Charlie Hebdo*, killing twelve persons. The next day, like all French newspapers, *Libération* was almost completely devoted to the tragedy: on the entirely black front page the headline was "Nous sommes tous Charlie" (We Are All Charlie). After a second attack was directed against a kosher grocery store two days later, killing five more people, the media continued to focus for the following month solely on these events and the reactions they provoked across the country.[1] Once again prison did not make the news.

Or rather it became a subject of interest for the press in a very singular way. It was discovered that Chérif Kouachi, the youngest brother involved in the first attack, had met his "mentor," Djamel Beghal, who was serving a ten-year prison sentence for terrorism-related acts, including the recruitment of jihadists, during his incarceration in a correctional facility, where he also befriended Amedy Coulibaly, the perpetrator of the second series of killings. Penal institutions suddenly appeared as sites of dangerous proselytism, a fact that did not prevent judges from sentencing dozens of men who, drunk or mentally disturbed for the most part, had publicly celebrated the death of the cartoonists to months or even years in prison for "vindication of terrorism." But while the concern may have been understandable given the circumstances, religious radicalization remained a very marginal phenomenon in prison, perhaps not even decisive in the case of the January attacks since their perpetrators' turn to the idea of jihad had mainly been the result of their frequenting a Paris mosque whose preacher was known for his extremist views. At the time of my research one or two of the nine hundred inmates in the facility I studied were deemed Islamists, and three or four others were suspected of being at risk of "conversion." The following year three young men returning from Syria were imprisoned on the suspicion of jihadism, bringing the total number of the radicalized Muslims to half a dozen.

Yet in all the interviews I gave during the month of January, the journalists apologized in advance for having to start by asking me what should be done to prevent religious radicalization in prison, a question I was almost as incapable of answering as the correctional officers and wardens at the facility where I conducted my research, since they had not been confronted with the phenomenon until very recently. I was therefore rather evasive as to whether and how Muslims suspected of indoctrinating their fellow prisoners should be isolated from the rest of the incarcerated population. Instead I seized this opportunity to emphasize the importance of developing alternatives to prison for minor offenses in order to avoid exposing offenders to religious proselytism inasmuch as my research showed the rapid growth of incarceration rates for misdemeanors in recent decades. But relativizing the statistical significance of radicalization and suggesting a more discriminate use of incarceration was not the most audible response; this was a time when drama and harshness had greater currency in the public.

Almost a month later the journalist at *Libération* informed me that her two-page article on the book would finally appear in the newspaper on February 5, while the interview would be published online a few days after. Indeed, she explained, the editorial board had decided to devote a special issue under the sensationalist headline "How to Abolish Apartheid in France?" The prime minister, Manuel Valls, had provocatively declared two weeks earlier that the country suffered from "territorial, social, and ethnic apartheid," a phrase that generated numerous comments, some applauding his lucid outspokenness, others criticizing his irrelevant sensationalism. Since the president, François Hollande, was holding a press conference the following day and was going to address the question, it was for the newspaper an opportune circumstance to cover this improbable topic and include a two-page article on the correctional system. This piece focused on the overrepresentation of black and Arab men in prison, which was the subject of a chapter in the book, about which the journalist had interviewed me.

During my fieldwork I had conducted a survey that provided figures on this issue for the first time in France, where the identification of minorities in statistics is illegal; it revealed that two-thirds of the inmates were black or Arab men, a proportion that climbed to three-fourths among those under thirty years old. Anticipating the possibility that right-wing commentators could infer from these numbers that minorities produced more criminals than the rest of the population, I showed in an analysis of the legislative evolution and crime statistics as well as my observation of policing and justice practices how racial and ethnic discrimination within the penal system played an important role in the disproportionate representation of minorities— from the parliamentarians who determine which offenses should be punished by imprisonment to the officers who profile the individuals stopped and frisked and the magistrates who sentence certain culprits with particular severity. Although I considered this issue to be crucial, when I learned about the editorial project I expressed my discomfort at having my work discussed in reference to the notion of apartheid, which I found both sociologically inappropriate (since racial segregation had never been inscribed in laws or policies) and politically problematic (since the excess of language lowered the quality of the debate). Besides, the focus chosen by the newspaper singled out the racial dimension instead of inscribing it in a larger reflection on punishment and its unequal distribution, as had been initially planned. Still the special issue came out with an editorial by the director assertively stating that the special report proved the existence of apartheid in France: "Emergency" was the title.

These setbacks should definitely not be taken too seriously. Even if *Libération* had maintained its original coverage of the book and had discussed the questions raised about the prison system at length, this would not have changed the carceral condition and would probably not even have significantly modified the terms of the debate about the politics of retribution. Besides, even in its shorter version, the issues raised had not gone unnoticed. When, a month later, a collective of nongovernmental organizations led by Doctors of the World and the Representative Council of Black Associations launched a campaign entitled War on Drugs, Race War to denounce the disproportionate punishment of minorities convicted of using cannabis, they made a short film that ended with two quotations from the book, mistakenly attributed to the journalist. The error was later corrected, but it revealed that the activists had become aware of the study through the newspaper. Thus if I have presented this anecdote in some detail, it is because the unlikely episodes of the media coverage of an ethnographic work illustrate some of the issues faced when such works move from academic circles to the public sphere. As scholars we are obviously more used to the former than to the latter, even if a long tradition of public engagement exists within anthropology and the other social sciences. Yet the moment our writing is published, it encounters a public—or multiple ones. The present essay is about this encounter.

Ethnography can be said to have two lives. A first life consists of fieldwork. Its defining character is participant observation during long periods of time— being there and living among. A second life entails writing. It corresponds to the analysis of the empirical material and its elaboration into a theoretical framework that give birth to a document—a book, an article, or a film. There is of course some degree of intertwining between these two lives. Both cease, however, at least temporarily, with the publication. Not only is the final product of this process not modifiable from then on, but it is exposed to readers, viewers, commentators, critics—in a word: publics. Social scientists who practice ethnography often consider that their scientific work ends with its publication. This is not to say that they would forgo the after-sales service of science, that is, the traditional activities of seminars, lectures, or interviews, which are conceived as the continuation or even repetition of what has been produced during the lifetime, so to speak, of their ethnography. This is also not to say that they may not diversify their audiences and engage with them in various ways, from initiating debates within society on contemporary issues to collaborating with administrations to make policies or with activists to combat these policies. Such interactions with publics do exist and are important in the academic as well as social activity of scientists. Yet they are generally deemed a mere extension of this activity rather than a specific matter for research.

What I suggest instead is to consider the public afterlife of ethnography as a genuine object of inquiry.[2] Historians of anthropology have somewhat paved the way. The monumental, albeit fragmentary, *History of Anthropology* edited by George Stocking and later Richard Handler is certainly a landmark. Here and there in the twelve volumes the reader can find biographical elements about and anecdotal evocations of the public reception of anthropology or of the public engagement of anthropologists, but each series of essays is focused on the practice of anthropology, anthropological schools, specific themes, or particular contexts.[3] More relevant for the historicization of the public afterlife of ethnography have been later historical explorations of the reactions to ethnographic studies, the popularization of anthropological works, or the ethical issues raised by the political involvement, among others.[4] All the authors who adopt this diachronic viewpoint acknowledge that what Roger Sanjek calls "the third, postfieldwork and postwriting, stage," implying the communication of "anthropological findings and perspectives to 'society at large' is not a new development."[5] The inevitable reference in that matter—especially, for obvious reasons, in the United States—is Franz Boas's denunciation of the spying activity of unnamed colleagues working for the government during the First World War and his chastisement by the very organization he had founded.[6] But for many there is a profound rupture in the public engagement of anthropologists during the second half of the twentieth century, which Thomas Hylland Eriksen describes as a "withdrawal of anthropology from general intellectual discourse" and considers a "fact which needs no further qualification." So "what went wrong?" he asks.[7] There are certainly exceptions; for instance, Roberto Gonzalez gathered a series of public interventions by anthropologists in newspapers on topics related to wars and peace as examples of their engagement beyond the academy.[8] More recently several calls for public anthropology or engaged anthropology have been made, and various initiatives to create research centers or to open special sections in anthropological journals have been taken.[9] The topic is undoubtedly in vogue.

In this context my present contribution to the understanding of the public afterlife of ethnography is definitely limited. It is to examine, mostly through my personal experience yet with references to that of others, some of the questions and challenges that this afterlife raises. By focusing on my own encounters with various publics in the aftermath of the publication of several books, I surely do not want to present them as exemplars to be followed but as examples to be analyzed. More generally this essay is not one more plea for the public presence of anthropologists—although I am sympathetic to such pleas—but a reflection on what it implies and complicates in our scientific and social activity. It can be read as an autobiographic approach of the public afterlife of ethnography rather than a historical review of it. In this sense it is a call for a reflexive analysis of what becomes of our work once it is published—an exercise for which I claim no precedence.

In order to specify the various possibilities of publicizing ethnography, I suggest distinguishing three intellectual operations: translation, discussion, and expansion. Translation comprises the successive transformation of a text that has a format corresponding to academic norms into various forms adapted to different audiences and media, whether for an interview, a talk for a human rights organization, advice to policymakers on a specific matter, a testimony shedding light on a case in court, or a contribution to an artistic exhibition or performance. Discussion includes the multiple exchanges generated by the publication, the author's responses to questions, and reactions ranging from mere elucidation of unclear points to reformulation of previous statements and even complete revision after well-founded criticism. Expansion refers to the opening of novel and often unexpected perspectives on the social sciences as such through an epistemological or sociological questioning of the very process of research, whether it has to do with a critical inquiry into the ethnographic method, the sort of work that it can do and the limitations it encounters, or with an analysis of the process of publicization and what it uncovers of the functioning of the contemporary public sphere. These three operations are not exclusive of each other and together contribute to the intellectual fecundity of the public afterlife of ethnography.

In the following pages I illustrate these operations by taking three different angles, as delineated by the three terms of the title of the essay. I first discuss the importance of including the afterlife of our work as part and parcel of our research. I then turn to the diversity of publics and the difficulty of knowing who they are. Finally I consider the specificity of ethnography and the sort of productive uneasiness it generates.

Afterlife

"No poem is intended for the reader, no picture for the beholder, no symphony for the listener," writes Walter Benjamin.[10] Such an uncompromising affirmation probably proceeds more from an ideal representation of the artist entirely devoted to his art, resolutely indifferent to its reception, and freed from material considerations than from a faithful depiction of the artist in contemporary society. This is true in particular when the work of art is a literary piece, which at some point gets published and therefore receives public attention—except when the author decides otherwise, as did Kafka, asking his closest friend and literary executor to burn all his writings after his death, a request Max Brod did not comply with. But written production presents a major difference from painting or music: to travel across countries and cultures it needs a translation into other languages—and one could again mention the challenges of remaining faithful to the writings of Kafka, to whom Benjamin devoted two essays. According to the latter, this operation is radically different from creation, since "the task of the translator" is, at least in part, "to perform a transmitting function," which is ultimately destined "for readers who do not understand the original." The only possible raison d'être of a translation resides in the existence of a public unable to access the text unless it is written in a language that readers can understand.

This link between the two versions of a text resulting from such an operation is, in Benjamin's words, a "vital connection," in which "a translation issues from the original—not so much from its life than from its afterlife." Quite successful in literary studies, where it has generatively been applied to Dante's Beatrice as an inspiration for nineteenth-century Victorian literature and Chaucer's tales as a source for both television series and material consumption, among many others, the idea of an afterlife has often been strictly related to the translation or even "translatability," as Benjamin has it, of the original.[11] Nevertheless, rigorous reading of his essay—which, as is always the case with his prose, does not distinguish itself by its transparency—suggests that the translation reveals rather than produces the afterlife of the original. What actually defines the afterlife of the text, in its broader sense, is the encounter with a public, whether in its original version or as a translated piece. While its life implies an intimate link with the process of creation, its afterlife essentially depends upon its reception.

This distinction can also be heuristic for the social sciences. The process of inquiry as a whole, from the construction of the object, the elaboration of a problematic, the design of a method, and the conduct of an empirical study to the interpretation of the material and its transformation into a text, corresponds to the life of research. It takes different forms depending on the sort of research—deductive or inductive, quantitative or qualitative, formally designed or empirically driven—but beyond these differences it always involves a creation of ideas, techniques, and data. Arguably this creation is particularly consistent, recognizable, and acknowledged in the case of ethnography since, like pottery, it consists in the production of a form out of an initially amorphous material composed, in this case, of a multiplicity of facts, words, gestures, images, moments, among which a cautious but discretionary selection has to be made so as to produce a meaningful order. More generally the work of the social scientist can be regarded as the creation, however modest, of new knowledge about social worlds. Even though it includes interactions with both living colleagues and dead authors, this creative moment belongs to the researchers themselves. They are the authors of their works in the etymological sense of having authority over them as well as drawing authority from them. But this situation changes when works are published. They escape their creators. They are shared with a public. Their afterlife begins.

That authors should claim or reclaim this afterlife as part of their intellectual task is the argument of this essay. Such a task may be painful since it exposes the social scientist to become more aware of criticism than praise from colleagues and experts as well as from the general public. Yet this is certainly not a novel idea. A few years after the publication of their monograph on a township in upstate New York, *Small Town in Mass Society*, Arthur Vidich and Joseph Bensman discussed the hostile reactions it elicited among those they had studied.[12] They provided a detailed account—including full texts of letters and reviews—of the reception of their book by the inhabitants, the municipal authorities, and the local media and of the response by the research project manager and the university dean, both of whom sided with the population against the sociologists. These unanimous attacks focused on the violation of privacy despite the protection of the anonymity of the persons and the negative image of both the small town and its residents conveyed by their depiction in the study. In their account of their mishaps the authors nevertheless seemed more eager to justify their choices and contest their opponents than to provide a thorough analysis of the controversy. In fact, the real inquiry into this affair came from the contribution in the same edited volume by Howard Becker, who affirmed that social scientists and the people they study do not share a community of interest. The polemic and the investigation it has generated thus make the so-called Springdale case a pioneering exploration of the afterlife of a social science study.

Anthropologists, however, have not been spared by such controversies. Negative reactions from the people studied by anthropologists have multiplied as the former have become more aware of what was written about them and the latter became interested in literate groups. This new situation has been analyzed by Renato Rosaldo in a famous lecture entitled "When Natives Talk Back."[13] Here the word "natives" should be taken in its widest meaning of belonging. Thus Ofra Greenberg discusses the way the inhabitants of an Israeli town where she conducted her research vehemently reacted to her book after having read an inaccurate review in a local newspaper, and Nancy Scheper-Hughes recounts how she was rejected by her Irish subjects as well as colleagues and eventually chased from the village where she had carried out her study.[14] But criticisms of ethnographies do not come only from the natives; they can be articulated by outsiders. The two most notorious controversies pertain to the attacks launched by the anthropologist Derek Freeman against Margaret Mead's study in Samoa and by the journalist Patrick Tierney against Napoleon Chagnon's research among the Yanomami. In the first case the scientific value of the findings and of the anthropologist was at stake—with arguments that were later countered on the same grounds. In the second case the ethical qualities of the anthropologist and his work were condemned—which provided an opportunity for the discipline to develop in response a broader reflection on its practices.[15] Beyond the numerous differences between the two polemics, both had in common, first, that they were produced by intellectuals; second, that they were the object of analyses by others than the protagonists; and third, that they seriously affected the image of the anthropological profession due to the extensive coverage from which they had benefited in the media. But, at least in the best cases—which correspond more often to third-person than first-person accounts—such ordeals served as opportunities to reassess the anthropological project—in particular its ethical dimension[16]—and more generally to reflect on public developments in the afterlife of ethnography.

The publication of my study on the experience and politics of AIDS in South Africa gave me the opportunity to do so. Indeed *When Bodies Remember* confronted me with the usual problems encountered by public interventions in polarized contexts over controversial issues: whereas I intended it to be a fair analysis of the polemic in historical and sociological perspectives and to give voice and meaning to the opposite sides, it contributed to the division.[17] The result of five years of research in townships and former homelands as well as political and scientific realms, the book tried to make sense of what was usually deemed irrational and criminal, namely the contestation by the government of the viral etiology of the disease and of the efficacy of antiretroviral drugs. Without justifying this erroneous stance, I analyzed the deeper reasons of the mistrust expressed with regard to public health and of the wide popular support for the authorities; complicated the simple opposition between true and false, right and wrong, ethical and unethical; and explored how history and memory were both embodied and uncovered through this disquieting dispute. Whereas the book attracted positive attention in the international academic and political spheres, contributing to the understanding of a conundrum that was then merely an object of condemnation and to the shaping of programs of cooperation that were in jeopardy, the research got several negative reviews by South African activists and scholars in newspapers and scientific journals. Although these commentators acknowledged the relevance and sensitivity of my work with patients, they expressed their discomfort at my effort to comprehend the controversy, regarding it as too indulgent toward the government, one of them even invoking my "subtle racism." At some point their hostility also affected my relationships with colleagues engaged in the research.

This contrasting reception led me to develop a more general reflection on the sort of tensions I was facing, which took two directions.[18] First, I attempted to account for the increasingly antagonistic reactions of my South African colleagues and developed a framework to interpret the intellectual tensions between national and foreign researchers. Going beyond what could be too easily explained by circumstantial or even personal reasons, I showed that structural relationships were at stake with regard to four elements: authority (indigenous vs. ethnographic), loyalty (situated vs. unconditional), responsibility (consequentialist vs. deontological), and legitimacy (sovereign vs. universal).

Second, I tried to analyze the combination of the objections formulated by certain South African activists and scholars and the interest manifested by social scientists, decision makers, and nongovernmental organizations outside the country. In light of my experience I discussed the contradictory moral and political implications of a critical ethnography depending on whether it was read by local or global actors. In other words, the first paper outlined the sociology of transnational research in academic contexts of power asymmetry, while the second one sketched a reflection on the dissemination and translation of scientific works in various worlds.

In both cases the public afterlife of my ethnography, with its sometimes trying moments, opened new dimensions in my inquiry, which were not about my research as such but about what its publication revealed of contemporary tensions within international programs, including the sorts of scientific nationalism they exacerbated. It forced me to reflect on what the book did to the public as well as what the public did to the book. The afterlife of the study was more than a question of reception; it was also about how public reactions amplified it and enriched it. In that regard, returning to South Africa seven years later to discuss it with some distance was a learning experience. Although the epidemiological situation was still preoccupying, the controversy has ceased and a more serene conversation became possible with some of those who had been critical of my work, which was taught in social sciences departments and had been positively engaged in medical workshops, as I discovered on that occasion. The work of time should certainly not be overlooked in the analysis of the public afterlife of ethnography.

With the publication of *La Force de l'ordre*, my reflection took a different direction, allowing me to pay closer attention to the mediations involved in the process of publicization. The book is based on the study of a police district, specifically of an anticrime squad operating in the *banlieues* of Paris between the spring of 2005 and the summer of 2007, that is, more or less in the interval separating the last two major outbursts of urban disturbances that occurred in France following the deaths of adolescents and youths from housing projects during interactions with the police force in Aulnay-sous-Bois and Villiers-le-Bel.[19] Although for a quarter of a century all riots have been the consequence of deadly interactions between the police and inhabitants of housing projects, no ethnography of law enforcement in these environments had been carried out in France. At the time of the publication the presidential campaign had just begun, and the Conservative candidate, Nicolas Sarkozy, increasingly instrumentalized the law-and-order discourse of the far right to secure his reelection. The conjunction of the novelty of the research and the favorable political context led the media to show unexpected interest in the book. For weeks it was widely and positively presented in newspapers and newsmagazines; long interviews were conducted on radio and television; invitations multiplied to give talks to grassroots organizations and in forums known as "people's universities." After a month of complete silence from the authorities, the Conservative minister of the interior decided to respond indirectly to the growing debate the book had elicited about policing practices, in particular racial discrimination, harassment, and violence. On December 8, 2011, Claude Guéant announced that he would celebrate the thirtieth anniversary of the anticrime squads, which had in fact been created only seventeen years earlier, and award medals to several officers of these dreaded units, despite the fact that the latter had been involved in almost all fatal police incidents in France in recent years.

The daily *Libération* took the opportunity of this ceremony to choose the book as its "event," and this time no dramatic interference occurred. Playing with the words of my title, the full front page represented in dark tones the belt of a police officer bedecked with weapons and handcuffs with this headline in white letters: "Les forces de désordre" (Forces of Disorder). The following pages included an editorial entitled "Fear," an article about the book, an interview with me, a report on a housing project, and the reaction of police officials.[20] The publication obviously undermined the efforts of the minister of the interior to redeem the image of the anticrime squads. Pressed to respond to questions from journalists about the book, he answered in vague but dismissive terms. This gave me the opportunity of a reply in an opinion piece published a few days later by *Le Monde*. Thus even if the headline and the picture somewhat caricatured the almost four hundred pages of the book, the newspaper's use of it, over which I had absolutely no control, contributed to the emergence of a collective discussion on policing in the banlieues, which had been almost completely absent from the public debate. Yet there was a cost to this mediation. Not only did the richness of the depiction, showing the diversity within police practices, and the complexity of the interpretation, taking into account the historical context and sociological processes, disappear, but the very text also vanished. What most readers accessed was the special section in one newspaper and the opinion piece in another as well as the various other interviews and articles in the media. The numbers were telling. Only considering *Libération*, 156,000 copies had been printed, while one year after its publication just 7,000 copies of the book had been sold.

There were twenty times more potential readers for the daily than for the monograph.

More generally it is highly probable that the majority of the people who know about such research and its findings have learned about it through an interview of the author, of which they may have caught only a fragment on the radio or the television; through an article by a journalist who perhaps perused part of the corresponding volume and found his inspiration on the back cover; or even through the comment of someone who heard or read something about it. In other words, most of those who have some knowledge and often an opinion regarding a book have never even laid their eyes on it. The afterlife of the work can thus be described in large part as spectral: when people refer to it in a conversation, what they have in mind is often in fact its representation in various mediations. This is true of the general public as well as of academic audiences. Scholars frequently learn about and even judge books through reviews—hence the power of reviewers, especially those who have access to prestigious magazines such as the *New York Review of Books*. It is therefore hardly a surprise that the afterlife of social science works should frequently have this spectral quality of invisible presence.

Acknowledging this apparently trivial reality has important practical implications for the relationships social scientists have with journalists. As Francisco Ferrándiz expresses it, "Anyone who has had negative contact with the press knows the sense of betrayal and manipulation that the published press article or the cuts in taped interviews leave: a headline which contradicts all you have stated, words and expressions that you do not recognize as yours."[21] To avoid such inconvenience I progressively adapted my attitude toward the press. While I used to give oral interviews later translated by my interlocutors into a written format, which implied a reduction of the dialogue by five to ten times and sometimes a transformation of my words verging on misinterpretation, I now request to proceed via email in order to express my thoughts more accurately, which is particularly crucial since the topics I address are generally sensitive. For radio or television interviews the problem is of course distinct, but broadcasts are often live or, if prerecorded, generally are not cut. In these cases selection of reliable journalists and the building of relationships of mutual respect are critical.

However, possibilities of intervention in what happens to the published work in its afterlife remain limited. Much of its existence is not only out of reach but also out of sight. One does not even know what becomes of it. Occasionally months or years after the fact one discovers it has been reviewed in some unfamiliar journal, learns about reactions either enthusiastic or antagonistic that it has elicited but had gone unnoticed, or retrospectively uncovers the impact not always acknowledged it has had on students, scholars, activists, or policymakers. But for the most part this afterlife is opaque to the author. And it is probably fortunate that it should be so; this is, after all, the public's domain.

Public

"The usage of the words 'public' and 'public sphere' betrays a multiplicity of concurrent meanings," Jürgen Habermas notes in the opening page of his influential essay, adding, "Their origins go back to various historical phases and, when applied synchronically to the conditions of a bourgeois society that is industrially advanced and constituted as a social-welfare state, they fuse into a clouded amalgam. Yet the very conditions that make the inherited language seem inappropriate appear to require these words, however confused their employment."[22] Legacy of profound transformations in modern society, the polysemy of these terms is thus simultaneously an obstacle and a condition to understanding their contemporary meaning. From this perspective the linguistic signal of the modern transformation of these terms, according to Habermas, is the emergence of the substantive from the adjective at the end of the seventeenth century: in English, German, and French, *public* gives birth to *the* public.

The public differs from the people, that is, everyone, in three senses. First, it does not exist in a latent way: it is constituted through objects, which become matters of discussion. Second, it is not free-floating in the social space: it needs places, like cafés, and mediations, like the press. Third, it is not neutral: it lives as a critical domain, initially in opposition to absolute power. The central idea is that the public is not already there: it is "brought into existence," as John Dewey expressed it, whether it is after an injury or via a claim.[23] The same idea prevails concerning the much debated notion of public opinion: it is not this amorphous conglomerate of judgments about everything that polling institutes assume they can sum up; rather it is formed "as a function of a society in operation, through the interaction of groups," in Herbert Blumer's words.[24] In short, the public is a social entity that comes into being in specific sites, through particular mediations, as a result of interactions, and with a potential for critique.

This delineation also characterizes the public that social scientists deal with. To put it in simple terms, it is composed of those who interact in one way or another with their work after it is published. As indicated earlier, it is much larger than the readership since one can react to a book or an essay without having read it; an interview with the author, a presentation by a journalist, a review by a scholar, a mere conversation with a colleague or a friend can make people enter the public. Actually one does not even need to react explicitly to be part of the public; one may remain silent while being interested, affected, or transformed by a book or an essay. These two features obviously make the identification of the public quite uneasy. Being in excess of the readership and not having to express itself openly renders it largely elusive. It is generally impossible to seize it or even to delimit or describe it. To the definition Michael Warner gives of the public, which exists "by virtue of being addressed," I would actually add that it also exists by virtue of being concerned.[25] This addition is necessary to account for the bilateral exchange—rather than a one-way bond—between the authors and their public. As they write, the former imagine the latter, who in turn imagine them while reading, listening, or discussing. This reciprocal but asymmetrical relationship is what constitutes the public: it is imagined, but certainly not imaginary.

Whereas calls for a public social science have multiplied in recent years, the questions of who this public is, where it is to be found, how it is to be interacted with are rarely posed. The most prominent and most articulated of these appeals has undoubtedly been Michael Burawoy's plea "for public sociology," which has generated a substantial literature in response.[26] Nevertheless his distinction between "traditional public sociology" directed toward a general public (the readers of a book or the listeners of a lecture) and "organic public sociology" connected to a specific public (trade unionists, neighborhood residents, activists) leaves almost entirely open the question of the composition of the former and problematically includes in the definition of the latter individuals who rather correspond to coproducers (what he proposes has long been known as participatory research). Yet the elusiveness of the public should not prevent social scientists from attempting to explore its composition. But such a formulation implies acknowledging its diversity. Whereas I have thus far mentioned the word "public" in its singular form, the plural seems more relevant.

So who are the publics of a book in the social sciences? There are probably at least four categories of individuals that constitute distinct publics: those under study, who can be divided into those among whom research has been conducted and those belonging to the larger group that has been analyzed; those linked to the previous ones through a hierarchical relationship, across

institutions, or possibly as clients; those professionally or pedagogically interested in the topic as scholars, journalists, experts, politicians, journalists,
students; and those simply affected for more general reasons, even if these
reasons might in fact be quite specific, in relation, for instance, to a personal
experience. There is arguably a certain overlap between these categories as well
as a degree of imprecision for each of them, but at least they give a sense of the
heterogeneity of the publics, which I have defined as both addressed and concerned. To illustrate this heterogeneity I will contrast the reception—at least,
what I am aware of it—of the two studies on law enforcement and the prison
system, since they are embedded in the same national context and developed
within the same scientific project.

On various occasions I have been asked how the police in general and the
officers among whom I had done my research in particular reacted to the publication of *La Force de l'ordre* and the publicity it received. The short answer
would be: I don't know. There is a good reason for this: the police do not express themselves publicly. The very few who, in diverse circumstances, have
spoken out, written opinion pieces, or produced critical memoirs have paid a
high price for it. The only exception is police unionists or high officials. In the
case of my book there seem to have been instructions not to respond to the
numerous articles in the press and interviews in the media since a public relations campaign had been planned by the Ministry of the Interior with the
peculiar celebration of the anniversary of the anticrime squads. In the rare
comments I read, the agents who were authorized to express the position of
their union or their administration resorted to two rhetorical tactics: appropriation and minimization. On the one hand, they used certain findings of
the study as evidence of the validity of their own demands, such as the end of
officially imposed quotas, which led them to arrest undocumented migrants
and marijuana users instead of criminals. On the other hand, they recognized
the most blatant deviance described in the study, for instance racist practices
and the display of far-right signs, but said it was the exception rather than the
norm.

However, to my surprise, the spokesperson of the largest police union sent
me a personal message in which he stated that he agreed with much of my
analysis and even asked me to do an interview for his magazine. I immediately
accepted. He transmitted me his questions, to which I quickly answered. He
did the page setting of the article and told me the issue would be out within a
few days. Then he wrote back and indicated that the general secretary had

vetoed the publication at the last minute. Since the head of the union had initially consented to it, I supposed that the order had come from above. Beyond this anecdote it is noteworthy that all the interactions I had with the police were private, either through emails or as an aside after a talk. Several former officials of the Ministry of the Interior concurred with my findings. Various officers who indicated they had been punished by their superiors for having denounced their colleagues' deviant practices provided me with their files. In fact I did not receive any criticism from the police. But I would not infer anything from their silence. The great majority of them probably did not even know that my work existed. The few who did preferred not to express their opinion.

As for the precinct where I had carried out the study, because the turnover among young officers was high, there was little chance that I could find the agents I knew, whereas the commissioner, who had been transferred to another region, never replied after I sent him the book, which I interpreted as disapproval. Although I had expressed my interest in interacting with law enforcement administration and in teaching or lecturing at the police academy, I was never asked to do so, which should not be a surprise considering how reticent this institution is toward independent researchers and how my work has been publicly presented. The only invitation I received was during the summer that followed the publication, from the newly appointed Socialist minister of the interior, Manuel Valls, who spent one hour conversing with me about the book. Having been the mayor of a city with several large housing projects, he approvingly mentioned my depiction of the harassment and racial profiling in these environments, going so far as to suggest his chief of staff read it, and as he walked me out he privately explained to me that the difficulty in reforming the institution lay with the police unions—although, in retrospect, I realize that he never even tried to propose such reforms during his two years in office before becoming prime minister.

The response of the prison system to my ethnography of a correctional facility was almost the complete opposite. Although the media presented *L'Ombre du monde* as a critical analysis not only of the carceral condition but also of penal policies, which it is, I was invited by the central as well as local administration to present my work straightaway. At the national level I was asked to give a talk at a seminar for Department of Corrections officials and a lecture at the Correctional Officer Academy, and I had private conversations with the minister of justice, Christiane Taubira, and one of her predecessors.

This confirmed what I had already noted about the openness of the prison administration to outside perspectives, from which I was not the only one to have benefited, in sharp contrast with law enforcement.

In the facility where I had conducted my research, a series of two-hour seminars was organized with the guards and wardens, the counselors and parole officers, and a group of inmates in an atmosphere of congenial excitement. Among the correctional personnel several had read the book. A warden who, I was told, had spent a couple of hours each morning annotating it, kindly alerted me to a few factual errors and even specified the corresponding pages. A guard amusingly mentioned that despite the anonymity he had been able to recognize himself in the portrait of a man whose roughness with the inmates I had linked to his former profession of gendarme; he agreed with my depiction of him and assured me that in his new post he had a completely different attitude. A lieutenant said she had offered a copy to relatives of hers so they would learn about the "reality" of prison life, adding that she regretted only that I had not given the name of the facility to authenticate her gift. She indicated that, after having read about the "hardships" endured by spouses when visiting inmates, she was working with a colleague to modify the security procedure and make things easier. I was not entirely surprised at these reactions since during my fieldwork the correctional personnel had often complained about the terrible image of the prison in public opinion, which contaminated them morally to the point that half of the officers never say what their job is; the book, they hoped, would shed a different light if not on the prison at least on those who worked in it.

Few inmates had accessed the book because the copy I had given to the library was always checked out; this was not the librarian's fault, however, since although he had read it twice already he had bought his own volume. The discussion with the prisoners was of a different nature than the conversation with the personnel: it was tenser and more political as they denounced the injustice of the penal system and the constraints of the carceral world. To the credit of the coordinator of the educational programs at the prison, who had selected the inmates attending this discussion, and of the administration, which had provided him the leeway to do so, several of those attending the meeting were Basques, incarcerated for alleged terrorist activities, and Muslims, suspected of being engaged in a process of radicalization. As they were deemed more dangerous (they were known under a special label that implied stricter surveillance) and more politicized (although in very distinct directions), their presence gave the debate a more impassioned and polemical turn, which was nevertheless restrained by the fact that a lieutenant was sitting in a corner of the room where we met. In the discussion they were above all interested in the injustice of the penal system and the arbitrariness of the prison institution: how the former practiced discrimination among offenders and how the latter did not abide by the law—which, in both cases, was true. Apart from this formal encounter in my presence, lighter conversations were also taking place, as, after having read certain passages, inmates would try to identify fellow prisoners or correctional officers evoked in my work. The exercise became a joke, especially since they often made wrong guesses.

The contrast between the reception of the two books by the publics most directly concerned—if not most specifically addressed—should in itself be an object of inquiry. Such has been the case for certain domains. Thus Angelique Haugerud analyzes the difficulties faced by anthropologists who try to make a different voice heard in the field of economics and finance, while Hugh Gusterson examines the obstacles posed to anthropologists who study neoliberalism or militarism when they try to break through to the mainstream press.[27] In my case the most obvious explanation for the differences observed between the two publics is that whereas both studies are critical of the corresponding system in terms of its unfairness and violence, my depiction of their activities shows police officers being more aggressive, ruthless, and racist than correctional officers. This difference is even more remarkable since they have the same social background, come from the same regions, take the same initial tests, and are confronted with the same populations. But mine is not a psychological or moral account; I provide sociological reasons in terms of occupational activity, work organization, political context, and policy orientation. Despite this effort to distance my analysis from judgments and emotions, I could be regarded as unsympathetic toward law enforcement agents and understanding with prison guards, which would ultimately justify the difference in their attitudes toward the respective books.

Yet there is a more relevant interpretation, at least one that is more coherent with my empirical observations. In France the police institution is much more closed, secretive, and antagonistic than the prison administration. Information is much less accessible and permission much more difficult to obtain from the former than from the latter. More subtly, the police see the world as hostile to them and therefore reject it so as to protect themselves, which explains their opacity, whereas prison personnel suffer from the negative image of their institution and consequently try to reverse the stigma, which may in part explain a certain transparency in their activities and a relative welcoming of researchers. Identification logics proceed through the exacerbation of resentment in the first case and the repair of an injury in the second. In sum, as they were both confronted with a publication deemed critical, the absence of a reaction from the police institution (when I had feared potential judicial proceedings) and the warmth of the reception by the prison institution (when I anticipated some discontent) validated and refined my analysis. Thus I could integrate my interactions with these publics into a broader interpretation of their respective institutions.

Beyond the police and prison worlds, the response was no less interesting. The book on law enforcement elicited many testimonies: a magistrate wrote to me in an email that after having read my analysis she now understood that charges of insulting and resisting the police in cases in which the defendant was the only person hurt were commonly used to cover up police violence; youths from housing projects expressed, sometimes directly in conversation, sometimes through a colleague sociologist who was working with them, their satisfaction that their words, which were never believed by the judges and journalists, could for once be confirmed by someone with professorial authority; various individuals informed me about a friend or relative who had been a victim of various forms of abuse. Members of a campaign to end the police's use of Taser and Flash-Ball asked me to give a talk to their group, as did representatives of local branches of political parties eager to fight police discrimination. There were also contentious utterances: when an interview or article was published online, it immediately generated hundreds of angry exchanges between people protected by their screen names who commented dismissively about my work or aggressively against the police.

However, the most noteworthy, if not unexpected, reaction was probably that of the French experts on the police, about which a renowned North American criminologist observed in a public talk that he had never seen such a surge of animosity against a scholarly work that had received such praise and suggested that the latter circumstance could well be the cause of the former. This discrepancy was striking since I was simultaneously invited to give lectures on urban policing by criminologists and social scientists on the five continents. In scientific journals, on news websites, and sometimes during debates on the radio or the television, the range of criticisms was wide. The most charitable among my colleagues considered my study to be characterized by "ethnographic rigorism," meaning in particular that I had investigated only one precinct, which did not allow for any generalization of my observations on police practices. The least generous ones disqualified the research as being a sort of "lampoon" belonging to a long tradition of denunciation of the police and even the work of an "amateur ethnologist" ignorant of the basic rules of fieldwork.

These convergent attacks were addressed by members or former members of the same research center, where most French criminologists work with the financial support and under the administrative supervision of the Ministry of Justice. Having studied law enforcement for several decades they had developed close links with the institution, its officials, and its professionals, and since they relied mostly on interviews, surveys, statistics, and document analysis in their own research, they were unfamiliar with and obviously disturbed by my ethnography. But in the end their insistent criticism of my work came down to a denial of discriminatory or violent practices in law enforcement and was read by many as an implicit defense of the police, in line with the comments of the minister of the interior at the time. As a conspicuous expression of this strategy, a member of this research center published online three months after my book came out the complacent interview of an officer belonging to an anticrime squad, which shed a favorable light on the units I had studied. In spite of the somewhat disparaging character of most criticisms, I chose to reply almost systematically, leaving aside their polemical dimension and focusing on the theoretical and methodological points they raised. It thus became an occasion to discuss the epistemology of ethnography, that generalization was not only statistical but also comprehensive, as well as its politics, since it was clear that the lack of representativeness could become a general way to discredit critical findings using such methods. I later synthesized this discussion in the afterword I wrote for the second edition of the book.[28] What had initially been an unpleasant set of attacks thus turned into a broader debate on ethnography, which allowed me to justify my approach as well as refine my arguments.

In the end, however, authors know that the immense majority of the public remains invisible to them. Those with whom they interact directly or indirectly compose only a small part of a larger unidentifiable virtual network of individuals who, without even being aware of it, are likewise addressed or feel concerned by a text—one that happens to be an ethnography.

Ethnography

"Ethnographies sit between two worlds or systems of meaning—the world of the ethnographer (and readers) and the world of cultural members (also, increasingly, readers, although not the targeted ones)," remarks John Van

Maanen in his discussion of ethnography. This precarious equilibrium is maintained through two types of operation: fieldwork and writing. "Fieldwork is one answer—some say the best—to the question of how the understanding of others, close or distant, is achieved.... In print, the research is presented as occasionally boring, sometimes exciting, but virtually always self-transforming as the fieldworker comes to regard an initially strange and unfamiliar place and people in increasingly familiar and confident ways." These features render the publicization of ethnography both fascinating and delicate: fascinating because it re-creates a social world alien to the audience who can progressively explore and tame it, but delicate because there remain large continents of untranslatability and misunderstanding of which both author and readers must be aware. There is a false transparency of fieldwork and writing: the former as access to the "real world" and the latter as translation into "tales of the field," as Van Maanen has it.[29] Ethnographers are conscious of the danger of this apparent transparency and use various rhetorical devices to prevent it—sometimes, conversely, at the risk of rendering the restitution of their ethnography definitely opaque.

The false transparency of ethnography is particularly striking in the debate between the promoters of a political or moral engagement and the defenders of an objective or impartial approach. Yet, as Jack Katz observes, "in the conduct of fieldwork, methods and theory interests are so closely mixed with each other and with historically and socially contextualized relevancies that neutrality is relatively hard to come by." More explicitly he argues that "in a variety of ways, all ethnographies are politically cast and policy relevant."[30] It is well known that even allegedly apolitical depictions of society involve political decisions. This is why the public afterlife of ethnography is largely determined by its previous life as fieldwork and writing. Starting the narrative of this afterlife with the publication of a text, as I may have implied thus far, is therefore an incorrect representation. The sequence it suggests—publication, media coverage, solicitation by diverse audiences, reactions from various actors, and finally reflexive assessment—provides a reconstitution that does not accurately account for the whole process of publicization. This process has a prehistory. It comprises the very choice of the topic of the inquiry, the readings related to it, the methodology used, the relationships built in the field, the facts rendered relevant, the theoretical framework to interpret them, and the style and form of writing the account of the research. The fate of the text after its publication is highly dependent on what happened before.

While the occurrence of two major series of riots in the fall of 2005 and 2007 was obviously a coincidence in the case of the monograph on the police since my fieldwork started in the spring of 2005 and ended in the summer of 2007, the choice of law enforcement as my next object of study after I had conducted research on racial discrimination was not the result of serendipity. This was a time when the minister of the interior, stated that he would "clean out with a Kärcher" (high-pressure hose) the housing projects to rid them of "scum" (undesirable youths) and had declared a "war on delinquents," imposing on the police his "politics of number" (quota of arrests) with objectives attainable only with aggressive stop-and-frisks. Thus deciding to study law enforcement in the banlieues in that context could not be a neutral act, and my investigation showed how police practices reflected the shift that was occurring in national policies. Similarly, using participant observation as my main method, when my colleagues relied on indirect approaches, allowed for a less filtered access to the everyday interactions between the police and the population. Furthermore reading foreign criminological literature, which had long produced data and analysis on urban patrolling, racial profiling, police violence, and professional ethics, instead of limiting myself to the local scientific production opened new perspectives on topics that had received little attention in the French context.

The conjunction of these choices enabled me to identify and analyze issues that were usually neglected or euphemized. Discrimination and brutality, for instance, were rarely discussed, and when they were it was in terms of complaints from the public, the discourses of the officers, and the procedures of the disciplinary committees or judicial courts, which had an effect of derealization since the facts themselves were reduced to statements and arguments about them. Ethnography provided a different status for truthfulness. But the act of writing was itself crucial in defining what would be the process of publicization. It was conceived as an attempt to reach out to an imagined audience that would exceed the usual academic circles to include various publics, from the police themselves to citizens interested in understanding the democratic issues involved in current law enforcement practices. Concretely it meant renouncing scholarly conventions, hermetic phrasing, erudite digressions, and even section headings, developing instead a more literary form with descriptions and narratives where theoretical developments were embedded in rather than separated from the empirical material. The idea was to restore to ethnography its life. This restoration can be paralleled with that of an artwork for which the conservator cleans successive layers of varnish that have darkened the painting to reestablish its original freshness. But, as soon became obvious, this had two apparently contradictory aspects.

On the one hand I realized that ethnography had a potent impact on readers and listeners. The mere relation of an event or the sheer depiction of a scene, even when what was narrated or represented had no sensational character but corresponded to the mundane life of police patrols or correctional facilities, often generated powerful effects of three types: first, an effect of proximity, with an impression of presence at the event or at the scene; second, an effect of realism, with confidence that what was related or depicted did happen; third, an effect of truth, with a sentiment to access a deeper level beyond the fact. The dialogue between an officer and a youth during a stop-and-frisk, uncovering the harsh and scornful way in which the police interacted with certain populations, or the description of the sounds of closing doors and shouts in the prison, revealing the invisible oppression and unbearable noise from which inmates suffered, had a power of evocation along these three dimensions that the abstract analysis of harassment or confinement would never achieve.

As I noticed on several occasions from the vehement reactions of the audience after a talk, ethnographic writing produced an impact, which was paradoxically proportional to the triviality of the fact related and the sobriety of the depiction: whereas drama and pathos would certainly have been counterproductive, a banal scene recounted in a neutral way—which is what I endeavored to approach—was not only more suggestive but more heuristic, since it opened the public to further examination of the historical context and the sociological configuration in which the event was embedded. It should be noted, however, that a fourth effect, to which ethnographers attach importance, could not be conveyed: the effect of reflexivity. Actually, bringing the ethnographer into the picture to reflect on the way his position could affect both what he observed and how he observed it was often inaudible, as the audience, even when composed of social scientists, would infer from it a subjectivity discrediting the author.

On the other hand I discovered that ethnography was often untranslatable through the usual media. Articles in the press, conversations on the radio, debates on television, even talks to general audiences, on which it seemed possible to have more control, erased the expressiveness of narratives and the thickness of descriptions to leave only the dry, condensed, and simplified analysis of police discrimination or violence, for example. The interviews I gave after the publication of the study on the prison were particularly revealing in that regard; almost all the questions asked were focused on the first two chapters of the book, which discussed the evolution of the penal system, while there were hardly any on the nine others, which dealt with the carceral condition itself. Journalists seemed more interested in the causes of the dramatic increase and racial differentiation in the prison population than in what the life and worlds of the prison were, or they considered that it was what their publics expected. I would rather discard the hypothesis that they stopped reading when they reached the third chapter.

Significantly, however, there were two domains in which my interlocutors valued ethnography as such: judicial and artistic. First, I was solicited on several occasions to testify in court cases involving police violence or racial profiling. Although I had not witnessed the events related to these cases, I was invited as an amicus curiae to write a report describing and analyzing the typical situation similar to the one of the trial based on my fieldwork and supposed expertise. Ethnography served as a sort of certificate of authenticity, as can also be the case in other juridical contexts.[31] Second, I was invited to participate in two international art exhibitions. One was on the theme of power and violence, with installations and photographs, notably on the police. The other was on figures of alterity, in particular that of the "savage," which corresponds to one of the representations and designations of the youths of color by the police. In both cases, as also with a film director who planned to include several episodes narrated in the book as sequences in a movie he wanted to make, events and scenes but also the representations and images they elicited were what interested the curators. Ethnography acquired in these projects a new potentiality, parallel to its developments as performance.[32] More than in the work of translation to wider audiences through interviews or talks, it was in the enterprise of transcription for other worlds—those of justice and art—that ethnography found its place; rather than being paraphrased, it had to be transposed.

The complications of these processes of translation and transcription in the domain of policy became evident when I was invited to give a talk at a conference co-organized by the École des Hautes Études en Sciences Sociales and the Ministry of Justice in Paris a few months before the publication of my book on the prison. The idea of the initiators of this high-profile event opened by the president of the school and the minister of justice was to bring together researchers and officials so as to confront their views. On each panel, social scientists presented studies generally initiated and funded by the ministry while civil servants of the latter reflected on specific evolutions of their institution.

Because they had known each other for some time and shared a similar set of policy-relevant interrogations, they spoke a common language and displayed a form of intellectual affinity. Being on the last panel with the national director of the Department of Corrections, whom I had never met, I was the only one to have carried out an ethnographic work. After some hesitation about the best use of this approach and material for a fifteen-minute talk in conversation with an executive of the government, I chose to turn two of my objects of inquiry into what I called "modest realistic utopias," an oxymoron that took seriously the creative potentialities of ethnography as others did for sociology.[33] My argument went as follows. Instead of the "grand utopia" of a world without prison, one could explore "small utopias" that had two major characteristics: they were an outcome of fieldwork, which implied their being grounded in empirical observation, and they had a reasonable chance to happen in a not so distant future, as history suggested. I provided two examples.

The first utopia concerned cell phones. They are forbidden but ubiquitous in prison; in the facility I studied, 850 were found in one year through searches among 900 inmates, and this figure is most certainly less than the real number. Their prohibition has various consequences: it generates an illegal economy; it produces multiple punishments, including extended prison stay; it leads to power relations among inmates, with local leaders using the most vulnerable among them to get and hide these devices. Contrary to the administration's fear, cell phones were not used by the great majority of prisoners to organize plots or threaten witnesses but to call their wives, mothers, children, and relatives. The likely evolution I anticipated was that cell phones would soon be sold by the correctional facilities themselves, thus allowing for better control of their type and utilization. Such a solution would reduce trafficking, penalties, and violence. I established a parallel with game consoles, which were forbidden when I started my fieldwork due to the possibility of Internet access and had become a frequent purchase in the facility. In fact this prediction seemed hardly original since the General Inspector of Prisons, an independent public body writing reports and making recommendations, had already proposed that cell phones be authorized.

The second utopia pertained to solitary confinement, which is the most common form of punishment used by disciplinary boards, even for minor and unproven faults. Socially and psychologically fragile individuals are the most affected because they are particularly exposed to misbehavior and extremely sensitive to this penalty. I have witnessed harrowing scenes of suffering, including inmates setting mattresses on fire after they were locked up in solitary confinement cells, where the risk of killing oneself is eleven times higher than in regular cells. The tragic consequences of this punishment partly explain why the suicide rate has multiplied by five in the past half-century in France, which ranks first in Europe for this cause of death among inmates. Yet over the years the maximum duration of solitary confinement has been progressively reduced, from ninety to thirty days. The forecast I made was therefore that, in the future, solitary confinement would disappear and that, in retrospect, the institution would regard it as it now regards punishment by irons and straightjackets.

I concluded the talk by saying that I was aware of the unconventional character of this use of ethnography as a predictive instrument but that a conference such as the one we were attending provided the opportunity to imagine innovative contributions by the social sciences to policymaking. But in surprising contrast with the atmosphere of intellectual congeniality at the event, the reaction of the national director of the Department of Corrections was angry and dismissive. She disqualified my reflections as pure activism and refused to enter the discussion. The next day I wrote her a long letter explaining the difference between the sponsored research responding to the legitimate demands of the administration, which my colleagues were carrying out, and the independent research posing questions that were usually not raised, which I was conducting; she never replied. I was later told by one of her deputies that she had thoroughly read the six hundred pages of my book with a mixture of interest and irritation. My modest yet realistic utopias were definitely not timely suggestions.

Subsequent events confirmed this. In response to the attacks of January 2015 in Paris, the government announced that telephone signals would be scrambled around prisons, a technique that had already been tested and eventually abandoned because of its cost and inefficacy, and decided to segregate and confine inmates suspected of Islamist radicalization, a measure that could have negative effects by grouping together the most hardened prisoners. This was certainly an evolution that my ethnography had not predicted.

Conclusion

The evolution of the social sciences over the past several decades toward what is often described as professionalization but would probably be better analyzed in terms of "academicization," as Craig Calhoun qualifies it, has accentuated the separation between those who practice and teach these disciplines and those who are their objects or subjects of study.[34] This is especially true in the United States, where the concentration of social scientists is the highest in the world and where the gap between scholars and society is particularly significant; in fact deeper attention to the various national histories of the social sciences would allow for the identification of quite distinct academic landscapes.[35] In response to this trend calls for a more public presence of the social sciences have repeatedly been made, although they have remained relatively marginal within each disciplinary field. Interesting exceptions are history, whose authors have for a long time achieved flourishing careers in bookstores as well as on television, and economics, whose most prominent scholars endeavor to translate their work into accessible essays; in both cases the discipline seems to have developed a dual format of publication, one academic, the other popular. Anthropology is far from such accomplishment.

Public presence means at least two different, albeit compatible, things, as illustrated by anthropology. It can correspond to an engagement in the public sphere through participation in debates around themes of general interest, frequently related to cultural differences and ethnic minorities; Norway is often promoted as a success story for such engaged anthropology.[36] It can also refer to collaboration with certain groups that are dominated, dispossessed, or excluded; the defense of indigenous rights has been a major domain for such anthropological intervention.[37] The figure of the anthropologist is that of the intellectual in the first case and in the second that of the activist. In the present essay I have focused on the former aspect, while occasionally indicating situations that involve the latter.

But what I have proposed is to move a step aside. I argue in favor of a descriptive rather than prescriptive stance. I am not saying that social scientists should be more public, although I think they should. I am instead urging them to account for and reflect on what happens when they become public. And my starting point is rather straightforward: from the moment a text is published, by definition, it exposes its author to a public. However, it is worth distinguishing publication, the mere fact of rendering the text available to the public, and publicization, the active process through which the encounter with publics takes place. There are obviously degrees in the intensity of the publicization, from the monograph mostly found in university libraries and discussed within erudite circles to the best seller that generates wide media coverage and debates beyond the academy. The afterlife of social science works is therefore diverse. Until recently, however, with exceptions of which I have provided examples, this afterlife has not received the attention it deserves, in particular from the very authors who develop such public presence. I have suggested taking it seriously and making this analytical exercise a part of the research.

Exploring the afterlife of works thus extends and enriches the intellectual project of the social sciences. Rather than the usual normative stance, which presupposes that their publicization is a good thing, it implies a reflexive and critical examination of their public presence. Ethnography offers an interesting example in that regard because of the sort of knowledge it produces, the expectations of exoticism and difference it creates, and the specific problems its embedding in the public sphere entails. Ultimately, as shown here, such an inquiry into the public afterlife of ethnography can be viewed as an ethnography in its own right.

Notes

An earlier version of this epilogue was initially published under the same title in *American Ethnologist* 42.4 (2015): 592–609.

1   For a detailed analysis of the response to the *Charlie Hebdo* attacks, see Fassin 2015a.
2   For an early discussion on public ethnography, see Cunha and Lima 2010.
3   For the corresponding illustrations, see Stocking 1983, 1984, 1989, 1991.
4   On the reactions to ethnographic studies, see Brettell (1993), MacClancy and McDonaugh (1996), and Fluehr-Lobban (2003), respectively.
5   In *Ethnography in Today's World* (Sanjek 2014: 189).
6   The story of this foundational moment of public anthropology in the United States is presented and analyzed in Price's (2000) article.
7   In *Engaging Anthropology* (Eriksen 2006: 23), which offers a broad review of the "public presence" of the discipline.
8   This reader is somewhat heterogeneous (Gonzalez 2004).
9   For examples, see Beck and Maida 2013; Borofsky 2011; Vine 2011. Within the American Anthropological Association, the journal *American Anthropologist* has an annual review on public anthropology and the letter *Anthropology News* grants space to it in each of its issues.
10 In "The Task of the Translator" (Benjamin [1923] 1968: 69–71).
11 See Straub (2009) and Forni (2013), respectively.
12 See Vidich and Bensman (1964), and more specifically Becker's (1964: 273) comments.
13 The piece offers a strong critique of anthropologists' reactions to their interlocutors' reactions (Rosaldo 1986).
14 Greenberg 1993; Scheper-Hughes 2000.

15 The Mead controversy was launched by Freeman (1983) and is discussed in Shankman (2013). The Chagnon controversy was fueled by Tierney (2000) and is assessed in Lamphere (2003).

16 On the ethics of anthropology, see Meskell and Pels 2005.

17 The English edition (Fassin 2007) followed by two years the French original, *Quand les corps se souviennent*, which had not raised any controversy.

18 For a presentation of these two lines of reflection, see Fassin 2008, 2013a.

19 I refer here to the French version (Fassin 2011), which provoked debates in France, but a translation was published two years later with the title *Enforcing Order.*

20 This episode has been related previously in more detail (Fassin 2013c).

21 In Ferrándiz's (2013: 18) account of his experience with the exhumation of victims of the Franco regime in Spain.

22 In his habilitation thesis (Habermas [1962] 1989: 1, 26).

23 In *The Public and Its Problem* (Dewey [1927] 1988: 17).

24 Blumer 1948: 544.

25 Warner 2002: 50.

26 See the collective volume edited by Clawson et al. (2007), in which Burawoy's 2005 presidential address to the American Sociological Association is reprinted.

27 See Gusterson (2013) and Haugerud (2013) in a special issue of the British journal *Anthropology Today.*

28 This postface served as both a preliminary reflection on the public afterlife of ethnography and a rejoinder to the criticisms on the book (Fassin 2015b).

29 See Van Maanen's classic (1988: 4, 2).

30 See Katz's (2004: 282) epistemological article.

31 On the experience of an anthropology at the British Court of Asylum, see Good 2007.

32 On performance ethnography, see Denzin 2003.

33 The notion of "real utopia" has been developed by Wright 2010.

34 In Calhoun's (2008: xvii) text on activist research.

35 For such an approach, see Wagner et al. (1991).

36 On Norwegians' idiosyncrasy, see Howell 2010.

37 On activism about American Indians, see Hale 2006.

References

Beck, Sam, and Carl Maida. 2013. *Toward Engaged Anthropology*. New York: Berghahn.

Becker, Howard. 1964. "Problems in the Publication of Field Studies." In *Reflections on Community Studies*, edited by Arthur Vidich, Joseph Bensman, and Maurice Stein, 267–84. New York: John Wiley and Sons.

Benjamin, Walter. (1923) 1968. "The Task of the Translator." In *Illuminations: Essays and Reflections*, 69–82. New York: Schocken Books.

Blumer, Herbert. 1948. "Public Opinion and Public Opinion Polls." *American Sociological Review* 13.5: 542–49.

Borofsky, Rob. 2011. *Why a Public Anthropology?* Hawaii: Center for a Public Anthropology.

Brettell, Caroline, ed. 1993. *When They Read What We Write: The Politics of Ethnography*. Westport, CT: Bergin and Garvey.

Burawoy, Michael. 2005. "For Public Sociology." *American Sociological Review* 70.1: 4–28.

Calhoun, Craig. 2008. Foreword to *Engaging Contradictions: Theory, Politics and Methods of Activist Scholarship*, edited by Charles Hale, xiii–xxvi. Berkeley: University of California Press.

Clawson, Dan, et al., eds. 2007. *Public Sociology: Fifteen Eminent Sociologists Debate Politics and the Profession in the Twenty-First Century*. Berkeley: University of California Press.

Cunha, Manuela Ivone, and Antonia Lima. 2010. "Ethnography and the Public Sphere: Summarizing Questions." *Etnográfica* 14.1: 61–69.

Denzin, Norman. 2003. *Performance Ethnography: Critical Pedagogy and the Politics of Culture*. Thousand Oaks, CA: Sage.

Dewey, John. (1927) 1988. *The Public and Its Problems*. Athens, OH: Swallow Press, Ohio University Press.

Eriksen, Thomas Hylland. 2006. *Engaging Anthropology: The Case for a Public Presence*. Oxford: Berg.

Fassin, Didier. 2007. *When Bodies Remember: Experiences and Politics of AIDS in South Africa*. Berkeley: University of California Press.

———. 2008. "Répondre de sa recherche: L'anthropologue face à ses autres." In *Les politiques de l'enquête: Epreuves ethnographiques*, edited by Didier Fassin and Alban Bensa, 299–320. Paris: La Découverte.

———. 2011. *La Force de l'ordre: Une anthropologie de la police des quartiers*. Paris: Seuil.

———. 2013a. "A Case for Critical Ethnography: Rethinking the Early Years of the AIDS Epidemic in South Africa." *Social Science and Medicine* 99: 119–26.

———. 2013b. *Enforcing Order: An Ethnography of Urban Policing*. Cambridge, UK: Polity Press.

———. 2013c. "Why Ethnography Matters: On Anthropology and Its Publics." *Cultural Anthropology* 28.4: 621–46.

———. 2015a. "In the Name of the Republic: Untimely Meditations on the Aftermath of *Charlie Hebdo* Attack." *Anthropology Today* 31.2: 3–7.

———. 2015b. "La vie publique des livres." In *La Force de l'ordre: Une anthropologie de la police des quartiers*, 365–86. 2nd ed. Paris: Seuil.

———. 2015c. *L'Ombre du monde: Une anthropologie de la condition carcérale*. Paris: Seuil.

———. 2016. *Prison Worlds: An Ethnography of the Carceral Condition*. Cambridge, UK: Polity Press.

Ferrándiz, Fernando. 2013. "Rapid Response Ethnographies in Turbulent Times: Researching Mass Grave Exhumations in Contemporary Spain." *Anthropology Today* 29.6: 18–22.

Fluehr-Lobban, Carolyn. 2003. *Ethics and the Profession of Anthropology: Dialogue for Ethically Conscious Practice*. Walnut Creek, CA: Altamira Press.

Forni, Kathleen. 2013. *Chaucer's Afterlife: Adaptation in Recent Popular Culture*. Jefferson, NC: McFarland.

Freeman, Derek. 1983. *Margaret Mead and Samoa: The Making and Unmaking of an Anthropological Myth*. Cambridge, MA: Harvard University Press.

Gonzalez, Roberto, ed. 2004. *Anthropologists in the Public Sphere: Speaking Out on War, Peace and American Power*. Austin: University of Texas Press.

Good, Anthony. 2007. *Anthropology and Expertise in the Asylum Courts*. Abingdon, UK: Routledge-Cavendish.

Greenberg, Ofra. 1993. "When They Read What the Papers Say We Wrote." In *They Read What We Write: The Politics of Ethnography*. Edited by Caroline Brettell, 107–18. Westport, CT: Bergin and Garvey.

Gusterson, Hugh. 2013. "Anthropology in the News?" *Anthropology Today* 29.6: 11–13.

Habermas, Jürgen. (1962) 1989. *The Structural Transformation of the Public Sphere: An Inquiry into a Category of Bourgeois Society*. Cambridge, MA: MIT Press.

Hale, Charles. 2006. "Activist Research v. Cultural Critique: Indigenous Land Rights and the Contradictions of Politically Engaged Anthropology." *Cultural Anthropology* 21.1: 96–120.

Haugerud, Angelique. 2013. "Public Anthropology and the Financial Crisis." *Anthropology Today* 29.6: 7–10.

Howell, Signe. 2010. "Norwegian Academic Anthropologists in Public Spaces." *Cultural Anthropology* 51.S2: 269–78.

Katz, Jack. 2004. "On the Rhetoric and Politics of Ethnographic Methodology." *Annals of the American Academy of Political and Social Science* 595: 280–308.

Lamphere, Louise. 2003. "The Perils and Prospects for an Engaged Anthropology: A View from the United States." *Social Anthropology* 11.2: 153–68.

MacClancy, Jeremy, and Chris McDonaugh, eds. 1996. *Popularizing Anthropology*. London: Routledge.

Meskell, Lynn, and Peter Pels, eds. 2005. *Embedding Ethics*. Oxford: Berg.

Price, Richard. 2000. "Anthropologists as Spies." *Nation*, November 20.

Rosaldo, Renato. 1986. *When Natives Talk Back: Chicano Anthropology since the Late 60s*. Lectures Series Monograph, vol. 2, series 1984–85. Tucson: University of Arizona.

Sanjek, Roger. 2014. *Ethnography in Today's World: Color Full before Color Blind*. Philadelphia: University of Pennsylvania Press.

Scheper-Hughes, Nancy. 2000. "Ire in Ireland." *Ethnography* 1.1: 117–40.

Shankman, Paul. 2013. "The Fateful 'Hoaxing' of Margaret Mead: A Cautionary Tale." *Current Anthropology* 54.1: 51–70.

Stocking, George, ed. 1983. *Observers Observed: Essays on Ethnographic Work.*
  Madison: University of Wisconsin Press.
———. 1984. *Functionalism Historicized: Essays on British Social Anthropology.*
  Madison: University of Wisconsin Press.
———. 1989. *Romantic Motives: Essays in Anthropological Sensibility.* Madison:
  University of Wisconsin Press.
———. 1991. *Colonial Situations: Essays on the Contextualization of Ethnographic
  Knowledge.* Madison: University of Wisconsin Press.
Straub, Julia. 2009. *A Victorian Muse: The Afterlife of Dante's Beatrice in Nineteenth-
  Century Literature.* London: Continuum Books.
Tierney, Patrick. 2000. *Darkness in El Dorado: How Scientists and Journalists
  Devastated the Amazon.* New York: Norton.
Van Maanen, John. 1988. *Tales of the Field: On Writing Ethnography.* Chicago:
  University of Chicago Press.
Vidich, Arthur, and Joseph Bensman. 1964. "The Springdale Case: Academic
  Bureaucrats and Sensitive Townspeople." In *Reflections on Community Studies,*
  edited by Arthur Vidich, Joseph Bensman, and Maurice Stein, 313–49. New York:
  John Wiley and Sons.
Vine, David. 2011. "Public Anthropology in Its Second Decade: Robert Borofsky's
  Center for a Public Anthropology." *American Anthropologist* 113.2: 336–49.
Wagner, Peter, Björn Wittrock, and Richard Whitley, eds. 1991. *Discourses on Society:
  The Shaping of the Social Science Disciplines.* Dordrecht: Kluwer Academic.
Warner, Michael. 2002. "Publics and Counterpublics." *Public Culture* 14.1: 49–90.
Wright, Erik Olin. 2010. *Envisioning Real Utopias.* New York: Verso.

Contributors

—— NADIA ABU EL-HAJ is a professor of anthropology at Barnard College of Columbia University and codirector of the Center for Palestine Studies at Columbia. Her work straddles the disciplines of anthropology and history of science, concerned with the relationships among scientific practices, social imaginaries, and political regimes. Her current research traces shifting understandings of combat trauma from the post-Vietnam era to the present. Her publications include *Facts on the Ground: Archaeological Practice and Territorial Self-Fashioning in Israeli Society* (2001) and *The Genealogical Science: The Politics of Epistemology and the Search for Jewish Origins* (2012).

—— JONATHAN BENTHALL is an honorary research fellow in the Department of Anthropology, University College London, and director emeritus of the Royal Anthropological Institute. During his directorship he steered the Institute toward more participation in public affairs and was the founding editor of the journal *Anthropology Today*. Recently he has focused his research on the overlaps between religion and humanitarianism, with special reference to Islam. His publications include *The Best of Anthropology Today* (2002), *Returning to Religion: Why a Secular Age Is Haunted by Faith* (2008), and *Islamic Charities and Islamic Humanism in Troubled Times* (2016).

—— LUCAS BESSIRE is an assistant professor of anthropology at the University of Oklahoma who works on politics, media, and indigeneity in the Americas. He has made two documentary films and his publications include *Radio Fields: Anthropology and Wireless Sound in the 21st Century* (2012, coedited with Daniel Fisher) and *Behold the Black Caiman: A Chronicle of Ayoreo Life* (2014).

—— JOÃO BIEHL is the Susan Dod Brown Professor of Anthropology and a Woodrow Wilson School faculty associate at Princeton University and the codirector of Princeton's Global Health Program. He is the author of the award-winning books *Vita: Life in a Zone of Social Abandonment* (2005, updated 2013) and *Will to Live: AIDS Therapies and the Politics of Survival*

(2007). He coedited the books *Unfinished: The Anthropology of Becoming* (Duke University Press, 2017), *When People Come First: Critical Studies in Global Health* (2013), and *Subjectivity: Ethnographic Investigations* (2007).

— GABRIELLA COLEMAN is the Wolfe Chair in Scientific and Technological Literacy at McGill University. Trained as an anthropologist, she explores the intersection of the cultures of hacking and politics, with a focus on the sociopolitical implications of the free software movement and the digital protest ensemble Anonymous. She has authored two books, *Coding Freedom: The Ethics and Aesthetics of Hacking* (2012) and the award-winning *Hacker, Hoaxer, Whistleblower, Spy: The Many Faces of Anonymous* (2014).

— MANUELA IVONE CUNHA, an anthropologist and sociologist, is a senior research fellow at CRIA-UMinho and teaches at the University of Minho. Distinguished with a social sciences award for her ethnographic research on prisons, drug markets, and the penal management of inequality, she has also focused on informal economies, on emerging forms of vaccine refusal in Europe, and on intersections between criminal law, inequality, and cultural difference. Her recent publications include "The Ethnography of Prisons and Penal Confinement" (*Annual Review of Anthropology*, 2014) and *Gypsy Economy: Romani Livelihoods and Notions of Worth in the 21st Century* (coedited, 2016).

— VINCENT DUBOIS is a professor at the Institute for Political Studies and a member at the Institute for Advanced Studies, University of Strasbourg. A sociologist and political scientist, his research proposes a sociological approach to public policy in the fields of culture, language, poverty, and welfare. He is currently working on surveillance and sanctions of welfare recipients in the contemporary social state. His publications include *The Bureaucrat and the Poor: Encounters in French Welfare Offices* (2010), *The Sociology of Wind Bands: Amateur Music between Domination and Autonomy* (2013), and *Culture as a Vocation: Sociology of Career Choices in Cultural Management* (2015).

— DIDIER FASSIN is the James Wolfensohn Professor of Social Science at the Institute for Advanced Study and a director of studies at the École des Hautes Études en Sciences Sociales. A sociologist and anthropologist, he is interested in contemporary political and moral issues and has conducted research in Senegal, Congo, South Africa, Ecuador, and France. His most recent work proposes an ethnography of the state through a study of police, justice, and prison in France. His publications include *Humanitarian Reason: A Moral History of the Present* (2011), *Enforcing Order: An Ethnography of Urban Policing* (2013), and *Prison Worlds: An Ethnography of the Carceral Condition* (2016).

—— KELLY GILLESPIE is a senior lecturer in the Department of Anthropology at the University of the Witwatersrand. She received her PhD in anthropology from the University of Chicago with a dissertation titled "Criminal Abstractions and the Post-apartheid Prison." Her research interests include criminal justice, social justice, political and legal anthropology, race, and sexuality. She is finalizing a book manuscript provisionally titled "Idle Acts: Criminality and the Dialectics of Punishment in Post-apartheid South Africa." She is the cofounder and convener of the Johannesburg Workshop in Theory and Criticism.

—— GHASSAN HAGE is the Future Generation Professor of Anthropology and Social Theory at the University of Melbourne. He works in the comparative analysis of colonialism, nationalism, multiculturalism, and racism in Europe, Australia, and the Middle East. His books include *White Nation* (2000) and *Against Paranoid Nationalism* (2003). His most recent work is *Alter-Politics: Critical Anthropology and the Radical Imagination* (2015).

—— SHERINE HAMDY is an associate professor of anthropology and a faculty fellow at the Watson Institute at Brown University. She is interested in health, medicine, and social inequalities as well as contemporary Islamic thought and the formation of Muslim identities. She is currently working with Soha Bayoumi on the role of Egyptian doctors in the 2011 political uprisings; on a graphic novel, *Jabs*, about a Muslim American college student struggling to find her own voice; and on a collaborative graphic novel, digital-platform, documentary film project called *Lissa (Still Time)*. She is the author of *Our Bodies Belong to God: Organ Transplants, Islam, and the Struggle for Human Dignity in Egypt* (2012).

—— FEDERICO NEIBURG is a professor of social anthropology at the National Museum of the Federal University of Rio de Janeiro. He is also the lead researcher for the Brazilian National Research Council and a coordinator with Fernando Rabossi of the Center for Research in Culture and Economy. He has conducted research in Mexico, Argentina, Brazil, and Haiti. In recent years he has concentrated on the ethnography of the relationships between forms of government and ordinary economic practices. His publications include the coedited volume *Empires, Nations, and Natives: Anthropology and State-Making* (Duke University Press, 2005) and articles in *Cultural Anthropology*, *Social Anthropology*, *Hau: Journal of Ethnographic Theory*, and *Anthropological Theory*.

—— UNNI WIKAN is professor emerita in the Department of Social Anthropology, University of Oslo. She has done fieldwork in Egypt, Oman, Indonesia, Bhutan, and Scandinavia and has been a visiting professor at Harvard, the University of Chicago, and the London School of Economics, among others. Her books include *Tomorrow, God Willing: Self-Made Destinies in Cairo* (1995), *In Honor of Fadime: Murder and Shame* (2008), and *Resonance: Beyond the Words* (2012).

Index

Assad regime, 59–60

Assange, Julian, 20, 22

Association de Secours Palestinien (ASP), 167–68

ATD Quart Monde, 193

Atshan, Sa'ed, 287, 299, 301–3, 304–5

Australian minorities, 49, 54

autonomy in research, 186–87

Awad, Isabel, 40

Awla, Rasool, 251

Ayoreo Indians, 12; ABG subgroup, 139, 140, 143; Christian, 143, 148; cosmology, 148–49; federations, 140, 142–43; as marginalized, 138, 143; NGO affiliations, 139–41; as nomadic, 139, 142, 143; political agency, 151; public ethnography of, 138, 141–42, 146–47, 148–50. *See also* Indigenous peoples

Barnard College, 207–8, 213, 214

Barth, Fredrik, 3, 244

Bataille, Georges, 152

Bayoumi, Soha, 299

Becker, Howard, 319

Beghal, Djamel, 312

Benjamin, Walter, 317–18

Bensman, Joseph, 2, 318–19

Berlant, Lauren, 300

bioethics, Muslim, 14, 290

biosecurity, 218

Birzeit University, 47

blackplans (hacker), 36

blan, use of term, 120, 133n2

Blumer, Herbert, 324

Boas, Franz, 315

Bobcats of Israel, 214

Boellstorff, Tom, 40

Boltanski, Luc, 190

Bonte, Pierre, 189

Borell, John Anthony, 33

Bórmida, Marcelo, 148–49

Borofsky, Rob, 4

Bose, Nirmal Kumar, 2–3

Boston Globe (newspaper), 205

Boukman, Samba, 128

Bourdieu, Pierre, 13, 49–50, 62, 189, 193, 198

Bourgois, Philippe, 3

Boycott, Divestment and Sanctions movement (BDS), 58, 213, 219

Brandeis Center for Human Rights under Law, 220

Braum, Pedro, 119, 128

Brazilianized Haiti, 122, 135–36n20

Breckenridge, Carol, 251

Bremen, Volker von, 149

Brisebarre, Anne-Marie, 189

Brod, Max, 317

Brown, Barrett, 33

Brown, Nathan J., 167, 168

Brox, Ottar, 231, 253

Burawoy, Michael, 3, 185, 186, 194, 198, 325

Bush, George W., 165, 168–69, 209, 212

Butler, Judith, 266

Calhoun, Craig, 337–38

Camp David Accords (1978), 294

Campus Watch, 212, 215, 219

Canova, Paola, 143

CARE, 166

Carnival for Peace project, 129

Carter, Jimmy, 294

censorship: intellectual, 273; self-, 10, 13, 198; of social media, 36

Chagnon, Napoleon, 3, 319

Charlie Hebdo attack (2015), 19, 35, 312

Chomsky, Noam, 38

Church of Scientology, 22

Civil Defence Force, 172

civility, 13, 214–15, 216–17, 218

Clastres, Pierre, 6

Clinton, Hillary, 168–69

Cochrane Collaboration, 271

Cohen, Jared, 57

Cole, Jonathan, 208–9

Columbia Hillel, 213
Columbia University, 205, 212, 213–16, 222n4, 223n11
Commission for a National Anti-Drug Strategy, 105
Commission for Prison Reform (Portugal), 100–101, 103–4
commissions of inquiry, 86–88
Computer Fraud and Abuse Act (1986), 33
Coulibaly, Amedy, 312
critical sociology, 186, 190
Crotty, Paul A., 168
cultural production, 50–51
cyber warfare, 31, 35, 36–37, 43n23

Dabashi, Hamid, 215
Dalai Lama, 252
DAM hip-hop group, 297–98
David Project, 212, 215
Dawkins, Richard, 3
Dawson, Fabian, 251
Debaene, Vincent, 5–6
Deeb, Lara, 299
DeHart, Matt, 33
denial of service (DDoS) attacks, 23, 25, 31–32
de-pooring people, 264, 266, 277–79
Deseriis, Marco, 22
Dewey, John, 324
dialect and identity, 230
Diamond, Jared, 3
Dirks, Nicholas, 215–16
Disarmament, Demobilization and Reintegration program, UN, 134n13
Doctors of the World, 314
Domestic Violence Act (South Africa), 77
Dotcom, Kim, 31
drug crimes, 100–106
drug-trafficking networks in Portugal, 102
Duggan, Lisa, 300–301

Durand, Jean-Yves, 107
Dutch Orthodox Protestants, 108
Duvalier, François (Papa Doc), 120, 123

Eakin, Hugh, 232–33, 253
Egypt, public ethnography in: barriers to, 287, 288–90, 304; critical hopefulness in, 299–303; cynicism, rejection of, 297–99, 302; delegitimizing the ethnographer, 290–94; organ transplantation, 290–91; social gatekeeping and, 290; translating across audiences, 294–96
Elster, Jon, 254
emic vs. etic, 54
empathy, 29, 40, 236, 243, 245, 248–49
Enxet-Enlhet Indians, 142
ergon and myth, 148
Eriksen, Thomas Hylland, 2, 231, 248, 255n23, 315–16
Erikson, Susan, 271
Eskandari, Ahmed, 251
ethnography, 331–37; academicization of, 337–38; afterlife, 14, 314–24, 338–39; auto-, 48–49; black holes of, 240, 252; collaboration in, 261–62, 263–64; contextualization, 70, 82–85, 88, 110, 172–73; critical, 69–70, 83–84, 90, 108, 145, 151, 152n1, 184, 279, 298, 321; disengaged empathy in, 243; false transparency of, 332; fieldwork/writing operations, 14, 332; as method and writing, 1; multisite, 48; objects of, 84; policy, 13, 96–97, 184–87, 189, 192–94, 197–99; research funding, 189; responsibilities, 14–15; scale in, 83–84; truth-claims, 144–45, 147, 262; use of term, 199n3; veridiction-falsification in, 7, 147, 264, 265, 269, 280. *See also* public ethnography; truth
etic vs. emic, 54
European Centre for Disease Prevention and Control, 107

resilience and resistance, 62–66

resistance: empowerment and, 10–11; public intervention and, 55–62; resilience and, 62–66

right-to-health lawsuits. *See* judicialization of health in Rio Grande do Sul, Brazil

Riles, Anneliese, 275

Robbins, Bruce, 50

Roma (Gypsies), 101, 108

Rosaldo, Renato, 2, 319

Rosen, Lawrence, 161

Rothschild, Edouard de, 311

Rousseff, Dilma, 265

Rovner, Ilana, 175

Russell, James R., 209

Ruth, Arne, 249

Sabu (hacker), 28

Sadat, Anwar, 294

Said, Edward, 10, 50, 209, 210, 297

Saint Joie, Herold, 123

Salafi, 291, 294–95

Salaita, Stephen, 214, 216

Sanapaná Indians, 142

Sanjak, Roger, 315

Sarkozy, Nicolas, 195, 321–22

Sartre, Jean-Paul, 5, 31, 311

Schaeublin, Emanuel, 166, 168, 171–72

Scheper-Hughes, Nancy, 2, 319

Second Intifada (2000–2005), 211–12, 289

Sejersted, Francis, 237

self-censorship, 10, 13, 198

September 11, 2001, terrorist attacks, 210, 211, 219

Shaffer, Simon, 210

Shapin, Stephen, 210

Sha'rawi, Shaykh, 292

Sidhu, Jaswinder Kaur (Jassi), 251

silencing, processes of, 211, 214, 228, 229, 239, 255n23, 290, 299

Silvers, Robert, 243

slaves, well-being of, 64

Snowden, Edward, 37–38

Social Democratic Party (Brazil), 265

social engineering, 29, 31

Social Justice Coalition (SJC), 79, 80, 81

sociology: as combat sport, 198; critical, 186, 190; French context, 187–89; public, 3–4, 188–89, 198; sociological knowledge, 185; use of term, 199n3. *See also* policy ethnography

Solicitor General's Office (Brazil), 261, 274

solidarity tourism, 307n25

South Africa, AIDS study, 320–21

South African Police Service, 76–77

Springdale case, 319

Stewart, Frank Henderson, 246

Stocking, George, 315

Stoler, Ann Laura, 86–87

Strathern, Marilyn, 55

Students for Justice in Palestine (SJP), 213, 216

suicide bombing, 221, 223n17

Sunni Islam, 289, 291

Sürücü, Hatun, 252

Sweden: censure in, 253–54; honor killing in, 13, 236, 239–43, 245, 246–51; migration to, 238–39; multiculturalism in, 238–39, 243, 245

Synthetic Biology Engineering Research Center (UC-Berkeley), 263

Syrian authoritarian regime, 59–60

Tambou lapé (Drums for Peace) project, 123, 124, 125

Taubira, Christiane, 327

Taussig, Michael, 85, 150

tenure, academic, 205, 207–10, 212, 220–21

"Terre humaine" (book series), 6

terrorism, humanitarian assistance to. *See* Palestinian Islamic charities, terrorism links to

Thévenot, Laurent, 190